AF749100

Policing Serious Crime in China

Despite a resurgence in the number of studies of Chinese social control over the past decade or so, no sustained work in English has detailed the recent developments in policy and practice against serious crime, despite international recognition that Chinese policing of serious crime is relatively severe and that more people are executed for crime in China each year than in the rest of the world combined.

In this book the author skilfully explores the politics, practice, procedures, and public perceptions of policing serious crime in China, focusing on one particular criminal justice practice – anti-crime campaigns – in the period of transition from planned to market economy from the 1980s to the first years of the twenty-first century. Trevaskes analyses the elements that led to 'striking hard' becoming the preferred method of attacking the growing problem of serious crime in China before going on to examine the factors surrounding the failure of 'striking hard' as a way of addressing the main problems of serious crime in China today, that is drug trafficking and organized crime.

Drawing on a rich variety of Chinese sources, *Policing Serious Crime in China* is an original and informed read for scholars of China, criminologists generally and the international human rights community.

Susan Trevaskes is an Australian Research Council QEII Research Fellow at Griffith University, Australia

Routledge Studies on China in Transition
Series Editor: David S. G. Goodman

The Democratisation of China
Baogang He

Beyond Beijing
Dali Yang

China's Enterprise Reform
Changing state/society relations after Mao
You Ji

Industrial Change in China
Economic restructuring and conflicting interests
Kate Hannan

The Entrepreneurial State in China
Real estate and commerce departments in reform era Tianjin
Jane Duckett

Tourism and Modernity in China
Tim Oakes

Cities in Post-Mao China
Recipes for economic development in the reform era
Jae Ho Chung

China's Spatial Economic Development
Regional transformation in the Lower Yangzi Delta
Andrew M Marton

Regional Development in China
States, globalization and inequality
Yehua Dennis Wei

Grassroots Charisma
Four local leaders in China
Stephan Feuchtwang and Wang Mingming

The Chinese Legal System
Globalization and local legal culture
Pitman B Potter

Transforming Rural China
How local institutions shape property rights in China
Chi-Jou Jay Chen

Negotiating Ethnicity in China
Citizenship as a response to the state
Chih-yu Shih

Manager Empowerment in China
Political implications of rural industrialisation in the reform era
Ray Yep

Cultural Nationalism in Contemporary China
The search for national identity under reform
Yingjie Guo

Elite Dualism and Leadership Selection in China
Xiaowei Zang

Chinese Intellectuals Between State and Market
Edward Gu and Merle Goldman

China, Sex and Prostitution
Elaine Jeffreys

The Development of China's Stockmarket, 1984–2002
Equity politics and market institutions
Stephen Green

China's Rational Entrepreneurs
The development of the new private business sector
Barbara Krug

China's Scientific Elite
Cong Cao

Locating China
Jing Wang

State and Laid-off Workers in Reform China
The silence and collective action of the retrenched
Yongshun Cai

Translocal China
Linkages, identities and the reimagining of space
Tim Oakes and Louisa Schein

International Aid and China's Environment
Taming the yellow dragon
Katherine Morton

Sex and Sexuality in China
Edited by Elaine Jeffreys

China's Reforms and International Political Economy
Edited by David Zweig and Chen Zhimin

Ethnicity and Urban Life in China
A comparative study of Hui Muslims and Han Chinese
Xiaowei Zang

China's Urban Space
Development under market socialism
T. G. McGee, George C.S. Lin, Mark Y. L. Wang, Andrew M. Marton and Jiaping Wu

China's Embedded Activism
Opportunities and constraints of a social movement
Edited by Richard Louis Edmonds and Peter Ho

Marketization and Democracy in China
Jianjun Zhang

The Chinese State in Transition
Processes and contests in local China
Edited by Linda Chelan Li

China's Governmentalities
Governing change, changing government
Edited by Elaine Jeffreys

China's Cotton Industry
Economic transformation and state capacity
Björn Alpermann

Policing Serious Crime in China
From 'strike hard' to 'kill fewer'
Susan Trevaskes

Policing Serious Crime in China

From 'strike hard' to 'kill fewer'

Susan Trevaskes

UNIV DUNELM

Routledge
Taylor & Francis Group
LONDON AND NEW YORK

30 SEP 2010

364.40951
TRE

First published 2010
by Routledge
2 Park Square, Milton Park, Abingdon, Oxon OX14 4RN

3031986

Simultaneously published in the USA and Canada
by Routledge
270 Madison Avenue, New York, NY 10016

*Routledge is an imprint of the Taylor & Francis Group,
an informa business*

© 2010 Susan Trevaskes

Typeset in Times New Roman by Swales & Willis Ltd, Exeter, Devon
Printed in the UK by the MPG Books Group

All rights reserved. No part of this book may be reprinted or reproduced or utilized in any form or by any electronic, mechanical, or other means, now known or hereafter invented, including photocopying and recording, or in any information storage or retrieval system, without permission in writing from the publishers.

British Library Cataloguing in Publication Data
A catalogue record for this book is available from the British Library

Library of Congress Cataloging-in-Publication Data
Trevaskes, Susan, 1964-
Serious crime in China : policing and politics / Susan Trevaskes.
p. cm.
Includes bibliographical references and index.
1. Criminal justice, Administration of—China. 2. Law enforcement—China.
3. Crime—China. I. Title.
HV9960.C53T74 2010
364.951—dc22
2009052577

ISBN10: 0–415–56447–6 (hbk)
ISBN10: 0–203–84893–4 (ebk)

ISBN13: 978–0–415–56447–2 (hbk)
ISBN13: 978–0–203–84893–7 (ebk)

In memory of my dear father
Graham Trevaskes

Contents

List of illustrations

Figures

Tables

Acknowledgements

I would like to thank colleagues Borge Bakken, Michael Dutton, Mary Farquhar, Mark Finnane, David Goodman, David Johnson, Sang Ye and Maureen Todhunter for their insightful and generous comments and help. I very much appreciate their expertise and advice. Thank you to the Australian Research Council for funding this project and to the Griffith Asia Institute for providing editorial and travel assistance.

I would also like to acknowledge permission granted to reprint parts of two articles that appeared in the following journals in Chapters 2 and 3 of this book: Susan Trevaskes, '"Strike Hard 2001": form and strategy in a Chinese anti-crime campaign', *Australian and New Zealand Journal of Criminology* 36 (3), 2003, pp. 272–92; and Susan Trevaskes, 'Severe and Swift Justice in China', *British Journal of Criminology* 47 (1), 2007, pp. 23–41.

Lists of abbreviations and pinyin words

Abbreviations

CCP	Chinese Communist Party
CL	Criminal Law
CMPO	Comprehensive Management of Public Order
CNCC	Counter Narcotics Control Commission
CPC	Central Party Committee
CPL	Criminal Procedural Law
NCD	Narcotics Control Department
NPC	National People's Congress
PLA	People's Liberation Army
PSB	Public Security Bureau
SPC	Supreme People's Court
SPP	Supreme People's Procuratorate

Pinyin words

congzhong congkuai	severely and swiftly
douzheng	(political) struggle
e'shili	evil forces
fa'an	crime incident
fa'an lü	crime incidence rate
fangfan	crime prevention
gong'an	public security
gong'anju	public security bureau
gongjianfa	police, procuratorate and courts
heishehui xingshi zui	mafia-style crime
heishehui xingshi jituan	mafia-style criminal syndicates
hexie shehui	harmonious society
jituan	group/syndicate
kuanyan xiangji	balancing leniency and severity
li'an	registered criminal case
li'an lü	registered crime rate
po'an	solved case
po'an lü	clear-up rate

shehui zhian	public order
shehui zhian zonghe zhili	comprehensive management of public order
shehui zhixu	social order
yifa congzhong congkuai	(punishing) severely and swiftly according to law
yanda	to strike hard
yanda douzheng	Strike Hard struggle (campaign)
zhengfa	politico-legal
zhengfa jiguan	politico-legal organ
zhengfa weiyuanhui	politico-legal committee
zhuanxiang douzheng	specialized struggle

Introduction

In contemporary China the story of how serious crime is policed and punished revolves around the political importance attached to order and stability in the nation's quest for modernization and prosperity. Criminal justice rhetoric and practice betrays the markings of a political culture in which order and stability take centre stage. Order–stability is the primary axis on which politico-legal debates about controlling serious crime is articulated. Hence, policing and punishing in order to protect the open reform agenda has been a key and enduring development goal for three decades.

Local political intervention and human rights abuses in individual criminal cases have been an important preoccupation in the field of China law studies in the West but it is not the focus of this book. This study examines the broader spectra of policing serious crime in China, focusing on one particular criminal justice practice – anti-crime campaigns – in the period of transition from planned to market economy from the 1980s to the first years of the twenty-first century. This is a 'war on serious crime' unlike the US war on crime, which some commentators have argued, came about in response to a distinct shift in the ideology of punishment in late-modernity from a philosophical emphasis on utilitarian punishment philosophies such as rehabilitation, toward retributive and punitive goals.[1] In contrast, no fundamental rupture occurred between the Mao and Deng regimes in China in relation to the importance placed on policing serious crime as a key goal of state development.

'Politics' in Chinese criminal justice practice is expressed not so much in terms of hands-on interference in individual cases but rather at the policy heart of criminal justice operations. I argue in this volume that a culture of 'campaign justice' was cultivated in the first 25 years of the post-1978 reform period as a model or template by which central policy makers in the Chinese Communist Party formulated policy guidelines for criminal justice practitioners in the management of serious crime. Campaigns were the vehicle or conduit through which policy goals in relation to outbreaks of serious crime formulated at the central level of state power were disseminated and realized at the local level. They came to define how criminal justice authorities responded to outbreaks of crime at the local level. Hence, 'campaign justice' is not a transitional 'moment' so much as an undercurrent that undergirds late twentieth century criminal justice practice, which is fundamentally rationalized as order-stability not human rights.

A culture of campaign justice, which flourished as a consequence of this preoccupation with order-stability, is loosely based on the Maoist ideology of political struggle (*douzheng*) and as we find in this study, the reliance on campaigning only began to wane in the first years of the twenty-first century. Because of the highly problematical and controversial nature of campaigns, this format of crime control became increasingly open to internal criticisms from practitioners and legal reformers alike. Campaign justice itself therefore became the object of political contestation. While campaigns were ubiquitous in the 1980s and 1990s, they have now largely fallen out of favour. This study traces the rise and fall of campaign justice, focusing on the thematic of 'politics', or more precisely, the political culture that informs state responses to serious crime. This study is an exemplar of how politics plays out in one area of social regulation in China. By following the rise and fall of campaign justice, we can observe the broader machinations of power arrangements in this transitional period, particularly as they emerge in the dynamic mix between rhetoric, institutional practice and party control. From this mix, we can observe how policing authorities in China have been hobbled, in myriad ways, by the challenges of policing serious crime in a transitioning economy, by the continued influence of a Maoist culture of crime control borne of the recent past and by the political importance attached to controlling serious crime 'severely and swiftly' as an overarching imperative of the Communist party's reform strategy.

The point of this study of campaigns is not to argue that they are the sole response to serious crime since the early 1980s but that their frequent occurrence has helped to entrench a particular mentality of crime control that uses 'political struggle' as its leitmotif of policing and punishment. Anti-crime campaigns are therefore an exemplar of what Chinese criminal justice operations look like when politics is in full command. Overall, this study of the politics of policing serious crime bears witness to the rise and eventual (relative) decline of a particular culture of harsh justice that came to define post-Mao criminal justice operations against a wide gamut of serious and other crimes.

Anti-crime campaigns take two forms, depending on their scale. One is the generic Strike Hard campaign, which runs for up to three years and focuses on a variety of crime targets, often involving the combined efforts of the nation's criminal detectives, judges and prosecutors who are referred to collectively as the politico-legal organs (*zhengfa jiguan*). The second is the 'specialized struggle' that uses 'Strike Hard' policy to target a specific category of crime – such as drugs or organized crime – over a period of months or years. Strike Hard campaigns and specialized struggles target outbreaks of serious crime or worrying crime trends through interagency cooperation, where the three agencies of criminal justice – the Public Security Bureau (PSB), the procuratorate, and the courts – make a concentrated effort over a specified time period to attack targeted crimes 'severely and swiftly'. 'Severe and swift punishment' is the material expression of campaign justice. The first generic Strike Hard campaign was carried out from 1983 to 1986, the second in 1996, and the third from 2001 to 2003. In the intervening years – indeed, every year since the 1980s – one or more specialized national campaigns were launched and dozens more initiated at the local level. It is this relentless pace that allowed a culture of campaign justice to flourish at a time of rapid economic transformation. This rollercoaster ride of successive campaigns against serious crime served to entrench an ethos of harsh punishment in the Chinese context. 'Strike Hard' is a term that encapsulates this punitive approach.

Serious crime, Strike Hard and political struggle

Serious crimes are defined as behaviours that gravely infringe or damage the social order or the public order.[2] Such crimes include robbery, rape, homicide, assault, bombing, kidnapping, arson, crimes committed by crime syndicates and other organized criminal groups, drug manufacturing and trafficking, and even property crimes such as major theft and other offences that pose a serious threat to public security.

Serious crime indeed constitutes a serious problem in today's China. It presents a major challenge to the nation, the government and the authorities who are responsible for crime control, especially as maintaining social stability remains the top national priority. Data on the registered incidence of crime nationwide reveal major annual increases in serious crime from the early 1980s. According to a confidential report by the Party Central Committee, there were 64,000 recorded cases of serious crimes in China in 1982. By 1999, the figure had reached over one million, which represents a 1,460 per cent increase in serious crime over this period.[3] In many Chinese provinces, what is regarded as serious crime normally comprises over 40 per cent of total registered crimes.[4]

Crime figures from two provinces alone bring home the gravity of the situation. In Yunnan Province, in the 23 years from 1979 to 2001, the number of crime incidents recorded on police files increased 690 per cent, an average annual accumulated increase of more than 10 per cent. Reports of violent incidents placed on police files for investigation rose 750 per cent, with a slightly larger annual increase. The number of criminal cases resulting in the death of a victim increased 380 per cent – an accumulated increase of 7.7 per cent per annum.[5]

In Sichuan Province, from January 1980 to June 1983, almost 3,000 people were murdered. This compares to the year 2000, when in a single year the figure was 3,845, which amounts to 30 per cent more people murdered in one year than in three and a half years in the 1980s.[6] The number of violent crimes in Sichuan has increased continuously for more than two decades. The percentage of violent crimes in Sichuan in relation to overall crime more than doubled, from 8.9 per cent in 1982 to 19.4 per cent in 2000.[7] These comparisons are disquieting, but even more so when we acknowledge that police statistics in the early 1980s were much more accurate than they are today; for almost two decades now, police across the country have routinely underreported crime incidents.[8]

Chinese authorities have been all too aware of the social impact of this exponential growth in the incidence of particular types of serious crime that is a corollary of China's post-Mao economic transition towards the market. The timing and nature of the emergence of this serious crime phenomenon indicate that, in China as elsewhere, serious crime is both enabled by and linked inextricably with national economic growth and rapid social change. Yet, whatever the similarities with other national examples in terms of the incidence of serious crime and its relationship to economic growth through market development, China is clearly *sui generis* in terms of its national response. Beginning in the early 1980s, the Chinese authorities' response to the dramatic rise in violent and other serious crime was to *Yanda* – literally, 'to strike hard' – through anti-crime campaigns.

Severe punishment has paralleled striking increases in serious crime.[9] The death penalty stands out here since it has been imposed, comparatively liberally, upon those found guilty of homicide, serious assault, robbery, rape, drug trafficking, serious theft and other crimes. The number of people executed in China each year remains a state secret but up until 2007, it was thought to be anything from 2,500 to 15,000 per annum. The most widely accepted estimate is between 8,500 and 10,000.[10] If this estimate is correct, over the last 25 years up to or around 250,000 people have been sentenced to death and most likely executed. At the very least, according to Amnesty International reports, newspapers report on around 2,500 to 3,500 executions per year. The increased application of the death penalty is consistent with campaign philosophy. Death to those found guilty is indeed a severe punishment; most would call it the most severe punishment.

'Strike Hard' policy is a means of asserting state authority and intention to prevail over serious crime. As the state's key weapon against serious crime since the 1980s, campaigns have been as intensely political as they are relentless. Campaigns are also a leading cause of the high number of executions in China. Yet Chen Xingliang, one of China's leading death penalty experts, maintains that most Chinese academics writing on death penalty policy have either inadvertently failed to take into account Strike Hard's magnitude or deliberately neglected the impact of Strike Hard policy on the number of people executed across the nation.[11]

The present study opens a window onto the politics, practice, procedures and public perceptions of policing serious crime in China today, focusing on campaigns between 1986 and 2007. In mapping campaigns as a multi-faceted and neglected aspect of Chinese criminal justice since the mid-1980s, we are able to gain a deeper insight into social regulation during this period of economic transformation. We are also able to gain a deeper understanding of how the political realm – ideology, party organization and institutional politics – operates to secure one particular aspect of social policy. Campaigns, I argue, developed as a model for dealing with crime problems that arose out of the three-decade long reform process. And just as campaigns are a model, this study of the politics of policing is also a model or exemplar of how politics work to implement social policy and to maintain party rule in present-day China.

Anti-crime campaigns as a 'model' of the Chinese state's response to serious crime

In China, crime prevention practices that operate within a system called 'comprehensive management of public order' are the state's key stated approach to the control of minor crime. By contrast, the management of serious crime has tended to favour an 'attack' or 'strike' approach. The 'attack' on crime is exemplified by the Strike Hard policy of 'severely and swiftly punishing in accordance with the law'. As the state's primary response to soaring rates of serious crime through severe and swift punishment for more than two decades, Strike Hard-style measures have dominated criminal justice responses to serious crime in China from the start of the Reform period in the early 1980s to well into the first decade of the twenty-first century.

The meaning of the characters that comprise the term '*yanda*' or strike hard is clear: *Yan* means 'harsh' or 'severe' and *da* means 'to strike'. 'Strike Hard' itself is shorthand for 'strike hard at serious crime', but use of the term is slippery, partly because of its twin lives as noun and verb. As a noun, the 'Strike Hard' label denotes both a type of generic anti-crime campaign and a criminal justice policy put to work within, but also independent of, the generic campaign. As a policy, 'Strike Hard' is cast as a mechanism for punishing serious criminals 'severely and swiftly'. This 'severity and swiftness' is applied to specific crimes that are considered a serious threat to order. 'Severity' signifies a sentencing rationale, and has essentially entailed meting out comparatively severe punishment within the scope of the law, while 'swiftness' refers to accelerating and simplifying criminal procedures to deal with targeted criminals. Swiftness is rationalized in terms of its perceived deterrence value: the shorter the time that elapses between the commission of a crime and the punishment meted out by the justice system, the greater are said to be the social benefits of punishment in terms of its deterrence value, and the more conspicuous the relationship between crime and punishment becomes in the minds of the public.[12] When Strike Hard policy has been applied, heavy punishment has been generally handed out across the board for the targeted crimes. This is significant in the sense that part of Strike Hard's purpose is to serve as a deterrent to crime through the application of severe punishment. The logic here is that the message of deterrence needs to reach people across the country, while simultaneously legitimizing the hard-line approach and mobilizing those who are to implement or participate in campaigns.

As a verb, 'to strike hard' takes on a life of its own as a politically charged rallying call against serious crime. In China, both generic and specialized campaigns are referred to as 'struggles'. As both verb and noun, Strike Hard has cultivated a culture of 'campaign justice' based on the ideology of 'political struggle'. Over the last two decades or more, these struggles have further entrenched a pre-existing tendency in Chinese law towards 'heavy penaltyism' that only in recent times has begun to wane.

China's traditional system of codified law was overwhelmingly penal in nature. Whereas the Confucian tradition of social control stressed preventative measures through the observance of *li*, an internalized code of civility and propriety in a strict social hierarchy, the legalist tradition was conversely an externalized system of social control through harsh punishments, based on the primacy of state power and sovereign dominion as the sole legitimizing rationale for punishment. In contrast to the highly codified nature of criminal law in traditional China, criminal justice practice within the socialist legal tradition in post-1949 China relied on 'principles' that directly related to the development and the protection of the state. The defining rationale informing criminal justice policy in post-1949 China was a particular political interpretation of the concept of 'social harm' or social dangerousness. The nature of harm assigned to a particular criminal behaviour was defined in terms of the degree of social harm inflicted on 'socialist social relations' in general. Social harm, therefore, was that harm which is caused when one or more socialist social relations had been violated as a result of the act under prosecution. In this sense, crime control became an intrinsically political issue as a direct link was made between social harm, the state development goals of social stability and the role of the party-state in protecting social relations.

In the PRC, a comprehensive criminal law was not to be enacted until 1979. In the post-1949 period, there were only a handful of regulations and statutes that guided judicial officers in the task of trying and punishing offenders. The two main criminal statutes implemented in the pre-1979 period were the Statute on Punishment for Counterrevolutionary Activity and the Statute on Punishment for Corruption.[13] Counterrevolutionary activities identified in the statute ranged from acts committed by persons maintaining links with imperialists (Article 3) to those by persons who, through the act of spreading poisons, caused social harm to people, livestock or crops (Article 7). Serious crimes such as murder, arson and poisoning were considered counterrevolutionary, as threatening the social order was deemed a political act. As the first statute did not detail definitions of specific criminal acts, there was no precise provision in the law for any criteria determining criminal liability and other concepts such as criminal intent, negligence and so on. Prescriptions for punishment were also laid out in very general and simplistic terms.[14] Punishments listed for most of the major crimes such as treason, espionage, incitement, 'spreading poisons', assassination, sabotage or killing included the three principal forms of punishment: the death penalty, life imprisonment or a fixed term of imprisonment. Ninety-five per cent of crimes listed in the statute were punishable by life imprisonment or death.[15] This is the basis of what many describe as a culture of 'punitiveness', or in Chinese, '*zhongxing zhuyi*', literally, 'heavy penaltyism'.

A culture of punitiveness, Borge Bakken argues, 'is learned in an historical and political context, which is manipulated by strong states'. He contends that it does not 'simply arise from an alleged inertia of deeply rooted popular cultural sentiments'.[16] Mao, for instance, utilized the cultural tradition of 'the people's revenge' (*minfen*) to legitimize his rule and to eliminate his enemies. He did so well into the post-revolutionary period by employing pre-modernist nomenclature, thereby placing harsh punishment and 'the people's revenge' not within a modern law context but rather a revolutionary framework of 'good' and 'evil', 'friend' and 'enemy'. This nomenclature to some extent persisted into the Deng's era of economic transformation, becoming a legitimizing argument for anti-crime campaigns, Bakken argues.

> Ever since the reform started in the late 1970s, the harshness of sentencing and the *yanda*, or 'hard strikes' against crime, have dominated the penal credo in

> China. Harshness in itself has become the core of the argument in criminal justice policy . . . Deng Xiaoping saw executions as [an] indispensable means through which the masses could be educated . . . Deng Xiaoping thus forfeited a golden chance to get rid of the violent tradition from war, revolution and Cultural Revolution . . . Instead, he utilized the *minfen* of the alleged angered masses for his own political purposes.[17]

For Bakken, the difference between Mao and Deng was that while Mao preferred 'justice in the public square' (*guangchanghua*), Deng's proclivity for 'justice in the theatre or the courtroom' (*juchanghua*) moved the punitive regime away from direct revenge of the masses to a modernist, law-governed state form of retribution, 'enabling him to expropriate the people's revenge'.[18] 'Harsh punishment', delivered through campaigns, was appropriated into the party's political language of reform and it became synonymous with a different type of 'order' in China, one in which the political imperative of social stability required criminal justice functionaries to control perceived outbreaks of serious control crime by 'attacking' severely and swiftly.

Campaigns in post-Mao China became a particular expression of a mode of governance, one in which retributive justice and 'heavy penaltyism' remained the prism through which state responses to serious crime were to be approached. This reworking of revolutionary era retributive and punitive goals occurred in tandem with a focus in rhetoric that promoted social stability as the means for ensuring economic success in this crucial era of unprecedented economic growth. In this context, political leaders placed criminal justice workers 'on a war footing' to protect the very success of the economic reforms. A significant expectation was placed on police, prosecutors and judges who were to play a key role in guaranteeing a successful transition to economic modernization by ensuring a zero tolerance towards criminal deviance.

While some Chinese scholars attribute the tendency towards heavy penaltyism as a phenomenon intrinsic to Chinese cultural tradition, this present study takes a different stance.[19] Rather than isolating 'culture' as an 'analytical abstraction, artificially separated from the other motivations and constraints that shape social action',[20] my approach here will be to move towards a framework that explores the significance of political culture to crime control practices. The way in which a particular regime punishes over time is a political choice rather than merely the reflection of an immutable cultural norm. What is deeply 'cultural' about heavy penaltyism in the PRC is the political culture that has sustained and legitimized the function of harsh punishment as a core component of social control in the PRC. The point here is that in mapping out an explanation of the enduring nature of anti-crime campaigns in China, we need to move towards an examination of 'culture in action'.[21] As David Garland reminds us, we need to show

> more than just a correlation, or even an elective affinity, between culture and conduct . . . In order to move from the analysis of culture to an explanation of action, we have to show how culture relates to conduct, how specific symbols,

> values and ideas come to be a motivational force or operational basis for action . . . If the analysis of culture is to inform the explanation of conduct we need an account of the processes and mechanisms that translate (or enact, perform, inflict, express and rework) culture into action . . . If a 'cultural tradition' is to be accorded causal efficacy in explaining present day penal action, we need an account of the *mechanisms* that transmit this cultural attitude through time, and reproduce it in the present.[22]

A core aspect of my argument about the politics of criminal justice in this study is that the anti-crime campaign has been employed as the very template or mechanism through which a pre-existing political culture of punitiveness has been able to be sustained and encouraged in a period of rapid economic transformation. By embodying quasi-Maoist nomenclature and practices, campaigns have acted as a bridge between past and present, a bridge that political authorities believed to be a necessary way of negotiating through the potentially unstable path to social and economic transformation. Just as Chinese leaders used designated places – for example, Daqing and Dazhai (Mao)[23] and later Shenzhen (Deng)[24] – as national models, campaigns were perceived as the conceptual 'model' for the Chinese criminal justice system's policy towards, and response to, serious crime. This is perhaps not surprising when we consider that the first anti-crime campaign in post-1949 China – the Suppression of Counterrevolutionaries Campaign beginning in 1950 – became the model for criminal justice in the Maoist period.[25] Similarly, the first Strike Hard Campaign from 1983–86 became the Deng regime's model for approaching serious crime and disorder in post-Mao China. Campaign justice as a model of crime management embodies the Chinese party-state's fixation with stability-order. This book maps the role and significance of campaign justice, which operates within a political landscape that not only prioritizes stability-order as a key party-state goal, but also pathologizes disorder.

The political nature of policing serious crime in China

For well over two decades from the early 1980s to the first years of the twenty-first century, the party-state in China articulated campaigns as instrumental to the Reform program which involved a climacteric process of initiating a market economy. Serious crime was not a serious problem in the PRC until the emergence of market reform in the early 1980s. The newly emerging markets in China represented an opportunity to impose regulation that would prevent crime from gaining a foothold. But impatience to fast-track economic reform and a lack of experience of what, how and how far to regulate in order to prevent crime inhibited such preventive action. Chinese authorities chose to control serious crime through what was called the 'Strike Hard' approach rather than to re-regulate the market with laws that could prove an impediment to market development. The wave of serious crime linked to the social and economic dislocation caused by the marketization process caught China's leaders unawares. They were also unprepared for the propensity of free market conditions to inspire and provide fertile soil for criminal activity. The growth in serious crime throughout the reform period and until very recently suggests that, in the early years of market reform, inexperience in market regulation and eagerness to maintain market growth allowed some forms of serious crime to flourish without an effective curb.

Post-Mao Chinese authorities used campaigns to attempt to inhibit the serious crime that introduction of the market both inspired and enabled, in an expanded repertoire and at a much higher level than in the Mao period. Cast as a means to help achieve Reform, campaigns employed the flagrant regulatory potency of 'severe and swift punishment' to help secure the social stability on which China's burgeoning market economy depended. Social stability was elevated as a primary precondition to economic prosperity. The starting point for this examination of the politics of policing in China is therefore an assertion that the policing and punishment of serious crime after Mao necessarily remained within a discourse of the 'political' because social stability has been considered the essential pre-condition for economic development since the early 1980s.

Michael Dutton in his seminal text, *Policing Chinese Politics: a history*, describes the Great Leap Forward in police reform in the post-Mao era, which closely reflected the contours of economic reform – contractual arrangements, the responsibility system and the monetarized reward system – of Deng's modernization drive in the economic sphere. Couched in the rhetoric of 'rule of law', these methods which Dutton describes as the commodification of policing were meant to inspire the criminal justice system to develop in practice, a new culture of professionalism which would parallel moves in legislative circles towards the promotion of a socialist rule of law. What emerged within criminal justice circles, however, was not a new political space governed by the mantra of a rule of law but rather a kind of crossbreeding of Maoist and Dengist rhetoric and practice. Along with this new system of contract-policing, we find an uneasy co-mingling of mass-line practices and rhetoric. Dutton's description of the landscape of policing in the 1980s provides a useful launching pad for this reconsideration of 'the political' in post-Mao criminal justice practice:

> In 1988, when police began to formally question their status as a tool of the people's democratic dictatorship, the script line for their new life as a law enforcement agency seemed clear enough. For economic reform to succeed, stability must prevail, and that, in turn, depended upon overcoming any remnants of the so-called rule of man in favour of the rule of law . . . The growth of police academies and the teaching of legal studies within them, coupled with a new professional attitude and desire for specialization, all suggested that police were in step with these changing times. As the role of the dictatorship in legitimating police actions diminished, law came to replace it [the dictatorship], and, as it [law] did, it [law] more and more framed police actions. Law proved central to economic reform because it was through law that stability could be achieved and calculable outcomes forecast . . . [However] while economic reform required stability, it did not produce it.[26]

Dutton begins his study by arguing that the model that dominated not only policing but the entire gamut of social regulation in Maoist China was the binary of friend/enemy. At the core of his work on the history of Communist policing is the argument that 'for both the party and its security forces, good and bad could not be read outside of a politics of friend and enemy'[27] – that is, friend and enemy as defined by Mao.[28] He asserts that while this 'politics of binary options'[29] completely dominated law enforcement in the Mao era, the post-Mao period experienced a 'de-politicization of friend/enemy generation'.[30] In policing, the replacement of political capital with the profit motive signalled 'a transition out of an era of political distinction and into one of economic distinctions'.[31] As he explains, economic reform

> transformed the single political question of friend and enemy into a multitude of discrete and largely non- or even de-politicizing questions . . . What slowly came to undergird all these disparate questions of the reform era was the single issue of profit and loss. The new consumer ethos that grew in this era required a new form of policing that was not political in the same way as it had been in the past. Economic development, it was argued, required stability and it was the task of the police to ensure this. Policing stability, not the revolutionary line, became the new order of the day.[32]

The post-1979 Communist regime pursued a path to legitimacy through the dual promises of maintaining stability and promoting economic development. As Dutton explains, the consequences for criminal justice organs of making social stability the precursor to economic growth were that although police continued to employ mass-line techniques in response to the social tensions that the policing of stability exacerbated, a profit and loss approach to policing saw a shift towards contract policing that deprived mass-line policing of its *raison d'être* in the way police did their business.[33] This is because the mass-line organs developed in the era of political campaigns of the 1950s and 1960s relied on 'harnessing political passion for revolutionary ends'.[34] But now these revolutionary ends and this passion were transformed. While the state was still 'ideologically committed to a limited and de-politicized version of the Maoist mass-line policing model', the commodification of policing and the 'contract' that it entailed came to define how the police went about their work.[35] Contract-style policing gained a distinctive foothold in framing the day-to-day operations of policing in particular, performance-based monetary incentives and bonus programs, as well as contracts to carry out specific policing tasks. The shift in style and ethos of policing through commodification meant that police and politico-legal cadres 'would be retrained and disciplined into the work habits of the market economy' and by commodifying mass-line policing . . . [authorities] 'would unwittingly transform the mass-line into one long conveyor belt of capitalist values'.[36]

The present study has taken a somewhat different empirical focus, which is not on the techniques of general policing, but on the political response to serious crime – its policing and punishment – in the post-Mao era. I argue that the political function of the policing and punishment of serious crime in the reform period did not disappear along with the binary of class struggle and continuous revolution. Rather, it was transformed. The political struggle ethos continued to dominate serious crime control post-Mao, post-Deng and beyond even though the political binary of friend and enemy and the concept of class struggle could no longer be used to generate the passion and determination that drove mass-line policing under Mao. The 'comprehensive' nature of the mass line was indeed no longer possible.

Recognizing this transition in the philosophy and practice of policing, I contend that the 'politics' involved in policing and punishing serious crime in contemporary China has been transformed rather than diluted or eliminated. The control of serious crime has been repoliticized rather than depoliticized. Policing has been forced to move well beyond the repression of political dissent as, post-Mao, the state recognized that the primary purpose of crime control was to rein in the forces that threaten social stability. This view perceives criminal activity through a lens informed by different values and different understandings – of the party, of the role of the state and of the type of society the state should work to achieve. While stability replaced the revolutionary line as the order of the day, this shift served to create a different manifestation of policing the political. Political struggle was given a new form to address the new areas of crime that began to thrive with the introduction of the market. To be sure, campaign methodology fed directly into a commodification of policing mentality such that targets and arrest quotas helped to 'quantify' success. Campaigns constituted the ultimate performance-based outcome of a police culture increasingly ruled by the ethos of the market and the contract. But crime control against serious offenders remained understood and practiced as a type of 'political struggle' and would therefore remain not only a political tool but a distinct expression of the political.

Three distinct 'threads' of the political are the essential yarn that binds together this almost three decade-long narrative of campaign justice; one ideological, another organizational and third, institutional politics. These three threads form the basis of the story of campaign justice in China and are each discrete expressions of the political in socialist marketizing China that will be explored in this volume.

The ideological foundation of campaigns: 'political struggle'

Since the late 1960s, the United States has been in the midst of a 'war on crime' which has distinguished the criminal justice system as increasingly characterized by retributive punishment, punitive populism, draconian sentencing laws and a vast expansion of the prison system. Punishment scholars have now largely rejected the simplicity of the 'responsive state' thesis as an explanatory model for this change. There is something endemic to the changed nature of governance in the United States that suggests that the remarkable politicization of law and order in this period goes well beyond the uncomplicated cause and effect scenario that attributes increases in the control and punishment of crime solely to increases in the crime rate. A sense of general insecurity within communities that was a by-product of the economic and social conditions of late-modernity has led to the development of a mentality of risk management in American society whereby people have grown to expect an instant governmental response to their feelings of insecurity. This has allowed legislators to place themselves on a 'war footing' in relation to crime, and to exercise direct control over sentencing levels.[37] Discourses of executive power which now focus on criminal victimization, vengeance and severe punishment, became a means of framing politicians' objectives in prosecutorial terms. Concomitant to these new discourses was the gradual shift of criminal justice power in America away from judges and toward prosecutors and politicians. So, within the criminal justice system itself, the valorization of police, victims, prosecutors and legislators has come to dominate a new political landscape in which courts have been 'hobbled' by the emergence of a new way of thinking about criminal justice, one in which 'the ability to consider different voices and many kinds of information have come to be seen as flaws that bespeak of a lack of alignment between judicial judgment and the common good'.[38]

The political nature of the Chinese party-state's response to serious crime is different from the politicization process in the United States for significant reasons. Any modern political system whether liberal-democratic, authoritarian or socialist has within its grasp the potential power to galvanize public support for 'get tough on crime' policies and, as is clear from the American experience, to politicize crime control for purposes beyond the immediate concern with high crime rates. But there is a distinction I wish to make between the type of war which grew out of the politicization of crime control in the US and China's War on crime: it is that the management of outbreaks of serious crime in post-Mao China, at least until very recently, has been regarded by political authorities as an intrinsically political activity because protecting social stability and order is regarded as an intrinsically political issue. This is a claim that senior officials in the party have made.[39] My point here is that in contrast to the American war on crime, the Chinese response has been to treat outbreaks of serious crime as collective threats to state development. As collective threats they are envisaged as requiring a collective and united response.

Campaigns in China in post-Mao China are officially called 'struggles' because they have the hallmarks of the kind of political struggles that characterized Mao's China. To those familiar with Maoist ideology, 'political struggle' is a call to arms that dominated the revolutionary and post-revolutionary era in China. Mao Zedong saw political struggle as the essence of the philosophy of the Chinese Communist Party.[40] He regarded the process of 'struggle' – both between classes and within the ranks of the proletariat – as a primary means of facilitating social progress.[41] Post-1949 Chinese history is largely the history of struggle. And, as I argue here, this ideology has lived on in the post-Mao period through campaign justice, which is essentially an ideology of policing and punishment in which the notion of political struggle fomented during the Mao period is translated into a legal 'struggle' against a specific target or targets for a specified period of time.

On one level, this interpretation of campaigns as political in nature is not a problematic or controversial interpretation, since generic Strike Hard campaigns are, after all, officially called 'Strike Hard struggles' (*Yanda douzheng*) or 'Strike Hard

Rectification and Struggles' and similarly, specialized campaigns are known as 'specialized struggles' (*zhuanxiang douzheng*). But the idea of 'political struggle' stretches far beyond its inclusion as an appendage to the name of campaigns. To be sure, explaining Strike Hard's political hue is also much more complex a matter than simply locating political 'interference' in policing business. The politico-militaristic naming of campaign features hints at the campaigns' political nature but even these features are not at the heart of why we can describe campaigns as political. During campaigns in the 1980s and 1990s, criminal justice workers were officially directed to 'make the enemy surrender or annihilate them'. Policies were referred to as 'deployment plans' and the 'struggle' was divided into major 'offensives' and 'battles'. At the launch of many campaigns, especially the generic Strike Hard drives, propaganda billed the struggle as 'a great decisive battle'. Organizationally, the concentrated powers of the Public Security Bureau (PSB), courts, and procuratorate were referred to as the state's 'concentrated military strength', with the PSB's position in Strike Hard campaigns called 'the front line of battle'. Campaign successes were referred to as 'meritorious military achievements' and outcomes as 'fruits of battle'.[42] This rhetoric indeed says much about the pre-eminence of the 'attack' mode of criminal justice work against serious crime, but it is also an expression of a deeper political underlay.

Campaigns are 'politicized' beyond labelling with revolutionary-militaristic jargon to talk up policing strategies. The idea of the 'political', which I pursue here as noun rather than adjective, speaks of a quality more intrinsic than the imposed paraphernalia of militaristic rhetoric. The political – or what is political about campaigns; its politics – does not 'seep' into or foist upon what is otherwise a politically neutral operation of policing. The state's response to serious crime in post-Mao China is an ideologically inspired regulatory strategy embedding the political at the very root of criminal justice operations and organization. In any modern legal system, responding to serious crime is an act, or at least initiative of the state for achieving social order. Usually it is punitive and thus a coercive tool. Because of this, there is an inherent tension between the shared desire of the state and the public to maintain law and order and to protect the legitimacy of the law and the rights of the accused. The politics I talk of in this volume goes beyond the state–individual interests' divide we find in legal systems in all modern states. Serious crime in contemporary China has been conceptualized within the ideological prism of political struggle. 'Struggle' is itself conceived within the broader conventions of what the state casts as socialist legality that continue to prefigure the ideological agenda of crime control in China today. Indeed, the very format and content of the anti-crime campaign is rooted in the concept of political struggle involving 'strikes' against the enemies of the people, as the description below of a 2001 campaign in Xinjiang in China's west suggests:

> Since launching the 'Strike Hard' campaign, political and law organs in Urumqi have constantly intensified the efforts to crackdown on the 'three kinds of elements' [national separatists, religious extremists, and terrorists] and on criminals who commit serious crimes, thereby effectively deterring the

> arrogance of criminals and helping maintain social stability in Urumqi city. The criminals sentenced at the open sentencing meeting were all those who committed crimes in spite of the announcement of the 'Strike Hard' campaigns and whose crimes were so heinous that unless they were given severe punishment, the people's anger could not be alleviated.[43]

As we find in the chapters that follow, campaigns have relied on a well-established format of selecting a target, struggling against the target, shaming the target and solving a 'social contradiction' through public shaming and punishment. These three practices of severe and swift punishment are at the heart of what I describe as campaign justice.

The Communist party's organizational leadership of campaigns

Arrest, prosecution and sentencing are legally sanctioned mechanisms to regulate human conduct and social relations and as such are used to achieve not just social order but also particular types of political order. In China, this political order is largely determined by the party. The political role of the ruling Communist party in China in crime control is writ large within the structure of crime management not simply because of its position as 'leading party' in a one-party state but because of the organizational arrangements that underpin the leadership over and within the criminal justice system.

One important continuity in both the generic and specialized campaigns is the leading role of the Communist party in criminal justice policy through its politico-legal committees. The party justifies its 'centre-stage' role in directing and coordinating responses to serious crime by asserting that social stability is the collective responsibility of the party-state, and that those who threaten social stability therefore threaten the party-state. This situates both Strike Hard campaigns and specialized struggles at the core of the party's response to serious crime, and also renders them an expression of the political will of the party.

However, central party authorities in Beijing have used a distinctly hands-on leadership role over campaign implementation not only as a way of maintaining decision-making over crime management but also as a way of unifying the interests of the nation's police. Party control over campaigns therefore also has a unifying function. For decades, police have experienced the push and pull of the competing interests of local and central authorities. Local police have two masters – one professional and one financial. On the one hand they are under the vertical professional control of the superior Ministry of Public Security in the central government, and on the other they are subject to the horizontal control of the local party and government agencies that are in command of their budgets and personnel.[44] Given this context, central authorities have used the call 'to strike hard' in an attempt to keep the crime-fighting spotlight on serious crime. This spotlight has come under competition from local government authorities that have different priorities. The main policing efforts of the local governments that have financial power over police are not necessarily focused on serious crimes, which are difficult to solve and considered a drain on resources. This suggests that without consistent, hands-on leadership by the Central Politico-legal Committee in Beijing over the committees in local jurisdictions, the energies of local police might otherwise be channelled more into local government (revenue-building) priorities such as policing traffic fines and tax evasion than into fighting serious crimes. Campaigns have functioned as the ideological and organizational glue that unites local party and central party-state authorities against serious crime, and the central party's leadership over Strike Hard policy has been an important means of providing at least some degree of conformity and unity. In other words, the campaign template has performed a unifying mechanism that draws together disparate and decidedly fragmented local public security agencies in China whose local agendas often take precedence over the larger political interests of social stability and national reform.

Institutional politics

A study of anti-crime campaigns presents us with an opportunity to snapshot a particular instance of institutional transition in China that bespeaks of some problems that governmental agencies face when there is an imperative to fast-track the development of professionalization and institutional legitimacy. In the post-Mao period, criminal justice agencies in China faced an imperative: to create a new institutional culture by modifying their image of authority and modifying their authority relations with other government and Party agencies, and within the wider community. This required a 'fast-track' repositioning of practices and appearances that would reflect a change from a Maoist to a Dengist political culture. Developing an authoritative persona meant that criminal justice agencies would need to develop legitimacy by securing obedience to their decisions as a function of 'having made them through appropriate institutional procedures'.[45] Criminal justice agencies sought to accelerate the construction of a new public identity based on a new-found ethos of governance in China: regularity, procedural propriety and bureaucratic rationality. This journey into the realms of professionalization and procedural propriety meant that in the decades from the early 1980s to the first years of the twenty-first century the political imperative to strike hard through campaigns was not universally welcomed within the ranks of criminal justice agencies whose leadership was well aware of the potential contradictions between 'political struggle' and professionalization.

In the past, some Western scholars held an essentialist view of the Chinese criminal justice system, which presumed that criminal justice agencies' motives and interests were by dint of their position in the authoritarian state, aligned exclusively to party motives and interests. The reality in China is that, as elsewhere, institutions tend to take on a life of their own. Contestations about the efficacy of campaigns and the damage these campaigns have inflicted on their burgeoning public persona of professionalization came out in the debates within policing and judicial circles in the years following the first generic campaign in the twenty-first century from 2001 to 2003. These debates highlighted the need for a more nuanced approach to describing the relationship between the ruling political authorities and the practitioners that manage crime control. Nowadays, we find, criminal justice work in China is fashioned as much by routine considerations such as resources and organizational ties with other governmental organs as it is by ideology. Police, prosecutors and court workers are equally vulnerable to the broader social conflicts, public expectations about their performance and economic constraints as they are to political and ideological issues.

A more nuanced approach to understanding the relationships between political authorities and practitioners also recognizes that while 'political struggle' in campaigns has indeed frustrated progress towards institutional reform in policing, procuratorial and judicial circles, the post-Mao party is not a natural enemy of institutional reform. It is no doubt tempting to pit 'party politics' and institutional reform as natural enemies, but I would argue that strong party leadership over politico-legal organs is not always an anathema to the development of professionalism. Certainly (and as Chapter 4 bears out) many campaign practices work against institutional goals such as professionalism. In general terms, the impressive leaps of institutional reform in China that have been well documented in the literature, have been achieved largely through the blessing and assistance of the party. This recognition muddies the waters, requiring that we move away from an 'either/or' approach towards viewing Chinese criminal justice institutions as multifaceted in motive and interests.

Sociology of punishment scholar David Garland observes that social institutions in general are the scenes of particular conflicts as well as being means to a variety of ends. Therefore, it is no surprise to find that each particular institution combines a number of often incompatible objectives and organizes the relations of often antagonistic interest groups.[46] The practices of the police, prosecutors and judges embody a variety of competing objectives from often rival sources which do not always fit into some unified pattern of a uniform set of measurable principles or a united political stance.[47] As we will find with this study of campaign justice, a large number of conflicting forces are at work within the criminal justice system. And as Garland describes the social institution of punishment in general,

> [b]road ideological ambitions may run up uncomfortably against immediate financial constraints, political expediency may conflict with established sensibilities, the perceived requirements of security may differ from those of morality, the professional interests of one group may be in tension with those of another, and the pursuit of any one value will generally involve the violation of several others.[48]

This theme of how criminal justice institutions in China, particularly the police, have dealt with the contradictions inherent between politicization and professionalization is brought out in the story of the rise and fall of campaign justice.

Within criminal justice bodies, campaign justice is a model of crime management that has been increasingly contested and shrouded in ambiguity. The landscape of campaigns in this period of remarkable economic transformation is replete with legal codes, party politics and debates between institutions such as the courts and the police on the appropriateness of harsh punishment. It is coloured by drama and death, particularly since severe punishment has, until very recent times, often meant the death penalty. It is therefore a changing landscape textured with public concern about crime and institutional and legal reformers' concerns about injustice, cruelty, and misanthropy. Clearly, the intersection between politics and law in the Chinese state's response to serious crime renders the campaign landscape not just dynamic and diverse but also contentious and contested from within the organizations that operationalize campaigns.

The rise and fall of campaign justice

Many of the issues and events that populate the academic literature on Chinese criminal justice in the 1980s are now well rehearsed and no longer ambiguous or contested. It is now well established in the literature that in 1979 the PRC's first Criminal Law and Criminal Procedural Law were introduced, and shortly thereafter the politico-legal authorities began to launch anti-crime drives that targeted crimes against the economic and social order. A party-initiated moral panic about increasing crime rates in the early 1980s gave rise in 1983 to the first generic Strike Hard campaign, which ran for three years. The nation's legislature passed three 'Decisions' in September 1983 to facilitate the 'severe and swift punishment' policy. The first stipulated that punishment beyond the existing maximum penalty under the Criminal Law could now be applied for a number of serious offences. The NPC's second decision focused on prompt adjudication, reducing the time limits for prosecution and appeal, and its third ruling, on 'Revision of the Organic Law of the People's Courts', lowered the level of the court of authorization for approval of the death penalty from the Supreme People's Court to the higher people's courts at the provincial level. During the first national Strike Hard campaign, 1.7 million people were convicted and sentenced in courts across China, with over 780,000 receiving sentences that ranged from five years in prison to the death penalty.[49] Some reports put the number of people sentenced to death over this three-year period (including those sentenced to death with a two-year reprieve) at more than 30,000.[50] The empirical story of campaign justice during this period is documented by Harold Tanner, Murray Tanner and Susan Trevaskes in their respective studies and will not be rehearsed at length in this volume.[51]

The 1983–86 campaign did not solve the crime problem; nor did it create the necessary preconditions for social stability and economic prosperity, and soon after the campaign ended, crime rates began to soar. Borge Bakken argues that the result of this first campaign created a 'brutalizing effect' in society.[52] This brutalization is not only reflected generally in the dramatic rise in violent crime but also in the fact that criminals committing property offences during campaign times are much more likely to use violence and, in many cases, to murder their victims to avoid the anticipated 'severe and swift punishment' that they would receive were they to leave witnesses. Despite multiple miscarriages of justice and wrongful arrests and executions during the three years of the campaign, Strike Hard policy was not laid to rest but continued throughout the 1980s and 1990s in the form of specialized drives that replaced the generic campaigns as the most common form of anti-crime initiatives.

While the first Strike Hard campaign from 1983 to 1986 is now well documented in both Chinese and Western literature, subsequent campaigns, particularly the specialized struggles against serious crime, have not yet been the object of sustained analysis outside China. Specialized anti-crime drives began to be employed as essential armour against serious crime almost immediately after the first Strike Hard campaign ended in late 1986.[53] It must be stressed again that Chinese society – or a sizeable proportion of it – has been 'struck hard' every year from 1983. There have been three main generic Strike Hard campaigns (1983–86, 1996 and 2001–03), as well as dozens of specialized anti-crime campaigns that have been implemented on a national level between generic drives. The short list below offers but a brief glimpse of the ubiquitous nature of nationwide anti-crime drives over the two-year period from 1987 to the end of 1989. It includes only the nationally initiated drives; many more anti-crime campaigns were launched by provincial and local county authorities during this period, making for an unyielding and exhausting rollercoaster ride for local policing, prosecution and judicial officers.[54]

1987 Specialized struggle against theft and smuggling of antiquities
Specialized struggle against prostitution
Specialized struggle against trafficking in women and children
1988 Specialized struggle against gambling, bombings and other violent crimes
Specialized struggle against robberies committed on major highways and freeways
1989 Specialized struggle against itinerant criminals
United operations against the 'six evils'[55]

The relentlessness of campaign-style justice is striking, even in the twenty-first century. A specialized drive against organized crime in 2000 was followed by a two-year Strike Hard campaign (2001–03), a 'People's War on Drugs' (2005–07) and another specialized drive against organized crime from 2006 to 2007. All were modelled on China's first Strike Hard campaign, which itself reflected the experience and events of the mass political campaigns of the 1950s.

The first four chapters of this book interrogate the landscape of campaign justice and practice in the late twentieth and early twenty-first centuries. They trace how generic campaigns, Strike Hard policy and specialized campaigns merge into a larger rhetoric about national development goals that underpins the post-Mao criminal justice system. This system perceives Strike Hard as the 'severe' answer to the problem of serious crime, but a series of debates in policing circles during 2002 and 2003 suggested that campaign justice itself may be part of the problem. Once these doubts and questions about the policy had been voiced, there appeared to be a change in the emphasis on Strike Hard policy, or at least in how it was portrayed in party pronouncements. Strike Hard policy began to be articulated in party circles after 2003 as a policy that needed to be embedded and 'regularized' in everyday policing practices. This subtle shift in terminology from an emphasis on Strike

Hard as a discrete 'political struggle' to the elusive concept of its 'regularization' is significant and marks a turning point in the story of campaign justice's rise and fall.

Because of the deeply political nature of Chinese criminal justice – and the fact that it is generally debated in private, especially in the case of the growing disquiet about campaign justice and its efficacy – it is difficult to pinpoint with any authority the precise nature of the discussions that took place at the highest levels of the party in the early years of the twenty-first century. What we do know is that a number of senior police openly began to speak out against Strike Hard policy in 2002 and 2003, and that at the 20th national public security conference in November 2003, China's Minister of Public Security, Zhou Yongkang, moved to shift emphasis from Strike Hard to crime prevention. We also know that from 2003 to 2007 the campaign landscape changed, at least in terms of the theatrics of 'severe and swift punishment'. The second part of this volume, Chapters 5 to 7, examines the landscape of serious crime in the post-2003 period and the resulting de-emphasizing of Strike Hard policy. These chapters demonstrate that while Strike Hard policy is still paid lip service as part of the armoury of crime control, it is increasingly controversial, and specialized struggles are increasingly initiated without the fanfare that characterized campaigns in the late twentieth century. Thus, despite the absence of formal announcements, subtle reforms to the system were 'appended' to the wider political momentum of 'harmonious society' rhetoric that was gathering pace in 2003 and began to sweep China in 2004 and 2005. We find now that the 'shock and awe' aspects of campaigns, such as mass sentencing rallies, have been largely discarded and replaced by a more professional approach to crime control, albeit one that continues to favour specialized targeting of particular criminal categories. Campaign justice has increasingly come to be seen in official and non-official circles as an anachronism whose political use-by-date has expired, despite the continued survival of a diluted form of Strike Hard policy.

Interrogating the rise and fall of campaign justice

The interrogation of campaign justice in this study focuses on the political realm, since politics is central to campaign policy and practice. The first generic Strike Hard campaign that was followed almost immediately by a series of specialized struggles across the nation, supplied these specialized drives with a template that included rationale, format and rhetoric. In turn, the specialized struggles, carried out between the larger Strike Hard initiatives, provided a thread of continuity between generic campaigns that gave campaign justice its seamlessness and momentum. The sheer pervasiveness and relentlessness of these specialized drives sustained and entrenched the culture of campaign justice. Chapter 1 explores these law-and-order practices, first through an overview of the history of specialized drives across the nation, and then by focusing on one jurisdiction – Beijing – from the mid-1980s through to 2000.

Chapter 2 explores campaign justice as a model or template of the state's response to serious crime. The story here begins with the argument that in China the regulation of criminal behaviour through the employment of 'severe and swift punishment' and other campaign tactics conveys a distinct political function of criminal law. This is because of the direct link that is perceived to exist between serious crime and the development goal of social stability in a transitional period of market reform and rapid economic and social transformation. It is in this context that responses to serious crime in the post-Mao era are articulated with reference to the ideological concept of 'political struggle'. This chapter examines campaigns as a model for criminal justice in relation to serious crime in post-Mao China by outlining what I describe as the template of campaign justice. I explain this template first in relation to its foundation in socialist law theory; second, in relation to its scaffolding or support structure; and third, its 'bricks and mortar', which is the policy and practice of severe and swift punishment. This policy is the overarching discursive framework for campaign justice, while the specific bricks and mortar which comprise the core of its template is threefold: campaigns combine the *targeting* of specific categories of crimes, with legal elasticity or *flexible* criminal justice practices and with an *educative* function which requires criminal justice workers to not only deal with crime through punishment but to express punishment and retribution in judicial ritual.

Chapter 3 examines how the first generic Strike Hard campaign of the new century was implemented in light of the template outlined in Chapter 2. Exploring the strategies of Strike Hard 2001–03 campaign, we find that although campaign operations are more sophisticated and specialized in the twenty-first century, the broad strategies of Strike Hard 2001–03 do not differ fundamentally from those of the first campaign in the 1980s, despite the rising public expectations of professionalism from the police, prosecuting bodies and courts.

The survey of anti-crime campaigns canvassed in the earlier chapters points to a number of fundamental problems with campaign justice, and these are taken up in Chapter 4, which examines the campaign's effects on crime, crime control and the legitimacy of the law in the eyes of those at the coalface. We find here that the post-2003 political landscape is increasingly tolerant of domestic criticism of the abuses of human rights and procedural justice that these anti-crime campaigns encourage, and this chapter brings to light the serious cracks in the campaign armour. It begins by detailing the official achievements and victories of the 2001–03 campaign, but follows this with an examination of the flipside to these successes. An unprecedented debate involving both local-level police and some of the nation's top police officials took place in 2002 and 2003 in the pages of the nation's top policing journal and local police academy journals. During this debate, the 2001–03 campaign was criticized for its failure to curb the tide of serious crime. This was followed in late 2003 by the announcement by Luo Gan, the head of the party's politico-legal committee and the nation's chief Strike Hard proponent, that Strike Hard would be 'routinized' or 'regularized' into everyday practice. This concept of 'regularizing' Strike Hard was given no concrete meaning or application, and there is no indication even today that it has moved beyond the campaign format to be an embedded part of policing serious crime. I argue here that this announcement was a merely a way of downsizing Strike Hard, and that it marked the beginning of the policy's subtle fall from grace.

New and emerging serious crimes in the PRC in the new century have rendered campaign justice increasingly anachronistic. Using campaign justice against simple street crime and uncomplicated violent crime may have seemed an efficacious approach in the 1980s and early 1990s, but in the twenty-first century the serious crimes that are considered to pose the greatest threat to social stability are the very crimes that are relatively difficult to 'strike hard' because they are hidden, complex and relatively sophisticated.

Authorities have identified two types of crime as particularly egregious, because of both their high incidence and the severity of the problems they create for Chinese society – drug crime and organized crime. Chapters 5 and 6 examine these two areas of crime, demonstrating how the drug and organized crime that increasingly accompany China's economic development are both enabled and sustained by the introduction of the market economy. We see here that the nation's relatively swift transition from a planned to a more market economy initially outpaced the capacity of the nation's crime control authorities to curb the growth of opportunities for these particular types of serious crime to flourish.

Chapters 5 and 6 move the focus away from state responses, to the problem of serious crime itself. Chapter 5 takes up the growing problem of drug crime, which increasingly involves the production of drugs inside China, as well as the carriage of hard drugs such as heroin into China for internal consumption or in transit to a third destination. China's geographic position adjacent to the Golden Triangle not only facilitates drug trafficking but also, as with other serious crime, provides opportunities for criminals to deal with and learn from their foreign counterparts, especially since China now has the means to produce and sell drugs domestically. Because drugs can easily be an entry point into other forms of crime that destabilize society, the criminal justice agencies now recognize preventing and severely punishing drug crime as a special imperative. This belated recognition of the seriousness of the drug problem coincided with a change in Strike Hard policy that was in part a result of the debates mentioned above and in part the consequence of a new national emphasis on a more gentle approach to dealing with social problems. Hu Jintao's new development goal of 'socialist harmonious society' rose to prominence after 2002 and brought with it an expanding recognition of the value of a more measured, less draconian approach to regulating social relations. This emphasis sparked a change in the rhetoric and policy direction of policing serious crime, emphasizing 'all-round policing' and interagency cooperation, and downplaying party control. The 'People's War on Drugs', a two-year specialized campaign which began in mid-2005, shows a renewed emphasis on an all-round approach that highlights both the 'attack' and 'prevent' arms of crime control, and avoids the 'shock and awe' tactics of earlier campaigns.

Chapter 6 explains the exponential growth of organized crime syndicates since the mid-1990s, not just in number but also in scale, as they evolved from much smaller and less sophisticated 'hooligan' gangs. The 2006 campaign against organized crime yielded a massive increase in the number of mafia-style syndicates and members of organized crime gangs prosecuted for lesser, but still serious or violent, crimes related to gang activities. In this chapter we see how the development of the national economy has provided the wherewithal for organized crime to take new forms, expand, finesse operations and learn from foreign associates, creating the need for ever more professional policing capacity to address the serious crimes that result. Clearly traditional Strike Hard tactics are out of place in this sophisticated crime environment.

The final chapter concludes the volume by looking at the failures and future of campaign justice. Criminal justice policy in China will continue to be political business for the foreseeable future but it is unlikely that generic Strike Hard campaigns will be the conduit through which party policy toward serious crime is implemented. Chapter 4 covered the problems identified by police and this final chapter deals with some problems that judges and legal commentators have observed. The final part of this chapter then asks how it might be possible to turn around a regime of punishment that has for decades been inclined towards 'heavy-penaltyism'. To this end, we briefly discuss the application of the death penalty in twenty-first-century China as it is conceived by legal experts, politicians and reformers, and analyse the death penalty debate in the context of the new discursive atmosphere of tolerance and harmony that emerged in the 'socialist harmonious society', a resolution issued by Hu Jintao in October 2006. While generic campaigns are likely to be a thing of the past, Strike Hard policy (particularly severe and swift punishment) will likely remain. The debate about heavy penaltyism in today's China has now shifted to the question of *whom* to strike hard – that is, to restricting severe punishment to a smaller cohort of the 'most serous criminals'. The issue of which categories of crime continue to deserve swift and severe punishment boils down to the more specific and fundamental question of what constitutes the most serious crime. Narrowing the goalposts that legally define serious crime limits harsh punishment to fewer categories of offenders and could therefore remove the need to 'strike hard' large sections of the criminal community. For legal reformers, this is a practical way of dismantling – by stealth – the culture of heavy penaltyism and campaign justice. The argument that severe and swift punishment should only be meted out to an extremely small minority of heinous criminals takes the sting out of Strike Hard's once pervasive tail.

Concluding remarks

This book is about the politics of dealing with a major social and political issue at a crucial juncture in China's development path. Strike Hard is clearly significant in the criminal justice landscape. It is more than just a criminal justice policy. It is a window into the debates that have shaped Chinese law in the era of transition from planned to market economy. Primacy given to the development goal of social stability has meant that policy towards serious crime has been dominated by politics. Criminal justice responses to serious crime in post-Mao China have necessarily been articulated in political terms because protecting social stability is political business in China. Because of this perceived necessity of protecting order-stability that has been regarded as a political imperative of the party-state, the response to the rise in serious crime has necessarily been political in nature and implementation.

Despite a resurgence in the number of studies of Chinese social control over the past decade or so, no sustained work in English has detailed the recent developments in policy and practice against serious crime, despite international recognition that Chinese policing of serious crime is relatively severe and that more people are executed for crime in China each year than in the rest of the world combined. This book demonstrates that party politics is ineluctably at work in China's war against serious crime. 'Politicking' is also manifest within criminal justice institutions, especially in the increasingly heated debate over the efficacy of retaining campaigns as the state's primary weapon against serious crime. The state's political role in protecting the development of the Chinese nation and society through the tenuous transition period is writ large in campaigns.

This book uncovers a growing recognition in China that Strike Hard – at least in the form of generic campaigns – does not and cannot deliver the desired outcome of preventing or even reducing serious crime during the current stage of economic, political and social development. The trend in the first decade of the twenty-first century has been to move towards a discursive and institutional alternative through which the Chinese criminal justice agencies are able to strengthen their own institutional authority. This alternative proffers a more institutionally professional approach to crime control that relies less on campaigns' draconian law-and-order tactics and more on the bureaucratic rationality of judicial institutions with their own guiding logic and language, which are based on a more 'scientific' approach to crime control. The emergence of this new trend, like the developments explored in this volume, demonstrates that as a primary criminal justice policy Strike Hard is highly contestable in an era in which marketization reshapes power relations between the party, criminal justice practitioners, the government at all levels, and the people who are governed by them.

1 The rise of campaign justice

The purpose of this chapter is to illustrate the unremitting nature of the onslaught of specialized struggles that occurred in China from the mid-1980s to the end of the twentieth century. The nation's first Strike Hard campaign, which ended in late 1986, produced offspring in the form of 'specialized struggles' that would propel the culture of campaign justice into the twenty-first century. We find that targeting specific crime groups signifies a reworking of the generic Strike Hard campaign (1983–86) into a more particularistic approach. Although these specialized struggles have been a mainstay of criminal justice operations against serious crime in China since the mid-1980s, they have not been examined in detail in literature outside China.[1] In this chapter we explore the recent history of nationally implemented specialized drives and then move to a particular focus on one jurisdiction – Beijing – from the mid-1980s to 2000.

The repeated listing of campaigns and their targets tabled in this chapter serves the purpose of supporting my argument, which is that the ubiquitous nature of specialized struggles during the 1980s and 1990s cemented the popularity of campaign justice, if not with grassroots police then at least with key figures in the party. Specialized struggles created a chain of continuity that gave momentum and cohesion to the model of campaign justice. It is the ever-present and unrelenting nature of these campaigns that helped to entrench the culture of campaign justice in the 1980s and 1990s.

As early as 1988, Public Security Bureau (PSB) researchers had begun to recognize and report on what they saw as an uphill battle by the state to halt the march of crime. Murmurs of discontent pointed to the inability of campaigns to live up to their ambitious deterrence goals. Internal criticisms within the PSB, however, failed to halt the march of campaigns in the 1990s despite the presence of evidence that suggested the counterproductive effects of campaigns. The final section of this chapter relates the beginning of attempts by policing authorities to sidestep party officials' insistence on using campaigns as the sole panacea for the control of serious crime. Here we briefly outline the reaction of public security practitioners to the relentless succession of campaigns during the 1990s, as we find that the surface appearance of unity and harmony of interests within the ranks of criminal justice began to be challenged by the stirrings of internal discord.

The birth of the specialized struggle

Let us begin this examination with an observation by Borge Bakken, not about specialized campaigns, but about the state-induced moral panic that impelled the call to 'Strike Hard' in the first generic campaign in 1983.

> Alarmist viewpoints about crime reached high proportions at the beginning of the economic reforms in China. The recorded 'crime boom' of the early 1980s, and the alarmist atmosphere which triggered the draconian anticrime campaign of 1983 . . . was to a large extent caused by panic about soaring rates of reported crime by juveniles . . . It adds to the argument about a moral panic that not only were the Chinese crime rates among the lowest in the world, but also that when the Strike Hard campaign was launched in September 1983, the crime rate was the lowest since 1979.[2]

The 1983 Strike Hard campaign began when a group of party leaders decided there was a need to restore the public order situation in post-Mao China to levels enjoyed in the halcyon days of the 1950s. These leaders believed that the criminal justice agencies had been too soft on crime in recent years and that a policy of dealing 'severe and swift' blows to criminals was required to turn around the situation. The observation by Bakken above provides a useful starting point to this study of specialized struggles because it reminds us that a simple 'responsive state' thesis is inadequate to explain the popularity of campaigns amongst the political elite. The party-led onslaught of campaigns was not the result of a simple cause-and-effect scenario – that is, a dramatic rise in serious crime in the early 1980s leading to a dramatic state response. This is because the goal of campaigns was never merely to effect a decrease in crime but to enable the appearance of a level of social stability comparable to the golden years of social order in the 1950s when (as the myth goes) it was not necessary to lock one's door at night. This point is important because it indicates that from the start, the goal of campaigns was based on an idealist vision of order-stability, not on contemporary managerial goals of containment.

Strike Hard 1983 began – and ended – with directives from the top echelons of Politburo power. In the mid-summer of 1983, Deng Xiaoping summoned the newly appointed Minister of Public Security, Liu Fuzhi, to a seaside resort at Beidaihe to order him to launch a new offensive against serious crime. Deng saw the crime epidemic as a result of the public security forces' unwillingness to attack crime, the inability of the procuratorate (the public prosecution) to conduct timely prosecutions, and the courts' leniency towards criminals.[3] Peng Zhen, head of the Central Politico-legal Affairs Committee, was also at this meeting. Supporting Deng's view, Peng claimed that his repeated calls to attack crime 'severely and swiftly' had been largely ignored by the criminal justice organs and that this lack of enthusiasm and vigour in dealing 'severely and swiftly' with crime would be interpreted by Party authorities as tantamount to 'encouraging crime'.[4]

The targets of the 1983 campaign were individuals and groups who endangered economic reform and social stability, specifically criminals whose crimes disrupted the public order or the social order. Official assessments indicated that the hooligan – who was the main target of Strike Hard 1983 – was the main cause of the deteriorating social and public order in China in the immediate post-Cultural Revolution period. The main targets of Strike Hard 1983–86 had therefore been first of all 'collective' offenders – groups of unemployed youths who committed property and public order offences – and secondly, 'individual' offenders – more serious offenders who committed murder, robbery, arson and rape.[5]

Strike Hard 1983–86 was described in the official rhetoric as a 'political struggle' that required mass participation and support. To mobilize the masses in 1983 and gain their support, the momentum which was needed to kick-start the campaign came in the form of a policy of meting out punishment to criminals 'severely and swiftly', and doing so in public arenas that provided the greatest possible publicity. Two key criminal justice activities created momentum: first, 'united operations' that caught suspects in 'one fell swoop', which involved police and parapolicing forces converging on the streets en masse in 'search and inspection' operations and second, public sentencing rallies. Thousands of rallies were conducted nationwide during the campaign, and in two provinces alone there were over 5,000 rallies (2,336 in Liaoning and 2,780 in Guizhou) held between August 1983 and January 1987.[6]

Beijing became the national model for Strike Hard implementation during the first campaign in 1983. On 9 August, a 'Strike Hard Office' was established and a meeting was held at the Capital Stadium and attended by 10,000 criminal justice personnel. The Beijing Strike Hard Office designed the overall plan for the national offensive. On 30 August, the first public sentencing rally, organized by the Beijing Municipal Party Committee was held at the Workers' Stadium and attracted an audience of 100,000. At the rally, the President of the Beijing Intermediate Court, Judge Liu Yuanfeng, announced the death sentence for 30 convicted criminals, 19 of whom had been convicted of murder, 10 of rape and one of armed robbery. The crowd applauded enthusiastically at each announcement of the death penalty. On 17 August, in preparation for the rally, the Beijing Municipal Party Secretary had invited 60 non-CCP politicians, workers, union members, and well-known identities to discuss the plans and rationale for the 30 executions. They were briefed on the circumstances surrounding the crimes and shown the available evidence. They had all agreed to the executions.[7] These scenes were repeated hundreds of times over throughout the country in the three years of the campaign and, as we mentioned in the Introduction, it has been estimated that over 30,000 people were sentenced to death. From August 1983 to the end of 1986, more than 1,400,000 cases involving 1,721,000 people were tried in the criminal courts nationwide.[8] The 1983–86 generic Strike Hard campaign provided the specialized drives with a ready-made template that informed their rationale, format and rhetoric. 'Specialized struggles' came to the fore within months of the end of Strike Hard in 1986. They appeared on the scene in early 1987 as periodic 'attacks' on one type of crime and operated under the guiding principle of police 'uniting in battle'. These campaigns developed a way of combining police powers into a concentrated force where police from different fields and specialties would unite against a common target.[9] Most specialized drives, like their parent the Strike Hard campaign, employed Strike Hard policy and followed a four-pronged implementation format. The first step is the announcement at a national public order conference or forum that crime rates have become unacceptably high and have created the need to 'Strike Hard' at certain targets. Second, a series of 'offensives' are scheduled over a period ranging from weeks to months. After this, a discrete set of enemies to be targeted is determined, and finally a public show of force is organized in the form of large-scale police stings followed by public arrest and sentencing rallies.

Specialized struggles take two main forms – stand-alone campaigns and those implemented as part of the generic Strike Hard campaigns. Some begin as stand-alone drives and end up enmeshed within generic campaigns. For example, a specialized campaign against mafia-style organized crime was run as a stand-alone campaign in 2000, and was subsequently merged into the generic Strike Hard campaign of 2001–03. Under the umbrella of generic campaigns, specialized struggles frequently operate by launching successions of different offensives against a variety of targets, as the campaign drives in Inner Mongolia in 2002 below indicate. Here the Strike Hard offensive consisted of a series of specialized struggles that ran over a nine-month period from January to September 2002 as part of a generic campaign.

- Struggle 1: Public order struggle to protect spring festival
- Struggle 2: Offensive to improve the clear-up rates and to catch fugitives
- Struggle 3: Offensive against robbery and bag snatching
- Struggle 4: October and November offensive to protect the 10th Party Congress and 100-day operation to protect public order and public security.
- Struggle 5: Winter offensive, from October to the end of the year.[10]

Both formats (embedded and stand-alone) employ the policy of 'severity and swiftness' to target and punish criminals and use concentrated and policing power in 'intensified anti-crime operations'.[11] The following description of 'Operation Hurricane B' operations in Chengdu city, Sichuan Province, illustrates the style of 'intensified anti-crime operations'.

> On 20 April 2001 at precisely 10:00 p.m., Public Security Bureau [PSB] officers across the province launched 'Operation Hurricane B'. They apprehended many criminal suspects who were brought to an arrest rally the following morning, attended by over 10,000 people. In the Sichuan provincial capital of Chengdu alone, over 400 suspects were publicly arrested. From mid-evening on 20 April, the police command centre received numerous reports from PSB branches all over the province. By midnight, Chengdu PSB reported that 2,100 suspects had been apprehended and 43 firearms and 150 kilograms of explosives had been seized.[12]

The Chengdu Municipal police chief was quoted in the local press as stating that 'Immediately after receiving the order to start, 11,000 PSB officers, 1,100 military police and more than 20,000 party, government and security officials were on the move'. Altogether, more than 50,000 police and 100,000 government and party personnel and civilians participated in 'Operation Hurricane B' that evening.[13]

Specialized struggles are planned at the national, provincial and even county level. County-level struggles sometimes target crimes that are a particular problem in the local area. Tables 1.1, 1.2 and 1.3 detail campaigns in three different counties

Table 1.1 Specialized struggles and Strike Hard campaigns in Yuanling County, Hunan Province, 1987–95

1987	Two anti-theft struggles
1987	Struggle against common assault
1988	Two anti-theft struggles
1989	Four struggles: (1) anti-gambling struggle; (2) anti-theft and robbery struggle; (3) struggle against the 'six evils', including human trafficking; (4) struggle againstitinerant criminals
1992	Two anti-theft struggles
1994	Struggle to restore public order in urban areas
1995	Local 'Springtime' Strike Hard campaign

Source: Yuanlingxian jianchayuan jianchazhi. neibu faxing gao (Reference Resource Material for the Annals of the Yuanling County Procuratorate), pp. 95–103.

Table 1.2 Specialized struggles in Yongshan County, Yunnan, 1987–89

March 1987	Struggle against homicide and other Strike Hard crimes Struggle against the 'six evils' and itinerant criminals
April–May 1987	Struggle against theft, gambling, pick-pocketing and minor assault
August 1987	Struggle to solve long-pending unsolved cases
September–December 1987	Struggle against human trafficking
February–April 1988	Struggle against pick-pocketing and theft
May 1988	Struggle against human trafficking
January 1989	Struggle against theft, gambling, fraud using superstition
May–June 1989	Struggle against itinerant criminals
October–December 1989	Struggle against the 'six evils'

Source: Liu Wanpin (ed.), *Yongshan xianzhi* (Yongshan County Annals), unpublished restricted materials.

Table 1.3 Specialized struggles and Strike Hard campaigns in Lu Quan County, Yunnan Province, 1992–2000

1992	County-initiated 'Strike Hard' to combat major crimes and itinerant criminals and to capture fugitives (focus on murder, robbery, rape, major theft and human trafficking)
1993	Struggle to combat gang crime and itinerant crime
1994–95	Struggles against (1) robbery and mugging; (2) gang crime; (3) itinerant crime; and (4) fugitives
1999	'100 Day Battle' to ensure public order for the 50th anniversary of the PRC and the Kunming International Flower Festival
2000	County-wide Strike Hard campaign against theft, robbery and gang crime

Source: Wu Mingze (ed.) *Luquan yizu miaozu zizhixian 1991–2000* (Annals of the Yi and Miao minority in Lu Quan Autonomous Region 1991–2000), pp. 380–833.

to illustrate the proliferation of both nationally initiated and more localized struggles in these counties during the 1980s and 1990s.

The term 'specialized struggle' was not commonly used until 1987. An earlier incarnation of these struggles was the Mao-era 'intensified anti-crime operations', which were conducted in an *ad hoc* manner in various regions but rarely constituted nationwide struggles. Table 1.4 illustrates this earlier phenomenon with a list of the operations and their targets in Shenyang city from 1948 to 1979.

Beijing detectives Qian Qiang, Li Yaojie and Li Suoping consider that the specialized crime struggle in post-Mao China was a result of a particular set of conditions during the first decade of the post-Mao reform period that conspired to create uncertainty and instability in public order.[14] The detectives claim that the almost continual specialized crime struggles of the 1980s and 1990s were implemented because serious crime was seen as posing a grave threat to the success of economic reform.[15] Specialized crime struggles were conceived as a positive propaganda tool for expressing the government's determination to deter and punish crime.[16] The post-1978 use of 'shock and awe' tactics such as public sentencing rallies and parading criminals in trucks can be interpreted as a remnant of the ideological belief in the power of propaganda work that was popularized in the 1950s mass campaign era.[17] Yet, the campaigns of the 1980s and 1990s were organized according to a distinct post-Mao economic model of contract-based policing that rewarded job performance and offered monetary incentives for reducing crime. Above all, specialized struggles thrived in post-Mao China because they were perceived

Table 1.4 'Intensified anti-crime operations' in Shenyang City, October 1948–April 1979

October 1948–December 1949	Operation against bandits and robbery gangs
January–March 1953	Operation against habitual thieves, offenders concealing booty, and those teaching others how to commit crimes
January–December 1955	Operation against common crimes such as theft, fraud, concealing booty, hooliganism, gambling, drug trafficking and smuggling
September–December 1957	Operation against common criminals
May 1958	Operation against itinerant criminals
January–December 1961	Operation against thieves and hooligans
March–June 1962	Operation against hooligans
November 1962–January 1963	Operation against itinerant criminals and hooligans
February–August 1963	Operations against those committing premeditated crimes and itinerant criminals
September–October 1963	Operation against murderers and robbers
October 1964–December 1965	Operation against male teachers sexually assaulting female students
July–September 1965	Operation against itinerant criminals
August–October 1974	Operation against hooligans, thieves and smugglers
July–September 1975	Operation against robbers, murderers, hooligans, thieves, gamblers and those stealing food
March–April 1978	Operation against common crimes

Source: Shenyangshi gonganju diaocha yanjiusuo (eds), *Shenyang gonganzhi chugao* (Draft Annals of Shenyang Public Security), Shenyang: unpublished reference material.

within party circles as a useful means of overcoming the problem of inadequate funding for basic police work.[18] They were therefore employed to 'fill the gaps' in resources by replacing normal police work with 'intensified anti-crime operations'.[19] The proliferation of specialized crime struggles in the 1980s and 1990s was fuelled by the perception that the 'powerful effect' of combining police powers in a concentrated and forceful body would be enough to curb the rise in crime. Launched with speed and gusto, the attacks were directed precisely to hit hard at a specific crime problem.[20] Specialized struggles in the 1980s and 1990s were most commonly used to attack emerging crime concerns. Anti-crime struggles in Guangxi Province illustrate this well.

The increased incidence of cross-border trafficking in Guangxi Province in the late 1980s was believed to require a swift campaign-style response. Authorities employed two Strike Hard-type practices, one involving the prosecution and court getting involved in the investigation cases ahead of standard time, known in Chinese as *tiqian jieru* and the other, the practice of severely and swiftly punishing criminals who were trafficking in firearms, people and drugs. These were emerging crime problems that had begun to have a major impact on the social order in the late 1980s. Trafficking in firearms became a problem as firearms left over from the Vietnam War found their way into the marketplace, and between 1983 and 1996 the courts heard 968 cases involving 1,252 people convicted of selling firearms – 42 per cent of these received sentences that ranged from five years to the death penalty. Authorities claimed that the problem had been turned around from 1993, due to the 'severe and swift punishment' policy applied to these cases.[21]

The problem of trafficking in women and children had also become a significant problem a few years earlier in Guangxi Province, which borders Vietnam. In 1980, courts in Guangxi heard 94 human trafficking cases, but by 1984 the figure had risen dramatically to 1,149. Punishments for human trafficking were relatively lenient in the 1980s, with some offenders even given exemption from punishment but the rapid increase in the number of instances of human trafficking resulted in more severe punishment. The 1991 National People's Congress' (NPC) 'Decision to Severely Punish Criminal Elements who Buy and Sell Women and Children', and the subsequent SPC judicial interpretation of the NPC decision, legally differentiated between the types of offences that would be deemed 'serious' and those that would be deemed 'extremely serious'. The latter offences would attract sentences of life imprisonment or the death penalty. This interpretation of the law helped inform the Guangxi Higher Court's formulation of its judicial interpretation of the sentencing rationale for human trafficking crimes. Of the 578 criminals convicted for human trafficking in Guangxi in 1993, 72 per cent received punishments that ranged from five years to the death penalty.[22]

Specialized struggles in Beijing

The discussion above provides a broad outline of the rationale and implementation of specialized struggles. Let us now shift our focus to one geographical area to illustrate the ubiquitous nature of campaign justice from the late 1980s to the turn of the century. Beijing was the first place in China to employ specialized struggles that were essentially miniaturized versions of the larger campaigns after the first national generic Strike Hard campaign ended in late 1986. The first specialized struggle in Beijing, from 7 February to 30 April 1987, was a campaign to weed out criminals from 'crime dens'. Police had become aware that known criminals often combined forces to buy or rent apartments or hotel rooms to use as the base for their operations. Most were career thieves, but some were armed robbers and rapists. By focusing their attack on one target – those taking refuge in these 'crime dens' – police were able to solve a large number of cases relatively quickly.[23]

This first struggle in Beijing uncovered 1,200 crime dens and 1,600 residences of minor offenders responsible for illegal (although not criminal) activities, and police were able to 'crack' 3,600 cases. The struggle caught the attention of the Central Party Committee's Politico-legal Affairs Committee, which saw the potential of such initiatives to reap timely results. On 23 April 1987, the Central Politico-legal Affairs Committee, impressed with what they saw, wrote a report asking other areas to note the success of this mini-campaign in the capital. Campaign-fever spread and had intensified by 1988, as Table 1.5 indicates. Beijing's second specialized struggle, from 1 February 1988 to 15 April 1988, was an attack on the increasingly prevalent offences of robbery and major crime – by January 1988 the incidence of robbery in Beijing had increased by 130 per cent and that of major crime by 70 per cent over the previous year.[24]

The period from 1990 to 1993 was dominated by campaigns launched at a national level and implemented by local jurisdictions, which chose their specific crime targets based on local circumstances. As Table 1.6 indicates, the targets of these crime struggles ranged from theft to human trafficking.

Table 1.5 Specialized struggles in Beijing, 1987–89

7 February–30 April 1987	Struggle to weed out criminals from 'crime dens'	This campaign targeted known criminals who bought or rented apartments or hotel rooms to use as a base. These criminals were mainly career thieves but included some armed robbers and rapists.
1 February–15 April 1988	Struggle to combat robbery and major crime'	In January 1988, robbery in Beijing registered an increase of 130 per cent and major crime 70 per cent over the previous year. Thieves began to conduct robberies in broad daylight.
13 June–15 June 1989	Struggle to combat crime committed by itinerant workers	This was a national campaign.
5 September–25 September 1989	Struggle to combat crime committed by itinerant workers	This struggle aimed to clean up before celebration of the 40th anniversary of the founding of the PRC on 1 October.

Source: Zeng Guangwen (ed), *Beijingzhi: gong'anzhi* (The Beijing Annals: chronicles of the Beijing public security), pp. 150–52.

Table 1.6 Nationally implemented 'Strike Hard' campaigns and 'specialized struggles', 1990–92

1990	The 'six evils' campaign
	Specialized struggle against trafficking in women and children
	Specialized struggle to catch fugitives
	Strike Hard campaign
1991	Specialized struggle against prostitution
	Rectification campaign focusing on hotels and clubs
	Specialized struggle against theft
	Specialized struggle against trafficking in women and children
1992	Specialized struggle against crime on trains

Sources:Guo Xingguo (ed.) *Jianguo yilai gongan gongzuo dashi yaolan*, pp. 645–1299; Bi Xiqian and Chen Juan 'Yanda zhengzhi douzheng de huigu yu zhanwang', pp. 45–50.

On 5 May 1990, the Party Central Committee's Politico-legal Affairs Committee convened a nationwide teleconference at which the Secretary of the Committee and Politburo member, Qing Shi, announced the need to launch a general Strike Hard campaign in most provinces to fight the growing crime problem.[25] The law and order situation in Beijing in 1990 was deemed to be particularly poor: from January to August, 10,874 criminal cases were officially 'registered on file' with the police, a significant increase over the figure of 9,241 crimes placed on file for the whole 12-month period. Rising crime rates were a particular concern because the first major international event in post-Mao China, the Asian Games, was scheduled to be held in Beijing later that year. But guaranteeing the security of the Asian Games was not the only objective of Strike Hard 1990, which also sought to ensure stability on the first anniversary of the Beijing Tiananmen Incident and to 'guard' National Day in early October.[26]

The Strike Hard campaign in 1990 ran from May to the National Day holidays in October. The targeted crimes were: murder; bombing; theft and robbery including theft of firearms, highway robbery, and major theft; crimes using firearms; damaging state-owned electrical and communications equipment and construction equipment; trafficking in drugs, firearms, and women and children; major fraud; and major smuggling. The types of criminals targeted by the campaign were hooligan gang ringleaders, ringleaders of prostitution rackets and counterrevolutionaries (from the Tiananmen incident). Deputy Secretary of the Politico-legal Affairs Committee and President of the Supreme People's Court, Ren Jianxin, announced that regions could also select their own Strike Hard targets to address local crime problems.

Criminal justice agencies were told to maintain the policy of 'severity and swiftness in accordance with the law' while at the same time upholding the policy of attacking crime 'surely, accurately, and relentlessly'. The generic Strike Hard campaign ran from 16 May to the end of September in Beijing, and over this five-month period, police cracked 2,357 major crimes including 77 murders. Minor crimes, misdemeanours and public order problems were also a focus of the campaign: 696 prostitutes were removed from the streets; police checks were made on 17,940 homeless individuals with mental illnesses, resulting in 1,458 being sent to hospitals or hostels; and 4,727 beggars were returned to the countryside.[27]

In September 1990, Beijing's law-and-order scene was the most incident-free and peaceful it had been in years, according to policing authorities.[28] Strike Hard 1990 concluded with 966,002 suspects brought in for questioning across the country, 796,171 cases cracked (including 155,725 major criminal cases) and 337,098 gang members apprehended. At a national teleconference in October that year, the Secretary of the Politico-legal Affairs Committee congratulated criminal justice agencies on their success, but added that they needed to 'maintain the Strike Hard momentum'. Deputy Secretary Ren Jianxin, however, added that crime rates had not fallen substantially, and that major crime in particular was still rampant. He announced that 'severity and swiftness' would therefore not be relaxed in the coming years. Immediately after the conference, two additional specialized struggles were announced – one targeting major crime and gang crime, and the other focusing on the 'six evils' of prostitution, pornography, gambling, drug taking, using superstitious activities to defraud, and trafficking in women and children.[29]

At a March 1992 national teleconference on combating and preventing serious crime, the Minister of Public Security announced that the number of murders and bombings had increased substantially across the country, and that the spate of bombings of large public venues was of particular concern. In accordance with directives from the Politico-legal Affairs Committee, public security organs were ordered to continue employing Strike Hard policy to address their specific local crime problems and to carry out specialized struggles in their local areas as required.[30] A national conference was held in Dalian city from 15 to 20 August 1992 to reflect on the national anti-theft campaigns. At this conference, the Minister of Public Security stated that from September 1991 to March 1992, over 650,000 cases of theft had been resolved across the country.

According to police records collated by the National Comprehensive Management of Public Order (CMPO) Committee, 1992 marked the first signs of a degree of frustration in public security circles with the continuous anti-crime drives. The Minister of Public Security reported that some police were opposed to the whole idea of using campaign justice as a weapon in the war on crime, and that many police officers did not want to put their already depleted energies into fighting theft.[31] But this frustration with the constant campaign operations did not the dissuade authorities from continuing to launch specialized struggles, as Table 1.7 demonstrates.

To the probable frustration and despair of the exhausted police force and the criminal population, there was no end to nationwide campaigning from 1993 to 1996 as Table 1.8 indicates.

At the National Public Order Work Conference in Beijing from 21 to 25 December 1993, President Jiang Zemin outlined the three main public security priorities for the coming year: to maintain political stability and protect national security; 'to maintain Strike Hard policy to severely and swiftly attack crime; and to handle contradictions between the people' to prevent civil disputes escalating into

Table 1.7 Specialized struggles in Beijing, 1990–93

1 February–30 September 1990	Struggle against gang crime Struggle to ferret out criminal dens Struggle against the 'six evils' Struggle against major crime Struggle to capture fugitives	These struggles were all launched mainly to ensure public order for the start of the Asian Games.
1 March–15 April 1991	Struggle to combat major armed robbery and car theft	This was a national campaign.
1 June–30 June 1991	Struggle to combat prostitution and to strengthen control over hotels and entertainment venues	This was a national campaign.
20 August–20 September 1991	Struggle against possession of illegal firearms and explosives	
20 October–10 December 1991	Struggle against car and bicycle theft and break and enter crime	This campaign was implemented in response to public outcries against the dramatic increase in these crimes.
15 May–30 May 1992	Struggle against gang crime and possession of firearms	
15 September–24 September 1992	Struggle against gang crime and major crimes	This struggle was launched to ensure public order for the start of National Day celebrations and the 14th Party Congress in Beijing.
17 October–27 October 1992	Struggle against gang crime and major crimes, and struggle to catch fugitives	The Ministry of Public Security decided that some key crime hotspots in China needed to organize 'joint operations' to combat these crimes.
15 November–25 November 1992	Struggle against gang crime, major crimes, crimes committed by itinerant workers, and struggle to catch fugitives	Poor itinerant workers from other provinces who did not have Beijing residency permits would often commit crimes during this period to obtain money and goods to take home to their families for New Year celebrations.

Source: Zeng, *Beijingzhi: gong'anzhi*, pp. 150–55.

crimes.[32] A national struggle to embed Strike Hard policy 'deep into society' and to rectify public order problems was announced in July 1994, and each province and region was encouraged to choose its own crime targets to focus on crimes prevalent in their area. More than 882,000 cases were cracked nationwide from August 1994 to January 1995, including 249,000 major crimes.[33] In February 1995, the Minister of Public Security announced a new Springtime Strike Hard Offensive, again allowing local areas to choose their own targets. Beijing chose to target itinerant criminals. Strike Hard work groups were established in most provinces, and included the Party secretary and heads of criminal justice agencies.[34]

Table 1.8 National Strike Hard campaigns and 'specialized struggles', 1993–96

1993	Specialized struggle against robberies committed on major highways and freeways Specialized struggle against trafficking in women and children Specialized struggle against prostitution Specialized struggle against illegal border crossing
1994	Specialized struggle against manufacturing fake business receipts Specialized struggle against damaging railway tracks, major transportation routes and oil fields National Urban and Rural Offensive to Strike Hard at Crimes and to Rectify the Public Order
1995	Specialized struggle against trafficking in women and children Springtime Strike Hard Offensive

Sources: Guo Xingguo, *Jianguo yilai gongan gongzuo dashi yaolan*, pp. 645–1299; Bi Xiqian and Chen Juan, 'Yanda zhengzhi douzheng de huigu yu zhanwang', pp. 45–50.

A national Politico-legal Affairs Committee conference was held from 18 to 21 December 1995 to plan the direction of criminal justice policy for the next 15 years. This conference determined that for the period ahead the basic tasks of criminal justice work during this period would be to 'strike hard' at both serious and economic crime. President Jiang Zemin blamed the crime problem on the inability of police to enforce the law and punish those responsible, and commanded Party committees at all levels to resolve the problem by 'striking hard' at political enemies, common criminals and economic criminals; by attacking mafia-style crime; and by resolutely combating prostitution, pornography, and gambling offences.[35] Table 1.9 highlights Beijing's efforts to fight serious crime through specialized struggles from 1993 to the end of 1995.

Table 1.9 Specialized struggles in Beijing, 1993–95

1 May–30 June 1993	Struggles against crimes committed by members of the floating population and struggle to weed out criminals from 'crime dens'	These were identified as worrying crime trends in Beijing.
1 September–30 October 1993	Struggle against illegal possession of firearms, and struggle to clean up entertainment venues	These struggles were launched to secure public order for the start of National Day celebrations and the 7th National Games in Beijing.
20 February–20 March 1994	Struggle to combat gang crime	Gang crime, especially crime involving firearms, was rife.
29 March–25 April 1994	Struggle against theft, and damaging rail lines, oilfields, and communications equipment	This was a national campaign.

Table 1.9 Continued

1 April–30 June 1994	Struggle against the manufacture and selling of counterfeit receipts	Forging receipts had become a worrying trend in 1994.
21 May–30 June 1994	Springtime Offensives	These were struggles against all forms of common crime and street crime, run as a publicity event to harness public support for Beijing police.
1 June–30 September 1994	Struggle against illegal possession of firearms and crimes involving firearms	The use of firearms in the commission of a crime was becoming a worrying trend in Beijing.
25 February–30 May 1995	Springtime Offensive against itinerant crime	Crime committed by itinerant workers was again on the increase in Beijing.
15 June–30 August 1995	Summertime Strike Hard campaign	This was a struggle mainly against crimes involving firearms.
30 August–8 September 1995	Struggle to combat prostitution and to strengthen control over hotels and entertainment venues	This struggle was launched to ensure stable public order before the start of the World Women's Conference in Beijing.
15 November–10 December 1995	Struggle to resolve long-pending cases and other crimes	These struggles were an attempt to take the initiative and 'get in early' to prevent crimes before the New Year holidays.

Source: Zeng Guangwen (ed.), *Beijingzhi: gong'anzhi*, pp. 153–55.

As Table 1.10 shows, the national law-and-order scene from 1996 to 2000 continued, predictably, to be dominated by a combination of national campaigns and local specialized struggles.

Table 1.10 National Strike Hard campaigns and specialized struggles, 1996–2000

1996	Strike Hard campaign Winter Strike Hard offensive
1997	National anti-drugs campaign Strike Hard offensive (in some provinces)
1998	Specialized struggle against bombing, illegal possession, and sale of explosives
1999	Specialized struggle against the Falungong and superstitious sects Specialized struggle to apprehend fugitives
2000	Specialized struggle against trafficking in women and children Specialized struggle against counterfeit currency 'Typhoon Offensive' against counterfeit trademarks Specialized struggle against prostitution Specialized struggle against tax evasion Specialized struggle against 'mafia-style' crime

Sources: Guo Xingguo, *Jianguo yilai gongan gongzuo dashi yaolan*, pp. 645–1299; Bi Xiqian and Chen Juan, 'Yanda zhengzhi douzheng de huigu yu zhanwang', pp. 45–50.

The largest generic 'Strike Hard' in more than a decade was conducted in 1996. As with previous campaigns, it was launched on the coat-tails of a national law and order conference. Ren Jianxin, Deputy Secretary of the Central Politico-legal Affairs Committee, announced that the law and order situation across the country was appalling; in particular, the growing number of criminal syndicates and other 'heinous' organized crime gangs had contributed substantially to the increase in murder, robbery and drug crimes over the past few years. The decision to 'strike hard' yet again was made by the Central Party Committee, and party and government organizations across the country were told to unite in leadership, to concentrate their strengths on mobilizing the masses and ensuring that enthusiasm for Strike Hard on the part of criminal justice workers did not falter.[36] Initially, this campaign was scheduled to run from April to June 1996 and to focus on crimes that seriously damaged public order, serious crimes, and public order misdemeanours that were a threat to the public. Its objective was to employ the speediest means available to effect a turnaround in public order. The campaign received a powerful kick-start from an urgent meeting of criminal justice workers on 22 April, at which President Jiang ordered all local party secretaries to personally take command of the campaign in their area.[37]

On 2 May 1996, a delegation of national leaders, including Party Deputy Chairman Hu Jintao, Secretary of the Central Party Committee's Politico-legal Advisory Committee, Luo Gan and other members of the Politburo, appeared at a sub-bureau in Fengtai district in Beijing and at police stations in nearby Taoranting and Gaobeidian counties, making surprise visits to observe Strike Hard in action. They subsequently issued a report on their visits that indicated that they were unimpressed with their findings, and Hu urged PSB officers and authorities to show a greater understanding of the importance of striking severe blows and the need to create momentum for the campaign by mobilizing the masses. He also called on them to spearhead the attack on specific targets and to concentrate their efforts on combating major crimes and catching members of organized crime gangs and fugitives.[38] In terms of the sheer numbers of offences and the complexity of the crimes involved, the crime situation in Beijing in 1996 was said to be at its most disturbing since 1949,[39] and in another indication of the escalation in crime activity the previous year, police and criminals had fired openly on each other in the streets in two major incidents. During the 1996 Strike Hard campaign, the Beijing PSB solved 211 high-profile major cases, detained 5,599 suspects and apprehended 546 fugitives. The most obvious effect of Strike Hard 1996 was that it brought crime under control for a short period, seeing the number of crime incidents (*fa'an lu*) in 1996 down 17 per cent compared to the previous year.[40]

The last major specialized struggle launched in Beijing during the 1990s was part of a nationwide struggle to apprehend fugitives. This campaign was made possible by technological advances in crime control – namely, improvements made to the police intranet database system, at least in the more affluent parts of the country such as Beijing, where those working in crime control could afford computers. The cost to Beijing police for catching one fugitive in earlier campaigns averaged 10,000 yuan, which the PSB claimed it could no longer sustain.[41] The

50th anniversary of the founding of the PRC was approaching, as was the Macao handover of sovereignty. The general law and order situation was relatively stable, both in Beijing and nationwide, but fugitives and escaped prisoners were considered by party authorities to be a growing threat to public order. This led police across the country to launch a specialized struggle to catch fugitives on 3 August 1999, under the guidance of the Central Politico-legal Affairs Committee. As part of this initiative, each bureau and sub-bureau in the country placed information on the intranet database relating to: cases from as far back as 1990 in which a suspect had already been identified; suspects whose arrest had already been approved; escapees from labour camps or from 'reeducation through labour' institutions; and major cases that had occurred before 1990 in the above categories.[42]

At the end of the campaign 200,000 fugitives had been apprehended. This was not good news for those in the public security forces who were tiring of the relentless push to Strike Hard, as it proved those police who wanted to argue that striking hard did not work effectively to reduce crime (at least in the short term) wrong. The sheer number of fugitives caught, however, gave the CPC Politico-legal Affairs Committee cause for concern; at the start of the campaign, the Ministry of Public Security had calculated the number of fugitives on its books to be around 100,000 – only half the number apprehended during the struggle. According to Lin Zhongliang of the Central Party Politico-legal Affairs Committee, this campaign put an end to the argument that specialized struggles that focused police powers and concentrated their efforts did not have any real impact on the crime situation.[43]

Contesting campaign justice

For reasons that are self-evident, the official literature on police work in China paints a picture of unity between criminal justice agencies and the party in relation to the continued emphasis on anti-crime campaigns throughout the 1990s. Yet, controversy and debate about the overuse of campaigns began to surface in police circles as early as the late 1980s.[44] Murray Scot Tanner's study of insider criticisms of campaign-style policing revealed that within PSB circles some had been 'chipping away' at the official pro-Strike Hard stance of the party and the PSB since the mid-1990s. A number of local and provincial police chiefs began to publish their carefully worded reflections on campaigns in local and national public security journals, especially around the time of the national 1996 generic Strike Hard campaign.[45] Although the police restricted their criticisms to the more 'narrowly professional' realm rather than attacking the ideological or political foundations of campaigns, a high degree of frustration if not outright dissent within policing circles during this time was apparent.[46]

Some critics noted the negative impact of interference by generalist party committee officials in police work, whereby party officials in some areas issued maximum case quotas for police to follow, 'either forbidding them to officially open more cases than this during a year, or imposing substantial wage, bonus, and promotion penalties on departments' that failed to comply with quotas.[47] Police in many areas falsified crime statistics, artificially inflating arrest rates by 'rearresting and recharging past criminals for "newly discovered offences"' and inflating arrest rates in order to appear to be 'striking' more effectively.[48] It has been widely reported that, since the end of the first Strike Hard campaign in 1986, police have routinely raised their case-cracking rates (i.e. solved crimes) by refusing to officially register particularly hard-to-crack cases. Others 'deliberately refrain from arresting criminals that they should arrest, "saving them up" to arrest during the next campaign when superiors were watching'.[49] These endemic practices were difficult to stop, creating a vicious circle that police chiefs, fearing future criticism of their campaign performance, were reluctant to break, as one senior analyst described in Tanner's observations about campaign-style policing:

> such inflated social order statistics are politically 'sticky' because any current official who ignores the exaggerated good crime statistics of the past and begins reporting more 'honest' current figures (which are usually more pessimistic) lays himself open to a charge that 'social order has deteriorated' on his watch.[50]

We recall from the Introduction that crime prevention practices in China operate within a system known as 'comprehensive management of public order', and these practices (including crime prevention work) are the state's key approach to the control of minor crime.[51] On the other hand, the management of serious crime has favoured an 'attack' or 'strike' approach that is exemplified in the 'Strike Hard' policy of 'severely and swiftly punishing in accordance with the law'. As we will find in the chapters that follow, one of the most enduring criticisms of campaign justice since the mid-1990s has been that the 'attack' emphasis of campaigning has discouraged the development of a stronger emphasis on (more resource-intensive) preventative policing. Preventative policing includes the strong street presence of patrols, household registration, neighbourhood watch groups and the management of firearms, explosives and other dangerous weapons.[52] This tendency to downplay preventative policing is partly a consequence of a long-term lack of financial commitment to such measures on the part of local governments. Tanner's research revealed that, as early as 1993, one provincial police chief urged senior authorities to allow the province's police to suspend the relentless practice of 'concentrated attack operations' and focus on developing their investigatory skills, their ability to hunt down wanted criminals, to train new police officers, and to improve the basic policing skills of current officers serving in the police force.[53]

Tanner observed the tension between those in policing circles who advocated greater use of crime prevention and social management measures in the 1990s and those who continued to advocate draconian 'severe and swift punishment' measures. As he noted, Jiang Zemin's report to the 15th Party Congress in 1997 for the first time placed 'crime prevention' on a higher plain than 'striking hard', through the formulation that police 'must combine striking hard with crime prevention, taking crime prevention as the key element'.[54] But, in practice, at least in the fight against serious crime, this realignment of emphasis was not reflected in any real change in party policy.

Murmurs of discontent over the overuse of campaigning reached national level in 2000. The Party Central Politico-legal Affairs Committee head, Luo Gan, enthusiastically announced the first national anti-crime struggle against organized and gang crime in 2000. Yet, before the panic concerning crime syndicates had reached fever pitch in 2000, China's Minister of Public Security had predicted a relatively quiet year for public security officers in China, a year in which striking hard could be put on hold. A national public security conference in early January 2000 considered the public security work performed in 1999 and planned the national priorities for 2000. On the final day of the conference, Jia Chunwang, the head of the police in China, summarized the public security situation in 1999 stating that public security organs achieved considerable successes in fighting and containing superstitious sects (read *Falungong*), apprehending fugitives, fighting transnational crime, controlling civil disturbances and strengthening the professional, financial and political infrastructure of the police force. However, he also noted that the public security forces were experiencing systemic problems in adapting to the market economy. They therefore needed restructuring to improve fairness, encourage a 'civilized' approach to policing, and incorporate advances in science and technology. Jia contended that the domestic scene in China was still relatively stable at the beginning of 2000, providing an excellent foundation for planning the restructuring of public security over the year ahead. He also signalled his intention *not* to launch another campaign that year, claiming that

> We must strengthen the rule of law and get a better grasp on how to best serve the people and improve on the four areas of stricter law enforcement, improving procedural fairness, encouraging a 'civilized' approach to policing, and taking on board advances in science and technology.[55]

He asserted that, during 2000,

> Police must promote social order and social stability through educating citizens; and must emphasize the policy of 'stringent control' of crime [*yanguan*], 'stringent measures to prevent crime' [*yanfang*], and 'stringent measures to control crime' [*yankong*] to maintain the pressure on criminals.[56]

He made no mention of Strike Hard policy.

China's top law-and-order politician and Politburo member, Luo Gan, was next to speak at the conference. Noting the Minister's absence of Strike Hard rhetoric and in an obvious and resounding dismissal of the Minister's veiled attempt to put campaigning on hold for a year to give police forces time to strengthen basic police work (that is, crime prevention) rather than to aggressively and exhaustively Strike Hard, Luo announced that he expected Public Security Bureaus across the country to make a greater effort to understand the Central Party Committee's criminal justice policy of Strike Hard and consider the national criminal justice situation when developing their activities for 2000. Consequently, there was no respite from campaigning in 2000. Neither did the disjuncture between certain senior party and police opinion dissipate, despite the continuation of the campaigning juggernaut through to the first decade of the twenty-first century.

Concluding remarks

Specialized struggles have proliferated in post-Mao China for political and practical reasons. Conditions during the period of rapid economic transformation in the first decade of the post-1978 reforms gave rise to a relatively uncertain and unstable public order. The post-Mao ideology of 'political struggle' involved responding to threats to order through a process of blaming and shaming the enemies of socialist modernization.

In practice, Strike Hard-style struggles proliferated from the 1980s through to the first decade of the twenty-first century, partly because they were organized according to a distinctive economic model of contract-based policing that rewards officers for their performance and provides monetary incentives for solving crimes. Specialized crime struggles also thrived because they were perceived in senior party circles as a useful way to overcome the problem of inadequate funding for basic police work, effectively 'filling the gaps' in resources by replacing normal police work with 'intensified anti-crime operations'. Because specialized struggles could focus police powers into a concentrated body that could respond with force to the serious crime problem, they were used to 'attack' new crime problems as they arose. This chapter's examination of specialized struggles has demonstrated how the generic Strike Hard campaigns and specialized struggles complemented and reinforced one another to sustain and entrench the culture of campaign justice. Yet, as we have seen in the final section, this relentlessness took its toll on policing forces, which had thoroughly tired of campaign justice by the end of the twentieth century. We take a closer look in the following chapter at the practices of severe and swift punishment and the ideological reasoning behind these strikes.

2 The campaign template[1]

Anti-crime campaigns struck society hard for well over two decades in China. As a catchcry, to 'strike hard' has the verbal clout of a spirited urging, while also asserting state authority and intention to prevail over serious crime. What can be acknowledged so far from our examination of specialized struggles in Chapter 1, and recognized immediately from Table 2.1, is the relentlessness of the campaigns. Unacknowledged, though, in this assertion to Strike Hard, are vital questions about the strike – by whom, at whom, for what, to what end, and how hard – which this chapter aims to address.

Chapter 1 asserted – and indeed the list below indicates – that campaigns were an undeniably frequent occurrence on the law-and-order calendar in the two decades or more beginning at the outset of Deng Xiaoping's reform program. But sheer relentlessness in itself cannot be a solitary determining factor for campaign culture's longevity and political popularity. The endurance of campaign justice says something important about the nature of the way deviance is regulated in China. Therefore, an examination of the impact of campaigns on this relatively unexplored policing landscape presents possibilities for obtaining deeper insights into the regulation of Chinese society during the current reform period. We argued in the Introduction that campaigns became the vehicle or conduit through which central authorities implemented serious crime policy, beginning in the early 1980s. Just as campaigns emerged as a model for dealing with serious crime, this study of the politics of policing is likewise an exemplar for how politics works in implementing crime management policy in present-day China.

A deeper insight into the mechanism of the campaign juggernaut itself, however, requires us to reach back into the recent history of twentieth century China, in particular, the immediate post-revolutionary period of the early 1950s when the foundation of criminal justice in the PRC was laid. Regulation and management of serious crime in the post-Mao reform period has drawn its operational and ideological inspiration from a political culture borne out of the nomenclature and practices of Maoism. Anti-crime campaigns have been the vehicle through which a pre-existing Mao-inspired political culture of harsh punishment has persisted in the reform era. I argued in the Introduction that campaigns have acted as a bridge between past and present that political authorities believed necessary in order to negotiate through the potentially unstable path to social and economic transformation. Following the

Table 2.1 List of nationally Implemented Strike Hard and specialized campaigns

Year	*Campaign*
1979–1980	Campaign against social and public order crimes
1981	Campaign against social and public order crimes
1982	Campaign against economic crime
1983–1986	Strike Hard campaign
	Specialized drive against theft and smuggling of antiquities
	Specialized drive against prostitution
	Specialized drive against trafficking in women and children
1988	Specialized drive against gambling, bombings and other violent crimes
	Specialized drive against robberies committed on major highways and freeways
1989	Specialized drive against itinerant criminals
	United operations against the 'six evils'
1990	The 'six evils' campaign
	Specialized drive against trafficking in women and children
	Specialized drive to catch fugitives
	The Strike Hard campaign (in a number of regions)
1991	Specialized drive against prostitution
	Rectification campaign focusing on hotels and clubs
	Specialized drive against theft
	Specialized drive against trafficking in women and children
1992	Specialized drive against crime on trains
1993	Specialized drive against robberies committed on major highways and freeways
	Specialized drive against trafficking in women and children
	Specialized drive against prostitution
	Specialized drive against illegal border crossing
1994	Specialized drive against manufacturing fake business receipts
	Specialized drive against damaging railway tracks, major transportation routes and oil fields
	A National Urban and Rural Offensive to Strike Hard at Crimes and to Rectify the Public Order
1995	Specialized drive against trafficking in women and children
	Springtime Strike Hard Offensive
1996	A Strike Hard Campaign
	Wintertime Strike Hard Offensive
1997	National anti-drugs campaign
	Strike Hard offensive (in some provinces)
1998	Specialized drive against bombing, illegal possession, and selling of explosives
1999	Specialized drive against the Falungong and superstitious sects
	Specialized drive to catch fugitives
2000	Specialized drive against trafficking in women and children
	Specialized drive against counterfeit currency
	A 'typhoon offensive' against counterfeit trademarks
	Specialized drive against prostitution
	Specialized drive against tax evasion
	Specialized drive against organized and gang crime
	National Strike Hard campaign
2005–2007	The People's War on Drugs
2006–2009	National specialized drive against organized and gang crime

first Strike Hard campaign of 1983–86, campaigns have been utilized as the conceptual 'model' for the Chinese criminal justice system's response to serious crime. In this chapter, I scrutinize what I interpret as a three-fold dimension of this model or template within which the anti-crime campaign is rationalized and operationalized: its foundation stone, its scaffolding and its bricks and mortar.

The foundation stone, interrogated in the first part, is the socialist concept of crime and its relation to the punishment of enemies that was developed in the immediate post-revolutionary era. While I do not argue that post-Mao campaigns are rationalized in an unmediated way on the basis of Maoist ideals, Mao era concepts of crime and law nevertheless inform two key principles that give post-Mao campaigns their guiding rationale: the concept of social harm and the principle of tempering harsh punishment for a minority of serious criminals with leniency for the majority of (minor) offenders.

The second dimension of the template, what I interpret as the scaffolding, is the structure of the communist party organization that provides leadership and direction in campaigns. Understanding who takes charge of these campaigns, and why they do so, is crucial to our appreciation of the ubiquitous and enduring presence of anti-crime drives over the decades since the economic reforms began. According to the Central Party Committee's Politico-legal Committee, the party's overall national tasks over, and responsibilities towards, the nation are threefold: to reform, to develop and to ensure stability for the country.[2] The task of guaranteeing social stability is regarded as a political necessity to be carried out under leadership of the party at all levels.[3] According to one party insider, party management and coordination in implementing campaign policy has been necessary because criminal justice agencies are inadequate to perform the task without this leadership.[4]

The bricks and mortar examined in the third part of this chapter is the practice and policy of 'severe and swift punishment'. 'Severe and swift punishment' is operationalized through three essential elements of campaigns: the targeting of specific categories of crimes; the legal elasticity or flexible criminal justice practices; and the educative function which requires criminal justice workers to not only deal with crime through punishment but to express punishment through judicial rituals. Along with criminal justice organs, the party assumes a tutelage role, 'charged with infusing the masses with a belief system', which is based on an assumption of 'pedagogical and tutelary responsibility'.[5]

The purpose of outlining this template in this chapter is to show how politics becomes practice in criminal justice operations. A secondary aim is to inform an explanation of why campaign justice has persisted in contemporary China. In the final section we address the question of why campaign justice continued to be the hallmark of criminal justice operations against serious crime well after Maoism had disappeared from the centre stage of Chinese politics. The argument of this final section involves what I have identified in the Introduction as three aspects of the political that convey the narrative of campaign justice. Three distinct threads of the political – one ideological, another organizational and third, institutional politics – inform the storyline of why campaigns persisted in contemporary China.

The foundation stone: crime and the political nature of crime control in the PRC

We begin our discussion of the relationship between politics and crime in China with three twenty-first-century vignettes that exemplify the culture of campaign justice, revealing some ways in which political struggle is manifest in criminal justice work. These instances may be construed by some as simply aberrations of the Maoist mass campaigns of the 1950s. But, as I will demonstrate, they entail a more complex political dynamic, revealing a campaigning ethos that is more than a mere cultural remnant or shell of Maoist mass-line policing. They illustrate how the enduring notion of political struggle still works powerfully in the PRC's approach to serious crime, even if the context is a marketized rather than a Maoist China.

The bad seeds of Baozi Town

In June 2001 in the small township of Baozi in Gansu Province, the Deputy Mayor Tang Shenghan announced to local residents that the town governing authorities (not the criminal justice agencies) would launch its own local Strike Hard campaign in response to the national call to Strike Hard in April that year. Casting it as a 'comprehensive management of public order' Strike Hard campaign, Tang announced a plan to rid the area of 'bad seeds' (*liejiren*) by forcing townsfolk and surrounding villagers to nominate members of the local population who exhibited any of 14 'bad seed' behaviours. These 'bad seed' behaviours reached dramatically beyond those one might reasonably expect to be officially recognized and treated as criminal, and were certainly not among the official targets of the national Strike Hard campaign that was launched two months before. Half of these behaviours were the explicitly illegal activities of: (1) illegally selling gold pieces, (2) using illicit drugs, (3) assaulting others, (4) gambling illegally, (5) trafficking in women and children, (6) evading tax and (7) thieving. The other half derived from a very different understanding of morality, law and crime: (8) fornicating, (9) causing fights with neighbours, (10) not raising children as moral citizens, (11) being drunk and disorderly in the past, (12) disrespecting parents; and the gender specific violations of (13) males having long hair and (14) women wearing improper or glittery clothing. Notably, these categories of behaviour had been devised by Baozi Mayor Bao and Deputy Mayor Tang.

Tang explained that, although the official targets of the latest national Strike Hard campaign in 2001 were mafia-style syndicates and 'heinous' crime gangs, as there were none of these types of criminal in Baozi, the targets in the township would instead be 'bad seeds'.[6] The Deputy Mayor declared that a representative of each family within the township's administrative reach would be required to vote on the top five bad seeds, who would be required to perform community service for five days. Those deemed 'bad seeds' were expected to bring along their own food and tools and pay a fine of 200 yuan (approximately US$30).[7]

One resident selflessly chose himself, his wife and his three children because he was unwilling to choose his neighbours.[8] Another, a 68-year-old farmer, was fined for 'refusal to work', even though he was unable to perform his usual farm work because a storm had washed away all the good soil and he had no other means of making a living. He was forced to sell his possessions, including his coffin, to pay the fine.[9] Some months later Mayor Bao and Deputy Mayor Tang were arrested. Bao did not participate directly in shaming and punishing villagers but he was nonetheless considered culpable. Both men claimed they were trying to play their part in implementing the policies of the central party authorities, citing 'strike hard' and 'comprehensive management of public order' in their defence.[10]

Even though the actions of the mayor and more particularly the deputy mayor in pursuing this quasi-Strike Hard drive in Baozi are extreme and contravened the law in many respects, the mentality of 'struggle', that is, struggling against a perceived enemy, has all the hallmarks of a real Strike Hard campaign rooted in the concept of political struggle: selecting a target or targets, struggling against the targets, shaming the targets, and solving a 'social contradiction' through shaming and punishment. This case is an extreme example of a local-level campaign, but its rationale is not so different from the typical application of campaign justice to punish serious crimes that has been in operation since the beginning of the reform era.

Liaoning's hundred-day Strike Hard in 2005

The Liaoning Provincial Public Security Chief convened a media conference on 19 September 2005 to announce the immediate launch of a province-wide campaign known as the 'Hundred-Day Strike Hard Decisive Battle to Assault Fortified Positions' (*Yanda bairi gongjian huizhan*). This battle targeted all violent and life-threatening crimes, as well as other crimes such as armed robbery, mugging and theft. Information about 1,351 murder suspects who were on the run was carried in television and newspaper advertisements, and the public was offered rewards for information leading to their arrest.[11] With the announcement of the launch of this campaign, the front page of the *Liaoning Shenyang Evening News* delivered a stern declaration to the public, including all involved in policing, that those responsible for law enforcement would be punished for any failure to conduct the campaign successfully.[12]

Xu Wenyou, Provincial Head of Criminal Investigations for the Liaoning Public Security Bureau, threatened serious consequences for senior police who failed to meet the stipulated quotas. The first quota related to the number of indictments made during the 100-day campaign, which was expected to exceed the average annual number of indictments made over the previous three years. The second quota concerned the number of violent criminal cases (murder, arson, bombings) solved during the 100-day campaign, which needed to surpass the total number of cases solved in that year to date – i.e. from January to September. At the end of each month, the 'worst performing' municipal sub-bureau head and its chief of criminal investigations would be summoned to a seminar of all sub-bureau heads to discuss performance problems. The career futures of the worst-performing bureaus heads would also be decided at these seminars. In addition, the head office of public security would provide cash awards of a million yuan for the five top performing municipal bureau heads, who would each receive an additional 200,000 yuan in funding for their organization. Awards and promotions would also be given to the top-performing police investigators.[13]

The officials' wives' tale

Former deputy bureau head of the Bureau of Town Planning in Taixun County, Zhang Shanping, and his wife Miao Biyun, who were indicted on charges of corruption and accepting bribes, were put on public trial at the local cinema on 22 September 2005, and were both sentenced to five years' imprisonment. County and town leaders including party secretaries and mayors and their wives, and all deputy government department heads and their wives were invited to attend the trial.[14] More than 1,000 attended, 300 of whom were officials' wives.

Zhang Shanping and Miao Biyun were ushered into the court at 5:30 a.m. During the trial, Miao Biyun wept continuously. Zhang Shanping pleaded his wife's innocence, claiming that the criminal responsibility for accepting the bribes was entirely his, and implored the court to show his wife leniency. The procuratorate argued that on a dozen or more occasions Zhang had received bribes totalling more than 268,000 yuan from construction companies that were building apartments on newly developed land. The bribe money had been paid directly to Zhang's wife. The court was hushed during the trial, and many of the officers' wives expressed sadness upon seeing Miao Biyun crying, according to the news report on the trial. One of the women told a journalist that the trial had made a deep impression on her, and that the experience of Miao Biyun should serve as a warning to others. Another was quoted as saying, 'We need to learn how to manage our households properly. We will need to pay closer attention to three aspects of our husband's life: his current finances, our family unit and our future'.[15] The Taixun County government head who organized attendance at the trial explained that 'We are using this opportunity to teach the wives a lesson, to teach them to help their husbands to be honest in performing their duties'.[16] Thus is the tutelage role of the criminal justice organs.

Our narratives from Baozi town, Liaoning Province and Taixun County above have the hallmarks of the institutionalized doctrine of 'political struggle' as their ideological basis. The idea of struggle, which I examine here, is an ideologically inspired regulatory strategy that embeds the political at the very heart of criminal justice operations and organization. While arrest, prosecution and sentencing are legally sanctioned mechanisms to regulate human conduct and social relations, they are employed to achieve a politically inspired type of social order. This type of 'political struggle' itself is conceived within the broader conventions of what the state casts as socialist legality that continued to foreshadow the ideological agenda of crime control in post-Mao China.

Crime and criminality in Maoist China

In common law systems, the framework of understanding that underpins the experience of law for professionals who work in the field is based on a conception of law as 'institutionalized doctrine'.[17] Institutionalized doctrine comprises a set of 'established rules, regulations, procedures, guiding principles and normative concepts'.[18] This 'rules-centeredness' has evolved from the positivist tradition that recognizes the value of law and the instrumentality and efficacy of rules. In Western liberal systems, institutionalized doctrine provides the means of ordering procedural practices, precedent and prescription and the legitimization or authentication of them. In these systems, ideally at least, the application of strict legal rules reflects the liberal principles upon which the authority of the law is presumed to rest.

The 'institutionalized doctrine' of criminal law in the PRC was not based traditionally on the application of strict legal rules that gave the law its authority. Historically, the 'rules' that provided the basis for interpreting and applying legal prescriptions were the regulations, procedures and guiding principles of party policy that aimed to legitimize and protect state development. Perry Keller and others have argued convincingly that the Chinese communist approach to law has shared with traditional Chinese concept of law a central perception that certainty and predictability originate in a 'broad social context' rather than in a narrow formalist exposition of legal rules and texts.[19] The dominant theme in the operation of law in Chinese legal institutions has been an emphasis on 'the instrumental use of law and its essential openness to its context'.[20] In the immediate post-revolutionary period of the 1950s, the 'context' for this instrumentalist use of law was guided by Maoist interpretation of Marxist discourse. What was known as the people's democratic legal system in the Mao period employed as the ideological foundation of socialist justice key discursive and operational approaches to justice administration from the revolutionary days of wartime communism that led to the creation of the PRC.

Such concepts as 'democratic centralism', 'collective leadership', 'mass-line' and 'mutual coordination' between the three arms of criminal justice – police, procuracy and courts – informed the organizational rationale of the basic tasks of criminal justice work from the 1950s to the late 1970s. These representational, discursive and ideological fixtures were part of a claim to legitimize and consolidate party dictatorship over the proletariat and to suppress what the party leadership identified as the enemies of socialism. Most importantly, for an understanding of campaign justice in the post-Mao period, the party leadership claimed that the law was to serve as an instrument for implementing party policy through the politico-ideological agendas of criminal justice work and the operation of the people's democratic legal system.[21] The official articulation of such a statement by the party leadership rendered explicit the political nature of criminal justice, particularly in terms of the political concept of crime as an act that is primarily a violation against the state. The foundation stone of campaign justice in China was built on the political belief that because crime impacts on the political fortunes of the state, the state's response to crime is necessarily a political one.

Campaigns and criminal law in Maoist China

In his 1957 'Report on the Work of the Government', Premier Zhou Enlai accounted for the absence of comprehensive criminal and civil codes in the PRC by explaining that, 'it was difficult to adopt a civil or criminal code prior to the completion of the socialist reform of the system of private ownership of the means of production and the complete establishment of the system of socialist ownership'.[22] Only when the new system was more developed would the country adopt fundamental laws on the basis of 'summarized past experience'.[23] Following the Soviet Union, a theory of socialist law in China came to be articulated as a system of legal principles based on the historical realities of socialist revolution and the role of the state in realizing communism. The PRC theory of socialist law borrowed heavily from the Soviet model, in particular, Soviet philosopher and jurist Andrey Vyshinsky's theory of the law and the state.[24] But this theory of law was never construed as a theory of positivist law but rather as a set of aspirational goals.[25]

It is not surprising then that only two penal 'codes' existed prior to the PRC's first Criminal Law in 1979; the 1951 Statute on Punishment for Counterrevolutionary Activity and the 1952 Statute on Penalties for Corruption, written during and enacted after the launching of the Suppression of Counterrevolutionaries Campaign and the 'Three-antis' and 'Five-antis' campaigns respectively. Crimes such as murder, arson and poisoning were considered counterrevolutionary. They threatened the social order, therefore were deemed a political act. As the statute did not detail definitions of specific criminal acts, there was no precise provision in the law for any criteria determining criminal liability and other concepts such as criminal intent, negligence and so on. Prescriptions for punishment were also laid out in very general and simplistic terms.[26] Punishments listed for most of the major crimes such as treason, espionage, incitement, 'spreading poisons', assassination, sabotage or killing included the three principal forms of punishment: the death penalty, life imprisonment or a fixed term of imprisonment. Ninety-five per cent of crimes listed in the statute were punishable by life imprisonment or death.[27] The articles in the statutes were in essence a list of penalties for various crimes and the crimes themselves were not defined in the statutes nor did the statutes include any sentencing rationales or guidelines for the appropriate application of sanctions.

Rather than being based on positivist definitions, these codes were said to have been formulated on the basis of the 'summarized' and 'objective' conditions of social development and revolutionary work.[28] From the first years of the founding of the PRC, the norms expressive of the 'objective circumstances of social development' were those political goals of consolidating the dictatorship of the proletariat and constructing a socialist economic base. The management of crime control was approached as part of the programmatic goals of the state, conceived as an important component of the mass campaigns that dominated the 1950s. Positive law was to evolve from the 'objective circumstances of social development' through the mass movements. As President of the Supreme People's Court, Dong Biwu, noted with regard to the relationship between law and the mass campaigns of the 1950s:

> Of what nature is a mass movement? A mass movement is a type of violent and stormy revolutionary movement; it relies primarily on the direct action of the

> masses, and not on the law. In the past, land reforms, suppression of counter-revolutionaries, the three-antis and the five-antis, all relied on mass movements; they do not derive their origins from the law. Our laws have been created from the mass movements.[29]

The First National Conference of Judicial Workers of the People's Republic of China that convened within a few months of the establishment of the people's courts laid the foundation of policy groundwork based on the ideals of mass participation in politico-legal work. The spirit of the conference was encapsulated in Peng Zhen's address to judicial professionals:

> Administrative and legal work is not merely routine and documentary work to be performed in an office. It must be extensively combined with the mass movement, linked directly and closely with the masses.[30]

The first president of the Supreme Court, Shen Chun-ju, followed up this call to mass action with the statement, 'Our judicial work must serve political means and must be brought to bear on current central political tasks and mass movement'.[31] From 1950 to 1953, the central political tasks referred to in Shen's speech were implemented through a series of mass political campaigns initiated to effect social change, consolidate the national power base of the government, to give the peasantry a vested interested in the new order and to pave the way for economic construction by eliminating class enemies and encouraging a class consciousness among the people.[32] The 'political ends' which criminal court work were to serve in the initial stage of the post-liberation period were manifested in three main movements: the 'Land Reform and Democratic Reform' movement, the Suppression of Counterrevolutionaries Campaign and the Three and Five Antis Campaigns. Each campaign dealt with specific 'targets of dictatorship'.

An important consequence of Dong Biwu's statement that 'our laws have been created from mass movements' was the political belief when adjudicating cases, judges' interpretations of criminality would need to be flexible and malleable, changing in accordance with changes in the political environment. Positive law could not be set until a more 'permanent' determination of the objective conditions and experiences of social development could be made, ideally, after the socialist reform of the system of private ownership of the means of production and the establishment of the system of socialist ownership. In the meantime, judicial officers were expected to rely on particular political criteria to judge an act as either criminal or non-criminal in nature. This is the legacy of Maoist justice that, in part, informs campaign justice in the post-Mao period.

Despite the introduction of the Criminal Law of 1979 that aimed to provide stability and predictability in the application of the law, the ethos and logic of this kind of 'flexibility' that has been described above continued to guide the rationale of generic campaigns and specialized drives in the post-1978 period. While it has been claimed that post-Mao campaigns have been implemented 'in accordance with the law', they were nevertheless also the catalyst for major changes in the Criminal

Law. Former Supreme People's Court President Dong Biwu's assertion in the 1950s that 'our laws have been created from the mass movements' rings somewhat true for the post-Mao period when we consider that the party's announcement of first Strike Hard campaign in late August 1983 was enabled by legislative changes to the new Criminal Law and Criminal Procedural Law in early September that year following the announcement. Three 'Decisions' were passed by the National People's Congress in September 1983 to facilitate the 'severe and swift punishment' policy: the first extending the range and severity of punishments beyond the existing maximum penalty under the Criminal Law for targeted crimes; the second accelerating the trial process and reducing the time limits for prosecution and appeal; and third, lowering the level of the court of authorization for approval of the death penalty from the Supreme People's Court to the higher people's courts at the provincial level.

The concepts of social harm, criminality and the dialectics of 'punishment and leniency'

If the foundation stone of campaign justice is based on an unambiguous political concept of, and response to, crime then it is important to understand the jurisprudential logic behind the definition of criminality, that is, how crime is perceived in terms of the harm it causes society and how the state responds to this harm. In the Mao era, a crime was defined as a socially dangerous act and the degree of social dangerousness of this act inflicted upon society was the main criterion for demarcating the boundary between a criminal and unlawful act. An act or particular behaviour was considered a crime based on three main factors: the nature of the crime (as defined by the seriousness of the act), the amount of damage caused by the act and the state of mind of the offender.[33] The interpretation of the 'seriousness' of the act which determined whether the act is a crime or a misdemeanour, altered from one political period to another. For instance, during periods when socialist construction was emphasized as a national priority, economic offences were regarded as more serious than would normally be the case. An act that would normally not be considered a crime in one period might be determined as a crime in another period. In other words, interpretation of the relative degree of social danger of a particular act depended on a certain political interpretation of the nature of the act and the class nature of the accused and the interpretation of both would necessarily change in line with the currents of political change occurring in the wider political sphere.[34] For example, the difference between the Cultural Revolution act of 'malicious political slander' (*e'du gongjizui*) and uttering 'inappropriate expressions' (*cuohua*) depended on whether the person who committed the act was considered one of the 'people' or an enemy of the people. In some cases, supposed members of the 'people' who committed crimes that were not characteristic of 'the people' were assessed as the 'enemy' and were dealt with through the method of 'dictatorship' (i.e. punishment) rather than through less punitive methods such as 'reeducation through labour'. As interpretation of the membership of the people and thus the nature and dangerousness of an act tended to alter from period to period, the judicial interpretation of the degree of social harm of an act had to be flexible and could not be set in positive law.

The concept of social harm or social dangerousness continued to provide a key framework for a description of the rationale and tasks of anti-crime agendas in China in the post-Mao period in the 1980s. However, whereas social harm in the first 30 years of official literature on socialist law was closely connected to class struggle, we find the idea of social harm from the 1980s onwards was more intimately linked to objectives of economic reform and social stability. Therefore, while criminal justice work in the 1980s continued to serve political ends, the 'political' was defined not so much in terms of the objectives of revolutionary 'class struggle'-type mass movements but in terms of the current agendas of reform: economic construction and its pre-condition, social stability. We find then that in post-1978 China, that the political ends served by criminal justice work were no longer ideologically linked to class struggle and the 'liberation' of the forces of production but were correlated to the changing modes and relations of production engendered by economic restructuring.[35]

It follows from this that although notions of social harm in the reform period continued to underlie the principles, functions and implementation of criminal law since 1979, the notion of the 'social' was broadened to incorporate the ever widening complexity of social relations engendered by economic modernization. The concept of social harm, which informed the PRC's first comprehensive criminal code, passed in July 1979, reflected these changes. What constituted 'social harm' during campaigns in the 1980s and beyond was not so much a depoliticized form of the principles of social harm found in the 1951 Criminal statute. It was, rather, a reformulated version in which the interpretation of the seriousness of a crime was linked to the agenda of national economic reform.

Post-Mao socialist law and doing justice 'in accordance with the law'

Deng Xiaoping's reform promise to 'institutionalize democracy' and promote a rule of law in China in the aftermath of the Cultural Revolution did not precipitate a concomitant revolution in the way in which socialist jurisprudence was articulated. Legal historian Zhao Zhenjiang reminds us that Lenin's theory of socialist law was adopted in the PRC at a time when consolidation of the regime through class struggle was a predominant political concern. In the immediate aftermath of liberation in 1949, the main tasks of law were to consolidate the dictatorship and suppress the enemies of socialism. But in the immediate post-1978 period the basic concepts of socialist law that informed the PRC's first criminal law were neither replaced nor substantially developed beyond the strictures of traditional socialist law, despite the profound changes to the PRC's social and economic structure. As the 1979 Criminal Law revealed, the realm of criminal law in China remained closely tied to the aspirations for state development and economic reform, even though this reform was to produce a very different type of economy than in Mao's time. Even after the 1997 amendments to the Criminal Law, the criminal justice organs were still expected to

> use criminal punishments to fight against all criminal acts in order to safeguard security of the State, to defend the State power of the people's democratic dictatorship and the socialist system . . . to maintain public order and economic order, and to ensure the smooth progress of socialist construction.[36]

Zhao Zhenjiang has observed how this situation created an incongruous relationship between two fundamentally different phenomena – the theoretical foundation of socialist law in the revolutionary socialist period under Mao and the actual requirements of law in a marketizing economy.[37] In other words, the reformist claim to 'institutionalize democracy' and promote a rule of law in China in the aftermath of the Cultural Revolution required acknowledgement of this basic incongruity, and a conceptual and practical response that took it into account. Yet there was no substantial change in the way socialist law was officially articulated in the new reform climate. Politico-legal literature in the post-1978 period continued to characterize socialist law as an expression of the 'objective circumstances of socialist development',[38] and the notions that criminal law existed first and foremost to serve state interests and to safeguard the socialist system even though the socialist economy was now to be subject to market forces. Hence, the socialist legal principles framed in the 1979 Criminal Law did not demonstrate any real acknowledgement of the possible consequences of economic marketization and restructuring for the conduct, policing and punishment of serious crime.

Despite this disconnection between the principles of socialist law and the emerging system of capitalism and marketization, ongoing campaigns in the post-Mao era have been prosecuted within a legal system that promotes itself as operating under a socialist rule of law. The rhetorical core of the new socialist rule of law was a catchphrase 'in accordance with the law' (*yifa*) which was progressively introduced into the lexicon in the early 1980s. Little legal rhetoric since then has been promulgated without having the words '*yifa*' appended. Phrases such as 'making arrests in accordance with the law', 'handling cases in accordance with the law', 'punishing in accordance with the law', 'putting to death in accordance with the law' and 'managing state affairs in accordance with the law' have been the rhetorical staples of everyday criminal justice-speak in official circles since the 1980s. Arrest, adjudication, sentencing, punishment and execution – all actions cradled within the meta-narrative of the Chinese rule of law – share this discursive space with one of China's most controversial criminal justice policies, that of doing justice 'severely and swiftly in accordance with the law'.

In the early 1980s, an unconventional marriage developed between these two disparate catchcries, *yifa* (in accordance with the law) and *congzhong congkuai* (severely and swiftly). This relationship can be traced back to Deng Xiaoping's call to institutionalize law in the early 1980s, which was always articulated with a decidedly utilitarian commitment to 'legalization'. Deng qualified the legal reforms and the 'socialist rule of law' he introduced in 1979 with the warning that these developments should never hinder the party's obligation to 'severely punish' those who threatened the social or public order:[39]

> [T]he legal system will be improved only gradually in the course of practice, and we can't wait for that. When we fail to mete out stern punishment to so many criminals, can we even speak of having a legal system? All those who undermine stability and unity in any way must be dealt with sternly, according to the merits of each case.[40]

Hence, 'legalization' and 'democratization' in the post-Mao period 'did not entrench an unqualified new paradigm of "jural" development', as Ronald Keith and Zhiqiu Lin explain:

> Codification, in 1979, did not presume to challenge the 'political-legal system' (*zhengfa*). This system had always pushed the law and politics together, hence the formal application of law in the criminal justice system was part of a 'comprehensive' socio-jural approach that called for concurrent 'Strike Hard' political mobilization, prevention of crime, and the 'comprehensive management of public order' (*shehui zhi'an zonghe zhili*).[41]

More than a decade after the first Criminal law of 1979 and the first Criminal Procedural Law of 1979, revisions to these laws – the Criminal Procedural Law in 1996 (CPL96) and the Criminal Law in 1997 (CL97) – revived hope among some jurists in China that procedural changes could offer long overdue protection against the tendency towards a liberal use of harsh punishment, especially during campaigns. Ultimately, however, these new provisions did not have a significant impact on the severity of punishments. In fact, the number of capital offences rose dramatically from 38 in the 1979 Criminal Law to 68 in the amended code of 1997. Moreover, while the CPL96 and CL97 were undoubtedly a substantial improvement on the 1979 Criminal Law and Criminal Procedural Law in terms of their potential to protect the rights of criminal defendants (at least in black letter law), the socialist concept of 'crime' itself was not amended in the revised laws. Crime in China remained defined in terms of its 'social danger' or 'social harm', primarily in relation to the harm it causes society or the state as a whole, as Article 13 of the CL97 suggests:

> A crime refers to an act that endangers the sovereignty, territorial integrity and security of the State, splits the State, subverts the State power of the people's democratic dictatorship and overthrows the socialist system, undermines public and economic order, violates State-owned property, property collectively owned by the working people, or property privately owned by citizens, infringes on the citizen's rights of the person, their democratic or other rights, and any other act that endangers society and is subject to punishment according to the law. However, if the circumstances are extremely minor and the harm done is not serious, the act shall not be considered a crime.[42]

In post-1996–97 criminal law practice, during campaign periods, a clear interpretation continued to be given to punishing crimes that cause a specific – and indeed politically informed – sense of 'social harm'; that is, crimes that subvert society's sense of security and those that threaten social stability. While in non-campaign periods, individual criminal cases were seldom politicized. Crimes during campaign periods targeted outbreaks of certain types of crimes as collective threats to social stability.

The dialectics of tempering heavy punishment with leniency

Another enduring notion in the post-1996–97 environment was the recommitment in rhetoric, if not in black letter law, to the concept of tempering the 'severe' punishment of a minority of criminals with comparatively lenient punishment of those whose crimes were deemed less threatening to society. 'Combining punishment with leniency' was a leading rationale for the harsh punishment meted out to serious criminal offenders in anti-crime campaigns in the 1980s and 1990s. 'Combining punishment with leniency', enshrined in Article 1 of the 1979 Criminal Law, is a policy of trying to 'win over and reform the great majority of criminals while isolating and punishing the minority' through a variety of means including punishing principal offenders severely and dealing with non-principal offenders relatively lightly, punishing recidivists harshly and first time offenders lightly, and imposing harsh punishment on those who fail to confess to their crimes while treating leniently those who surrender themselves to police or perform meritorious service.[43] 'Combining punishment with leniency' is based on a principle of punishment which historically relied on the concept of utilitarian dialectics: 'the people' versus 'the people's enemies'; the 'majority' versus the 'minority' and 'the general enemies' versus the 'immediate enemies'. It has roots in the revolutionary era and was further developed in the post-liberation era as a particular means of 'dividing and breaking up' criminals to 'win over and reform' the majority (using lenient treatment) and to isolate the minority (using heavy punishment).[44] The dialectical balance here between severity and relative leniency reflects a mode of flexibility or elasticity that is a hallmark of the Chinese criminal justice system, as Keith and Lin argue:

> While Communist dialectical analysis often formally highlighted the need for both severity and leniency in a self-conscious response to the feelings of the masses who suffered social harm, it, nonetheless, highlighted the primary purpose of criminal law as providing social control in the wider interests of the masses. The latter, of course, is very much a matter of self-conscious political division and has resulted in cyclical 'cracking down' or '*yanda*' (Strike Hard).[45]

This dialectic between severity and leniency emerged as part of the repertoire of criminal law rhetoric of the 1950s socialist regime that aimed to reform society by transforming the majority of people while at the same time punishing a minority of class enemies. But this simple friend–enemy binary became more problematical as a rhetorical reference point for sentencing rationales in criminal cases in the decade or so after the advent of Strike Hard policy in the 1980s, as Strike Hard's more or less across-the-board 'severe and swift punishment' for serious crime came into conflict with the idea of selecting only a small minority of criminals to punish severely. Chen Xingliang argues that Strike Hard's overly liberal use of harsh punishment clashed both rhetorically and operationally with the idea of combining punishment and leniency. As he explains:

> Strike hard is a war against serious crime initiated by [state] authorities and carried out by criminal justice organs using the practice of 'severe and swift punishment' . . . Conventional readings of the issue might suggest that the policy of combining punishment and leniency and the policy of 'severe and swift punishment' are compatible because the policy of combining punishment and leniency can be regarded as the broad umbrella concept under which its specific application – i.e. severe and swift punishment – sits.[46]

Chen sees nothing questionable about the basic logic whereby a general policy tends to be all-encompassing and a specific policy usually constitutes one aspect of the manifestation of a more general policy. However, he does not believe that the relationship between 'combining punishment and leniency' and Strike Hard policy constitutes the relations between a general policy and one of its specific manifestations, because during the 1980s and 1990s criminal justice organs constantly made excessive use of severe and swift punishment. The harsh punishment side of the 'combining punishment and leniency' equation, in other words, became the sole focus of criminal justice agencies in their fight against serious crime.[47] Chen contends that Strike Hard policy made severe punishment more severe without a parallel increase of the 'lenient' component of the equation. For Chen, Strike Hard policy did not function legitimately within the principle of combining punishment with leniency; rather it developed as an antithetical principle, coming into conflict with the basic tenets of the principle of 'balance'. Further to this, he believes that in the 1980s and 1990s, 'combining punishment and leniency' was all but abandoned in favour of Strike Hard policy, largely to prop up the rationale that 'when there is the option to choose whether or not to arrest, [the suspect] should be arrested' (*kezhua kebuzhua, zhua*) and 'when there is a choice either to kill or not to kill, choose to kill' (*kesha kebusha, sha*). Chen maintains that such a rationale is hostile to the policy of tempering punishment with leniency.[48]

The Criminal Law was amended in 1997 and no longer contained any direct reference to combining punishment and leniency. The conventional justification for its removal from the Criminal Law 1997 (CL97), Chen contends, was that because the spirit of combining punishment and leniency already permeated all of the CL97's sentencing provisions, it was no longer deemed necessary to spell it out in black letter law as it had been in the 1979 Criminal Law. Chen's own interpretation of the reason for its removal from the CL97 was that its omission accommodated the smoother implementation of Strike Hard policy.[49] Removing the idea of tempering harsh punishment for the minority with more lenient punishment for the majority precipitated the heavy-handed use of harsh punishment during campaign periods. It has been this ethos of 'kill more' which has been a leading reason for the overzealous application of the death penalty in China.[50] Encapsulated in the policy of 'severe and swift punishment' and manifested in the idea of *kesha kebusha sha* – 'when there is a choice either to kill or not to kill, choose to kill' – the ethos of 'kill more' gained impetus with the continued implementation of Strike Hard's policy of swiftness and severity from the 1980s through to the first years of the twenty-first century.

The scaffolding of campaign justice: party leadership

Thus far we have examined one particular aspect of criminal law that has sustained and entrenched campaign justice in post-Mao China, its ideological basis. Let us now turn to another factor that has sustained the culture of campaign justice. We step outside an examination of the ideology and principles that are used to rationalize campaigns and punishment to consider one crucial constant in both the generic and specialized campaigns – their political leadership. Here we probe the organizational framework of party leadership over criminal justice policy through politico-legal committees and their role in the grassroots implementation of specialized and generic campaigns. We do so by exploring the role of the Central Party Committee's (CPC) Politico-legal Affairs Committee in promoting and sustaining the Strike Hard approach to crime control. Central to the party's justification for its prominent role in managing and coordinating the response to serious crime is that the party gives itself ultimate responsibility for maintaining social stability. Threats to social stability jeopardize the very future of the party, as President Jiang himself declared in 2001.[51] An outline below of an announcement of the final major national specialized campaign of the twentieth century in China kick-starts our discussion. It signposts the important nexus we find that exists between the role of criminal justice agencies in fighting crime and the broader political role of state-building.

Beginning in the mid-1990s, organized crime had been identified on the political radar as a serious social problem. A major specialized campaign was therefore predictable. A notice titled 'Certain issues regarding the launch of a specialized campaign to fight mafia-style syndicates and heinous gang crime' was jointly issued by the Supreme People's Court (SPC), the Supreme People's Procuratorate (SPP), the Ministry of Public Security (MPS) and the Department of Justice in 2000. In it, it stated that organized crime had increased dramatically in recent years, with some smaller criminal groups expanding into what authorities coined 'mafia-style' syndicates, arguing that the crimes committed by these syndicates were becoming increasingly serious, spreading like a cancer across society and causing growing public concern. The notice announced a campaign to strike hard at mafia-style syndicates and gang crime in order to protect the social and economic order, which would be known as the campaign to 'Strike down mafia-style syndicates and deals with heinous gang crime'. The notice advised that:

> We must gain a deeper understanding of the real threat these gangs present to society and we must understand the absolute necessity of this campaign. We

> must fortify leadership of the campaign and strengthen coordination [between the three criminal justice agencies]; apply the law correctly to severely and swiftly punish mafia-style syndicates and heinous gang crime; destroy protective umbrellas within the government; improve efficiency in case handling; speed up the pace of dealing with cases to send a strong message and ensure the campaign has a real impact on society; and mobilize the masses . . . to create a positive mood for the campaign.[52]

On 11 December 2000, the MPS launched the campaign at a teleconference at which Mr Luo Gan – then politburo member and chief Strike Hard advocate and head of the party's Central Politico-legal Committee – gave a speech that unequivocally outlined the political obligations of the police, procuratorate and courts to cooperate in the fight against organized crime:

> I must stress the political responsibilities of the criminal justice agencies in this campaign. They must fortify their leadership over this campaign because the protective umbrellas in government and other networks will attempt to pervert the course of justice during the investigation and trial phases of cases. Under these circumstances, it would be difficult to obtain the desired outcomes by relying solely on the three organs of criminal justice. Party committees and key government officials at all levels must therefore strengthen their leadership over the campaign. Criminal justice agencies must cooperate closely to ensure real results.[53]

Luo Gan's statement opens a window onto the landscape of campaigns and party politics.[54] In it, he went on to urge the nation's police to demonstrate a greater understanding of the Central Party Committee's criminal justice policy and consider the national perspective on criminal justice in developing their Strike Hard measures. Three main points he made provide a useful reference point for considering the party's role in criminal justice operation in China. First, he claimed that the party and criminal justice agencies needed to be unshakeable in protecting social stability and continue to 'strike hard' at all types of serious crime, targeting and homing in on specific hotspots and emerging crime trends. Second, party committees needed to assume a greater leadership role over the police, with the main political and party leaders personally taking over leadership of police work in their jurisdictions. Police, in turn, were urged to be unstinting in implementing their leaders' directives. Third, police were urged to improve the professionalism of their officers and increase their 'combat power' in order to strengthen their force.[55] Luo Gan's three points neatly echo three of the essential ingredients of the party's role in anti-crime initiatives: the maintenance of social stability is given as Strike Hard's *raison d'être*; party committees are seen as the organizational means of implementing Strike Hard; and Strike Hard's strength articulated as residing in the combined 'combat force' of criminal justice agencies that unite in battle.

The party's role in controlling campaigns is articulated clearly in the above statements. Both Strike Hard campaigns and national specialized drives are initiated by the CPC's Politico-legal Affairs Committee in Beijing and conducted under the leadership of the party at national, provincial, municipal and county levels. China's constitution entrenches party leadership over all aspects of state power. While party officials are not permitted to 'interfere' in individual cases, party committees nevertheless have decision-making power over specific anti-crime policies and other criminal justice strategies that directly affect the work of the police, prosecution and courts in their fight against serious crime. This is seen not as interference but as one side of the equation that prefigures the inherently political nature of criminal law in China. The other side of this equation is the political responsibility of criminal justice workers to ensure the smooth progress of socialist construction, as outlined in the criminal law. As one central party bureaucrat asserted in 2004:

> China must maintain the policy of severity and swiftness in relation to serious and violent crime . . . Criminal justice organs cannot abrogate responsibility for striking hard. Each and every judicial officer must maintain a heightened sense of political responsibility. Officials who are soft on crime should be regarded as traitors [*beipanzhe*], or at the very least their actions should be regarded as a serious dereliction of duty.[56]

The party maintains control over campaigns through a web of committees that reach down from central to county level. As Figure 2.1 shows the Politico-legal Affairs Committee, which operates under the leadership of the CPC, is the organization within the CPC charged with responsibility for criminal justice policy

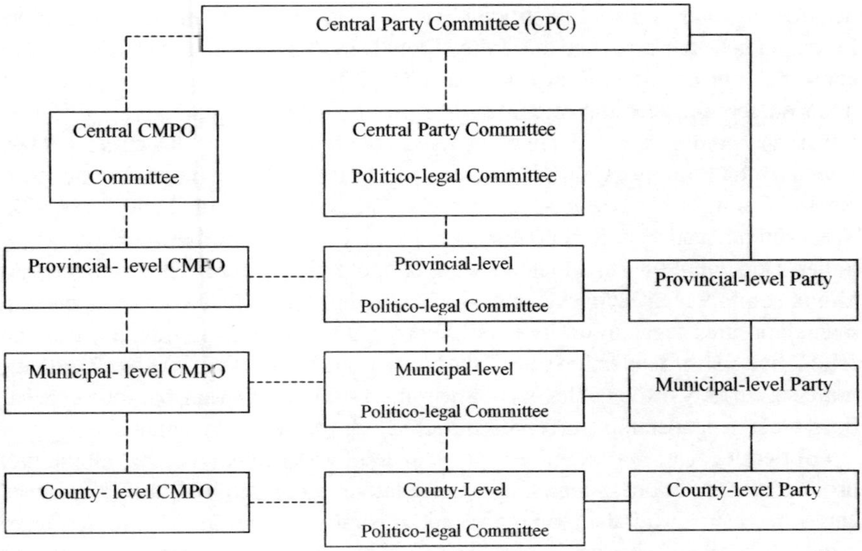

Figure 2.1 Organizational chart of the Central Party Committee, provincial committees, politico-legal committees and CMPO committees

matters at all levels of government. It is regarded as the 'staff officer' or 'assistant' to the party committee at all administrative levels.[57] Personnel and financing tie this committee inextricably to the umbrella party committee at its corresponding level. Its membership comprises personnel appointed by its parent party committee, and its budget is provided by the party committee and government at each level. While subordinate to the party committee, each politico-legal affairs committee has a 'guidance' role over the politico-legal affairs committee at the level below it. This means that each politico-legal affairs committee must comply with orders and decisions from the party committee at its own level, and report to and 'seek instruction' from the politico-legal affairs committee at the level above it.

According to one CPC Politico-legal Affairs Committee insider in Beijing, there is little detailed knowledge outside the upper echelons of the party of the specific role and rationale of the CPC Politico-legal Affairs Committee.[58] Although the Committee has operated under its current title since 1980, the first and only comprehensive account of its operations (a book-length account) was distributed as a restricted-circulation document to senior party hacks in 2004. This book, *Geji dangwei zhengfa wei de zhineng ji hongguan zhengfa gongzuo* (*The Functions and Macroscopic Tasks of the Politico-legal Affairs Work of Politico-legal Affairs Committees at all Levels of Government*), was written by Lin Zhongliang, head researcher of the CPC's main law-and-order 'think tank', the Politico-legal Affairs Committee Research Unit, and outlines the organization, tasks and rationale of the Politico-legal Affairs Committee and its self-appointed role of maintaining social stability in China.

The authority of the politico-legal affairs committee is similar to that of other departments within the party structure such as the Organization Department, the Propaganda Department and the United Front Department. But its role is not just to coordinate and advise, as is the case with other party departments. Lin contends that it has an actual leadership role in its area of jurisdiction, a qualitatively different role than 'guiding' or 'advising' government functionaries.[59] Document 94-9, issued by the Politburo Central Office on 12 March 1994, stipulated that the Party Central Committee's Politico-legal Affairs Committee is charged with leadership over criminal justice matters in China. On 7 June 1995, the Politburo Central Office issued Document 95-28, which stated even more clearly that 'The politico-legal affairs committee at each level is the branch within the party that takes leadership over all politico-legal affairs matters'. According to Lin, this provides a legitimate foundation for the leadership role of the politico-legal affairs committee. The committee is not only responsible for administration and coordination, but forms part of the collective leadership and represents all politico-legal affairs organs.

Politico-legal affairs committees at all levels of government (county, municipal, provincial and national) comprise representatives from criminal justice agencies and a secretary-general in charge of administrative affairs. Each politico-legal affairs committee secretary-general is also either the secretary-general or deputy secretary of the parent party committee. In most cases, then, the committee secretary is not the head of the public security bureau, procuratorate or court at the corresponding level, but a full-time party official. General membership of the committee usually includes the head of the local government in that jurisdiction (such as a county government head who has administrative control over the county's criminal justice organs), a court president, a head procurator, and a public security chief. At senior levels, it also includes a national security head, justice department head, or a PLA head. The only member with a full-time administrative position is the secretary-general, who carries out the politico-legal affairs committee's everyday work.[60]

As with other party organizations, while the party has its politico-legal affairs committee, the government has a mirror organization, the comprehensive management of public order (CMPO) committee at each level of government (see Figure 2.1). The politico-legal affairs committee and the CMPO committee are almost identical in terms of personnel, organization and work tasks.[61] The CMPO committee is the (public) governmental face of the politico-legal affairs committee. Strike Hard campaigns and national specialized drives are led either directly by the politico-legal affairs committee or through its government handmaiden, the CMPO committee. The CMPO committee is a joint government and party organization, charged with the 'comprehensive management' of criminal justice work.

The rationalization of party leadership: social stability

Central Politico-legal Committee head researcher Lin rationalizes the work of the politico-legal affairs committee as follows. Officially, the overall tasks of the party in the modernization era are threefold: to enable reform, to encourage development, and to maintain social stability. Protecting social stability is the collective responsibility of the party and the government leadership, and must be carried out under the combined leadership of the party and government at all levels.[62] While the criminal justice organs are the specialist organs for protecting public order, social order and social stability, the politico-legal affairs committee is responsible for the overall management and coordination of the specific tasks involved in protecting social stability.[63] These responsibilities are outlined in the 1995 party document No. 28 issued by the General Office of the Politburo, which states that 'Being duty-bound and without shirking responsibility, the politico-legal affairs committee must understand and properly grasp the entire picture concerning the protection of social stability and must therefore research and devise an overall plan to enable it to fulfil this responsibility'.[64]

Lin provides further rationalization of the party's leadership over criminal justice agencies. He claims that because many factors affect social stability, there need to be many separate organs responsible for understanding and dealing with these factors. It is therefore not possible to manage the complex task of protecting social stability without centralized and unified leadership, and this is the responsibility of the party. The politico-legal affairs committee is charged with devising plans at regular intervals to protect social stability.[65] The party rationalizes its supervision and coordination of criminal justice organs on the grounds that it cannot simply assume that they will properly implement the party's plans. The various work units, which involve criminal justice agencies across far-reaching geographical regions, need supervision and coordination to ensure that they are 'united in their thinking' and synchronized in their approach. As Lin Zhongliang explains metaphorically, 'If there was no central leadership, the criminal justice organs would simply be "a host of dragons without a head" (*qunlong wu tou*)'.[66]

The party's role in implementing campaigns

Lin explains that Strike Hard policy cannot be separated from party leadership and coordination because it is 'simply not enough to rely on criminal justice agencies' to do the job.[67] To be sure, the party's leadership is rationalized as a necessary way of channelling dispersed power into a united and powerful 'fist'. Indeed, the police, procuratorate and courts have a political duty to work together to concentrate human, material and financial resources to participate in a Strike Hard offensive or a specialized drive for a specified period of time. According to Lin, campaigns are considered necessary because the four fingers of criminal justice (the police, procuratorate, courts and the Ministry for Justice) normally perform separate operations that make it difficult for them to come together to address emerging crime trends. But when the fingers form a fist, their power becomes more concentrated and stronger. Lin adds, however, that 'A big brother [*laoda*] is needed to control this power'.[68]

Party leadership of large-scale anti-crime activities has been part of the political furniture of criminal justice operations since the revolutionary period in the 1930s. The following, a report written by the county party committee in the remote county of the Xiaoyi in Shanxi Province, exemplifies party involvement in anti-crime activities at the grassroots level in the early 1980s, an involvement that was replicated in thousands of counties. A pre-Strike Hard period national anti-crime campaign in 1981 was implemented in Xiaoyi County by 'strengthening the party's leadership' over the police, procuratorate and courts (known collectively as the *gongjianfa*) on the one hand, and on the other hand, by mobilizing an array of social institutions to help 'severely and swiftly attack crime' in accordance with the law. In one month after the start of the campaign, 227 cases were solved including cases involving 11 hooligan gangs with a total of 75 members. The public, the report noted, had remarked that in the past the *gongjianfa* had been 'acting like a marble lion, snarling its teeth but not biting anyone, not making an effort to attack criminals'. They remarked that they were frightened of their homes being robbed or being pickpocketed on the streets, and even more scared that criminals would seek recriminations if they called the police.[69] The anti-crime drive in Xiaoyi County was implemented in four stages. First, the party committee relayed the news from the province capital of the necessity of the campaign and organized personnel to lead the campaign. Second, campaign targets were set. Third, work practices were made 'flexible' in order to attack crime 'severely and swiftly'. Finally, the masses were mobilized and sentencing rallies convened to educate the masses and frighten would-be criminals. The county party committee took over the leadership of the *gongjianfa*. A 'rectifying the public order leadership group' was formed, comprising the county deputy party secretary, the county government head, the heads of the county police, prosecution and court, and the deputy head of the party propaganda department. The office established a number of 'teams' including a 'case cracking team', an 'investigation team', a 'propaganda team', a 'crime prevention team' and other smaller leadership teams at grassroots level.[70] Four work teams were sent to the four hotspots. Team 1 was headed by the county head procurator, Team 2 by the county court president, Team 3 by a county deputy head of public security and Team 4 by the county Bureau of Justice head. The head of the public security bureau remained in the county capital to help the county party committee to coordinate affairs. The other deputy PSB head also remained in the capital to lead the criminal investigation unit and to lead the fight against active criminals who were continuing to commit crimes after the launch of the campaign. The four work teams were responsible for organizing and prioritizing which types of criminals to target in their areas.

The local *gongjianfa* in Xiaoyi County acknowledged that law and order was a complex social issue and that in order to tackle crime they would need to unite and closely coordinate their activities and to place all available manpower into anti-crime activities. The job of mobilizing the masses and propagating the campaign involved the following activities:

- encouraging families to persuade their criminal relatives to surrender themselves to police;
- distributing 3,000 'open letter' leaflets propagating the drive;
- convening 130 law education sessions through slide shows at cinemas, on street corners, or on radio programs;
- holding sentencing rallies.

The county court organized five sentencing rallies around the three mining towns and a total of 30,000 members of the public turned out to attend these events which the county report stated were convened 'to educate the masses and frighten criminals'.[71]

Party involvement in campaigns had not changed fundamentally at the turn of the new century. At the start of the 2001 Strike Hard campaign in Henan Province, for instance, it was reported that criminal justice authorities 'sprang into action' immediately after the national announcement of the campaign. 'They studied and implemented the policies and spirit of the Central Party Committee and the provincial party committee's directives and established a Strike Hard Leaders' Group under the command of Party officials.'[72] In Shanghai, the Court President of the Shanghai Higher People's Court observed on 21 April 2001 that

> Courts across the city have all followed the Strike Hard policy of the Central Party Committee in achieving all aspects of work in the Strike Hard Campaign. We have implemented the Strike Hard Campaign in accordance with the Party's anti-crime policy, focusing our attack on serious criminals who undermine public order.[73]

As with previous campaigns, the call to battle in Strike Hard 2001 transformed party officials into temporary criminal justice managers. The Jiangxi provincial party head Meng Jianzhu, for example, stated that he had ordered the party secretary in each county and city in the province to head of the Strike Hard leadership team. These leaders were expected to be there in person working in the Strike Hard office at crucial periods of the campaign. He explained that party control of Strike Hard avoided potential problems in the organization of the campaign.[74] Xu Xiaogang, Deputy Public Security Chief of Jiangxi Province, puts this spin on it, describing criminal justice work in the 2001 Strike Hard campaign:

> Courts, prosecution and police work in close cooperation to create a pooling of forces. Because the party secretary at each level is the senior Strike hard official in the area, this person is able to facilitate the cooperation of the three arms of criminal justices so that they are able to work together smoothly and in unison. In addition, we have the Ministry of Justice, the Ministry of National Security, the military police, the people's militia and army reserves.[75]

Not only does grassroots party leadership over criminal justice organs remain a hallmark of anti-crime campaigns in the twenty-first century, but the party continues to demand political commitment from police, courts and prosecutors. As Lin Zhongliang noted in 2004:

> There are two sides to the coin [in tackling crime in China]. First, in fighting crime we must handle cases in accordance with the law and within the dictates of the rule of law. We must perfect the criminal law and other regulations and strengthen judicial interpretations in line with changing social conditions. This side of the coin relates to strengthening the law-making aspect of legal development. This is fighting crime through legislative development. But the other side of the coin, law enforcement, is even more important. China must maintain the policy of severity and swiftness in relation to serious and violent crimes.[76]

These two sides of the coin neatly encapsulate the perceived need for party leadership over criminal justice policy: one, a necessity based on the party's tutelage role in bringing about a party-led law-governed society, and the other, through overt punitive displays which reinforce the necessity of a strong party-state in order to fight effectively against the enemies of economic modernization. In both instances, the aim is to maintain and strengthen the party's contemporary role in Chinese society.

The bricks and mortar of campaign justice: severe and swift punishment

While the rationales and ideology of socialist legality inform criminal justice policy in post-Mao China that responds to outbreaks of serious crime, and while party organizations provide the structural scaffolding that supports the implementation of campaigns, it is the bricks and mortar of 'severe and swift punishment' that form the centrepiece of campaign justice. In order to unpack the implications of this expression, we need to flesh out three essential elements of 'severe and swift' punishment in campaign practice: the selection of targets for severe and swift punishment; the readjustment of the routine practices of criminal justice agencies to expedite the judicial process; and the propagation of punishment through rituals of public shaming.

Regardless of the length of time they run and their scale, both generic and specialized anti-crime campaigns operate under the common policy of striking hard by 'severely and swiftly' targeting and punishing serious crimes. Swift and severe punishment is therefore a key policy measure involved in striking hard through campaigns. Campaigns typically progress in the following manner: (1) a campaign is triggered by the announcement by state officials that the crime rate in relation to a particular crime category has become unacceptably high and crime targets are established. Criminal justice workers then launch a succession of 'offensives' that involve joint operations; (2) routine police and detective work is put on hold, and criminal justice operations move into a 'flexible' work mode in order to punish criminals 'severely and swiftly' with maximum effect; and (3) a 'great momentum' for the campaign is created through propaganda measures, particularly by conducting mass sentencing rallies. We explore below these three components of the campaign template by focusing on the bricks and mortar of severe and swift punishment policy – targeting, flexible practices and propaganda. It is these components of Strike Hard policy and practice that best informs our understanding of how campaigns operate on the ground and the rationale that underpins them. We begin this discussion with a 2007 vignette from Zhengzhou City in Henan Province that exemplifies the machinations of severe and swift punishment and campaign justice.

On 9 September 2007, as part of a local anti-crime drive, five separate public arrest rallies were convened in a united operation by the police of Zhengzhou City to warn and deter both active and would-be criminals. The first rally was held in three villages on the outskirts of the city. In a bid to attract the attention of as many early morning t'ai chi practitioners as possible, the open trucks that would transport the criminal suspects drove out of Zhengzhou People's Park at 7:30 a.m. towards the city watchhouse. At the watchhouse, police took 31 suspects, seven of them handcuffed and shackled, to parade in the open trucks around several districts. The suspects were publicly arrested at Yangjunliu village, again in Chenzhai village, and a third time in Zhangjia township. Each prisoner was guarded by two heavily armed police officers.[77]

The second rally, on the campus of Zhengzhou Teachers' University, was attended by students from campuses across the city. One by one, the arrests of 15 criminal suspects accused of theft, rape, robbery and assault were announced to the audience of several thousand students. According to Xinhua News Agency, one student observed that 'These suspects are all around the same age as us so it's distressing to hear about the crimes they have committed. Hearing it reminds us that we need to vigilantly self-regulate our behaviour so we can remain good citizens'. The third rally, at the May 1st Public Park, was convened to arrest 30 suspects. Xinhua reported that a small child in the audience was heard to comment: 'Mummy, look! Those wearing the black hoods are baddies.' While the black hoods protected the identities of the suspects, it also emphasized their status as 'baddies'. After the rally, the suspects were taken to Xushui town to be rearrested.[78]

The fourth rally was held in the public square of the Parkson Shopping Centre. The 30 murder and robbery suspects transported to the rally in three open trucks wore black hoods en route to the shopping centre but were made to remove the hoods when they arrived at the mall for their public arrest. They were forced to kneel on the ground in a line while their arrests were publicly broadcast. Surrounding the square were 200 police and 30 military police armed with semi-automatic machine guns. The fifth rally, at the Sanxuan Food Factory, was a repeat of the earlier public arrest of the 15 suspects at the Zhengzhou Teachers' College. The suspects were paraded on the podium when their arrests were announced. Most were males born in the 1980s – three had only just turned 18, including Liu Xuebin, who was accused of committing murder in the process of stealing 200 yuan. According to Xinhua, one onlooker claimed that Liu Xuebin 'should not be shot. He should suffer the punishment of being cut into ten thousand pieces'.[79]

The Zhengzhou rallies provide a graphic illustration of the campaign justice in action. In general, campaign justice is marked by three main features. The first is the categorization of targets: this involves the determination of the most 'serious' crimes in order to enable particular types of criminal to be targeted during anti-crime campaigns.

A second feature of campaign justice's 'severe and swift punishment' is the *flexibility* afforded to criminal justice practices, especially where this is required to achieve Strike Hard's trademark 'swiftness'; while its third discursive feature is the framing of criminal justice practice in terms of the didactic or *educative* role of police, prosecution and courts as agents of social change as well as social control. The symbolic and educative functions of criminal justice work rest on the assumption that citizens' values and understandings of law and justice are shaped by means of explicit education and deterrence programs that pit the enemy (the criminal) against 'the people'. Since the end of China's latest national two-year Strike Hard campaign in 2003, public arrest and sentencing rallies and other forms of expressive punishment have become much more infrequent, but as the Zhengzhou rallies and the show trial described above demonstrate, they have not directly been outlawed.

The targets of campaign justice

Campaign policy and practice is conceived in terms of attacking 'enemies' who threaten social stability and economic reform, who are seen ultimately as enemies of 'the people' in general. Indeed, since 1949, 'the people' have confronted many (party-identified) enemies, or at least one main enemy, with each new political event or economic construction program. In the 1950s, the enemy was landlords and counterrevolutionaries, and later, the rightists. In the immediate post-Mao era, it was hooligan gang members,[80] and in the twenty-first century it became organized criminals and violent offenders such as armed robbers. All of the anti-crime campaigns from the early 1980s to the present have targeted particular categories of criminals. The official justification for targeting particular groups is that their crimes pose a threat to the prevailing national priorities of economic reform and social stability. The operational basis for punishing serious criminals post-1978 has rested on a particular approach to distinguish 'serious offenders' from common criminals, which has its roots in the historical revolutionary mode first used to determine criminality and punishment in the 1950s – distinguishing between 'the people' and 'the enemy' and between different types of enemies.

The types of crime that most frequently come under campaign attack are those that disrupt public order (such as trafficking in, transporting and manufacturing narcotics, and organizing prostitution rackets) and violent crimes that infringe the social order and violate the rights of the person (such as homicide, rape, robbery, assault, arson, kidnapping and bombing). The main targets of campaigns are the enemies of socialist economic modernization who endanger the public and social order. They pose a threat to economic development, and because they endanger the very success of the reforms, they become the enemy of the people.

Flexible criminal justice practices

We noted above that in socialist legal theory, the principle of flexibility in applying criminal law in judicial procedures is promoted as a legitimate way of adapting to the rapid changes in the political and economic conditions of social development and consequently the changing nature of threats to the social and public order. The openness of the interpretation of criminal law to the ever-changing social, political and economic context has meant that party supremacy in policy making and the party's instrumentalist conception have relied heavily on the principle of 'flexibility' in administering justice. Criminal law was to serve the ever-changing priorities of state-building as well as ever-evolving social development, and so must be flexible.[81]

'Flexibility' is manifest in malleable conceptions of the degree to which certain crimes pose a danger to the social order, and in the ways in which criminal justice agencies respond to these crimes. Because in the Mao era socialist development was recognized as an evolutionary process, flexible application of the criminal law in judicial procedures was promoted as a legitimate way of adapting to changes in the political and economic conditions of socialist development and responding effectively to the changing threats to social and public order. Similarly, in all post-Mao anti-crime campaigns in China, the degree of severity attributed to particular crimes such as murder, arson, rape, theft and armed robbery, drug trafficking and organized crime has been informed by changes in official interpretations of the 'social danger' posed by these crimes in certain periods.[82] For example, as Harold Tanner points out, in the 1983 Strike Hard campaign, the 'new, more politicized characterization of crime explicitly refuted the idea that youth offenders were in some way victims of their socio-economic environment'.[83] Now they were seen as saboteurs of the socialist social order and economic modernization. As a result, when instability in the social and public order were deemed to threaten the very success of national reforms, adjudication and sentencing practices were 'simplified' and 'fast-tracked' to ensure the success of the campaign. Sanctions for 'social order' and 'public order' crimes were increased at times when these crimes were deemed a threat to social stability. Similarly, when corruption and profiteering were deemed a threat to economic success, sanctions were increased substantially.

This flexibility with regard to sanctions is still practised in many crime hotspots in China today. For example, theft cases are dealt with either through the system of administrative punishment or through the court system, depending on the severity of the crime (i.e. the monetary value of the property stolen). During some anti-crime campaigns, police have been known to reduce the existing monetary benchmark at which a theft misdemeanour is deemed to cross over the line into an act of criminality and therefore subject to criminal prosecution so that the case can be heard in a court of law and dealt with more severely than would be the case if it was dealt with as a summary offence or misdemeanour through administrative punishment.[84]

In criminal justice practice, the ethos of 'flexibility' in anti-crime campaigns also involves intra and inter-agency coordination of activities such as 'united operations' and the 'severe and swift' punishment criminal groups that are a particular problem in local areas. Inter-agency cooperation requires the three agencies of criminal justice – the public security bureau (PSB), the procuratorate and the courts – to work together for a specified period to attack crime targets 'severely and swiftly'. Flexibility during campaigns allows for the employment of 'severity and swiftness' to deal with criminal cases that are considered a major threat to public or social order. The concept of 'severity' as a sentencing rationale entails meting out relatively severe punishments within the options set down by the law. In normal criminal law practice in China, judges have considerable discretion; there is judicial space for the judge to assess a case according to her/his own judgment of circumstances of the crime. Judges are expected to hand down relatively 'severe' punishment for crimes with aggravating circumstances and lighter punishment for cases in which there are mitigating circumstances. For example, under normal criminal law, the penalty for a rape crime ranges from five years to life, and in extremely heinous cases, the death sentence; the judge must exercise discretion when passing judgment. However, when Strike Hard policy is applied to particular targeted crimes, judges are given much less discretion in determining the severity of punishments, and little room to consider any mitigating circumstances that might mitigate the length or severity of punishment. When Strike Hard policy is applied, judges are often required by the state to routinely apply a greater level of severity across the board for all targeted crimes.[85]

Severe and swift punishment

Originally employed in the immediate post-Mao period, 'severity and swiftness' was cast as the most effective way of dealing with emerging social order crimes, particularly those committed by juveniles and hooligans. Politico-legal authorities stressed that 'severity' must be applied within the constraints of the available penalties and within the time limits set out in the law. But this style of severity differs explicitly from the 'severity' principle that is applied to aggravating circumstances of a crime in normal criminal law practice. During campaigns, severity is encouraged across the board for all targeted crimes, regardless of the circumstances of individual cases, and requires judges to choose a relatively severe penalty from the available sentencing options. In short, it is the mandatory application of heavy punishment compulsory to all targeted crimes that distinguishes Strike Hard justice from the everyday criminal justice process. Table 2.2 shows the punishment range for crimes that were the main targets of the 2001–03 campaign.

'Swiftness' mandates the speeding up of criminal procedure to deal with targeted criminals quickly, often within two weeks of arrest. It entails the prompt investigation, prosecution and adjudication of a case within the time limits set out in the Criminal Procedural Law.[86] During anti-crime campaigns, 'swiftness' means accelerating the speed at which a case is moved through court by employing the

Table 2.2 Scale of punishments for crimes targeted in Strike Hard 2001

	Sentences ranging from 0 to 3 years imprisonment	*Sentences ranging from 3 to 10 years imprisonment*	*Sentences ranging from 10 years to life*	*Death penalty*
Arson, breaching dikes, causing explosions, spreading poisons			*	*
Manslaughter, attempted murder, murder			*	*
Serious assault causing severe injury or death			*	*
Rape		*		
Multiple rape or rape causing death			*	*
Trafficking in women and children		*	*	*
Kidnapping			*	
Kidnapping resulting in death				*
Forming, leading or taking an active part in an organization of the nature of a criminal syndicate		*		
Common robbery		*		
Serious robbery			*	*
Habitual theft	*			
Serious theft		*		
Major theft			*	*
Drug smuggling, manufacturing or transporting heroin (50 grams or more)			* (15 years)	*

Source: Criminal Law of the People's Republic of China, 1997.

policy of the 'two basics' and by avoiding the minutiae of case detail. The principle of the 'two basics' essentially lowers the standards that are used to determine guilt. This policy requires judges to be satisfied only that (1) the basic facts are clear, and (2) the basic evidence is conclusive. The 'basic' facts are those that can be considered the main components of the crime, and the 'basic' evidence is the essential evidence – and only that evidence – required to ascertain criminality and guilt. Following these two 'basics' enables the rapid conduct of cases that 'swiftness' requires.[87] 'Swiftness' is also achieved through other flexible work practices such as 'entering the judicial process before the scheduled time' (*tiqian jieru*) to adjudicate cases at lightning speed. Court workers, police and prosecutors work together to process cases as quickly as possible.

Adjudication and sentencing practices are 'simplified' and 'fast-tracked' to ensure the success of Strike Hard campaigns at times when the unstable state of the social and public order has been characterized as a threat to the success of economic reforms.[88] Commentary on legal trends in *The People's Daily Online* spelled out the wider rationale to the general public during a campaign in 2001:

> [Courts] work in close consultation with the public security bureau and the procuratorate before any serious or difficult cases are put on trial in order to fully grasp the situation pertaining to the crime and to ensure that all potential problems concerned with evidence or the facts of the case are sorted out before the indictment is given to the court, to ensure a speedy trial and judgment.[89]

The policy of severity and swiftness was never actually enshrined in the Criminal Law; as noted earlier in the chapter, it was legislated through supplementary regulations passed by the National People's Congress at the start of the first Strike Hard campaign.[90] This legitimated the use of punishment over and above the existing maximum punishment in the Criminal Law for a number of serious offenders, and extended legitimate use of the death penalty to the seven main categories of crimes targeted in the campaign (murder, rape, robbery, arson, bombing, major theft and hooliganism).[91] The 1983 provisions that form the basis of the 'severe and swift punishment' policy remain in the Criminal Law, and have been applied to serious crimes including robbery, rape, murder, kidnapping, and even non-violent crimes such as serious theft for the last two decades or more. In short, the rationale for swiftness is its perceived deterrence value. The assumption here is that the less time that elapses between the commission of a crime and the punishment of the guilty party, the greater the social benefits of punishment. This maximizes deterrence value because swiftness helps to cement the conspicuous relationship between crime and punishment in the minds of the public.[92]

The role of propaganda

Framing criminal justice work in terms of the educative role of police, prosecution and courts as agents of social control and change is the third feature of the bricks and mortar of campaign justice. During the mass campaign period that spanned the decade of the 1950s, criminal justice workers assumed an educative role in the fight against social harm in an effort to effect social transformation of individual and society. Criminal justice work was perceived as a didactic interpreter of public morality and social conduct, and as a facilitator of change in the social and moral nature of the individual.[93] This educative role continued in the post-Mao period, mainly in the form of punishment rituals such as the Zhengzhou rallies described above.

The sentencing rally in China is a shaming ritual enacted in public for educational and deterrence purposes, whereby case judgments and the sentences of convicted criminals are announced at a public forum. The audiences for rallies are usually organized en masse by work units and local Party committees, and can range from a few dozen to more than 100,000. These events are not sites for adjudication and determination of guilt, as the judgment in each case has already been determined by the court; rather they are a judicial setting in which the emotive acts of public shaming and gestures of moral indignation can be acted out in public. As I have noted elsewhere, rallies provide 'an important organizational format through which the communicative acts of blaming and shaming are constituted and relayed to their social audience as a message from the state that "crime does not pay"'.[94] Rallies are, in essence, degradation ceremonies:

> The sentencing rally is removed from the formal and unemotive trial proceedings of the courtroom and is usually held away from the courthouse in a venue that belongs to the public, not the court. It is conducted at sites such as market places, stadiums, community halls, at the crime site, or the criminal's workplace. It can be convened to pronounce sentences on a few individuals or a large group of convicted criminals, usually for serious crimes that attract some public attention or specific crimes that are the targets of anti-crime campaigns. The rally usually opens with a succession of offenders brought out on to a platform or stage, handcuffed and under the guard of a line of court police. Offenders sometimes wear placards around their necks and tied to their backs, which detail the criminal's name, the nature of the offence, and the sentence. The offenders usually stand at the front of the stage under guard, while Party and government dignitaries stand or are seated behind them at the centre of the stage or in other prominent positions. Senior heads of the police, procuratorate, and courts stand or sit together with local government and Party dignitaries as a sign of unity. After a succession of speeches, a senior judge or court president is called upon to declare sentencing. Offenders are then placed in court vehicles, sometimes in open trucks, and led either to their deaths at the local execution grounds or to prison.[95]

Rallies remained a popular component of campaigns at the turn of the new millennium. The most common manifestations of Strike Hard momentum in the 2001–03 Strike Hard campaign were three different types of sentencing rallies: 'simultaneously convened rallies', rallies convened for a specific audience called 'specialized sentencing rallies', and 'joint public arrest and sentencing rallies'[96] Simultaneously convened rallies were coordinated by central authorities to magnify the deterrent effect of rallies. The 'special purpose Strike Hard sentencing rallies' catered for a boutique audience such as high-school students. For example, on 25 April 2001, a local court in Haizhu held a rally to educate high-school students and frighten would-be criminals in the audience. In front of the 1,300 students and teachers in attendance, three armed robbers from the local community were sentenced. The local evening newspaper reported the rally's 'positive effect' on the school environment: students who had been troublemakers suddenly experienced a positive attitudinal change and troublemakers who had been hanging about outside the school dispersed in fear.[97]

In China's first generic Strike Hard campaign of the twenty-first century, the most popular form of sentencing rally was the 'joint public arrest and sentencing rally'. A hybrid of the 'public arrest rally' and the conventional sentencing rally, the joint rally was a Strike Hard 2001 creation. Typically, a rally begins with a line-up of detained suspects who are paraded on a stage or podium and publicly arrested by PSB officers, handcuffed and (sometimes) paraded around the grounds of the rally site. After police publicly arrest a batch of suspects, court judges sentence another batch of suspects who have been found guilty, very often of crimes similar to those for which the suspects have just been charged. Police and judges work closely together in these rallies to demonstrate unambiguously that those who are arrested are punished severely.[98] Less frequent are show trials to which a specific audience is 'invited' to learn the lesson that crime does not pay.

In summary, campaign justice requires a public stage from which to shame and punish its enemies. Selecting a target, struggling against the target, and shaming the target through the process of public humiliation and degradation are therefore important parts of the campaign process. The five separate public arrest rallies on 9 September 2007 in Zhengzhou City, Henan Province, which were convened to frighten and deter both active and would-be criminals and to impress upon law-abiding citizens that the 'shock and awe' approach to crime control is indeed effective in deterring crime. Rally No. 1, which was held in three villages on the outskirts of the city, began with a number of open trucks departing from a public park in order to attract as many early morning t'ai chi practitioners as possible. At Rally No. 2, one university student at the Zhengzhou Teachers' University remarked to the Xinhua News Agency that attending the rally 'reminds us that we need to vigilantly self-regulate our behaviour so that we can remain good citizens'.[99] Rally No. 3, at the 'First of May' Public Park, was convened to arrest 30 suspects, all wearing black hoods to protect their identity, but also, presumably, to set them apart from the law-abiding citizens in the audience.

In short, rallies are a product of a certain socialist reasoning that assumes human behaviour and attitudes toward crime can be manipulated by conscious acts of persuasion and ideological education, using representational formats that project negative models as a guide to attitudinal and behavioural change.[100] Police and court workers select model cases strategically to 'give wide publicity and magnify their social effectiveness'.[101] Politico-legal authorities are encouraged to select cases that send a clear message about the state's response to crime to both frighten would-be criminals and inspire the masses to action. Moral indignation expressed in arrest and sentencing declarations effects the ritual destruction of the individual by constructing the status of the accused as the antithesis of the values and moral order of the majority.[102] We find therefore at Rally No. 4 in Zhengzhou in September 2007 that the 30 murder and robbery suspects were made to kneel on the ground in a line while their arrests were publicly broadcast, and while 200 police and 30 military police surrounded the square armed with semi-automatic machine guns. At Rally No. 5, suspects were made to stand and face the crowd, one by one, as their arrests were announced. These are small-scale examples of the 'shock and awe' function of rallies writ large in the national campaigns, as will be evident in the discussion in Chapter 4.

Concluding remarks: why campaigns persisted in a marketized China

We conclude this discussion of the campaign template by teasing out some explanations for the endurance of Strike Hard practices. Why campaigns ended up as the key political expression in criminal justice operations against serious crime in the 1980s and 1990s through to the first years of the twenty-first century is largely to do with the primary contention of this study: that the policing and punishment of serious crime in this period has remained within the realm of the 'political' because social stability has been considered the essential pre-condition for economic development. Criminal justice responses to serious crime have therefore necessarily been articulated in political terms because protecting social stability is political business in China. Following on from this assertion, we can address the question why campaign justice continued to be the hallmark of criminal justice operations by bringing back into focus the three aspects of 'the political' that informs the storyline of campaign justice – one to do with the ideological rationale of criminal law and practice, another related to party politics and the third concerning institutional politics.

In the wake of the atrocious failures of the Maoist reforms and the Cultural Revolution, courts, prosecution agencies and police embarked on another revolution in organization and operation in response to the Communist Party's call for a new approach to socialist legality in December 1978. The intended metamorphosis was a significant shift in an approach to justice administration in the wake of wide-scale political, economic and social changes occasioned by the open reform policies under Deng Xiaoping. But, all of these developments occurred at a time when the local criminal justice agencies had not yet even been given the funding to build their own courtrooms and facilities and at a time when the majority of judges had a level of education and training far inferior to their Western counterparts. Until the mid-1980s, the majority of courts in China conducted their trials in office rooms and rented auditoriums. Despite the aspirations and intentions to professionalize the workforce, the majority of judicial staff in courts did not have a university degree let alone a degree in law. The situation was similar for police and prosecution bodies.

Despite the lack of material conditions for professionalization to occur, the post-1978 legal reforms engendered an expectation that law would function as a means of delivering the democratic ideal of governance promised to the nation in December 1978. The 'systematization' and 'institutionalization' of democracy in law was conceived as a socio-educative process whereby institutions would foster a sense of respect for law amongst the citizenry. These expectations of legal reform also placed legislative and procedural changes in a moral context of developing a sound spiritual civilization. Part of the process of developing sound spiritual civilization was for criminal justice agencies to professionalize their ranks. But during this process of reform and restructuring in the 1980s, there emerged a tension between the expectation of social and institutional reform and the reality of the limitations of professionalism within criminal justice circles.[103] Criminal justice functionaries were expected to act as models of propriety but the reality was a scenario of very limited judicial experience with procedural regularity. Hence, there emerged a significant constraint on the promotion of a new legal culture and the path towards legitimacy. The chronic shortage of trained and educated justice professionals militated against the promotion of criminal justice officials as credible and authoritative administrators of justice. In addition to this problem, there were a number of other systemic conditions that also militated against an environment of professionalism that can be attributed to both the longstanding militaristic culture and the 'mass line' populist culture of criminal justice work.

'Populist' law's endurance in post-Mao China has to do with ideological and institutional factors as well as the central role of the party in criminal justice work. Ideologically we can approach this endurance from an understanding of how 'context' prefigures Chinese criminal justice practice. Chinese socialist jurisprudence has required criminal law to be instrumental, and such instrumentality depends on official political interpretations of the 'broad social context' of any given period rather than from the certainty and predictability of the formal exposition of legal rules and texts. This understanding is true of campaign justice – its rationale and relentlessness – which required criminal justice work to be continually flexible in order to address unpredicted consequences of the marketized economy. In a marketized China, campaigns, it was hoped, would meet the new regulatory requirements of a vastly different socio-political context. The old China, under Mao, was marked by a politics peppered by capricious ideological passions. The new China was an evolving political economy transforming through gradual introduction of the norms and values, as well as the concrete infrastructure that has driven market-oriented economic development. Yet, 'the instrumental use of law and its essential openness to its context'[104] continued to dominate the responses of politico-legal institutions to serious crime because criminal justice practices continued to base their tasks on the programmatic agendas connected to state development, which largely interpret serious crime as a threat to social stability and thus to economic reform.

As is the case in most developing economies, the unpredictability of social and economic trends presents challenges to those whose task it is to secure the type of stability required for an attractive investment environment. In marketized China, new and emerging pockets of serious criminal activities that appeared in certain localities, and in particular periods of economic liberalization, required authorities to target these outbreaks using established models familiar to the political mindsets of criminal justice practitioners. The campaign template provided what politico-legal authorities saw as the most flexible mechanism for responding to the ever-changing social context of the economic transformation process. The enduring ethos of socialist legality – 'openness to social context', as Perry Keller puts it – provided a ready-made rationalization for authorities to put criminal justice workers on a war footing against serious crime, a war footing that allowed them to bend their practices – by increasing the using of harsh punishment and by interagency cooperation to ensure greater and speeder levels of criminal convictions.

Giving precedence to social stability as an essential prerequisite for economic development in the early 1980s provided the basis for reshaping the political imperative of criminal justice work to fit the contours of a post-Mao, post-revolutionary rule-governed state, and gave the policing and punishment regime its political *raison d'être*. At their core, criminal justice agencies in China remained agents for social and political change, and continued to be known as 'politico-legal organs'. Crime deemed serious enough to threaten social stability and thus the very success of reform continued to be met with a political response in the post-Mao period and into the twenty-first century. Policing serious crime was now read outside the bounds of revolutionary politics and class enemies, but it remained within a discourse of the political.

By assigning social stability as the primary pre-condition for the success of the economic modernization agenda, Dengist reformers placed a heavy burden on criminal justice agencies to deliver this stability. The criminal justice agencies, however, were not adequately prepared to undertake this grand endeavour. As Murray Scot Tanner argues, the dictum that 'stability overrides everything' cast criminal justice agencies in the role of protector, which they were hopelessly incapable of fulfilling, given their fundamental lack of resources and professional training.[105] He explains:

> Historically, China's vast size and population have prevented any Chinese state from supporting professional police forces that comprise anywhere near as large a percentage of the population as police forces do even in many adjacent developing countries, let alone in industrialized countries. Drawing on its ancient Legalist traditions, China attempts to overcome police shortages 'on the cheap' by severely punishing offenders to 'deter' crime.[106]

For instance, in Yiyang City in Hunan Province in 1983, only 21 criminal detectives (including a police dog handler and a forensic examiner) were employed in a city with a population of 163,240. What they lacked in numbers they made up in shock and awe campaigning, as the compilers of the local archives describe:

> The main method used in the first 'Strike Hard' battle in 1983 in Yiyang City was to 'catch criminals in one fell swoop'. In all, there were three main

> offensives and 11 battles from 1983 to 1986. The first main battle went from early to late August. The municipal party secretary was appointed head of the Strike Hard office and 210 government employees from outside the criminal justice sector were seconded to work full time in the Strike Hard office. The first main 'united operations' were launched in early September in which 5,500 members of the public along with public security personnel took part in police stings and 'investigation points', checking over 500 public areas and buildings and 2,500 private residencies of people of interest to the police. In total, 203 suspects were brought in for questioning . . . Two more battles were waged in the months that followed. In order to mobilize the masses, 2,640 Strike hard-awareness propaganda activities had been arranged, including 1,400 visits to public schools and 93 large and small-scale sentencing rallies. Police arranged for a roving propaganda van to drive around the streets and a propaganda boat to ply the river. In order to amplify the fruits of the Strike Hard battle, they arranged three kinds of shows, 'public pronouncement of punishment' events, public announcements of crimes and misdemeanours and public parading of offenders in trucks along the street.[107]

Importantly, campaign emphasis on the rhetoric of mass-line justice and comprehensive support from the people derived from what the authorities perceive as the need to restore, what Murray Scot Tanner calls, 'the balance of awe'[108] – that is, to recapture the 'social mood' and community confidence in criminal justice agencies. As Tanner points out,

> To decisively 'puncture the arrogance of criminals' and revive popular faith in state power needed, quite literally, an 'awesome' (*shengshi*) display of that power. It required, as the Central Committee stressed, 'using methods that had proven effective in the past': a police campaign, mass rallies and publicized executions.[109]

The practice of subcontracting policing through people's militias, security protection agencies within enterprises, and community and village residents' committees declined dramatically in the reform era. During the early 1980s the party-state's declining ability to police the grassroots through these organizations, coupled with a perceived decline in the level of fear and rise in arrogance among the criminal population, inspired a political imperative to regain the 'balance of awe'. The method was a 'cheap' alternative to the 'subsidized' policing of the Maoist era. Rather than relying heavily on 'non-productive' security activists, politico-legal authorities in the party sought to recreate the 'shock and awe' mass campaigns of the 1950s, but without the political commitment of the masses.[110]

The endurance of campaigns was also very much a consequence of shifting central–local relations. Campaigns provided the format and platform for central party authorities to maintain a hold on policing activities at the local level. Party leadership over campaigns has been an important means of providing at least some degree of conformity to the disparate and decidedly un-unified local public security agencies, whose local agendas have often taken precedence over the larger political interests of social stability and national reform. The party has initiated and led the implementation of all major campaign policy, and has exerted pressure on public security officials at the grassroots level to employ Strike Hard policy to attack crime. However, this situation has come about not only because of the 'social stability' rationale described above, but also because of the leadership structures under which the public security organs operate. Administratively and financially, police are controlled by the local government and local party committee at the same administrative level, but professionally, they operate under the leadership of the higher-level public security organs at the provincial and national levels.[111] This dual leadership arrangement has created a tension in policing in the post-Mao era. This is because police have been under increasing pressure to professionalize their operations in order to combat serious crime more effectively. Operationally, though, the pressure to professionalize has been heavily influenced by the declining availability of funds at the local government level.[112] One source states for example that in Sichuan, the government only funded one third of the police budget. The police have had to supplement their funding by conducting non-police work for example, enforcing the one-child policy or collecting fines and fees.[113]

Murray Scot-Tanner and Eric Green describe this 'interlocking system of vertical professional control by superior public security organs, and horizontal control by local party and government organs' as a 'principal-agent' structure.[114] Police are 'agents' who are subject to often competing principals, and because 'the balance of central–local power is substantially affected by the nature of the policy issues at stake',[115] the Central Party Committee's Politico-legal Affairs Committee deems it necessary to exercise power over local police through its leadership over the politico-legal committees at local levels that exercise leadership over local police in policy making and implementation. So, while local governments control the purse strings, the Central Party Committee has retained its policy and leadership role over policing serious crime in the post-Mao period. Both Strike Hard campaigns and national specialized drives have been initiated by 'Party Central' in Beijing and coordinated by the party at provincial, municipal and county levels, precisely in order to keep the crime-fighting spotlight on serious crime. This necessity for party authorities to keep the focus on serious crime is a consequence of workaday resources considerations as much as it is about ideology. Local governments hold financial sway over the police and thus determine their main operational priorities. And the priorities of local authorities have not necessarily focused on serious crime, which is both difficult and costly to police. Thus, without a sustained, hands-on approach by the Central Politico-legal Committee in Beijing over committees in local jurisdictions, local police efforts would otherwise have been diverted away from the fight against serious crime and towards revenue-raising local government priorities such as pursuing traffic fines and tax cheats. In this sense, then, campaigns have provided the organizational glue that enables local party and central party-state authorities to unite against serious crime. The leadership of the central party over campaign policy is an important means of creating at least some uniformity and cohesion of state responses to serious crime when more than any time in recent history we find an ever-deepening disparity between local and central interests. In short, campaign philosophy and practice has worked to provide a unified sense of purpose for the disparate local public security agencies across China, whose individual priorities often threaten to obscure the larger political interests of social stability and national reform, in the fight against serious crime.

This chapter has investigated the *what* of campaign-style justice – its foundation stone, scaffolding and bricks and mortar – and the *why* – why it persisted beyond the political context of Maoist China. The following chapter examines the *how* of campaigns – how a campaign is implemented both nationally and in regions. Here we find all elements of the campaign template at work as authorities attempt to control the tidal wave of serious crime that followed the economic tide of hyper growth in the first years of the twenty-first century.

3 Striking hard in the new millennium[1]

The chronicling of campaign justice's rise and fall continues in this chapter as we consider the first major generic Strike Hard offensive of the twenty-first century which ran from 2001 to 2003. Here we explore the campaign template in action. First, let us consider a more general observation about the continuing wave of campaigns and their effect on the crime-fighting landscape.

Some observers have argued that the proclivity for campaigns has itself to some extent fuelled the dramatic upsurge in violent crime, especially gang and organized crime. Eminent Peking University scholar of criminal law, Chen Xingliang, believes that 'campaigns' and 'organized crime syndicates' are natural enemies that have encouraged each other's growth. He considers that the roll out of each successive campaign has exacerbated the deterioration in the social order. After the first three years of Strike Hard came to a close in the mid-1980s, Chen argues, 'striking hard' became an ongoing policy. From this time, he says, '"striking hard" and "crime" had been locked into a daily seesaw struggle in a protracted war against each other', with the number of violent and serious crimes having increased exponentially on an annual basis, while at the same time, the level of financial investment in the prison system had fallen dramatically at the same rate. Prisoners, he said, who had served their sentences and were released, along with those who escaped prison, emerged from prison with a death wish against society.

> They organized themselves into gangs and mafia-style syndicates, forcing the Central Party Committee into declaring another Strike Hard campaign in 1996 . . . The outcome of the 1996 campaign was even more woeful. Not only did striking hard not keep a lid on murder, kidnapping, robbery, bombing and mafia-style syndicate crime, it did not even have a definite conclusion, but just fizzled out . . . Therefore, the increasingly violent crime situation forced the party into another, even bigger, Strike Hard campaign in 2001.[2]

This 'even bigger' Strike Hard campaign that began in April 2001 is the subject of this chapter, which examines the strategies of Strike Hard in 2001–03 in light of the campaign template set out in the previous chapter. Chen Xingliang's observations about the dangerous symbiosis between organized crime and Strike Hard are important points to reflect on at this juncture in the story of Strike Hard's rise and fall. This is because in this chapter when we examine each of the three main strategies of Strike Hard 2001, we are also providing a backdrop to explanations put forward in the following chapter about Strike Hard's fall from grace.

The nationwide Strike Hard campaign that ran from April 2001 to April 2003 involved a number of short-term 'offensives' against particular targets. The two-year campaign was roughly divided into three main offensives, but their exact timing varied from region to region. The first and main offensive from April to June 2001 aimed to stimulate public awareness of and momentum for the campaign. Although operations were more sophisticated and focused than in the 1983–86 Strike Hard campaign, the broad strategies of Strike Hard 2001 did not differ substantially, despite the fact that the preceding decade had seen much greater expectations of professionalism from the police, prosecuting bodies and courts. Each strategy reflects in its own way one or more of the three discrete but interconnected expressions of the 'political' that inhabit criminal justice operations that have been examined in the previous chapter – first the ideological framework of campaigning expressed as a form of 'political struggle', second the organizational framework of Party leadership over criminal justice policy through politico-legal committees and third, institutional politics. This chapter examines the intermingling of these three expressions of the political manifest in the key strategies for Strike Hard implementation:

1. the announcement at a national conference that crime rates are unacceptably high and that only 'striking hard' at crime will control crime rates, then establishing a discrete set of targeted crimes for each offensive;
2. the introduction of more flexibility to the criminal justice process to enable criminals to be punished 'severely and swiftly';
3. the creation of a 'great momentum' for the campaign by 'mobilizing the masses' and through acts of expressive punishment such as mass sentencing rallies.[3]

As we will find, the crusade to preserve social stability continued as the central battleground of criminal justice in China in the first years of the twenty-first century. But, one vital difference between the party-initiated moral panic in 1983 and the situation in 2001 was that at the turn of the new century, serious crime really was becoming a serious issue in China. More than 1.5 million criminal cases were registered in China in 1996. The figure rose to over 2 million in 1998 and 2.2 million in 1999; and in 2000 the number of registered crimes reached 3.6 million.[4] And, whereas only 9 per cent of registered crimes in 1985 were considered major crimes, the figure had climbed to 21 per cent by 1990, and had reached 42 per cent by 1995.[5]

We begin this examination of Strike Hard in the twenty-first century by claiming that while this most recent national campaign was conducted much more within the realm of law than the 1983 campaign, and whilst twenty-first century criminal justice operations were comparatively more sophisticated, the overall strategies of Strike Hard 2001 nevertheless did not differ fundamentally from those employed in 1983, despite the growing expectations of professionalism of the PSB, procuratorate and courts. This suggests a continued reliance in Strike Hard 2001–03 on the rhetoric and practice of campaign justice described in the previous chapter.

Strategy 1: Bring a group of experts together at a conference to evaluate the crime situation and inform the government, local party committees and the public that crime rates are unacceptably high, and then announce that the intended targets of the campaign are 'enemies of the masses' and saboteurs of socialist modernization

The 1983 campaign began with a group of party leaders deciding that although crime rates had decreased in the year preceding the campaign, public order in post-Mao China would need to be restored to levels enjoyed in the 1950s. The criminal justice agencies, it was decided, had been too soft on crime in recent years, and a policy of dealing 'severe and swift' blows to criminals would be required to turn the situation around. Strike Hard 2001 began in the same way as the 1983 campaign – it was launched by party leaders at a national conference on public order that was held in Beijing. Key personnel from the three arms of criminal justice attended. They were told by experts and politicians that China's crime rate was unacceptably high and that a 'Strike Hard and Rectification Struggle' was to be launched to redress the situation. As with the 1983 campaign, it was emphasized at the 2001 conference that even though the criminal justice agencies had achieved various breakthroughs in reducing crime, their results were inadequate, and a new Strike Hard campaign was needed 'to attack the arrogance of criminals and effect a complete turnaround in social order within two years'. Political-legal agencies throughout the country were urged to mobilize the masses in the attack on all kinds of crime, so that 'criminals would scatter for cover like rats on the street' (*xuanyu laoshu guojie*).[6] The conference also considered recent crime statistics, which gave added weight to the pressing need to 'strike severe blows' to curb rising crime rates. The December 2000 figure of 3.6 million registered crimes was a 61 per cent increase (1.387 million) over the previous year. In addition, the number of convicted criminals whose punishments were legally enforced in 2000 reached 646,431, an increase of 6.3 per cent over 1999.[7]

Rural itinerant workers make up China's largest change in social demographic and have brought about the largest change in the crime demographic since the reform era began in 1979. The following example of this demographic no doubt gave cause for concern for politico-legal authorities in cities where there has been a dramatic influx of workers from rural areas. In the city of Tianjin in 1986, theft accounted for 56.2 per cent of crimes committed by rural workers. The second highest category of crime committed by rural workers at this time was robbery (13 per cent) and the third highest was rape (6.7 per cent). In 2001, however, theft accounted for only 33.3 per cent of crimes committed by rural workers. Robbery now constituted 18.5 per cent of crimes committed by this population and serious assault was now the third highest category of crimes (8 per cent).[8] It is not surprising then that this unprecedented movement of workers – with over 150 million itinerant workers from the rural areas now residing in cities – has also changed the face of crime in urban areas. Since the early 1990s the sharp increase in crimes committed by rural workers residing in large cities has been astounding in some places.[9] In the city of Xiamen in 1993, for example, 82 per cent of all major cases involving violent and serious crime were committed by those identified as members of the itinerant worker population. Nationally, in 1999, 57 per cent of all crimes in urban areas were committed by rural workers and in some cities the figure was much higher. In Guangzhou, for instance, it had reached 88 per cent.[10] Even five years earlier than this date, in 1994, in all of China's 11 largest cities, itinerant workers had committed over 50 per cent of the total number of registered crimes. In Beijing, Shanghai, and four other large cities in 2001, 33.4 per cent of robberies, 80 per cent of smuggling cases, 42 per cent of homicides and nearly 100 per cent of drug trafficking cases, were committed by the itinerant worker population.[11] Many of these crimes were committed by itinerant workers who had joined criminal gangs.

Politico-legal authorities claimed that the dramatic increase in major and violent crimes in 2000 had seriously eroded the public's sense of security. There were also 4,074 bombing cases in 2000, an increase of 12.7 per cent on the previous year, and senior police officials were particularly concerned that 2,673 of these bombing incidents were the result of domestic disputes, crimes of passion, and retribution for the non-repayment of loans.[12] Nearly 13,000 arson cases (an increase of 42.9 per cent over the previous year) as well as a dramatic increase in the number of serious assaults, robberies, muggings, and bag-snatching incidents contributed to the perception that social instability and public disorder were again at troubling levels. While the murder rate had not increased substantially, there had been a 56 per cent increase in robbery cases. With 26,000 registered crimes that year which directly involved members of 4,480 crime gangs, it was not difficult to see another Strike Hard on the horizon.[13] In 2000, there were over 4,000 known mid to large-scale organized crime gangs in China reported to be 'sabotaging the economy'.[14]

Two disturbing crime trends were underscored at the national conference on public order. Economic and property-related crime had become more violent at the turn of the twenty-first-century China, and organized crime had become increasingly out of control and more reliant on corrupt government and party officials. It was this growth in 'mafia-style' criminal syndicate activity and violence, coupled with the alarming increase in the number of 'protective umbrellas' in government and party positions who facilitated and profited from organized crime that triggered Strike Hard 2001 in early April.[15]

Importantly, for the first time in any Strike Hard campaign, the entire membership of the national politburo attended the conference that launched the 2001 campaign, giving crime control instant status as the state's top domestic policy priority for the year. President Jiang Zemin gave an address to launch the campaign officially, declaring that Strike Hard was a key mechanism for preserving both the future of the economic reforms and, crucially, the future stability of party rule.[16] Following Jiang's speech, campaign policy was quickly disseminated through provincial party committees and national criminal justice agencies. The basic aim of the campaign was to attack serious criminal elements to procure a sharp decline in crime rates through the judicial practice of applying 'severe and swift' punishment to predetermined categories of criminals as a means of both deterrence and retribution. The 'enemies' who were to be targeted by the campaign were members of mafia-style gangs and other organized criminal groups, violent offenders, and corrupt government and party officials.[17]

Both individuals and groups who endangered economic reform and social stability, in particular, criminals whose crimes disrupted the public order or the social order were targets of the 1983 campaign. Similar collective and individual crimes were the main targets of Strike Hard 2001. It was announced at a national conference on 3 April that the major target of the campaign would be the 'mafia-style' syndicate member – the twenty-first-century version of the 1980s hooligan gang member. Other targets would include individuals who committed violent acts, as well as some non-violent crimes such as theft. In short, the three main target categories were:

- crimes by mafia-style syndicates and other organized criminal groups;
- serious violent crimes such as bombings, wilful murder, armed robbery and kidnapping;
- property crimes such as burglary, theft and other offences that posed a serious threat to the security of the masses, and crimes of corruption that involved government and Party official who offered protection for organized crime.[18]

Targeting organized and gang crime

Chinese criminal justice authorities recognize three main types of criminal groups as a threat in China – 'heinous' or 'dark' forces (*e'shili*), that range from small gangs to medium-sized but unsophisticated criminal groups; mafia-style syndicates (*heishehui xingzhi jituan*); and to a much lesser extent, Triads. Since the early 1990s, the gang and syndicate member has replaced the 1980s hooligan as the focus of fear and loathing in police circles in China. Some scholars put the number of gang and syndicates in China at around one million, with a membership totalling four million.[19] The particular focus of the campaigns against organized crime in the late 1990s and the first years of the next century were on mafia-style offenders. This mafia-style offender belongs to an often violent, but organizationally immature, criminal syndicate. Members of such crime groups in the PRC are not as tightly controlled as the traditional triad gangs and are therefore classed as mafia-*style* gangs.[20] Despite a lack of organizational maturity, they usually possess characteristics similar to those of conventional triad gangs. For instance, they are said to refer to each other as 'brothers', their organizations possess a measure of internal discipline, a discrete language and codes, and, importantly, they often work under the 'protective umbrellas' of government figures and have links to key corrupt bureaucrats and police.[21] Some gangs have a complex organizational structure that includes well-defined strata of leadership, consultants and assistants, and even a hierarchy among hit-men. Some syndicates have detailed compensation plans for the families of members who are convicted and jailed, while others have compiled their own rule books with disciplinary regulations against offences such as public drunkenness and lewdness.[22] There are also gangs that have a division of labour whereby one group of criminals might engage entirely in armed robbery or mafia hits, while others work in quasi-legitimate businesses.

Mafia-style syndicates typically have dozens of members, a stable and tight organizational structure, and a strict disciplinary code. Financial gain is their main *raison d'être*. They have financial interests in the market economy running 'front' companies and often having regular contact with legitimate companies and enterprises. Such syndicates have a monopoly over one or more industries in a geographic area, and their three basic tools are violence, terrorizing and bribery. And, as noted above, they are often protected from the law by corrupt officials in government, party or criminal justice circles.[23]

The Criminal Law was revised in 1997 to reflect the perceived danger posed by this new category of criminal. Although there was already provision under the 1979 Criminal Law for joint offences, the Law was amended in 1997 to include these relatively new mafia-style organizations. The mafia-style criminal syndicate includes any type of organizationally immature gang that commits illegal or criminal offences, and is referred to in the 1997 Law as an 'organization [which takes] the nature of a criminal syndicate' (Criminal Law 1997: Art. 294). The official explanatory notes that accompany the 1997 Criminal Law explain that, according to Article 294, it is a criminal offence, not only to form or lead a mafia-style syndicate, but also to have any connection with or take any kind of active part in such a syndicate. That is to say, an individual who is connected to a syndicate does not need to have actively taken part in a crime – being connected to a syndicate is a crime in itself.

Six main kinds of mafia-style gang activities dominate the organized crime scene in China: violent acts of terrorism, including murder and robbery; kidnapping, and protection rackets involving 'godfather' figures who control whole streets, roads or villages; criminal acts such as obtaining stolen goods by force; hired hits; and smuggling rackets that involve gangs outside China.[24] The most common types of group in recent years are those that control whole industries in one or more local areas. Other types include gangs that specialize in armed robbery, gangs of hit men for hire, district 'godfathers' who control whole geographical areas, organized smuggling and drug trafficking gangs, and money lenders. *Xinhua News* described the situation in one local area in 2001:

> In some cities, townships, and villages, all kinds of 'village tyrants', 'street tyrants', 'factory tyrants', 'mining tyrants', 'city tyrants' and 'trade tyrants' ride roughshod everywhere and fleece the ordinary people. [For example,] 'cotton tyrants' led by Fang Yiduo in Heba Township, Wuwei County, Anhui Province, seized the local cotton procurement market. Whenever they illegally ship out their cotton, more than 30 trucks line up. There are escorts in the front and at the rear of the convoy, swaggering around with unbridled arrogance.[25]

There are a number of reasons for the re-emergence of criminal syndicates in China, the first and most obvious being that the economic climate during the 1990s was ripe for this kind of criminal organization to emerge. In addition, the extent of official corruption in China has rendered it impossible to mount a serious attack on the problem. Yet, another possible factor was the increasing mobility of the population.[26] For example, one newspaper source notes that there were 3 million non-residents in Shanghai in 1998, compared to only 100,000 in 1950. In 2001, more than one third of all crimes committed in Shanghai were committed by non-official residents. Many of those who arrive from the provinces and are unable to find work organize into gangs that specialize in particular types of crime. The main pick-pocketing group in Shanghai in 2001, for instance, was controlled by a Moslem gang from Xinjiang in western China. The majority of organized fraud crimes in Shanghai are carried out by a gang from Guizhou Province, while organized household break and enter crimes are mainly the work of a gang from North Jiangsu.[27]

The most immediate party-state concern about the rise of organized crime organizations and gangs is the increasingly intimate relationship between crime and local government. Between April and early June 2001, in one province alone, 83 party and government officials were investigated for providing protection to criminal gangs.[28] In Nanjing, over a period of six months in 2001, 63 cases of corruption involving government and party bureaucrats at the level of county head or above were uncovered.[29] In Zhejiang Province, a local criminal, Zhang Wei, and his gang were found to have received protection from 42 government officials, including 15 who worked in the criminal justice system. A sign was even placed in front of Zhang's home to warn unwitting police officers that it was a 'protected zone' and beyond the reach of the law.[30] Increasingly, government and criminal justice agencies employ gangs either for corrupt purposes or to help 'restore' public order to an area. In Zhengzhou City, for example, the local PSB paid for a Chinese mafia-style gang – which called itself the 'Committee for the Management of Public Order' – to take charge of public order in an entire suburb. In fact, the gang was carrying out robberies and obtaining protection money from shop owners, handing over a cut of its profits to the PSB and local government.[31]

In April 2001, at the beginning of the Strike Hard campaign, the Ministry of Public Security issued a national circular describing these groups. It stated that large-scale syndicates and other smaller groups:

> run amok in some places . . . seriously impairing our social order and stability and jeopardizing the safety of the people's life and property. Some of them use violent and terrorist methods to commit various crimes unscrupulously such as murder, robbery, kidnapping, blackmail, raping and insulting women, smuggling and drug trafficking. Some operate underground casinos, sex-service facilities, or other illegal businesses . . . Some interfere in economic disputes and use violent and threatening methods to secure repayment of debts for others. Some interfere in judicial matters to settle disputes . . . Some attempt to usurp grassroots political power and act against party, government, or judicial organizations.[32]

Although organized crime syndicates were clearly the main target of Strike Hard 2001–03, one novel innovation of the campaign was that provinces were encouraged to 'proceed from reality' and observe 'concrete conditions' to target categories of crime in the region in addition to the main national targets. The examples below illustrate this boutique targeting of crime in three northern provinces.

Targeting separatists in Xinjiang

Xinjiang authorities merged the national Strike Hard target (gangs and syndicates) with their own local targets – the 'three evil forces' (terrorists, separatists and fundamentalists) – as Xinjiang's Party Secretary Wang Lequan explained in April 2001 at the region's work conference on public order that launched Strike Hard in Xinjiang:

> The [14 to 15 April] meeting has identified the key points for crackdown for the current 'strike hard' and rectification struggle. First, they are organized crimes conducted by people led by key elements of national 'splittism', elements who have committed violent crimes and terrorist acts, and elements of extremist religious forces; crimes committed by gangs that have connections with the underworld; and crimes committed by highway bandits and tyrants, rogues and evil forces. Second, they are serious and violent crimes such as explosions, murder, robbery, inflicting serious harm on others and kidnapping. Third, they are repeated crimes that seriously influence the sense of security among people, such as theft and robbery.[33]

By the end of May 2001, Xinjiang party and criminal justice authorities had begun to include separatist activities as a specific type of 'organized crime', thus making separatists (or 'splittists' as they are often labelled in the press) the key campaign targets. However, these targets were not necessarily charged with committing political crimes but with social crimes such as murder, armed robbery and drug trafficking. A work meeting convened by the Xinjiang Autonomous Region Party Committee for Party leaders on 30 May confirmed this move:

> Since the curtain was raised on the struggle to 'strike hard' . . . all areas of the region have acted in accordance with the demands of the central and regional authorities by regarding elements of three categories as focal targets for 'striking hard', and in particular have cracked down on organized crime committed by the elements of three categories; in Khotan and Kashgar, where ethnic separatist activities are rampant. Apart from the key targets for attack determined by the regional authorities, the localities have also added their own key targets in light of their prominent public security problems.[34]

Despite the region's targeting of the 'three evils', very little detail was given in the Chinese press on the specific kinds of political crimes committed by those convicted on charges of separatism.

By October 2001, the 'three evils' had become the primary target of Strike Hard in Xinjiang. 'A campaign to wipe out terrorism and separatist activity in the capital of western China's Muslim-majority Xinjiang region has begun', one report announced. The report went on to explain that 'Striking hard at violent terrorist activities and ethnic separatists is one of the main goals of the campaign'. It added that 'So far this year, ten violent groups have been "wiped out" as well as around 210 "hardened minority splittists", suspected violent criminal terrorists or religious extremists'.[35] By November 2001, police had shut down 13 illegal religious centres and arrested more than 50 people who were worshipping in the makeshift mosques.[36] Over a seven-month period from the start of Strike Hard until October 2001, police in Kashgar solved over 5,000 serious criminal cases including murder, armed robbery and serious theft, and 'crushed' more than 200 criminal gangs.[37] One of the only separatist cases in which the defendants' names were published in Xinjiang newspapers was the trial of two defendants named Abdulmejid and Abdulahmad, who were accused of participating in the 1997 Yining incident in which nine people were killed and more than 200 injured.[38] Both were executed immediately after sentencing, but scant detail was provided in the media about their precise involvement in the uprising.

One of the few terrorist cases in which details of the crimes committed by the suspect were released went to court after the conclusion of the Strike Hard campaign.[39] In October 2003, the *Urumqi Evening News* reported that the head of a breakaway faction of an East Turkestan organization who had allegedly instigated a number of terrorist incidents had been executed, after being successfully prosecuted for inciting a civil disturbance, organizing an attack on a police station, setting fire to a police station, setting fire to a local government building, bombing a cotton factory and attempting to bomb a prison. Ojememet Abbas, the head of a self-styled 'Jihad' organization, was sentenced to death on 22 October 2003 for his involvement in the 1997 Yining incident.[40] After escaping arrest following the incident, Abbas formed a new political faction known as the 'East Turkestan Moslem Freedom Party', which subsequently became the 'Moslem Jihad Organization'. He and his followers set fire to a police station in Sali Town in Zepu County, resulting in the death of a police officer and serious injury to a civilian. In another incident, they set fire to the town hall in Yingahwati, seriously wounding one person. They also bombed a cotton factory, killing one person and injuring six more, as well as killing a police officer and injuring six others in a shoot-out at the time of their arrest. Abbas also attempted to bomb the Xinjiang Prison in an effort to help a member of his organization to escape.[41] The Hetian Intermediate Court found him guilty of the crimes of leading and organizing a terrorist group, illegally manufacturing firearms and bullets, illegally manufacturing and selling explosives, and gathering people to raid a prison with weapons.[42]

Targeting the 'public order' in Beijing

Unlike other provinces that primarily set their own secondary Strike Hard targets according to the crimes that were most prevalent in the area, the aim in Beijing was to focus on keeping the streets incident free and 'protecting public order' in the lead-up to major national events in the capital. The first stage of Strike Hard, from 4 April to 30 September 2001, focused on guaranteeing public safety and security for the 80th anniversary of the CCP, and in the period leading up to the decision on hosting the 2008 Olympics, the World University Games and National Day. The second stage, from October 2001 to 28 February 2002, concentrated on guaranteeing public safety and security for the Sixth Plenum of the 15th Party Committee and the Spring Festival, and the third stage, from March to the end of June 2002, focused on maintaining public order for the annual National People's Congress. During the fourth period of the campaign, from July 2002 to April 2003, the emphasis was on guaranteeing security for the 16th National People's Congress and National Day. According to author Mu Yumin, a Beijing police officer, police were not required to meet arrest quotas, as were the police in most other provinces. The success or failure of Strike Hard in Beijing rested instead on guaranteeing security of major public events and the conferences, and maintaining average clear-up rates.[43]

Beijing authorities also launched specialized drives against mafia-style crime, 'longstanding unsolved cases', using police databases to locate fugitives, pick-pocketing and robbery. Of those arrested, formally charged and indicted, 10,995 were suspected of involvement in organized or gang crime, including 24 cases involving relatively large criminal syndicates and 2,784 cases involving group or gang crimes. The number of registered crimes fell by 6 per cent in 2001, with the largest decline being in robbery cases, which fell by 22.6 per cent, and theft, which was down by 18.4 per cent.[44] Beijing continued its use of specialized drives in 2002 with initiatives against mafia-style crime, bag snatching from motorbikes or bicycles, car theft, pick pocketing and drug-related crime, as well as a drive to track down fugitives outside Beijing using police intranet databases.[45]

Targeting border 'seepages' in Jilin

A confidential public security report on Jilin in the early years of the twenty-first century nominated crimes that resulted from human 'seepages' across the North Korean border as Jilin's most serious crime problem from 1999 to 2003.[46] 'Seepage' includes crimes such as people smuggling and drug trafficking as well as intelligence leakage by Chinese officials; illegal crossing into North Korea through legitimate companies; propaganda and intelligence activities from North Korea into China aimed at uniting Korean minorities in China with their compatriots in North Korea; and secret Chinese government defections to North Korea and the subsequent repatriation of these officials back to China to gather intelligence for North Korea. Jilin police also noted the prevalence of violent crimes committed by North Korean soldiers crossing the border to deliberately create social instability in China by committing robbery, murder, serious theft, drug trafficking and smuggling offences.[47]

The famine in North Korea in 1996 and 1997 created a tidal wave of illegal migration into Jilin Province, and in the years following the famine, many thousands continued to escape across the border to find work, to escape persecution in North Korea, or to use China as a route to a third country where they could seek asylum. A small minority of Koreans who crossed the border committed serious crimes – murder, robbery, smuggling, drug trafficking and human trafficking – in the pursuit of economic gain. Many of the victims of human trafficking were North Korean women. Jilin police also reported that many Chinese border patrol officers routinely colluded with professional North Korean criminals, providing them with easy access routes for their smuggling activities. At the turn of the new millennium, some prominent criminal groups were even smuggling top range European cars from Russia through North Korea and into China.[48] The forced repatriation of refugees back to North Korea became a key Strike Hard target in Jilin Province in 2001, with arrests, house-to-house searches and fines of up to 30,000 yuan for aid workers who harboured refugees.[49]

Once campaign targets had been set and media attention had been focused on the problem of gang activity and other targeted crimes, the next step in the campaign was the readjustment of law-enforcement practices to accommodate the 'severity and swiftness' required by Strike Hard policy.

Strategy 2: Ensure that judicial, prosecutorial and police practices are 'flexible' in application, and encourage cooperation between police, prosecutors and courts in a multi-agency approach to campaigning

Ordering and legitimizing legislative and judicial practices in the PRC have historically relied on programmatic agendas that are connected to state development. Within this logic of socialist legal ideology, the principle that criminal law serves as an instrument for the realization of party policy is said to be achieved through the politico-ideological agendas of the three arms of criminal justice. In official discourse, therefore, the criminal justice system in the PRC has existed essentially as a mechanism for advancing the cause of socialist state development and as a tool for implementing the requirements of national construction. This openness of criminal law to the ever-changing social context has meant that party supremacy in policy making and the party's instrumentalist conception of law have relied on the principle of 'flexibility' in the administration of justice. At times when the unstable state of the social and public order have been deemed to threaten the very success of the national reforms, adjudication and sentencing practices have been 'simplified' and 'fast-tracked' to ensure the success of the campaign. The penalties for crimes against the 'social order' and the 'public order' have increased during periods when such crimes have been considered a threat to social stability. Similarly, when corruption and profiteering have been seen as a threat to the market economy, sanctions have increased substantially. The ethos of 'flexibility' in Strike Hard campaigns is expressed first and foremost through the overall coordination of activities, such as 'united operations' within the police force, and between the police, prosecution and courts to form small joint 'case handling groups' to ensure the highest possible conviction rates. It is also achieved by adjusting adjudication and sentencing practices to punish 'severely and swiftly' the criminal groups that are a particular problem in certain local areas. In the 2001–03 Strike Hard campaign, criminal justice agencies were not only encouraged to practise close cooperation and 'mutual coordination' of activities but also to devise their own Strike Hard 'initiatives'. Most of these initiatives were devised at the provincial level and implemented at the local municipal or county level.

Initiatives included rearranging normal organizational arrangements. For example, according to Heilongjiang's provincial report to the Central CMPO Committee in 2004, organized crime had been a particular problem in the province for a number of years. Therefore, the Strike Hard campaign in Heilongjiang focused predominately on the targets of gang and syndicate crime. The campaign was launched in Heilongjiang on 6 April 2001 and on 19 April a Strike Hard Office was established comprising the following eight work teams under party leadership:

1 The 'co-ordination team', which was the main group charged with overseeing and coordinating between areas and distributing information and investigating work.
2 The 'supervision team' whose task it was to discover Strike Hard weak spots and advise these areas on how to proceed. They were able to veto recommendations from head office.
3 The 'strike' task force, which coordinated attack plans and organized joint operations. They were responsible for catching fugitives on the PSB national wanted list. They were also responsible for compiling arrest and other statistics.
4 The Strike Hard 'public order cleanup' task force which was responsible for areas in which law and order was particularly problematic and specific areas such as hotels and large schools and factories.
5 The 'crime prevention' task force was responsible for organizing and establishing an effective mediation system and establishing a system for controlling the floating population. It was also responsible for compiling statistics on community and neighbourhood watch groups.
6 The 'adjudication' task force (mainly court and prosecution) was responsible for mediating in a timely manner any disputes between police and courts over the nature of criminal charges and investigating reports from all regions and offering advice on policing issues. The task force were also responsible for distributing information regarding 'severity and swiftness' policy and practice, and all criminal statistics including number of people in prison, number of suspects arrested, number of criminal trials pending and so on.
7 The 'propaganda and news reportage' task force was responsible for Strike Hard propaganda and organizing, and monitoring media reports on Strike Hard.
8 The Logistics Department coordinated all Strike Hard finance-related matters, made Strike Hard budgetary recommendations and supervised Strike Hard funding expenditure.[50]

The first joint operation in Heilongjiang occurred in a 60-hour period from 12:00 a.m. on 16 April 2001 to 12:00 p.m. on 18 April. It was basically a series of 'search and investigate' operations involving thousands of personnel who searched public and residential buildings and performed stop and search activities on vehicles throughout the province. In the 60-hour period, 1,982 cases were cracked, 2,214 people were arrested, 165 fugitives were caught, and 541 kilograms of explosives and 771 firearms were confiscated. The 60-hour operation involved personnel from many government areas including 200 county heads, municipal heads and party heads, 86,000 police, 14,000 police vehicles and 1,271 stop and search roadblocks. Police searched and investigated 15,271 public spots such as hotels and clubs and 18,000 officers went into county areas or to establish stop and search roadblocks.[51] This kind of Strike Hard operation is commonly described in police reports as a tactic of 'waging war using a sea of humans'.

Some provinces opted for more dramatic and large-scale initiatives in the form of 'united operations'. Lu Zhao, head of the Sichuan provincial PSB, announced to reporters on 20 April 2001 that from 10:00 p.m. that night, PSB officers across China's most populous province had launched a united 'search and arrest' operation. This initiative led to the capture of many criminals who were paraded at an arrest rally attended by over 10,000 people the following morning. In the Sichuan provincial capital Chengdu alone, over 400 suspects were publicly arrested. From mid-evening on the night of 20 April, the police command centre received regular reports from PSB branches all over the province, and by midnight Chengdu PSB reported that 2,100 suspects had been caught and 43 firearms and 150 kg of explosives had been seized. According to the Chengdu Municipal PSB head,

> immediately after receiving the order to start, 11,000 PSB officers, 1,100 military police and more than 20,000 party, government and security officials were on the move. In total, more than 50,000 police and 100,000 government and party personnel and civilians participated in the crack-down on the night of 20 April.[52]

The Liaoning provincial PSB initiative in the north of China involved introducing a 'quota system' for arresting suspects. PSB bureaus and stations were informed that they must apprehend at least 50 per cent of wanted local criminals within a particular time frame or their pay would be docked; those who exceeded the quota by 25 per cent would receive a cash reward.[53] During the first phase of Strike Hard, which lasted around 50 days, 359 of the 1,100 criminals on Hubei Province's wanted list had been captured by the PSB. This impressive figure followed a Strike Hard initiative orchestrated by the provincial PSB to offer PSB officers a 20,000 yuan cash reward for the capture of any criminal on the province's wanted list. In the provincial capital, Wuhan, the municipal government chipped in, offering a further 5,000 to 10,000 yuan reward for the capture of local criminals, setting aside 5 million yuan from the city budget for a 'rewards for wanted criminals' fund.[54]

In other provinces, there were Strike Hard initiatives at the municipal level. Authorities in Qingdao City in Shandong Province made 'catching fugitives' their particular Strike Hard focus. PSB initiatives in the city included inviting family members of wanted criminals to sit down together at a meeting and watch a live cable broadcast of a public sentencing rally, attended by more than 10,000 people, at which 10 criminals were sentenced to death. According to family members who attended this broadcast, it was effective in putting pressure on them to give up their relatives.[55]

The courts were also required to implement Strike Hard initiatives by meting out 'severe and swift' punishment. From the start of the campaign in 2001, politico-legal authorities stipulated that the policy of 'severity' must be applied within the limits of available penalties and within the time limits laid down by the law. It was emphasized that Strike Hard-style severity differed from the 'severity' principle in normal criminal law practice, which is applied where there are aggravated circumstances surrounding a crime. In Strike Hard campaigns, unlike in the Criminal Law, severity is often applied across the board for *all* targeted crimes, regardless of the circumstances of individual cases. This means that judges must award a relatively harsh punishment within the available range of punishment options.

As noted earlier, the 'swiftness' side of the equation entails the prompt investigation, prosecution and adjudication of cases within the time limits laid down in the Criminal Procedural Law. The operation of this principle of 'swiftness' is described in a report from Xinjiang in 2001:

> Beginning in late April, the localities have . . . sifted through and selected a number of cases that had a significant social impact and caused concern among the masses; through careful organization, they have convened large public arrest and sentencing rallies, achieving good social effects. In accordance with the principle of acting with severity and speed, the region's political and legal organs have drawn up systems for speeding up the handling of cases to ensure that 'strike hard' cases are rapidly tried and concluded within the deadline set by the law.[56]

The two basics and speedy trials

In the context of Strike Hard 2001–03, swiftness meant accelerating the rate at which cases were processed through the court by employing the principle of 'the two basics' and by avoiding the minutiae of case details. Chapter 2 outlined how 'the two basics' refer to the principle whereby, during Strike Hard campaigns, judges need only be satisfied that the basic facts of a case are clear, and that the basic evidence is conclusive. The term 'basic', in this context, refers to the key facts that can be considered the main components of the crime, and the 'essential evidence' that is required to ascertain criminality and guilt. It is these two basics that facilitate 'swiftness'.[57] Xinjiang authorities enthusiastically adopted these flexible sentencing arrangements. A regional work conference on public order that was held in Xinjiang from 14 to 15 April 2001 identified the two basics as a key tool of Strike Hard. Authorities at the meeting stated that:

> It is necessary to adhere to the principle of 'giving severe punishment and processing cases in a prompt manner based on the law'; it is necessary to adhere to the principle of the 'two basics' which says that as long as the basic truth is clear and as long as the basic evidence is verified, prompt approval of arrest, prosecution and court decisions are required; it is necessary to adhere to the principle of being 'sure, accurate and relentless'; and it is necessary to adhere to the principle of 'integrating the special work of the mass line'.[58]

Even serial murderers received speedy trials in Beijing at the height of the campaign. Zhao Wenjun, a prison escapee from Liaoning, and Ma Jin from Inner Mongolia, were charged with murdering 12 Beijing residents and injuring 89 others between August 1999 and August 2000, bashing their unsuspecting victims in the back of the head with a hammer and robbing them. Their vicious crimes committed over a 12-month period received constant media attention, as they were particularly brutal and had occurred in dozens of Beijing underground walkways. The entire case took 52 minutes of trial time, which included 45 minutes to read the indictment and judgment notices listing the dozens of victims.[59]

'Flexible work practices' took on a variety of expressions at the grassroots level, mostly involving some form of expediting the investigation and prosecution process under party leadership. For instance, in July 2001, the Anhui provincial Higher Court reported as its campaign initiative in the first months of the campaign, a strategy of mass-line justice reminiscent of the 1950s mass movements. In the two months since the start of the campaign, the Anhui Higher Court had tried a massive 754 serious crime cases involving 980 criminals. The local party committee in the provincial court in Anhui established one 'Strike Hard leaders' group' and eight 'work groups' to 'adjudicate and punish swiftly'. The leaders' group coordinated the activities of groups of trial judges who were brought together to exclusively try cases relating to the three main campaign targets. The Anhui Higher People's Court also introduced a compulsory six-day working week for judges during the campaign. The Higher Court president and vice-presidents each took a group of judges to eight intermediate courts throughout Anhui to 'supervise' the implementation of the campaign, personally selecting judges for cases and ensuring that each trial that began on a particular day was completed the same day. The Higher Court instructed inferior courts that they only needed to satisfy the 'two basics' rule outlined above to make a conviction.[60]

The political obligations of defence lawyers

An even more worrying trend emerged immediately after the launch of Strike Hard 2001–03, when the Ministry of Justice chief, Zhang Fusan, issued a warning to defence lawyers throughout the country via the Chinese Bar Association and the bureaus of justice at each administrative level. Given that the Ministry is responsible for the registration and deregistration of lawyers in China, its demands constituted a serious threat to the defence process. Zhang stated that the role of defence lawyers in the campaign would impact directly on the 'swiftness and severity' policy and on the protection of people's democratic rights; it would also affect public respect for the law and how it was implemented. He also urged defence lawyers to pay close attention to the political situation, and to work in conjunction with the criminal justice organs when carrying out their defence work, based on the principle of 'using the facts as the criterion'. They must also emphasize the facts of each case, and only consider 'objective views' when arguments arose in relation to judicial process or the specific application of the law. They must help to improve the efficiency and quality of casework and, when arguing a point in court, they must support the application of the 'two basics', rather than searching needlessly for insignificant details in order to argue against the charges. It was the duty of the Ministry of Justice and the Chinese Bar Association to supervise and guide the work of defence lawyers, taking practical and effective measures to make appropriate arrangements for, and oversee, three main types of cases: cases of major importance that were widely reported in the media, major crimes such as murder and extremely serious crimes such as multiple murders. This was to be achieved by training lawyers to respect professional ethics and by taking disciplinary measures against recalcitrant lawyers. Lawyers were told to remember their responsibility towards defendants and, at the same time, not to forget their responsibility to society and the law. They were obliged to guarantee positive political, legal and social outcomes in their defence work and, in so doing, help to support the corrector prosecution of the law by judicial officers in their efforts to attack crime in a decisive and timely manner.[61]

Any doubts that the above directive might go unheeded due to the subtlety of its wording were put to rest with a second directive issued by the Minister to the Chinese Bar Association and all bureaus of justice in July 2001. This directive stated that, in order to guarantee the smooth implementation of the campaign, justice bureau guidance over defence lawyers needed to be strengthened in certain ways:

> [Defence] lawyers must without hesitation partake in all relevant aspects of Strike Hard. They must not deliberately complicate issues, must not pounce on specific wording or phrasing in an indictment simply to frame their defence in such a way that will negatively influence the prosecution of a case. During trials, lawyers must show self-discipline and not discuss the contents of the case with any outside bodies [read the media]. Justice bureaus at all levels must guide lawyers and supervise their work in order to guarantee quality and to advance the swift and efficient adjudication of a case.[62]

Prosecution bodies were not left out of Strike Hard's flexibility initiatives. The Beijing procuratorate, for instance, announced that it was working overtime during the five-day May Day holiday period to ensure that enough cases were processed before the completion of the first phase of the campaign.[63] In the city of Zhangzhou in the southern province of Fujian, 202 suspects involved in 149 separate cases were arrested over a one-month period in April–May. In 80 per cent of these cases, arrest warrants were written and approved by the procuratorate within 24 hours.

The local paper, *Minnan ribao* (*South Fujian Daily*), reported that the procuratorate had been ordered to approve all PSB arrests within a three-day limit, and that defendants were to be indicted within seven days of their arrest.[64] A special initiative in Zhangzhou City in the early stages of the campaign was the practice of 'getting involved [in prosecutorial work] ahead of time', whereby prosecutors became involved in the criminal justice process before a case had officially been handed over for prosecution, in order to reduce their investigation and preparation time. For example, on 29 April, in the case of Lin Taiping, who assaulted a police officer with a knife, the municipal procuratorate sent four prosecutors to 'get involved ahead of time'. Two of the prosecutors involved themselves in pre-trial proceedings, and the other two visited the crime scene to collect evidence.[65] Similarly, in Shanghai, the Municipal Party Secretary announced that the Shanghai initiative would include the procuratorate 'getting involved [in prosecutorial work] ahead of time', in order to 'arrest and prosecute swiftly'. The courts in Shanghai were also told to hold simultaneous sentencing rallies and to mete out the most severe punishment allowed for each crime brought before the courts.[66]

Strategy 3: Create 'momentum' for the campaign by mobilizing the masses and through acts of expressive punishment

To mobilize the masses in 1983 and gain their support, the momentum needed to kick-start the campaign came in the form of a policy of meting out punishment to criminals 'severely and swiftly', and doing so in public arenas that provided the greatest possible publicity. As noted in Chapter 2, two main criminal justice practices created momentum: first, 'united operations' that caught suspects in 'one fell swoop' and second, public sentencing rallies. Expressive acts of degradation and punishment with 'severity and swiftness' continued to be the leitmotif of Strike Hard 2001. A massive propaganda effort was therefore needed to reinforce Strike Hard's status as the top political priority for 2001. As one official media commentary explained at the time, 'without a strong momentum, it will be difficult to get the desired results. In the current struggle, we must create an awe-inspiring situation'.[67] The unleashing of 'severity and swiftness' throughout the country in April provided the momentum required for the success of the campaign. As part of the cooperative multi-agency approach to campaigning, a series of public sentencing rallies was organized nationwide, at which criminals were arranged in batches to be publicly humiliated before large audiences. These sentencing rallies were of three main types: simultaneously convened rallies; rallies convened for a specific audience or 'special sentencing rallies'; and 'joint public arrest and sentencing rallies'.

Joint arrest and sentencing rallies were held throughout the country on 11 April 2001 to 'formally start [the] large-scale and momentous "strike hard" anti-crime struggle'.[68] The curtain was 'drawn open' on the campaign in the capital, with the first batch of jointly organized arrest and sentencing rallies occurring in 21 districts across the city.[69] In southern China, the propaganda effort began in Guangdong at a large sports stadium in which a large-scale rally saw 40 suspects publicly arrested and numerous convicted criminals sentenced to death. Even though Guangzhou was experiencing a cold snap at the time, more than 30,000 members of the public turned up and applauded enthusiastically when each death sentence was announced.[70]

In the city of Fuzhou in southern China, on the same day, PSB officers publicly arrested 100 suspects and 21 convicted criminals were sentenced, at one rally, while in the central western city of Xian 10 criminals were sentenced to death at another rally. Also on 11 April, 92 members of criminal gangs, hooligans and other suspects were publicly arrested in Chongqing City in south-west China; and at a rally in Zhengzhou, in central China, 164 suspects were publicly arrested and 17 death sentences were announced.[71] In Shanghai, 136 convicted criminals were sentenced.[72] In all, at least 89 criminals were executed nationwide on Wednesday 11 April, which was known as 'great momentum day'.[73]

Another wave of public arrests and sentencings occurred between 17 and 23 April 2001, after which hundreds of criminals had been sentenced to death. The pace of arrests, rallies and executions was relentless. For instance, rallies were simultaneously convened across Guangdong Province on 21 April to 'publicly deal with' 5,485 suspects.[74] On 23 April, 1,168 serious criminal offenders were publicly sentenced in courts across Henan Province, and a number of death sentences were announced at the Sichuan Provincial Sports Stadium to an audience of over 10,000.[75] Similar rallies took place in Chengdu, where 45 death penalties we announced and more than 400 suspects publicly arrested.

From April to December 2001, police in Inner Mongolia launched four region-wide joint 'sentencing operations' involving 3,592 public arrests and 1,763 public sentencings. More than 1.6 million people in Inner Mongolia attended these rallies during 2001.[76] The Deputy President of the Xinjiang Higher People's Court announced at the beginning of the second main campaign offensive in late May 2001 that courts throughout Xinjiang had held massive public sentencing rallies since the start of the campaign. He noted that courts in Xinjiang,

> have held 62 such rallies to publicly pronounce sentence on 767 criminals involved in 432 cases; over 300,000 of the masses have attended these rallies. The success of the first batch of rallies has dealt heavy blows to the arrogance of criminal elements and frightened them, while also educating the masses . . . Since the first batch of sentencing rallies was carefully organized, they have had a big impact, and the masses have been enthusiastic about attending them, so the social effects have been marked.[77]

Xinjiang authorities announced on 31 May 2001, immediately prior to the second main offensive from June to November, that they had decided to 'select key areas and areas where crime is concentrated, such as Urumqi, Kashgar and Yili, to convene the second [batch of] public sentencing rallies at the end of May to continue to maintain a high-pressure posture in "striking hard"'. They announced that a further series of concentrated sentencing activities would be held throughout the region in late June, 'when a new upsurge of "striking hard" will be whipped up and the struggle carried forward in depth. At the same time, the courts will also hold concentrated public sentencings in June in a number of cases of smuggling, fraud, tax evasion, circulating counterfeit currency, and other crimes that disrupt the order of the market economy'.[78]

Concluding remarks

This chapter has explored some of the practical implications of the political and ideological assumptions in China that criminal justice necessarily operates in the broad and fluid political context of national modernization and reform, rather than on the basis of formalistic, inflexible and immutable rules and regulations. Making criminal law open to the broad political context has meant that both historically and in contemporary China, criminal law relating to serious crime has had been made to serve the purposes of state development and has been exercised in a flexible manner. To this end, a number of strategies were applied to achieve the programmatic goals of the campaign. In particular, the principles of flexibility and 'mutual coordination' between the three arms of criminal justice that had been successfully applied in the late 1950s and during the 1983 campaign were resuscitated during the 2001–03 campaign in various forms, as were the requisite 'shock and awe' theatrics of sentencing.

The strategies of the campaign from 2001 to 2003 explored in this chapter are indeed at odds with the rhetoric and ethos of 'professionalism', 'rule of law' and 'independent administration of justice' that has been employed consistently for over two decades in the effort to develop credible and legitimate institutions of criminal justice in China. Along with catchcries such as 'equality before the law' and 'handling cases in accordance with the law', these catchcries of modernization have been promoted as part of a wider claim to a new model of institutional authority that is based on organizational reform and the institutionalization and regularization of legal and governmental processes in the wake of China's economic revolution over the last two decades.

Indeed, since the reform era began in 1979, the PSB, procuratorate and courts have had to negotiate a path to institutional reform based on the rhetoric of professionalization, regularization and procedural propriety while at the same time retaining their 'mass-line' ethos and rhetoric. They have responded to the rapidly changing social and political environment by attempting to develop their authority and legitimacy based on public, government and professional expectations of reform and a new openness. But for historical and political reasons, this authority has continued to be depicted as deriving from two sources. While it is described as residing in the professional execution of duties 'in accordance with the law', this authority has been promoted concomitantly as a direct expression of 'the will and interests of the masses'.

These dual characteristics of authority are expressed in two key requirements of legal institutions in the post-1978 period: first, to provide an organizational and structural basis for promoting economic modernization and foreign investment, and second, to provide a means of guarding against social instability (in other words, guarding against the inevitable negative social consequences of economic reform – crime and social dislocation). The irony of this tension, however, is that the official justification of Strike Hard 2001 – a dramatic rise in crime in 2000 – was in part a direct result of the decidedly 'unprofessional' system the police force itself used to calculate crime statistics. What was identified as a massive 50 per cent increase in the crime rate between 1999 and 2000 was to some extent the result of an internal police campaign to stop crime statistics being manipulated at the local level.[79] This crackdown on the under-reporting of crime incidents had the immediate effect of increasing the crime rate dramatically in 2000. Another explanation for the sudden upsurge in crime was the increasing number of repeat offences committed by recently released prisoners.[80] A high proportion of the prisoners who had received long prison sentences during the first campaign were released in 1999 and 2000, and many had not been successfully 'rehabilitated' during their time in prison. Although prisoners were provided with limited assistance with employment on their release, many of the government enterprises established to offer employment to ex-felons were inadequately funded. There were no 'half-way' houses, safe places, or interim arrangements for released prisoners, with the result that many went back onto the streets and joined mafia-style organizations or other gangs that committed serious offences.[81]

Indeed, it seems that the worst enemy of the criminal justice agencies at the turn of the century may not have been the criminals they were targeting, but the woeful inadequacies – both financial and professional – of the crime management systems within which practitioners were required to operate. Chen Xingliang's description of the war between 'strike hard' and 'crime', quoted in the introduction to this chapter, is pertinent well into the first decade of the twenty-first century, as the daily struggle between crime and punishment challenges Strike Hard's already limited capacity to contain, let alone protect, the social order. We explore these challenges and other inadequacies of campaign justice in the following chapter, which surveys police reflections on campaigns and outline Strike Hard's fall from grace.

4 Cracks in the campaign armour

Thus far, we have followed the trajectory of campaigns from their initial incarnation as generic anti-crime drives that began in the early 1980s, through a series of specialized anti-crime drives in the late 1980s and 1990s and into the first decade of the twenty-first century. This chapter will focus on the growing criticism of the failure of successive campaigns, in particular the 2001–03 campaign, to stem the tide of serious crime. It is at this juncture in campaign justice history that we can begin to trace its decline in prominence.

Here we examine the beginnings of these cracks in the campaign armour by focusing on discussions about campaign justice's shortcomings followed by an unprecedented debate among some of the nation's top police brass that took place over a number of volumes of China's top policing journal, *Public Security Studies*. After this debate, the trajectory took an unexpected turn. In late 2003, Luo Gan, the head of the Party's Politico-legal Committee and the nation's chief campaign proponent, announced that Strike Hard would be 'regularized' into everyday practice. The idea of 'normalizing' or 'regularizing' Strike Hard is – I would argue, deliberately – highly ambiguous. Given the abstract nature of the concept, the call to 'regularize' Strike Hard can be seen as a way of diffusing its political stigma and reducing the dominance of campaign.

The announcement of Strike Hard's 'regularization' was preceded by a series of debates in policing circles in 2002 and 2003 that suggested that campaign justice itself may be part of the problem. The first part of this chapter briefly surveys the mixed results of the 2001–03 campaign, while the second part takes up the criticisms that began to surface in a series of journal articles by junior police and provincial heads of public security during and immediately after the Strike Hard campaign. China's police had by this period, become increasingly professionalized. The transition to modernity for any criminal justice system requires a professionalized police body. Here we find that this body begins to speak out and 'the political' speaks back. The final part of the chapter describes the aftermath of the campaign, particularly the push to 'regularize' Strike Hard in everyday criminal justice practice. Here we find the beginnings of a turnaround in the approach to campaigns in public security circles, with a concerted but subtle attempt by the Minister of Public Security to clip campaign justice's wings. While previous chapters have focused on the first two expressions of the political identified in the Introduction, this chapter concerns the third aspect; institutional 'politicking'.

The mixed fruits of battle: the national appraisal of Strike Hard 2001–03

Barely a month into the Strike Hard 2001 campaign, its success had begun to be touted in the media, and a variety of indicators were wheeled out to illustrate its achievements. Politico-legal officials at the national level measured Strike Hard's success in terms of the number of suspects detained and the speed with which these suspects were arrested, indicted and punished. Strike Hard's achievements were even measured in terms of media exposure itself. The number of propaganda pamphlets that had been distributed in 2001 (2 billion) and the number of Strike Hard exhibitions and information boards that had been displayed in work units, schools and on streets (581,000) were all used as indicators that the campaign was indeed effective in delivering the message that crime does not pay.[1] It was widely reported that 99,947 suspects had been formally arrested and indicted by the procuratorate across China between 4 April and 1 May 2001, and that more than 1,000 criminals had been executed by the end of May.[2] By June, there had been at least 1,781 criminal executions reported in the Chinese press[3] – and the real figure was undoubtedly much higher.

Another purported indicator of Strike Hard 2001 success was the rise in the number of criminal cases finalized in the courts. A figure of 751,000 cases, a 16.2 per cent increase over the previous year, was seen as an indication that swiftness had been achieved.[4] In terms of the campaign's main target – syndicate and gang crime – achievements were measured in terms of the 420 cases (involving 8,355 suspects) cracked by police that had involved large mafia-style syndicates and the 6,321 cases (involving 36,000 suspects) that related to crimes committed by smaller organized crime gangs. Success in reducing the prevalence of 'protective umbrellas' was also measured as a campaign victory: 581 officials who had been providing protection for organized crime were arrested, including 79 government or party officials, 328 court or prosecution officials, and 16 members of the People's Congress.[5]

While authorities had indeed managed to capture thousands of gang and syndicate members, the campaign failed to put a dent in targeted common crimes such as theft; the campaign also did not manage to 'rectify' public order in crime hotspots, another of its stated aims. In ten major provincial jurisdictions including Shanghai, Jiangsu, Henan and Inner Mongolia, 2001 saw significant increases in the number of thefts, armed robberies and bag snatching incidents from motorbikes or bicycles – the 3.745 million cases in these three categories accounted for 84 per cent of all registered crimes, representing a massive 28 per cent increase in property-related crime. The number of registered cases of theft had increased in 2001 in all provinces apart from Shanxi and Beijing. Moreover, the locations of theft crimes were changing – from worksites, factories and farms, to residential housing areas.[6] In 2001, 43.4 per cent of the total of 1.268 million theft cases occurred in residential housing areas. Even more worrying was the dramatic increase in the number of cases involving armed robbery and robbery by bag snatching. There were 352,000 cases of armed robbery in 2001, an increase of 13.7 per cent over the previous year, and a 22.9 per cent increase (92,000 cases) in armed robberies that occurred in public areas, public squares or on large roads or streets. There was also a 35.8 per cent increase in the number of cases of bag snatchings from motorbikes or bicycles.[7]

The National Comprehensive Management of Public Order (CMPO) Committee in Beijing made four main recommendations on how Strike Hard 2002 should proceed, based on the results of Strike Hard 2001. Its first recommendation was to continue to maintain 'the high pressure of Strike Hard' using 'severe and swift' punishment, with a focus on violent criminals and repeat offenders who committed non-violent crimes such as theft. Authorities were advised to continue to infiltrate mafia-style organizations by destroying their financial bases and, where appropriate, to conduct specialized campaigns to target bombings. Police were also advised to continue to fight soft offences such as pornography and prostitution while continuing their main attack on violent crime. Second, authorities were advised to continue to solve public order problems in known crime hotspots, and third to make efforts to strengthen crime prevention and control and promote the three arms of police work – attacking, preventing and controlling crime. Finally, police were directed to look beneath the surface of the crime problem and focus on mediation to prevent marital or domestic disputes and neighbourhood problems from escalating into violent conflicts.[8]

The following year's CMPO Committee internal report on the campaign again announced mixed results. The Committee's 'Notice on Strike Hard 2002' reported that the total number of registered crimes in 2002 had fallen 2.8 per cent on the previous year, to 4.3 million. The number of victims injured during the course of crimes had also declined by 4.2 per cent to 221,000.[9] A fall of 5.6 per cent in the number of suspects formally charged during 2002 was reported as evidence that fewer people were willing to risk committing crimes during the campaign. A total of 2.4 million criminal cases had been cracked in 2002, an increase of 11.8 per cent on the previous year, while the clear-up rate remained steady at 45.5 per cent. A total of 765,899 people were arrested (512,540 cases), a decline of 5.6 per cent on the previous year, and 829,520 people (561,579 cases) were indicted for trial, an increase of 2.9 per cent.[10] In addition, 7.2 million people were apprehended for illegal acts such as prostitution, gambling and drug use that were subject to administrative rather than criminal punishment.[11] But despite all this, the number of crimes with the threat of violence had not declined in 2002, and 355,000 cases of robbery were recorded, an increase of 0.8 per cent over the previous year. Cases of street robbery and robberies in market squares also constituted 26 per cent of all types of robbery in 2002, which represented an increase of 2.1 per cent over the previous year; and robberies on freeways and highways accounted for 21.4 per cent of all robberies, a dramatic 12.3 per cent increase. The number of incidents of bag snatching from bikes and motorbikes also increased by 7.6 per cent in 2002, to a total of 197,000 cases.[12]

UNIV DUNELM

The CMPO Committee made three recommendations for the remainder of the campaign and beyond. First of all, while the established 'campaign path' should continue, the main post-campaign plan should be to regionalize the fight further by focusing on the particular crime problems of individual jurisdictions. The second recommendation was for criminal justice authorities to place greater emphasis on mediating social conflicts to prevent them from escalating into violence. The police, procuratorate and courts were advised to participate routinely in mediation activities, by properly investigating conflicts and handling them in a manner that would prevent social issues turning into crimes. The Committee's final recommendation was the promotion of a system that combined three aspects of crime control – combating, preventing and controlling crime – under the leadership of the party and government. This could be achieved through practices such as boosting police patrols in problem areas, strengthening neighbourhood watch programs, tightening controls over itinerant worker mobility, improving the management and supervision of newly released prisoners, and strengthening juvenile education and management.[13] These were all decidedly un-*Yanda*-like activities that favoured prevention over 'striking hard'.

Contestation in the provinces: police on *Yanda*

The following discussion of the failure of the 2001–03 *Yanda* campaign to deliver a noticeable improvement in public order is based on a candid appraisal by public security insiders, and provides the strongest indication to date of the level of frustration with campaign justice within both junior and senior ranks of the police in China. What emerged during the 2001 campaign and its aftermath was an increasing tension between the party's call to strike hard at serious crime and the alternative strategy favoured by the police – crime prevention. Within this context of institutional tensions, there was an impassioned discussion on campaign policy that involved both local police and provincial heads of public security in Chinese public security journals, both during and in the wake of the 2001–03 campaign. A minority of senior public security personnel were pro-Strike Hard and happy to admit it. For example, a deputy head of public security in Jiangxi Province boasted that 13,026 cases had been solved in the first 90 days of the 2001 campaign, from April to June 2001, which represented a 107 per cent increase over the January to March period. He also reported a reduction in the number of calls to the police emergency hotline in most parts of the province. According to this official, when Jia Chunwang, China's Minister of Public Security, had visited the province for an inspection tour, he had proclaimed Jiangxi a campaign success: 'Our accomplishments were unambiguous and some of the best achievements in the country'.[14] The pro-Strike Hard public security minority typically originated from the richer coastal provinces such as Zhejiang, where local government budgets were able to afford a Strike Hard campaign. But, for the majority of public security officials, Strike Hard rhetoric had clearly worn thin.

Campaign justice's ineffectiveness

We begin this discussion with a candid observation from a local public security officer. Campaigns are an inefficient waste of police resources, according to Rao Yuanming of the Lishui Municipal PSB in Zhejiang Province, who highlighted a number of problems with the implementation of the 2001–03 campaign that stemmed from poor organization of resources. During campaigns, Rao explained, there is a tension between campaign commitments and everyday police work.

> There is a saying that goes, 'there are one thousand threads to weave but only one needle to weave them' . . . When it comes to the grassroots level, 'Strike Hard' has to translate into specific tasks. Our jurisdiction is a county-sized city and quite apart from the tasks issued to us from politico-legal authorities at the provincial level, the party committees at the local level also give us specific everyday tasks to perform. On top of these tasks, we also have our own routine tasks that need to get done every day. But in such a long period of campaign – over two years – it's Strike Hard, not the everyday minor tasks that take up our daily work.[15]

Another inefficiency-related campaign problem concerned inappropriate spending, according to Rao. Joint offensives were used as a propaganda and deterrence exercise during the 2001–03 campaign. The human and other costs of staging a joint show of force such as a joint offensive that might last days or weeks greatly exceeded the budget in Rao's jurisdiction.

> It is highly uncertain that we get a return for our money . . . With one offensive after another, it is unavoidable that police begin to feel utterly sick and tired of striking hard and feel half-hearted about their work during these offensives.[16]

Another problem Rao raised was that the tactic of fast-tracking police investigations as a way to improve crime clear-up rates is in direct conflict with the meticulous work that should follow conventional routine policing. Over the last few decades, he explained, as populations have become more mobile, basic police work has become much more difficult. And the speedy (campaign-style) resolution of criminal cases cannot be compared favourably with solid basic police work.

> Basic policing is a slow and long-term job . . . In reality, the two don't mix. [Campaign justice] is hard-ball policing and basic police work is soft-ball in approach. So when these two come into competition, it is always basic police work that gets ignored.[17]

Police resources are always stretched, so when police are constantly required to take part in joint offensives, basic policing suffers.[18] Rao continues:

> After two decades of campaigning, some police have developed the mentality that if there are no campaigns there's no social stability. Other police cynically

> believe that Strike Hard is all about improving the career paths of their senior officials and that joint operations are simply a propaganda tool for senior police to show off to their superiors . . . Yet, there are other police who actually look forward to the next campaign because they feel that policing in normal times is eventless and mind-numbingly boring so they save all their enthusiasm for the next campaign.[19]

Rao's observations about the inefficiency of campaigns were backed up by another local police officer, Zheng Jianguo, head of the Pingyang County PSB in Zhejiang Province, who claimed that the 2001–03 campaign was laboriously slow and ineffective. Zheng outlined the circumstances faced by police in his area in the wake of the two-year Strike Hard campaign and the ongoing specialized drives claiming that the 2001–03 campaign had not led to an improvement in public order. Zheng writes that, over the two-year course of Strike Hard 2001–03, 'we exhausted all of our physical and psychological power and all that eventuated from this work was that the incident report rate had not declined and remained at a high level'. He contends that street robbery and bag snatching remained rife in his area, during and post-campaign, and considering that crimes were becoming much more high-tech, police were becoming increasingly less sophisticated than criminals. In the two years since the end of Strike Hard in 2003, he added, there had been non-stop specialized campaigns, and local police had routinely been working overtime and on weekends, and were not permitted to take any annual recreation leave.[20] Zheng claims that a key reason for the lack of positive outcomes from these campaigns is that the Strike Hard clock is forever slow:

> Campaigns are sluggish and stagnant. Each specialized struggle only gets launched after the crime targeted in the campaign is already rife in that area, therefore making it even harder to control . . . For example, after Strike Hard in 2004, the Ministry of Public Security launched a specialized campaign on internet pornography. This crime already had a serious impact on law and order before the drive was launched. In many areas, including our area, it had been going on for years but because we needed funds and didn't get them and because we needed more staff and didn't get them, we had no alternative but to wait until the announcement of the campaign before we could do anything. But if we keep waiting around until the next campaign [before we tackle the problem], we have lost any opportunity to take control of this problem before having to pour out massive expenses of time and money to solve it.[21]

Zheng claims that there is an over-enthusiasm for rapid results, whereas effective crime control is a more complex and long-term issue. Nevertheless, the very essence of Strike Hard's official goal is that it will effect a 'fundamental turnaround in the state of public order'. But Zheng questions how this can be possible when campaign tactics are so hopelessly outmoded:

> Society has changed dramatically in the last 20 years yet we are still using the same tactics that we did in Strike Hard 1983: 'specialized campaigns', 'joint

> offensives', concentrated police 'comb-outs', then public arrest rallies and later public sentencing rallies. The criminals have learned our Kungfu kick tactics very early on, but we don't have the time to research their moves.[22]

One commentator Liu Xuegang claims that the Maoist mass-line tactic of 'waging war using a human sea' – pouring thousands of police and parapolice onto the streets in united operations – is antiquated and should be made obsolete. The tactic of 'ferreting out the enemy' through search and stop operations on the streets and search and investigate operations in commercial, government and residential buildings is usually conducted at night, and is very labour intensive. Liu believes that these tactics were actually effective in seeking out suspects in the 1980s campaigns, but are now outdated. He explains:

> In Strike Hard 1983, the targeted offences were street crimes such as armed robbery. Many criminals could easily be caught in the act. Strike Hard was effective in catching these types of criminals. But during Strike Hard 2001, the targets were hidden underground as they were largely mafia syndicates and gangs and professional criminals. As soon as they heard the campaign battle cry they went into hiding. No wonder the situation we find ourselves in is that 'the net of Strike Hard is cast but there are no fish to catch'. The effort involved in casting a net is costly. Police cast their nets at night and don't catch anything and are then too tired to work the next day. This method of campaigning is now outdated.[23]

During campaigns, police are taken away from their routine crime prevention tasks, and this itself causes fluctuations in the crime rate. Bi Xiqian and Chen Juan explain that the emphasis of campaigns is firmly focused on attacking crime, with much less weight given to preserving the foundations of public order through crime prevention and managing the movements of the millions of people who make up China's itinerant population. The normal business of a police station is put aside for the duration of large campaigns, and the routine business of maintaining public order – for example, controlling key areas such as pubs and clubs – is put on hold. As Bi and Chen explain, this creates a situation where crime rates decline dramatically during campaigns, but after each campaign, rates increase to a higher level than before, because the routine work of regulating public order is ignored during campaigns. The benefits of the valleys in crime control are thus cancelled out by the peaks.[24]

An extreme example of campaigns' ability to blindside routine police work occurred during the first Strike Hard campaign when a serial killer murdered 48 people under the noses of police. Long Zhimin, a peasant in Sheng County, Shanxi Province, murdered 48 people between February 1982 and May 1985. All Long's victims were killed and buried in his home, and he had apparently hung out 391 items of the victims' clothing in his yard in full view of his neighbours. His modus operandi was simple – he used a pickaxe to hack his victims to death. He did not hide himself away, but lived only 7.5 kilometres from the county capital and 500 metres from the town centre. He stood out in a crowd, because he was extremely short at 155 cm in height, and had a criminal record for rape. Long committed most of the murders from January to May 1985, in the middle of the campaign, killing on average one victim every five days. During his killing spree, 38 family members of the victims reported their relatives missing, but none were put on file as missing persons, and only one police officer followed up on the relatives' statements. This was apparently because finding missing persons was not an objective of the campaign.[25] What makes this story even more extraordinary is that it was detailed in an internal national CMPO report published in 2003 as evidence that party officials and the Minister of Public Security knew as early as the 1980s that such problems were occurring.[26]

Public security officer Xiao Xiong describes another problem with campaign tactics that involve players outside immediate criminal justice circles. The targets of campaigns often expand at the grassroots level to incorporate social problems that are completely unrelated to campaign targets. This is because campaigns rely on a number of government and non-government actors for both workers and funding.[27] Local governments, which have financial control over local police, therefore consider that they have a right to take advantage of campaigns to pursue their own interests, as Xiao Xiong describes:

> In some areas, quite apart from the specified campaign targets, [local governments] are tacking on add-ons that have nothing to do with Strike Hard. Tax evasion, illegal business registrations, fraud through the issuing of false contracts, all kinds of offences and all ranges of severity are thrown into the campaign ring. As a result, the numbers of cases on police file and the clear-up rate statistics vary dramatically from place to place.[28]

Another commentator points out that, once social organizations and political institutions are mobilized to help in the fight against crime, these groups are likely to jump on the campaign bandwagon. For example, during Strike Hard 2001, the tax departments in some areas asked the police to crack down on tax evasion as part of the campaign. Local councils also took the opportunity to crack down on non-payment of council rates, and authorities in some areas even used to campaign to target infringements of the one-child policy. Even though these matters fall outside their legal jurisdiction,[29] the police are obliged to add them to their list of campaign targets because they are funded and resourced not by central authorities but by local governments. This makes them subject to the whims and interests of local officials.

Another inefficient campaign tactic is to set unrealistic time limits for solving criminal cases. According to Liu Xuegang:

> The worst news that local PSB bureau chiefs can hear is a message from their municipal or central superiors ordering them to crack a major crime within a particular deadline . . . The situation is such now that all crimes involving violent death must be cracked within a specified time . . . The position of the local bureau chief is threatened if he/she can't crack a case in the specified time. This

> is not only unscientific, it's irrational. The PSB then have no alternative but to use inefficient methods such as 'using several people to take turns to fight one opponent in order to tire him out' . . . No-one is allowed to return home until the case has been solved.[30]

Campaigns are rationalized as an operation that reflects the will of the masses and involves mass participation. News reportage of campaigns is often accompanied by mass-line rhetoric that alludes to public support or 'mass participation', but in the 2001–03 campaign there was little evidence of widespread public participation in the drive. As Zhai Jinping explains:

> Enthusiasm for campaigns is waning. This has something to do with the law of diminishing returns; that is, the more you do it, the less enthusiastic people will be about implementing it . . . Campaigns are a short-term measure to combat crime. If it continues to be used on a routine basis it will lose its effectiveness.[31]

The Public Security Chief in Nanchong City, Sichuan Province, believes that not only was public enthusiasm for campaigns waning in the 2001–03 drive, so too was enthusiasm for helping with law enforcement in general. He claims that the level of public participation in campaigns is insufficient:

> By the term 'participation', I do not refer to public audience participation during arrest and sentencing rallies. I mean that we receive very few calls from witnesses to crimes, who in times past would have called the police out of a sense of responsibility . . . There are now fewer and fewer members of the public who are willing to help police to arrest a suspect.[32]

A large-scale province-wide internal police survey of the Strike Hard Campaign in Fujian Province that was undertaken by police researchers and commissioned by the Fujian Province Public Security Department in 2001 found that the campaign was not getting the deterrence message across to the public or to criminals, chiefly because the operational methods used for propaganda were outdated. Li Shuangqi of the Fujian Police Academy outlines a number of problems related to the promotion of campaigns that are evident in the report's findings. First of all, police failed to create a proper campaign 'vibe' or atmosphere in communities, which means that criminals were not scared into submission and continued committing crimes throughout the campaign.[33] Li also notes both a fundamental lack of public understanding of the particulars of the campaign, and a lack of general awareness about the campaign process. A large proportion of the people surveyed were unaware that Fujian was even in the middle of a Strike Hard campaign. Other members of the public who were aware of the campaign were critical of police efforts to combat organized crime. The survey found that a large proportion of those surveyed in Fuzhou, Putian and Quanzhou cities considered that the PSB had not even begun to lift the lid on mafia-style organized and gang crime; some of those interviewed also said that they would be afraid to report any gang crime.[34]

The survey report also highlighted the relatively poor clear-up rate for common public order-related crimes. The public are naturally more concerned with crimes that are likely to affect them personally, such as burglary, car theft and purse snatching. These are the three most common types of crimes, but have the lowest clear-up rates. Li makes the point here that the public fail to see the benefits of striking hard if the campaigns fail to solve the very crimes that they are most concerned about.[35] The Fujian survey also pointed to the poor quality of criminal investigations. During *Yanda* 2001 in Fujian Province, the rate of indictments secured by the PSB actually declined, and there had been an increase in the number of cases sent back by the prosecution for reinvestigation. The PSB's emphasis on cracking cases at the expense of collecting solid evidence for the successful prosecution of the crimes meant that little time could be spared for the paperwork required to indict suspects, and the cases were therefore not prosecuted in a timely manner. At the time of the report's publication in 2002, there were 24,424 people remanded in custody in watchhouses in Fujian waiting to be indicted.[36]

Assessing **Yanda** *success: the problem of underreporting crime*

The falsification of crime statistics by local PSBs has been an endemic problem in China since the 1980s.[37] While this problem occurs worldwide, it is acute in China. Over the last three decades, the assessment of the state of public order has relied on two indicators: the number of crimes placed on police files (*li'an*) and the police clear-up rate (*po'an lu*). The number of crimes placed on police files is not the same as the number of actual incidents (*fa'an shuliang*) because local police exercise their discretion about whether or not to place individual cases on file. Because police measure their success using the rate of registered cases on file for investigation, they can claim better results than would be the case if they compared the number of cases solved to the actual number of crime incidents. Police can manipulate the statistics to conceal the real rate of crime – that is, the *fa'an shuliang* – by simply choosing to place only some crime incidents (usually those that are easy to solve) officially on file. Rao Yuanming explains that most stations have two different crime records on file: one for internal eyes only that records the real incident report rate, and a 'fake' record.[38] Police reports conceal the large number of cases they are aware of that have not yet been solved, and often only officially place them on file when they have been cracked, so that favourable evaluations can be made by comparing the number of cases on file for investigation and the number of cases that have been solved.[39] In 1998, the Ministry of Public Security Survey estimated that the official crime statistics represented only 20 per cent of the actual number of incidents reported to police.[40]

A 1998 internal survey on falsifying statistics commissioned by the Beijing PSB Party Secretary in three of Beijing's largest districts found an even greater than expected discrepancy between the reported incidence of crime and the actual crime rate. There were 7,225 incidents reported to police in Xuanwu, Haidian and Shunyi districts from January to July 1998. Of these, 733 were investigated and no crime was found to have been committed, so these cases were not pursued. In theory, the remaining 6,492 cases should have been officially placed on file and reported to superiors, but in fact only 1,331 were reported; this constitutes only 20 per cent of the cases that should have been investigated and officially put on file. Most major crimes such as murder, rape and violent assault were recorded, while the majority of the crimes that went unrecorded were thefts.[41] After the findings of the report were circulated, officials launched a campaign against falsifying crime statistics. Statistics on clear-up rates show just how grave the falsification problem was in the mid-1990s; police officer Mu Yumin compiled national statistics which indicate that the clear-up rate for crimes in 1994 and 1997 was 69 per cent and 81.2 per cent respectively – these are totally unrealistic figures that could not even be achieved in a developed country that could afford adequate police resources. The figure of 25 per cent for 1999, the period after the campaign against falsifying crime statistics, seems more realistic.[42]

A national campaign against falsifying crime statistics in 1999 led to a massive jump in the number of registered cases from 2.2 million in 1999 to 3.6 million in 2000. Ironically, this increase was a leading reason for launching the 2001–03 campaign. Despite the well-recognized tendency to falsify crime statistics, the success of generic campaigns and specialized drives continued to be measured by political authorities and public security bureaucrats in terms of the clear-up rate and the percentage decline in the registered crime rate. According to Rao Yuanming, this is highly problematic because it has encouraged local public security bureaus to falsify crime statistics during campaigns to an even greater extent. Rao claims that, in order to highlight the success of campaigns, police often move records from the previous (non-campaign) period to the campaign period to give the appearance of an improvement in the proportion of cases cracked during campaigns. By shifting solved cases from the previous year to the campaign year, the clear-up rates for the preceding year appear poorer, thus enhancing the rates for the campaign year. Some police stations even wait until an imminent announcement to 'strike hard' before arresting suspects; by doing so, they keep the suspects on the streets until it is in the interests of the police to arrest them.[43] Li Yaoming and Chen Jiwei, police officers stationed at the Beilun District PSB in Ningbo City, argue that concealing the real number of crimes is ultimately self-defeating because it fails to reflect the real crime problem. If police deliberately lower the incident report rate, the budgets they receive from local government will be reduced correspondingly.[44]

The system of using clear-up rates as the measure of success and relying on a rewards system based on the number of cases solved creates with it three additional problems, according to Xu Yinggui, Zhou Ying and Cao Chong. It means that police often concentrate on solving cases that involve only one criminal and a single crime incident, ignoring cases that may be complex and difficult to solve. Second, police only focus on the crime at hand and have no incentive to pay attention to crimes a repeat offender may have committed in the past. Finally, courts often drown in smaller (easy to solve) cases, creating a backlog that results in delayed prosecution of major or more complex cases.[45]

The use of the police incident report rate as the measuring stick for assessing ability or failure to maintain public order ignores the established fact that the crime rate inevitably rises in modernizing states, in direct correlation to economic growth, according to Liu Xuegang.[46] Liu believes that it is well understood in criminology literature that when economic development reaches a certain point in developing countries it tends to plateau, and the crime rate follows this trend. According to Liu, politicians in China refuse to acknowledge the relationship between crime, public order and economic development:

> They assess the state of public order entirely on the basis of the crime rate at the time. Officials then use the old tried-and-tested means of "waging war using a human sea" . . . Crime rates decline, but only in the very short-term.[47]

The problem of funding

The Fujian survey also highlighted the general over-emphasis on 'attacking crime' at the expense of routine detective work in the province. Crime scene investigation funding that had been earmarked for technology and forensic equipment in Fujian had been reallocated to fund the 2001–03 campaign. This meant that crime scene investigation work had essentially been put on hold. Funding for public security intelligence databases that needed to be bolstered to cope with the influx of campaign cases had not been increased.[48] Li argues that this problem occurred in Fujian because the overall funding level is far too low. For example, in Fujian, the funds allocated to the Criminal Investigation Branch in 2001 by the local government accounted for only 20 per cent of the entire police budget that year, and only 20 per cent of these funds were used for hands-on criminal investigation. Criminal detectives at the local county level had no alternative but to go to their local community councils and the local business community to seek additional funds. Li notes that they raised 30 per cent of their budget from these alternative sources. The remaining 50 per cent of their required budget was unfunded, and in some counties there was only enough funding to investigate one or two major cases – any remaining cases were put on hold. In addition, funding was only sufficient to employ three to six criminal detectives per county, and these officers were expected to perform specialist tasks they were not trained for, including crime scene forensic investigation. According to Ministry of Public Security guidelines for staffing numbers per head of population, Li calculated that in 2001 Fujian should have had a minimum of 740 detectives, but only 418 were employed, because there were insufficient funds to fill the other 322 positions. To compensate for this shortfall, each detective had to work overtime on a daily basis. There was no time for professional development, and criminal investigation equipment remained outdated, with most equipment dating back to the 1980s.[49] To emphasize the gravity of the situation in Fujian, Li notes that in 2001 the national Ministry of Public Security made a list of the minimum level of equipment for each region; in Fujian, only Xiamen City and 14 counties reached the minimum standard. In the other counties, the average value of existing equipment was 103,000 yuan, whereas the Ministry put the value of the minimum standard equipment at between 600,000 and 1.2 million yuan, depending on the size of the jurisdiction. The average value of equipment and police resources in municipalities in 2001 was 1.2 million yuan, but the Ministry put the minimum standard at 12 million yuan. It is little wonder, given this level of funding, that detectives were unable to investigate cases with any scientific precision. 'There isn't even enough time for investigation teams to meet to discuss a case', Li notes. To add to the funding misery, there was no provision in the budget to maintain even the small amount of relatively up-to-date equipment. According to Li,

> At our provincial central forensic unit, there is a 800,000 yuan shortfall in funding, with no funds to purchase even the simplest things such as paper and film. Ninety-five per cent of counties and cities are funded below the minimum standard and 20 per cent of these are completely incapacitated.[50]

The most alarming aspect of this is that Fujian is a relatively affluent province. Truly poor regions are even more vulnerable to the problems described above. Chen Zili, Public Security Chief of Nanchong City, asserts that, given the desperate lack of funds in poorer regions, many areas can ill afford campaigns.

> In a poor city like ours, there are not even enough funds to pay police. Municipal police wages come from the local municipal government. There is no guarantee at all that police have the basic funds to get a case to court. There's no point even mentioning such things as crime scene investigators. They don't exist here . . . During campaigns, there's one offensive after another. Police don't get any weekends off and they even have to work during national holidays.[51]

Liu Xuegang's research confirms this problem. He argues that the police are placed under considerable work, psychological and health pressure by campaigns, and claims that the most common reaction of police at the mention of the word 'strike hard' is an exhausted sigh.

> Why are they exhausted? There are not enough police to go around. There are not enough funds to cover policing costs and policing methods are insufficiently modernized. Because of this, the work of two people is done by one officer.[52]

When funds are insufficient, Liu notes, criminal investigators can't afford to fly in planes to a distant crime scene. Instead, they have to take a bus, which wastes crucial investigation time. If police have access to fingerprinting databases, a suspect's prints can be found in seconds, but if there is no access, police have to laboriously search through thousands of pages of material to match the print.[53]

Provincial heads on Strike Hard

At the height of the 2001 campaign, a number of provincial heads of public security across China began to participate in an unprecedented discussion that was conducted in the pages of the country's premier public security journal, *Gong'an yanjiu* (*Public Security Studies*). The head of public security in Sichuan sparked the debate by launching a scathing attack on the campaign. He critiqued three main issues. The first was the inadequacy of the deterrence function of Strike Hard 2001:

> The crime rates in the first offensive of Strike Hard 2001 from April to June, have not begun to fall. In 1983, during the first offensive of the campaign from September to November, the number of cases reported to the police declined by 50.5 per cent compared to the two months prior to the campaign. Of these, major crimes declined by 28.6 per cent. In this year's campaign, from April to June, 17,000 incidents have been reported to the police each month in April and May, which was an increase of 1,000 each month over the three months before the campaign . . . Violent and heinous crimes have not declined during the campaign. In some areas, non-stop violent murders and rapes have occurred right through the first months of the campaign . . . The number of people voluntarily surrendering to police has declined substantially. In 1983, during the first offensive from August to November, 10,355 suspects surrendered. In the 2001 campaign, during the same period, only 448 people surrendered, that is, only 4.3 per cent of the 1983 figure.[54]

Lu's second criticism was that 'the masses' had not really been 'mobilized' as campaign propaganda had boasted. During the first stage of the campaign, four million people in Sichuan were organized to attend public arrest or sentencing rallies. Information on crime was sought from the public at these rallies and through other means, but only 6,037 members of the public offered information, resulting in only 853 civil arrests. Lu compared this to the first Strike Hard campaign in 1983 when there were 21,600 sources of information, resulting in 5,810 civil arrests. He claims this demonstrates a lack of enthusiasm for *Yanda* 2001: 'The public just see *Yanda* 2001 as just another specialized campaign in a long line of campaigns . . . People are desensitized to campaigns and over-accustomed to the top-down approach to crime control'.[55]

Lu identified the internal issue of police funding and resources as the third main problem with campaign justice. While recent decades had seen some improvements in the quality of policing, these had been minimal. In 2000, there were 196,516 cases on police files in Sichuan, a 269.6 per cent increase over the 1983 figure of 53,161 cases. But in 2000 there were 58,459 police in Sichuan, compared to 23,032 officers in 1983, representing an increase of 153.8 per cent. He also noted that not all police in the province were guaranteed a full pay packet every month, and that police needed to pay for their own work-related expenses, including medical expenses. He reported in exasperation that:

> It is well acknowledged that crime rates in China are going to continue to grow, but the current problems with the PSB are not going to go away soon. PSB agencies are marching ahead laden with a heavy load and if our national leaders can't recognize these problems, it will not be possible to effect a lasting

> state of peaceful order simply by launching a couple of offensives. Campaigns need a new conceptual and operating framework . . . Since 1983, nearly every year there has been either a Strike Hard or a specialized campaign, but crime rates have continued to rise. The party is not satisfied, the government is not satisfied, and neither are the people. They have all lost their sense of security. Every year, the police run themselves haggard and they are sick to death of it all . . . So could we consider some alternative solution?[56]

As we have noted in earlier chapters, Chinese security organs operate under a dual leadership structure. Administratively and financially, police are controlled by the local government and local party committee at the same administrative level, but professionally they are managed by higher-level public security organs at the provincial and national levels.[57] Lu suggests that the solution to this problem is to 'smash' the current administrative arrangement at the county and local levels that gives local governments financial control over PSB funding. He sees this as not just a budgetary problem, but also a problem with the system of command.

> Commands should only go from one PSB head vertically down to the level below, not through local government officials . . . the costs, not only the benefits of campaigns should be considered. Compare how much we pay out to how much we get in return. The market economy is ruled by efficiency, so we should be too.[58]

The view from poorer regions was even more damning. Wei Zhenzhong, head of public security in Gansu Province, discovered on an inspection tour of the province in 2002 that police resources were so inadequate that even easy-to-catch fugitives were not being apprehended during the campaign.[59] Eighty-five per cent of wanted criminals still lived locally, and 94 per cent of the wanted criminals in Lanzhou City, the capital of Gansu, had not left the city during the campaign. In Qingyang City the figure was 93.5 per cent, and in Gangnan County it was 100 per cent. Wei claimed that most criminals had not bothered to flee very far, and most had been in phone contact with their families and had received money from them. In the countryside, wanted criminals often returned to their farms to help their families with farm work. In Qingyang City, 57.5 per cent of those apprehended in 2001 had returned home on occasion to see family, and 21.8 per cent had remained in constant phone contact. Thirty-two per cent relied on their families for food, and 93 per cent had worked or been self-employed at some stage while on the run.[60]

Wei saw this situation as partly a result of funding problems, but also due in part to poor basic policing skills. The common excuse for the situation that he was met with on his inspection tour was the lack of funding for catching wanted criminals. But even when local governments did provide funding to the PSB, the local police did not seem to know where to start looking for fugitives:

> I noticed during my visits that many local stations didn't even know the first thing about the wanted criminals they were supposed to be searching for. They

> only knew the person's name and didn't know where his/her family lived, the family's economic background, the suspect's educational background, occupation, his/her social ties or personality and temperament.[61]

Wei believes that campaign-style policing over the past two decades has engendered a policing mentality that has become desensitized to unrealistic campaign quotas. Police routinely fake crime statistics or fail to place known crimes on file or on police databases. As the Gansu police chief explained, in some counties in his province, police were reluctant to place details of their wanted criminals on the intranet as they lacked faith that substations in other parts of the country would help them trace these suspects. They feared that if they put the details on the intranet it would look bad for them because they had been unable to track down the suspects themselves.[62] In Jishan County, for instance, police apprehended 34 fugitives in 2001, but 72 per cent of these were not recorded on the police databases. Wei contends that police follow a general rule of thumb: they place major crimes such as robberies and murders on the database because they are difficult to hide, but do not record other, lesser crimes.

> Or, alternatively, if the police are fairly sure that they can catch a suspect, they place them on the database. If they think that the case will be difficult to solve, they don't place them on the database, and some even wait until they have already caught a suspect. They then put the suspect on the database as "wanted" and immediately report them as having been apprehended.[63]

The next provincial head of public security to enter into the debate in Public Security Studies was from Guizhou, another of China's poorest provinces. Jiang Yanhu believed that crime rates were actually on the increase during the Strike Hard campaign. In Guizhou Province between January and November 2001, 80,979 crimes were registered on police files, an increase of 36.5 per cent over the previous year. More worrying was the type of crime being committed. The main offences committed in Guizhou in 2001, starting with the most common, were theft, robbery, serious assault, rape, murder, bombing, arson and kidnapping. Theft, the most common crime, was the only non-violent crime on the list.[64] Explaining why the Strike Hard policy of announcing nationwide targets was not effective in his region, Jiang noted that Guizhou's population of 30 million people largely reside in mountainous regions and are largely unschooled. Many of these people did not consider the consequences before reacting violently to a situation. In Guizhou, cases that resulted in the death of a victim were often the result of common assaults that escalated to violence, minor disturbances, or perpetrators reacting violently to unfounded suspicions. Jiang argues that campaigns are not an effective deterrent to such unpremeditated types of crime. Moreover, in poor regions such as Guizhou, general campaign targets such as car theft are meaningless because there are few cars to steal – people in Guizhou steal cattle and horses not cars.[65]

The provincial chief of Yunnan, China's drug capital, also entered the debate the following year with a scathing attack on the ineffectiveness of campaign justice.

> We have been running around in circles for the last 20 years. Cases get reported, cracked, and then arrests are made; then more cases get reported, cracked, and even more arrests are made. The number of incidents reported to the police just gets higher and higher and the number of criminals caught just gets greater and greater. This rate of crime cannot be totally defeated and can never be completely prevented.[66]

He points to a number of reasons for this lack of progress that he claims are widely acknowledged within public security circles. The first is the sharp increase in the speed and volume of movement in people, finances and material goods, and the second is the increased disparity in incomes, which leaves many feeling that they have missed out on the benefits of reform. The third reason is the increased openness to new desires, values and moral views in China, and the fourth reason relates specifically to Yunnan's drug problem. According to Jiang, because the clear-up rate for cases in his bureau is low, a large number of criminals are still on the streets.[67]

Specialized drives, which were first employed in part as a solution to the problem of the lack of police funding and resources, encouraged strategies such as 'united operations' and 'stings' as an alternative to old-fashioned (and more resource-intensive) crime prevention. But as Yunnan's head of public security pointed out, the continual drain on police funding over the previous two decades meant that police investigation work, in both campaign and non-campaign periods, was rapidly outpaced by the dramatic increase in crime.

> In 1975, the year that specialized criminal detective units and crime scene investigation units were established in Yunnan, each detective managed an average of 7.5 criminal cases per annum and solved an average of 5.3 of those cases. In 2001, each detective had an average of 24.5 criminal cases per annum and solved an average of 11.7 of these cases. This is a fall in the clear-up rate because our staff numbers and the technology we use have failed to keep up with the crime rate . . . With the amount of 'surface-policing' [read campaign work] increasing, we have been unable to get a fundamental hold on crime. There has been wave after wave of Strike Hard campaigns and specialized drives over the last twenty years, and as soon as you finish a campaign, the crime rate increases dramatically, so the time between each Strike Hard or specialized campaign has shortened. The sheer amount of local police work that needs to be done is overwhelming. We only have a limited number of bricks to build up the defence wall. If someone wants us to build up the bricks on this part of the wall, we have to dismantle other parts of the wall to do so.[68]

Suggestions for alternatives to conventional campaigns abound in internal reports, the majority of which emphasize strengthening crime prevention strategies. The most popular recommendation in the literature around 2002 and 2003 was to bring back *yanfang* (stringently preventing) as a counterweight to Strike Hard. 'Stringently preventing' is not a new concept, but it is an approach that the majority of senior police have preferred to Strike Hard for decades. Senior police bureaucrats attempted to upgrade the status of crime prevention to place it on an equal par with campaigns as early as 2002 at a National Conference on Comprehensive Management of Public Order. At this conference, authorities announced that 'while "striking hard" police must also move to prevent crime, and make crime prevention the priority'. 'Stringently preventing' was seen as a key method of re-establishing public order

- by concentrating police power at the grassroots level, ensuring that police street patrols made up at least 70 per cent of police workloads at police substation level;
- further developing the system of private security and neighbourhood watch committees;
- making police officers more visible and accessible, and establishing small substations in areas that have a large concentration of people, such as large shopping centres;
- improving police response times in 110 emergency calls;
- developing and coordinating networks of street patrols that involved specialist police patrol officers and private security personnel;
- improving management systems to be able to react more speedily to crime in hotspots;
- managing, through closer surveillance, potential offenders who have committed illegal but not criminal acts.[69]

These strategies appear to constitute a much more rational and enlightened form of crime control.

The minister's voice: challenging Strike Hard from the MPS

Any challenge to campaign justice directed from the level of Minister of Public Security was always necessarily going to be presented in a highly nuanced and non-confrontational tone. The 20th National Public Security Conference in Beijing in November 2003 took on particular significance because of a number of points made by Minister Zhou Yongkang in his annual report to senior police, which indicated to those present that change was in the air.[70] Zhou announced that the specific tasks for police in 2004, in order of priority, would be to protect national security; to protect public order and social order; to protect the rights of citizens, the safety of their person and the freedom of the individual, and their legitimate property; to protect public property; and to prevent, stop and punish crime.[71] Senior police bureaucrats listening to Zhou's report picked up on a number of points in his speech that signalled a change in emphasis.[72] For the first time in over 20 years in an MPS Minister's speech at a national public security conference, the term 'strike hard' was not mentioned once. Second, the task of 'protecting *public* property' was consistently listed as a higher priority than protecting individual citizens' rights in every Minister's annual report on public security in the past. But in Zhou's speech, collective property came second to his listing of individual citizens' security and property in terms of police priorities. Zhou's final sentence was even more telling. Since the 1980s, Ministers had always called on police to both 'attack and prevent crime'. But in Zhou's 2003 speech, he amended the usual 'prevent and attack' catchphrase to 'prevent, stop and punish' crime, removing the campaign-tinged word 'attack'. This immediately drew the attention of senior police ranks in the audience.[73] The report also announced a new task known as the 'three basics':

1 'grassroots construction', which involved improving the quality of sub-stations and focusing more of the police budget at the grassroots level rather than in central offices;
2 'basic construction', which involved improving professionalization and specialization of tasks; and
3 'basic skills development', which involved improving police skills such as firearms training.[74]

Senior police inferred from Zhou's speech that a new line was being drawn in the sand, and that 'stringent prevention' was gaining the upper hand over Strike Hard policy at the highest levels.

After the November 2003 Conference, Zhou's Ministry commissioned 18 key national research projects to be conducted at the Public Security University, on topics such as dealing with mass protests in a peaceful manner, interagency cooperation, the development of early warning and rapid response systems, community policing, economic crime prevention, and reform of the police administration system. None of the 18 projects was remotely connected to 'striking hard'. By mid-2004, the Ministry of Public Security had added 33 smaller projects to the list – again, none was related to 'striking hard'. Moreover, the findings of some of these projects were at odds with the basic tenets of campaign justice.

One of these reports, by Professors Zhang Guoxing and Li Jingping, took aim at the traditional campaign practice of public rallies, recommending that police should halt any 'public activities' that were not directly related to police business. The report also contained oblique criticisms of politico-legal committee leadership over police work, in particular the politico-legal committee's routine requirement that police undertake propaganda tasks – namely, organizing arrest and sentencing rallies – that had nothing to do with real law enforcement. The authors believed that these non-policing activities damaged the public image of the police and the quality of police work, as they explain below.[75]

> The administrative power of the police is indeed under the general leadership of the party . . . but police cannot possibly be expected to complete the huge task of socialist modernization if they are doing non-police work and encroaching on the tasks of other criminal justice agencies, resulting in interagency conflict . . . It creates a situation in which 'the violinist is expected to play the drums and the flutist is made to play the cymbals'. It might look lively and it might create attention but it is noise not music . . . There are some [in the party] who analytically separate the two into 'good' police work and 'bad'

> police work [read 'rallies']. While they may acknowledge that 'bad' police work has nothing to do with law enforcement, they believe that it nevertheless procures good social outcomes. We believe that this is completely wrong. Calling 'non-policing activities' good or bad is akin to calling a personality cult a 'good cult' or a 'bad cult'. A cult is a cult and there is no 'good' or 'bad' about it.[76]

Zhang and Li considered that the best way to strengthen and improve party leadership over public security work in the new era of policing would be to allow police to divest themselves of the extra-policing aspects of their work.[77] It is likely that these sentiments are shared by many of the practitioners whose views have been aired in this chapter. It must be emphasized, however, that these momentous moves by senior police to distance themselves from draconian campaign practices did not occur in a political vacuum. It is no coincidence that the Ministry of Public Security's move away from the theatrics of campaigns coincided with the rise of a new and soon-to-be-ubiquitous political slogan – harmonious society – which was set to take China by storm in coming years, changing the face of campaign justice.

Regularizing Strike Hard

In China, a change in party semantics signals a change in policy direction, or at least a dilution of existing policy orientations. As John Delury argues,

> [T]he CCP pays more attention to the linguistic nuance than the average political organization . . . Every speech by a party leader and every proclamation by a party organ seems like a recording rather than a performance . . . And because of the care with which the CCP scripts itself, changes in terminology signify shifts in power or policy with greater predictability than is the case in more anarchic environments.[78]

It is in this context that the announcement in 2003 of a new term, 'regularizing Strike Hard', is significant. Because of the political nature of Chinese criminal justice, and the confidential debates behind criminal justice policy-making, it is difficult to determine accurately what the discussions and criticisms at the highest party levels in the aftermath of the 2003 campaign entailed. We do know, however, that after the Strike Hard campaign had come to a close in April 2003, the Central Party Committee Politico-legal Committee organized a politico-legal conference for provincial criminal justice officials and politico-legal committees to discuss the future of Strike Hard. At this conference, the Committee advised that Strike Hard's main tool – punishing criminals severely and swiftly in accordance with the law – was to remain a key policy against serious crime, but a new system of normalizing Strike Hard into everyday criminal justice work was to be devised. Conference participants were urged to consider specific ways to 'regularize Strike Hard' (*jingchanghua Yanda*) into everyday police work.[79] To confirm this new direction, two months after the 2003 campaign had ended, Luo Gan again announced that 'striking hard' would continue to be China's key response to serious crime. While the party would not abandon Strike Hard policy, Luo Gan gave the clearest indication yet that large-scale campaigns would be toned down.[80] In official terms, this meant that the policy of 'severe and swift punishment' would be localized – in other words, grassroots authorities would be given more freedom to choose their own targets and to launch their own offensives, without the need to wait for a large-scale campaign to be launched from Beijing. Luo Gan urged criminal justice authorities to continue to use Strike Hard policy, announcing to a CMPO Committee meeting that, even though social security had improved markedly, various types of criminal offences were re-emerging, pointing to the continued need for 'striking hard'.[81]

The idea of 'regularizing' or 'routinizing' Strike Hard is a slippery concept at best. According to the Central Party Committee's Politico-legal Committee, 'regularizing' Strike Hard involved embedding the policy into routine criminal justice work in an orderly and regulated fashion

> to make the policy of punishing criminals 'severely and swiftly' a pro-active approach to crime fighting, allowing for agencies to gain a clear focus on relevant targets and gain real results . . . The 'regularizing' of Strike Hard means that criminal justice agencies can 'attack crime trends proactively as soon as they rear their heads' thus maintaining pressure on criminals at all times.[82]

With this regularization, authorities believed that criminal justice organs would be able to attack the specific crime targets that were emerging in their area more effectively and in a timely way. One of the stated advantages of regularizing Strike Hard was that it would allow police to target particular crime categories and avoid casting the Strike Hard net too widely, which could be the case during national campaigns.[83]

The Politico-legal Committee stressed that criminal procedure would continue to rely on the policy of punishing serious crime 'severely and swiftly'. The difference was that criminal justice agencies were now required to be more precise in determining criminal targets based on the principle of 'combining punishment with leniency'.[84] In other words, criminal justice workers were urged to make clearer distinctions between those criminals who were to be treated with severe punishment and those who should be treated more leniently, due to either the nature of their crime or mitigating circumstances. According to one member of the Central Politico-legal Committee, criminal justice officials were urged to apply lenient treatment to first offenders, minor criminals and young offenders.[85]

In short, regularizing Strike Hard officially meant reconfiguring the policy of punishing criminals 'severely and swiftly' into a more pro-active approach to everyday crime fighting, but in a more precise and discriminating fashion. As one party insider put it, normalizing Strike Hard and by making it an on-going policy would give the criminal law a stronger sense of continuity and stability, as it would allow agencies to punish 'severely and swiftly' on a continual basis.[86] With emerging crime trends, the new requirements were to 'attack early' and 'attack trends when they were in their infancy'.[87] Again, while insisting that the party would not abandon Strike Hard policy, Luo Gan gave a clear indication that the generic campaigns would be scaled down. On 4 December 2003, he declared that Strike Hard (*yanda*) would be combined with 'stringently preventing' (*yanfang*), 'stringently controlling' (*yankong*) and 'stringently managing' (*yanguan*) as China's key state responses to crime.[88] And from December 2003, criminal justice agencies would be expected to integrate the policies and practices of the campaign into their normal routine by embedding the policy of punishing criminals 'severely and swiftly' into a more pro-active approach to everyday crime fighting, enabling local agencies to attack their own particular crime trends.

While detailed recommendations about exactly how police were to regularize Strike Hard were not forthcoming, it became clear in late 2003 that there was a push in internal police circles to limit campaign excesses. The campaign from 2001 to 2003 did not bring a fundamental turnaround in the state of public order. The Central Politico-legal Committee's move to regularize Strike Hard (whatever that meant in practice) coincided with moves in the Ministry of Public Security in late 2003 to downplay campaign justice as the key police instrument for controlling serious crime, and instead giving prominence to crime prevention.[89]

A new push for a 'rule of law'?

One aim of this book is to trace the particular journey of thinking about policing and punishing serious crime that began with the almost universal support for 'striking hard' in official circles in the 1980s and culminated in 2007 in a new push towards a more 'harmonious' and balanced approach to controlling serious crime that utilizes both the 'prevent' and 'attack' arms of the law. Since the early 1980s the 'attack' wing has been consistently favoured in dealing with serious crime. But, as this chapter has revealed, in the post-2003 environment Strike Hard's dominance was subject to challenge within criminal justice circles. After the 2001–03 campaign, 'striking hard' became increasingly contested in police, court and academic circles, in parallel with the promotion in these circles of a less theatrical, more nuanced approach to dealing with serious crime. We have observed a subtle realignment of official thinking about campaign justice, while police and courts have toned down the 'shock and awe' approach to crime control in official public security and court reports. A similar tone has also surfaced in party-run news outlets such as *Xinhua*. The traditional mass-line tactics of 'waging war using a human sea' – pouring thousands of police and parapolice onto the streets to perform 'concentrated united operations' and 'ferret out the enemy' through search and stop operations – is now increasingly recognized as having little deterrence value. Policing authorities have increasingly called for greater use of preventative measures as an alternative to the 'attack' mode of crime control.

One reason for softening the mass-line rhetoric and hard-line strategies such as public sentencing rallies is a recognition that these approaches do not work effectively on the types of crime that are currently most damaging to the social fabric: drug and organized crime. Drug and organized crime are more complex than earlier types of crime, and involve much more complicated social networks than individual crimes such as robbery, assault, rape and arson. This makes them harder to 'crack'. They cannot be dealt with effectively just by 'attacking' through theatrical 'joint operations', rallies and the like. Thus, since the end of 2003, while the system of launching campaigns has been retained, there has been less of the histrionics and more emphasis on a professional approach. This has required effective interagency cooperation not just between police, prosecution and courts, but also between police and other government agencies. In the context of the prevent–attack dialectic, 'crime prevention' has been increasingly touted as a viable alternative to campaigning in senior police circles. This movement away from 'attack' towards 'prevent', and towards a more professional and less theatrical approach, has important implications for the treatment of serious cases.

It is important to stress here that even though the taste for campaigns appeared to be waning, it did not represent a teleological retreat from the way of 'politics' towards a 'rule of law'. I have argued in an earlier volume that socio-legal scholars outside China Studies have recognized the limitations of bifurcating legal phenomena neatly between law and politics.[90] Alan Hunt, for instance, argued more than 30 years ago that major sociological works that range across the conceptions of Marx, Weber and Unger have all attempted to explain law to some extent in terms of an assumed dualism inherent in the nature of law, recognizing it as both a consensual mechanism of shared societal values and a coercive arm of state power. Unger articulates this dualism as a dichotomy between 'interactive' and 'bureaucratic' law; for Weber, it is a distinction between formal and substantive justice.[91]

As I argued in this earlier study, employing a teleological treatment of law to interpret its concrete operation carries the risk of explaining away criminal justice practices within the continuum of consensual/coercive modes of law.[92] Conceiving of law in this way ventures into philosophical badlands since, as Alan Hunt observes, it casts law as a 'single paradigm lying between the polarities of ethics and power, and its progress is marked by an increase in its ethical base and a decline in its reliance on power'.[93] This tends to result in 'an unstable analysis that lurches between the polarities set up', producing 'an "either–or" effect in emphasizing "either" the element of consent "or" the element of coercion'.[94] Such analyses consequently fail to articulate a clearly defined concept of law 'which is not reducible to a choice between opposites or to a fluctuation between them'.[95]

I am wary of arguments that claim the *inevitability* of advancement towards a rule of law in China. With specialized campaigns still in operation, the crime/punishment nexus is far too complex and still too fragile to declare a victory of law over politics. Crime control in China today is still intrinsically a political business. However, as I have argued earlier in this volume, the political does not simply 'percolate' into what would otherwise be the politically neutral operation of policing. Criminal law is political in any modern legal system, at least in relation to serious crime, since the practices of fighting crime, prosecuting, adjudicating, and sentencing are used to regulate social relations and human conduct. These practices are by their very nature political to some extent or another, because they are always forms of social control by the state. Serious crime connects directly with the dangers of social instability in this transitional period of market reform and rapid economic and social transformation in China. It is in this context that the tendency to politicize serious crime has worked within the ideological prism of communist 'political struggle' for the last two decades or more. However, as this chapter has shown, there is not only 'politics' at work in this sphere of law enforcement – there is also 'politicking'. Moving Strike Hard from centre stage required its detractors, in part, to argue their case in internal circles through practitioner journals. What makes this debate interesting, and indeed possible, is that it took place at a time when party authorities in China were allowing space for contention in internal policing circles if not in the wider media.

Concluding remarks

This chapter has focused on the growing criticism of the failure of successive campaigns to stem the tide of serious crime. A short-term decline in crime rates and various other campaign successes began to be touted in the media within weeks of the start of Strike Hard 2001 as evidence of the efficacy of 'severe punishment'. But by 2003, short-term declines in crime rates had been rapidly replaced by continued rises in crime. The number of registered crime cases in 2003 was 4.3 million; in 2004 the figure was 4.7 million. The relentlessness of campaigns, which featured so prominently in 1980s and 1990s discourse and practice began to be openly questioned by police, judicial practitioners and legal observers during the 2001–03 campaign, and the first foray of campaigns into the twenty-first century with this two-year generic campaign was cut short by the emergence of a new emphasis from around 2002 on professionalism in crime control and crime prevention measures, which stressed a more nuanced approach to regulating social relations through law in Chinese society. The party's increasing tolerance of criticism from within policing and judicial circles coincided with the growing prominence of the new political catchcry of a 'harmonious society' from outside the criminal justice arena.

The announcement of Strike Hard's 'regularization' was preceded by a series of debates in policing circles in 2002 and 2003 that suggested that campaign justice itself may be part of the problem. Although campaigns remained an accepted feature of the crime and punishment landscape (at least in terms of party rhetoric), it became increasingly controversial. Specialized struggles in this post-2003 climate began to be put into effect without the theatrics that had characterized campaign justice in the twentieth century and the generic campaign from 2001 to 2003. The 'shock and awe' aspects of campaigns such as mass sentencing rallies were largely discarded, and in their place came increasing calls for a more professional approach to crime control from within police circles. This turn of events is not without political context. The subtle downplaying of campaign justice and moves to emphasize 'prevention' over 'attack' followed close on the heels of China's renewed promises to improve its human rights record in the wake of its entry to the WTO. The political atmosphere of relative liberalization in 2003 was also due in part to the growing resonance of the 'harmonious society' rhetoric that began to gather momentum in 2003 and started to sweep China in 2004 and 2005.

As we have found in this chapter, criminal justice practitioners across China have been increasingly willing to express their disillusionment with campaigns publicly. Lu Zhuo, the provincial head of public security in Sichuan Province was critical of the failure of Yanda 2001 to effect a long-term turnaround in crime trends. He asked: 'if Strike Hard was such an effective way to control crime, how do you account for the rapid increase in crime rates after every generic campaign in the past?'[96] Or, as another commentator put it in the party's own mouthpiece, the *People's Daily*:

> Strike Hard is a vicious cycle, it's a treadmill that we can't get off . . . The more we attack the busier we get, the harder it is to keep up with the attacks, and the harder it is to prevent further crimes occurring.[97]

'Harmonious society' rhetoric was set to take China by storm in 2004 and 2005, but the moves against the theatrics of 'severe and swift' punishment were already taking shape in some areas even before the call to harmonize society went out. While police in some provinces continued to show pride in their campaign excesses in 2003, police in major cities such as Beijing had begun to detach themselves from 'shock and awe' tactics. Beijing police, for example, decided to articulate their 'success' in the 2001–03 campaign by distancing themselves from the hype and theatrics of expressive punishment. At the conclusion of the campaign in 2003, the public security forces in Beijing issued a news report entitled 'Beijing Bows Out Gracefully and Closes the Curtain on Strike Hard in a Civilized Manner, Overturning 35 Death Sentences'. According to this report, no criminals were paraded with placards tied to their front and back in Beijing during the 2001–03 campaign; nor were there any simultaneous sentencing rallies, public executions, or parades of criminals in open trucks. The suggestion here is that these activities were common elsewhere, in the not-so-sophisticated provinces. The report added that 'We have placed particular importance on the stipulation in the Criminal Law that only the most heinous criminals be given the death penalty'.[98]

We have seen in this chapter that the campaign justice gloss applied to success stories in the general media was not reflected in the majority of specialist appraisals of campaign policy in general and the 2001–03 drive in particular. The tactics and rationale of campaign justice had worn decidedly thin. These criticisms, in no small part a result of the inability of campaigns to curb serious crime, together with the rise of 'harmonious society' rhetoric, have forced authorities to rethink the value of 'shock and awe' tactics and heavy penaltyism. The following chapter surveys how the post-2003 'severe and swift punishment' terrain looks without the theatrics of traditional campaign tactics.

5 The people's war on drugs

One feature all post-Mao leaders in the PRC have had in common has been a penchant for espousing Mao-like catchphrases to define their political style and general leadership goals. For Deng Xiaoping it was the 'Four Modernizations'; for Jiang Zemin it was the 'Three Represents'. Hu Jintao's mantra of a 'harmonious society' came to rhetorical prominence alongside his secondary signature phrase, 'scientific development', after the Fourth Plenum of the 16th National Party Congress (NPC) in 2002. In subsequent years, 'constructing a socialist harmonious society' was explicitly proposed as one goal of 'governance capability' for the party-state, and as the foremost socio-economic goal for China in the new century.[1] A 'harmonious society', according to official interpretations, requires authorities to 'coordinate and regulate the interest relationships between different sectors, and adequately manage contradictions in society'.[2] This is said to be achieved through 'scientific development', a by-word for a particular governance technique that purports to 'take care' of the needs of the majority of Chinese, including members of 'the disadvantaged classes'.[3] This emerging emphasis on a more measured approach to regulating social relations also began to be reflected in a change in the rhetoric and policy direction of policing serious crime.

The Central Politico-legal Affairs Committee in late 2003 announced that part of the process of reshaping Strike Hard into a more effective mechanism for controlling crime would be to regularize Strike Hard into everyday police work.[4] And, as we saw in the previous chapter, 'regularizing Strike Hard' is at best a slippery concept that, in general terms, purported to reconfigure the on-again off-again policy of punishing criminals 'severely and swiftly' into a more proactive approach to crime fighting. Yet, rather than to regularize Strike Hard (whatever that might actually mean), counter-narcotics authorities decided to run a discrete anti-crime campaign in 2005 that reintroduced the rhetoric of 'mass-line' policing, albeit in a manner devoid of the masses. We find here the insertion of the contemporary language of crime management and the occlusion of shock and awe rhetoric.

This return to 'all-round policing' and 'the mass-line' in campaign rhetoric is significant. It is no coincidence that the 2005–07 campaign was named 'the People's War on Drugs'. Making the campaign a 'People's War' was a way of subtly shifting the political and organizational emphasis away from party control, towards interagency and intra-agency cooperation, professionalism and community policing. Unlike the 2001–03 campaign, though, this People's War did not actually involve 'the people'. Public sentencing rallies were a rare occurrence, and certainly not a feature of this campaign.[5] This 'People's War' was fought through what Chinese authorities describe as 'Comprehensive Management of Public Order' (CMPO) model – that is, interagency cooperation and all-round policing that emphasizes both prevention and punishment. Such an approach fits neatly into the rhetoric of 'socialist harmonious society' that was being touted in the main political arena as a more gentle approach to regulating social relations. The 'People's War on Drugs', which began in mid-2005, showcased a renewed emphasis on an all-round approach that highlighted both the 'attack' and 'prevent' arms of crime control, and eschewed the 'shock and awe' tactics of earlier campaigns. The idea of combining the 'prevent' and 'attack' arms of crime control is certainly not new in the PRC; neither is it new when applied to counter-narcotics activities. In the past, though, such combined strategies were mainly limited to minor offences such as prostitution, gambling and pornography, and minor drug offences.

We begin this chapter with a general survey of the drug situation in China, and then move on to consider counter-narcotics efforts in the two-year People's War from 2005 to 2007, examining how one area of policy – counter narcotics – functions within the operational and rhetorical rubric of two basic crime control policies: the CMPO and the Strike Hard approach. CMPO, when applied to policing serious crime, is a system that seeks to prevent and attack crime through interagency cooperation. Mo Desheng and Jin Changling explain CMPO as 'a way of rectifying public order through both attack and prevent modes of crime control by using political, economic, administrative, legal, cultural and educational measures under the overall leadership of the Communist Party'.[6] The People's War on Drugs marries a Strike Hard approach to crime control with CMPO rhetoric, emphasizing interagency cooperation and crime prevention for minor offenders and striking hard at serious offenders by means of severe punishment. Two main issues emerge from the discussion in this chapter. The first is that drug activity has proliferated in China in recent years and now constitutes a major crime problem. The second is that the enormity of this illegal drug problem in the post-2003 period has encouraged a more professional, more 'all-round' and less theatrical response to controlling this area of serious crime.

The drug trafficking problem

China's drug barons have enjoyed spectacular success in controlling the heroin trade in the region since the 1990s. One drug lord apprehended by Chinese police in 2007, for instance, was tried for trafficking nearly half a tonne of heroin.[7] More spectacular still, in 2004 Chinese authorities in Yunnan Province captured and tried a leading international drug lord, Tan Xiaolin – a Chinese national residing in Burma – who was responsible for bringing over 100 tonnes of heroin into China over a period of years. Tan Xiaolin worked his way up the ranks of a drug syndicate in seven years from a humble beginning as an itinerant worker in China. He began his criminal career in 1993 when he travelled to Burma from Sichuan to work as a shoe repairer, becoming the youngest drug lord in the Golden Triangle by 1995. Establishing his own private army, he became China's biggest drug baron, with a syndicate that controlled 40 per cent of the heroin coming from the Golden Triangle.[8] PRC police apprehended Tan with the help of the central Burmese government and the provincial authorities in Burma's No. 2 special economic zone.[9] Tan's base was in Mujie, just across the border in Burma, where the local Burmese referred to him as the 'short Sichuanese'.[10] His success derived from his development of two new drug routes into China – at first using small-scale drug mules who crossed the border on foot, and later using horses to carry the drugs across the mountains. His route avoided Reili City (a drugs stronghold in Yunnan Province) and his mules used only small village pathways to reach Linsang City in central Yunnan. The drugs merely had to pass through Linsang – essentially a trouble-free route – to reach the central drug market in Yunnan's capital, Kunming City. When police increased the pressure on drug shipments into Kunming, Tan's mules would cross the Burmese border and enter Baoshan district across the Nujiang River via makeshift footbridges high in the forest areas of Yunnan, and proceed on foot to Lijiang, avoiding the anticipated route into Dali City. The now-famous ethnic minority area of Lijiang was in the process of becoming a major international tourist site during the 1990s, and yet the airport's customs checkpoints had no X-ray machines. Direct flights to Hong Kong made Lijiang the perfect route for transporting drugs out of China.[11] On 10 May 2004, the Kunming Intermediate Court sentenced Tan Xiaolin and three others to death for smuggling, trafficking and transporting heroin and illegally selling synthetic drugs. Tan appealed to the Yunnan Higher Court, but his appeal was rejected. The Court found that Tan had organized the trafficking of two tonnes of heroin and three tonnes of ephedrine into China. (This amount was sufficient to secure a death sentence even though police knew he was responsible for trafficking more than a hundred tonnes.) Tan was publicly sentenced to death on 25 June 2004 at a large World Anti-Drugs Day rally and executed the same day.[12]

Tan's considerable success in hauling massive amounts of heroin across the border and avoiding detection provides one example of the seriousness of the drug problem in China today. Over a 23-year period from 1982 to the end of 2005, police in China cracked 166,500 serious drug cases involving 220,000 people and seized the following quantities of drugs: 710,000 kilograms of heroin; 576,900 kilograms of opium; 7,500 kilograms of methamphetamine (ice); 1,840 kilograms of morphine; and 2,840 tonnes of precursors.[13] In the year 2005 alone, police uncovered 6.9 tonnes of heroin, 5.19 tonnes of which was found in Yunnan Province.[14] The following year, police cracked 46,300 serious drug cases involving 56,200 suspects, 47,290 of whom were later formally charged. In all, 5.79 tonnes of heroin, 1.69 tonnes of opium, and 5.95 tonnes of methamphetamine were seized in 2006.[15] In the month of March 2006 alone, police apprehended 1,698 people suspected of serious drug crimes (including trafficking, transportation and manufacture), and seized 462.5 kilograms of heroin, 225.4 kilograms of ice, and 158.2 kilograms of opium. The following month police apprehended 2,515 people (in connection with 2,172 serious cases) and seized 1,429.5 kilograms of narcotics.[16] In 2007, authorities seized 4.6 tonnes of heroin, 1.2 tonnes of opium, 5.8 tonnes of liquid methamphetamine, 7.6 million methamphetamine pills (86.4 per cent more than the previous year), 2.2 million ecstasy pills (3.9 times more than the previous year) and 6.9 tonnes of ketamine (2.4 times more than in 2006).[17]

For close to two decades, Chinese drug trafficking groups have been extremely active in importing and supplying heroin to the international market both through ports and overland. As a result of Thailand's success in controlling the flow of heroin in the 1990s, most of Burma's heroin now travels through China. The domestic drug manufacturing market in China is now booming, thanks to the worldwide increase in demand for amphetamine-type stimulants (ATS). The US State Department's International Narcotics Control Strategic Report (INCSR) for 2007 states that China is one of the world's largest producers of precursor chemicals, and is a major international supplier of the illicit ephedrine and pseudoephedrine used in the production of methamphetamines.[18] The flow of drugs in and out of China is now clearly a major international concern, not only for the Asian region but also for Europe and the USA. The UN Office on Drugs and Crime Report on ATS patterns and trends for 2006 estimates that Asia produces one-half of the world supply of ATS – of this, China produces 50 per cent and Burma 43 per cent.[19] China's involvement in the international drug market is therefore no longer merely as a transit route for Golden Triangle drug trafficking to Europe and the USA. Domestic drug manufacture and consumption is now a major social issue in China, significant enough to warrant – at least according to political authorities – the 'People's War against Drugs' in June 2005. This is just one in a long line of anti-drug campaigns in China since the late 1980s.[20]

The counter-narcotics research unit in the Yunnan provincial Public Security Bureau (PSB) has analysed the dramatic increase in the flow of drugs since the mid-1990s, concluding that it indicates four main trends. First, large quantities of drugs continue to pour in across the Burmese and Lao borders, despite dramatic declines in poppy production in Burma. Second, there is an increased demand for drugs in China, and third, a new trafficking strategy of using non-traditional transport routes into China has emerged. Finally, the strategy in Burma and Laos is now to package heroin in smaller lots and employ more mules with lighter loads, who then cross the border concealing the heroin on their persons.[21] In addition to these general trends, Chen Beidi adds the following observations. First of all, because the traditional border routes have been under constant attack by Chinese police since the mid to late 1990s, new routes have been established to carry drugs out of China. Drug hotspots have recently emerged in Nanning (Guangxi Province), smaller port cities and Liupanshui in Guizhou Province, and Dongxiang in Huanghe County, Gansu Province. All are located in China's poorest regions, where police resources are particularly strained. The Golden Triangle is the source of drugs into Liupanshui, while the source into Dongxian and Guanghe is the Golden Crescent via India and Tibet. These economically underdeveloped regions rely on poor people to act as mules and carry the drugs across national borders. Guizhou and Gansu provinces are major transport routes for drugs entering the European market via roads inland through the Middle East to Amsterdam.

The focus of the People's War on Drugs in 2005 was on south-west China – especially Yunnan Province, China's drugs capital, which has borders with the Golden Triangle countries of Burma and Laos and, to a lesser extent, Guangxi Province, which borders Vietnam, Burma and Laos. A mere 70-kilometre stretch of road leads through Laos to the Thai border from Yunnan. The Yunnan border stretches 4,000 kilometres, and there are just 11 official customs entry points along these borders. At the same time, there are 111 counties that border on Laos, Vietnam or Burma, which can be reached by road and countless numbers of less conspicuous minor roads and pathways. Adding to the difficulties of border patrols are the 17 different ethnic minority groups who share cultures with people across China's borders, and whose movements in rural areas and across borders are essentially impossible to police. It is because of this socio-geographical situation that international drug traders in the 1970s saw China as an ideal access point into international drug markets.[22]

Four main types of narcotic were the focus of the campaign: heroin, opium, crystal methamphetamine (ice) and ecstasy (MDMA). The manufacture of precursor chemicals such as ephedrine, both domestic and imported, is a problem that has increased dramatically since 2003, and the manufacturers of such drugs are therefore also a key target of the campaign. Chen Zhonglin and Huang Kaicheng identify five major drug crime trends in China at present. The first is the overall increasing trajectory of serious drug crimes. The number of serious drug crimes registered in China in 2005 was 4.15 times the 1991 figure. The second trend is the growing frequency of major drug cases that involve more than 10 kilograms of drugs, and the third is the increasing diversity in the types of drugs available. Heroin is the main problem drug in China, but refined ATS are also increasingly flooding into the market in major centres such as Guangzhou and Shanghai. The fourth trend is the regionalization in drug crime distribution. We have already noted that the majority of heroin trafficking now occurs in the province of Yunnan, and to a lesser extent in the neighbouring province of Guangxi, both of which border Golden Triangle countries. However, trafficking activity in Xinjiang in China's west, which borders the Golden Crescent region (of Afghanistan and Pakistan), and in the provinces in China's north-east that border North Korea is also thriving. The final trend is the increasingly two-directional flow of drugs, both in and out of China. The drug-consuming market in China has exploded in recent years.[23] And, increasingly, markets in Europe and the USA are turning to the Chinese drug market for their supply of precursor chemicals such as ephedrine.

Drug trafficking activity into China

The Golden Triangle region remains a challenge for authorities concerned with the importation of drugs into China. In 2005, the region had more than 100,000 acres of poppy plantations, which potentially translates into 3,600 tonnes of opiate manufactured into over 300 tonnes of heroin per year. There were also over a hundred local production facilities in the region in 2005. Even though the Burmese government announced in 2005 that it had dramatically slowed poppy production in the north and proclaimed that the No. 2 special economic zone was no longer one of the biggest plantation areas in the region, Chinese satellite images still detect significant poppy plantations.[24] While UN reports in 2005 stated that Burma's poppy production was down 80 per cent from its peak in 1996, and that Burma accounted for only 21 per cent of total poppy plantation and 7 per cent of heroin production, the reality is that drugs continue to flow into China. There may well be a number of complex reasons for this, but at the very least, as analyst Liang Jinyun points out, it reveals that the quantity of drugs in storage facilities in the Golden Triangle region is still enormous.[25]

Thus, despite the introduction of alternative development cooperation with the Burmese, heroin continues to pour across the border – albeit to a reduced extent. In the three-month period from January to March 2006, Chinese police cracked 3,271 cases involving 3,038 suspects, and seized 2,098.3 kilograms of heroin. This drug haul was a 34.3 per cent increase on the same three-month period the previous year. The number of cases involving more than 10 kilograms of drugs was 42.2 per cent higher in this three-month period than in the same period the previous year.

In 2006, authorities focused on blocking off areas for wholesale sale and transportation, and launched a large-scale search and check of vehicles in the main access points of Reili, Jiankang and Menglian. Police in Kunming and Dali also performed large-scale stop and search operations that targeted vehicles leaving the city. Yunnan remains 'ground zero' in the fight against drug trafficking in China. Since 2001, around 80 per cent of the total amount of heroin seized in China has been seized in Yunnan. In 2001, police seized 10,250 kilograms in the province, and a further 10,680 kilograms were seized in 2004. In 2005, the first year of the People's War on Drugs, the figure was 10,750 kilograms. While the 2005 figure is not dramatically higher than that for previous years, there was a 20.8 per cent increase in the number of cases cracked that involved drug trafficking and manufacture (22,946 cases), and a 16.2 per cent increase in the number of suspects apprehended (25,727).[26]

One aspect of China's marketization that has significant consequences for drug dealing is the increasingly diverse passages for illegal drugs that have been created by the burgeoning legal trade of goods and services into and out of China from regions other than the Golden Triangle. Heroin is increasingly trafficked from the Golden Crescent region of Afghanistan and Pakistan into China. The old Silk Road that leads out of China is another major international route, and is now nicknamed the 'Heroin Road'. Authorities believe that more than half the Golden Crescent drugs travel through the Republics of Turkmenistan, Uzbekistan and Tajikistan into international markets. The remainder goes through Pakistan, Iran, India or China.[27] Although the Golden Triangle is still the largest source of the heroin that enters China, Chinese authorities increasingly recognize the Golden Crescent region that borders China's Muslim-dominated Xinjiang Autonomous Region as a threat. Overland shipments of heroin from the Golden Crescent are also increasing in volume.[28] For example, on 5 October 2006, Kashkar Custom officials in Xinjiang found almost 6,000 small packs of heroin inside a shipment of 10,000 bottles of imported skin-care cream. Twelve days later they found another 590 packs inside a package containing 200 bottles of shampoo. The previous year, the

Hongqilafu police confiscated more than 20 kilograms of pure heroin contained in five cartons of preserved dates imported from Pakistan.[29]

Routes leading out of China

The four traditional drug trafficking routes leading out of China are (1) in Fujian Province, from Xiamen by boat to Taiwan; (2) In Guangdong and Shenzhen across the border into Hong Kong; (3) from Canton and Yantian ports in Guangdong to Hong Kong; and (4) in Liaoning Province in the north, from Dalian port to Hong Kong and on to Europe, Korea and Japan.[30] Chen Beidi notes five traditional routes from city to city across borders via air travel: (1) from Bangkok to Guangzhou to Hong Kong; (2) from Bangkok to Singapore or Kuala Lumpur to Guangzhou to Hong Kong; (3) from Hong Kong to Guangzhou or Shanghai to cities in the USA; (4) from Hong Kong to Beijing to Europe; and (5) from cities in the vicinity of the Golden Triangle to Kunming or Nanning and on Guangzhou or Hong Kong. In addition to these traditional routes, there are more recent routes from Kunming or Nanning direct to capital cities in east and north China.[31]

We noted above that approximately 40 per cent of the heroin that traditionally was trafficked from the Golden Triangle through Bangkok to Europe is now diverted through China. Most of this goes through Kunming or Nanning to Hong Kong. Another major route to Europe leads from the Golden Triangle through Kunming to Urumqi in China's north-east and on to the Republic of Kazakhstan, and a third major route for small shipments to Europe is from the Golden Triangle in rural Burma and Laos through to North Vietnam, and from there to rural parts of Guangxi Province. Fewer drugs now go through Bangkok, partly because of international pressure to stop drugs reaching the city from the Golden Triangle and partly because of the political instability on the Thai–Burma border since 2000.[32] North Korea poses an increasing threat to Chinese drug authorities. Along the 500-kilometre border between China and North Korea, there are around one million minority Koreans who are PRC residents. Their trafficking activities include ice, high-grade heroin and morphine (a legal drug).[33]

The main form of domestically produced drug trafficking out of China in the twenty-first century is raw or unprocessed materials, especially chemicals involved in the making of methamphetamine. These are known locally as 'easy-to-make drugs', because most of their components are legal substances (although their purchase for drug-making is a crime). The domestic production of ATS is becoming an increasing national and international problem. As noted in the Introduction, China is now one of the world's largest producers of precursor chemicals, and a major international supplier of the illicit ephedrine and pseudoephedrine used in the production of methamphetamines.[34]

Comprehensively managing crime

Now that we have canvassed the magnitude of the drug manufacturing and trafficking problem in China, let us turn to the government's recent response – the dual policy of attacking and preventing drug crime through CMPO. Criminal justice authorities in China articulate the work of crime control in terms of two broad elements – the prevent (*fangfan*) and attack (*daji*) modes. CMPO encompasses both elements but emphasizes prevention, through an 'all-round' approach to crime control. As Sarah Biddulph explains:

> The CMPO prescribes a combination of 'moral, material and coercive' measures and the combination of formal and informal techniques of social control . . . The CMPO seeks to replicate historical preferences for identification and control of social deviance at the local level, with formal intervention occurring only when the matter becomes sufficiently serious.[35]

CMPO is thus a system of both preventing and attacking crime – with the emphasis on prevention – through interagency cooperation. There are two main lines of defence for relatively minor crime, while Strike Hard 'attacks' what is deemed to be serious crime, as Biddulph outlines:

> The first line of defence against crime includes strengthening basic-level local community organizations and local police work such as maintaining the household register and registers of the local population and education, especially of juveniles. The second line of defence includes use of coercive administration measures, particularly administrative detention, targeting for reform, investigation and, where necessary, repatriation of juvenile delinquents, prostitutes, transients suspected of committing crime, vagrants and beggars. The CMPO calls for the severe punishment of crime by increasing cooperation between the public security organs, the procuratorate and the courts to strike hard against crime.[36]

CMPO has been a mainstay of criminal justice rhetoric since the early 1980s. It was first promulgated in 1981 as a key ideological and organizational tool for crime control in the new era, and developed as an all-encompassing policy that emphasized education and punishment of criminals through coordination and cooperation between the political, social, legal, economic, cultural and educational bodies involved in managing crime. CMPO involves interagency surveillance and control of populations (such as the floating population), specific crime categories (such as organized crime, prostitution rings) and localities (such as rental apartment blocks, regions on the outskirts of cities).[37] The rationale for CMPO is documented in two main government publications. The first and most detailed text on CMPO was the 'Central Party Committee and State Council Decision on Strengthening Comprehensive Management of Public Order' (19 February 1991),[38] and the second was the Central Party Committee and State Council 'Decision on Further Strengthening Comprehensive Management of Public Order' (5 September 2001).[39] The 1991 Decision affirmed CMPO as the key measure through which public order problems were to be tackled in China, arguing that 'attacking crime' alone would not bring about an end to the crime problem. According to the 1991

Decision, CMPO is employed to secure economic and social development and public order. It is an important aspect of the development of a spiritual civilization, and is an important form of the 'dictatorship of the people' as well as an important means of developing the legal system.[40]

The 1991 Decision also established CMPO committees at all levels of government. CMPO operates under the leadership of party committees at all levels of government, and all relevant government agencies – including community-based organizations, educational and criminal justice institutions – are expected to make CMPO part of their routine work. The 1991 Document also called for specific CMPO offices to be established at all levels of government with a dedicated hierarchy of leadership and staff.[41] Party and policing literature articulate the work of CMPO in terms of six specific aspects of crime control: 'prevent', 'educate', 'manage', 'construct', 'reform' and 'strike' (or attack).[42] These tasks are elaborated below.

Prevention **(fangfan)**

As the first main line of defence, *preventing* crime is described in the criminal justice literature as a combination of policing and community-based activities and control mechanisms that range from household registration and resident and village committees to police surveillance of suspect venues. Responsibility for crime prevention is therefore the task of not only police but also government agencies and social institutions. Prevention covers a broad gamut of activities that are monitored by public security agencies and local government agencies, and CMPO committees from the township level up to the provincial level coordinate such crime prevention activities.

Prevention work also incorporates routine policing tasks – such as inspections of crime-prone places such as clubs and other entertainment venues, hotels, ports, and markets – and regular street patrols of crime areas. For example, in October 2005, three months after the launch of the People's War Against Drugs, more than 10,000 entertainment venues in seven cities – Beijing, Dalian, Qingdao, Guangzhou, Harbin, Wuhan and Urumqi – were asked to join the War by pledging to 'fight against drugs with self-discipline, and not to permit any drug-related activities in their venues. They will also give publicity [to programs about anti-drug activities] . . . so as to help create a sound and healthy environment for common people'.[43] At the same time, staff at entertainment venues who were found guilty of drug crimes would be 'severely punished', while any government officials responsible for making spot checks on entertainment venues who failed in their duty would also be appropriately punished.[44] The Beijing PSB announced in June 2006 that any entertainment venue in which drug activity was discovered would be fined between 10,000 and 20,000 yuan and would be suspended from operation for six months; in serious cases, venues would have their business licences revoked.[45]

Prevention also includes monitoring non-police activities such as establishing safe environments – for example, ensuring that construction sites improve security arrangements such as fitting CCTV cameras and building security walls. City council arrangements for building approvals are now required to include CCTV and security doors as standard in building plans. In Beijing, more than 90 per cent of entertainment venues have now installed security cameras, and patrons of large venues are routinely asked to undergo security checks.[46] All entertainment venues in Beijing are required to employ security guards, and crime prevention as a whole in China now also incorporates the development of the private security industry.[47] In December 2006, there were almost four million authorized private security guards in China, a 100 per cent increase on the previous year.[48] The 2006 figure includes 930,000 security personnel who work for companies owned directly by China's PSBs, and three million personnel who work for companies monitored and managed by PSBs. The four million legitimate security personnel are the tip of a much larger private security iceberg. Millions of unregistered or 'black market private security' personnel currently carry out their duties in uniforms almost identical to those of their authorized counterparts, and in some areas the proportion of black market to legitimate guards is one to one.[49]

Prevention is also considered to be a responsibility of 'the masses'. Work units are encouraged to train workers to prevent crime by securing their possessions in a safe location in order to eliminate the factors that might lead to crime. Part of the task of neighbourhood watch committees and residents' committees is to help and resolve social contradictions and civil disputes before they escalate into violence.[50] Residents' committees are also involved in prevention activities in the fight against drugs. Zhou Yongming describes one local committee in Wuguo Street, Panlong, a suburb of Kunming, in the 1990s:

> The residents' committee has about 500 households under its jurisdiction. During an interview, its director, Mrs. Duan, acknowledged that there are eight heroin addicts on the street and her residents' committee has its own way of handling the drug problem. Once a person is found to be a drug addict, a help group, usually consisting of a local police officer, an official of the committee in charge of public security, and parents of the addict, is established. The help group visits the addict twice a month, to persuade him/her to give up the habit.[51]

Education (jiaoyu)

One of the main aspects of the education task of CMPO is to educate the masses in a general sense through moral and legal education drives and to encourage entertainers and producers of mass culture – including music, television and film – to pay close attention to the potential impact of their creative output on the moral fibre of society.[52] For instance, in May 2007, following the arrest of pop singer Xie Dong on minor drug possession charges, the Counter Narcotics Control Commission called for celebrities to act in a more disciplined manner and to play a positive role in the war against drugs.[53] The other main aspect of the education task is the education of juvenile delinquents, which is again regarded as a society-wide responsibility. Local councils, for instance, can help delinquents who have been released from custody to find gainful employment.[54] The People's War on Drugs included a mass education campaign in schools throughout China. While it is difficult to say how effective these propaganda drives are, Chen Xufu, general secretary of the National Counter Narcotics Foundation, claims that mandatory drug education in primary and middle schools throughout the country 'has made students more capable of identifying and refusing narcotics'.[55] *Xinhua*, China's official news agency, was eager to advertise the success of the education campaign:

> A recent questionnaire-based survey conducted in several major Chinese cities, including Beijing and Shanghai, showed that 99 per cent of the 3,000 students interviewed in primary and middle schools were aware of the dangers of drug addiction, and 87 per cent said that if somebody offered them drugs such as ecstasy they would refuse and report the incident to teachers or police.[56]

The task of education also involves anti-drug propaganda in the media, in the form of the announcement of high-profile drug cases. The most popular time each year for the announcement of court convictions, and public burn-offs of confiscated drugs is 26 June, the International Day Against Drug Abuse and Illicit Trafficking. For example, two offenders, Mu Yousu and Ma Wenhai, were sentenced on the eve of 26 June 2006. Mu was sentenced to death, and Ma sentenced to death with a two-year reprieve. Mu and Ma were convicted of manufacturing illegal drugs in Lanzhou City in the north-eastern province of Gansu. They had been producing ice in conjunction with Burmese and Chinese nationals, having built an ice-making factory with the potential to produce 10,000 pills per hour.[57]

Management, construction and reform (guanli, jianshe, gaizao)

The *management* task of CMPO involves 'managing' the registration of hotels, clubs and karaoke bars and the supervision of the activities of these venues to prevent possible crimes such as drug dealing, prostitution and illegal gambling. The *construction* task, on the other hand, relates to improving local political infrastructure at the village level through the establishment of party sub-committees whose key task is to monitor CMPO work at the grassroots level. The *reform* task entails developing programs to improve the lives of offenders by making employment opportunities available for released prisoners in order to prevent recidivism.[58] One other key aspect of the 'reform' task as it applies to drug abuse is detoxification programs. There are three organizational settings for detoxification in China: compulsory rehabilitation centres, re-education through labour facilities and voluntary detoxification centres. Those sent to re-education through labour facilities are recidivists who have been unsuccessfully treated in rehabilitation in repeated stints in compulsory rehabilitation centres. In 2004 there were 583 compulsory rehabilitation centres around the country.[59] Because of the dramatic increase in the number of users apprehended and registered by police in 2005 (an increase of more than 10,000), local public security regulations in Yunnan increased the period of compulsory incarceration for drug users from one to two years, and 13 additional compulsory drug rehabilitation centres were established around the province, providing 14,300 extra beds.[60] As of 2005, there were 56 compulsory drug rehabilitation centres in the province.[61] More than 269,000 people were sent to rehabilitation centres in China in 2006, and more than 71,000 recidivists were given administrative punishment and sent to re-education through labour facilities.[62]

Striking (daji)

According to the official police literature, counter-narcotics work in China involves all six of the above mechanisms of crime control and management of offenders. In reality, though, the policing and punishment of serious drug crime relies almost exclusively on the 'attack' arm, and to a much lesser extent on the 'prevent' arm. In practice, this translates into harsh punishment for those who are apprehended and prosecuted. So, while CMPO has rhetorical prominence in public criminal justice policy speeches and annual reports from PSBs to provincial people's congresses, in practice it has taken a back seat to Strike Hard's 'severe punishment' in the fight against serious crime. As discussed previously, the *strike* aspect of CMPO refers to the campaign policy of 'attacking severely' and is the exclusive domain of the criminal justice organs. Although Party propaganda paid lip service to the 'strike' mode as part of overall CMPO, until late 2003, it was not generally considered – or propagated – in policing circles as a CMPO strategy, but rather as a distinct campaign strategy.

The People's War as an 'attack' and 'prevent' mechanism

Although the People's War on Drugs advertised six modes of CMPO – strike, prevent, educate, manage, construct and reform – as comprising the 'all-round' strategy against drugs, in fact, the War on Drugs has concentrated on the dual strategies of 'strike' and 'prevent'. In the context of the campaign, these elements translate into the following programs: severely and swiftly punishing serious criminal offenders; interagency cooperation between police and customs, and police and forestry authorities; police border patrols and intra-agency cooperation across provincial borders; administrative supervision of the management of the manufacturing of (legal) precursor chemicals; compulsory treatment of drug users through the system of compulsory rehabilitation centres; detecting drug cultivation through aerial surveys and remote satellite sensing; and educating adolescents about the dangers of drugs.

The People's War on Drugs was run out of the Counter-Narcotics Department in the Ministry of Public Security (MPS). China's principal policing authority, the MPS, operates out of Beijing and comprises 27 specialist bureaus, including the Narcotics Control Department (NCD). The NCD has four deputy bureau chiefs, who are responsible for: (1) narcotics control; (2) drug prevention and rehabilitation; (3) drug crime investigation; and (4) drug education, community cooperation and international liaison. The NCD is answerable to the Minister of Public Security but also reports to the Counter-Narcotics Control Commission (CNCC), which is a broad organization comprising deputy ministers of Public Security, Propaganda and Public Relations, Health, Customs, and other relevant bodies. It is an advisory commission that is run by senior police to provide avenues for close cooperation with allied agencies such as Customs. Each public security department has its own counter-narcotics unit at the provincial level, which comes under the organizational leadership of the national NCD in Beijing. Some key drug provinces such as Yunnan and Guangxi also have a Counter-Narcotics Command Centre or a provincial Commission on Counter-Narcotics Activities, which is a subsidiary of the CNCC. Other provinces set aside specialist teams devoted to counter-narcotics work that are responsible for the operation of compulsory drug rehabilitation centres for drug users at the provincial level. With the exception of drug capitals such as Yunnan and Guangxi, there are no official specialist drug units at the county level, as general criminal investigation units handle the task of investigating drug crimes at this level.[63]

The current focus of counter-narcotics activities in general, and the People's War on Drugs in particular, is the fight against drugs crossing into China for internal consumption. In Yunnan, Chinese authorities now thwart the inward passage of drugs through a number of increasingly effective defence lines that include checkpoints along the national border, highway patrol surveillance, car and train inspections, and checks at local airports. Each checkpoint detects some inbound drugs, and traffickers who manage to pass through Kunming airport, the largest in Yunnan Province, are a minority. The effectiveness of this policing in reducing drug availability results in a huge difference in the price of drugs at rural and regional points close to the border and in cities such as Kunming. In 2005, for example, heroin users in small towns near the border needed an average of only 10 yuan (approximately US$1.30) a day to feed their habit, whereas in Kunming City, the capital of Yunnan, users needed an average of 100 yuan a day.[64]

The war on drugs in 2005

The war on drugs began with the implementation of a new 'three defence lines' policy against drugs being transported across the borders of Laos, Vietnam and Burma into China. The first was the main line located along key points of the national border, the second was at key points on the transport routes into major centres, and the third was at key locations on the borders of Yunnan and the neighbouring provinces. This proved relatively effective, according to (CNCC) statistics. The more than ten thousand drug cases that were uncovered at these checkpoints involved the seizure of 5.19 tonnes of heroin, 124 kilograms of morphine, 2.62 tonnes of ice, and 2.05 tonnes of opium. More than 13,500 suspected criminals were detained in 2005, an 8.7 per cent increase on the previous year. In addition, 50.4 tonnes of precursors were seized, resulting in 34 criminal cases involving 44 suspected traffickers.[65]

The national modus operandi of the campaign in its first year of operation in 2005 was to separate specific tasks into individual agency responsibilities rather than to use a cross-institutional method. The individual agencies involved included customs, railways, water police, airline security, forestry police and the postal services. In 2005, customs uncovered 409 kilograms of heroin, resulting in 150 criminal cases; railways uncovered 285 kilograms of heroin, resulting in 2,360 criminal cases (2,650 individuals indicted for trial); water police uncovered 49 kilograms (42 criminal cases, involving 65 individuals); airline security arrested over a thousand suspects; forestry police uncovered a major case involving 2.97 tonnes of heroin; and the postal services uncovered 30 cases. All other cases were detected by regular police. By the end of the year, more than 58,000 suspects had been questioned, and 46,359 of these had been formally charged and indicted for trial. Of those cases that ended in court convictions, 1,794 cases involved between one and 10 kilograms of heroin, and 343 cases involved more than 10 kilograms.[66]

In recent years, the war against drugs has taken to the air with ongoing surveillance of potential drug plantation areas. This strategy is also showing results. According to the CNCC report for 2005, the first year of the campaign saw a marked reduction in the number of domestic opium crops, which was partly attributed to improvements in satellite sensing and aerial surveys. Another factor was the new policy of making local government officials more responsible for controlling the problem in their area. Traditional opium plantations in Heilongjiang, Gansu, Sichuan and Fujian declined dramatically in number by 2004, and by 2005 were almost non-existent. Areas in Chongqing and Inner Mongolia that were still a problem in 2004 improved markedly in 2005, according to the CNCC annual report, which found no production in Tianjin, Shanghai, Tibet, Hainan, Qinghai and Ningxia that year.[67]

The war on drugs in 2006

There was an increase in the number of cases indicted for trial in 2006, as well as in the quantities of drugs seized – in particular, there was an increase in the number of cases involving large hauls of heroin.[68] There were 1,902 cases involving heroin weighing between one and 10 kilograms, and 409 cases involving heroin hauls exceeding ten kilograms. There was also a focus in 2006 on small-scale street dealing of heroin. Police found 26,000 cases of dealing that involved less than 10 grams of heroin, a result that was said to have weakened networks between dealers and users. Police also concentrated on breaking links between small-scale dealers in Sichuan, Guizhou, Gansu, Xinjiang, Chongqing, and Ningxia and their sources in Yunnan, catching 423 dealers entering Yunnan.[69]

More than 110 million yuan of central funding was poured into counter-narcotics 'three defence line' activities in Yunnan, and in support of the patrols on the borders in Tibet, Xinjiang, Jilin, Guangxi, and inland in Sichuan in 2006.[70] The major thrust of the campaign in its second year was to organize cross-institutional cooperation between the relevant government bodies on a region by region basis, rather than to separate individual tasks into individual agency responsibilities as had been the case in 2005. Regular police, Customs, railways, water police, airline security, forestry police and postal services all worked together, and the 'three defence lines' strategy was expanded further inland. Thus, the new campaign strategy in 2006 was a united operations approach – 'united' in both geographical and institutional terms. The country's counter-narcotics operations were divided into four main regions – north-west, south-west, north-east and south-east – based on inter-agency cooperation within each region. The success of this strategy resulted in a further dramatic decline in the quantity of heroin on the street, which further pushed up the price.

In the south-west region, operations centred mainly on Yunnan. Authorities launched a united operation known as 'Sky-Net 3', which solved 666 major drug cases, accounting for 66.9 per cent of all major drug cases in Yunnan that year.[71] Another operation known as the '2006 Border Hunt' uncovered 460 drug cases, and 1,002 other cases of drug transportation were uncovered on the airlines. In the neighbouring province of Guangxi, 165 cases of drugs crossing the Vietnamese border were uncovered during 2006.[72]

In the north-west region, the War centred mainly on Xinjiang, where the majority of cases involved the drug flow across the Chinese border from the Golden Crescent region of Afghanistan and Pakistan via the airports. Drugs found their way mainly to airports in Shanghai, Guangdong and Beijing. In all, 58 cases, involving 108 individuals and a total of 107 kilograms of heroin, were uncovered.[73] Overland shipments of heroin from the Golden Crescent are also increasing in volume.[74]

In south-east China, the main focus was on Guangdong, where drug trafficking occurred chiefly in Shenzhen, Guangzhou and further north in Zhuhai. One joint China–US operation, in particular, uncovered a drug trafficking ring of nine individuals bringing 142 kilograms of cocaine into China.[75] Another case involved 65 kilograms of heroin originally from North Burma that was transported by boat into Guangdong. From January to December 2006, police across Guangdong Province discovered 22 drug-making workshops and drug-processing facilities, confiscating 42 kilograms of heroin, 396.8 kilograms of ice, 698.6 kilograms of ecstasy pills, 347 kilograms of ketamine, 1,350 kilograms of unprocessed chemicals, and 18 million yuan in drug money.[76] In Shanghai, police uncovered an operation involving 100 kilograms of precursor chemicals intended for export, and police in Jiangsu uncovered a case involving 107 kilograms of cocaine.[77]

In the north-east, Heilongjiang and Inner Mongolia police ran a joint operation with Russian authorities that uncovered 14 criminal cases involving a total of 14.9 kilograms of heroin and other narcotics. Jilin Province began a new pilot operation on the North Korean border known as 'Border 110', which resulted in police cracking 174 cases involving 4.7 kilograms of ice.[78] The North Korean government denies the production and trafficking of drugs into China but it is widely known that this occurs, and it is regarded as a political act of sabotage. It is widely assumed by Chinese counter-narcotics authorities that Korean ships often carry large quantities of drugs into international ports. In the past, Korean ships would stop at Chinese ports, off-load cargo, and proceed to a third destination, to avoid suspicion by other countries. The third port was usually in the Pacific (Japan or Singapore). Chinese authorities became aware of this practice soon after 2000, and began to prevent suspicious Korean ships from docking in China. The current Korean drug shipment strategy is not to port directly in China but to offload drugs mid-ocean onto another vessel. Alternatively, ships offload their cargo in Cuba, where they are re-routed to other countries.[79] The only official relationship China has with North Korea concerning narcotics control is a training scheme run by the Chinese CND. According to one public security official, this is simply a means of keeping the avenues of communication open, but it also gives the PRC the opportunity to show off its Australian-trained drug dogs as a subtle warning to the Koreans.[80]

The war on drugs in 2007

In 2007, authorities across China seized 4.6 tonnes of heroin, 1.2 tonnes of opium, 5.8 tonnes of liquid methamphetamine, 7.6 million methamphetamine pills (86.4 per cent more than the previous year), 2.2 million ecstasy pills (3.9 times the figure for the previous year) and 6.9 tonnes of ketamine (2.4 times the 2006 figure).[81] Police also cracked a large number of cases involving more than 10 kilograms of drugs during 2007. For example, on International Anti-drug Day on 26 June, the Guangzhou Intermediate Court sentenced to death 'policeman turned drug baron' Liu Zhaohua for producing 12.7 tonnes of ice for a profit of more than 31 million yuan.[82] Two drug traffickers, Wang Zuguang and Xu Lianke, were also sentenced to death on 17 August for trafficking and selling 434 kilograms of heroin.[83] In October the same year, Chinese authorities uncovered the largest Golden Crescent case to date, seizing 4,848 kilograms of hashish and 67.5 kilograms of heroin concealed in 313 pieces of fibreboard in a container.[84]

We noted earlier that the manufacture and trafficking of ATS in China is now a serious international concern, and that China is one of the world's largest producers of precursor chemicals as well as a major international supplier of illicit ephedrine and pseudoephedrine used to produce methamphetamine.[85] In 2007 there was a dramatic increase in the amount of ATS seized in the three northeastern provinces of Liaoning, Jilin and Heilongjiang. In Liaoning, 65 kilograms of methamphetamine were seized (an increase of 163 per cent on 2006). In Jilin, police seized 220,000 methamphetamine pills and 63 kilograms of liquid methamphetamine (4.1 times more than the previous year), and in Heilongjiang 1,127 drug cases were solved.[86] In Yunnan, authorities cracked nearly 10,000 drug cases and seized 7.09 tonnes of various drugs during 2007.

International cooperation

A relatively recent addition to the counter-narcotics repertoire has been the development of international cooperation between police agencies in China and Southeast Asia. In 2006, for example, China extradited 37 Chinese drug barons from neighbouring countries.[87] The manufacture and trafficking of drugs by international syndicates is increasingly common. For example, in December 2006, Chinese and Philippine police jointly solved a major international ice trafficking case and detained 15 suspects. The syndicate was led by Shao Chuntian, a drug lord from Fujian Province who had been manufacturing ice in the Philippines since 2001. In mid-November 2006, Chinese police units had learned that Shao had been using containers to ship one tonne lots of ephedrine into China, and that he had set up drug processing plants in the Philippines. In a joint operation with the Chinese police, Philippine police captured three suspects in Manila on 19 December 2006, uncovering an ice-processing plant, and confiscating 350 kilograms of processed and semi-processed ice products, 10,000 cases of precursor drugs such as ephedrine, and 8 sets of drug-making equipment. Fujian provincial police arrested Shao, Wu Chuanxiang and 13 other suspects in Quanzhou City, confiscating 3.2 million yuan in drug money. Guangdong provincial police also confiscated one tonne of ephedrine from a Shenzhen warehouse.[88] In one of the largest cases in recent years, Han Yongwan, a Yunnan native and head of an armed drug trafficking gang, his nephew, and another suspect were arrested for trafficking 850 kilograms of narcotics. Between June and August 2004, Han had obtained 206 kilograms of heroin outside China, hiding it in teakwood containers. These drugs were confiscated by police. In August 2005, Han instructed other syndicate members to transport 383.3 kilograms of heroin, and these syndicate members were arrested by Chinese and Burmese police.[89]

Cooperative policing ventures between Chinese and Burmese people have increased in recent years, and the Chinese government has had some success in encouraging the central Burmese government and governors of special economic zones and autonomous regions in Burma's north to unite with Chinese police in the war on drugs. Burmese authorities now cooperate in fighting international drug rings and smaller Burmese drug traffickers (but not Burmese drug lords, who are likely to have strong ties to regional Burmese authorities).[90] Burmese and Lao police have also combined with Chinese authorities since 2002 to handle international drug cases as well as in united operations. In the two-year period from 2002 to 2004, there were 102 joint operations and jointly handled cases, that resulted in 2,300 kilograms of heroin being seized and 18 heroin production facilities being shut down. In 2006, there were 46 joint operations, including the destruction of poppy plantations and the seizure of 520 kilograms of heroin in Burma.[91]

Concluding remarks

Two main points emerge from this chapter's discussion of drug crime and the state's response to it in China. The first is that the severity of China's drug crime problem poses a serious economic and social threat to the nation. China's rapid economic growth in the post-Mao period has been paralleled by a huge rise in serious drug crime. As we have seen, until recently, even the government's stringent crime control measures could not prevent the exponential growth of drug crime. In the past, the campaign strategy of swiftness and severity in treating crime cases provided the punishment but not the deterrent effect that the authorities sought. In the meantime, socio-economic dislocation provided the reason, and the market provided the opportunity, for an unprecedented rise in drug crime. The socio-economic developments that brought both new individual responsibilities and possibilities and freedoms overtook the capacity of the national crime control authorities to curb the unprecedented growth in serious crime.

The second main point that emerges in this chapter is that the campaign from mid-2005 to 2007 was run as a People's War that took the spotlight off 'Strike Hard' and placed it onto CMPO. The discussion of drug crime and counter-narcotics operations in this chapter has inevitably shifted the focus to a change in the rhetoric of anti-crime campaigns in the post-2003 environment. The return of 'all-round policing' and 'the mass-line' to campaign rhetoric in 2005 is significant, as is the naming of the campaign – 'the People's War on Drugs'. A 'People's War' underscores community involvement and interagency cooperation, reducing the importance of the hard-core 'swift and severe' policing and punishment of earlier campaigns. However, as we have seen, this 'People's War' did not directly involve 'the people'. Rather, it was fought through what Chinese authorities describe as 'comprehensive management of public order'. It is no coincidence that the renewed emphasis on interagency cooperation and all-round policing fits neatly into the rhetoric of 'socialist harmonious society' that was being touted in the political arena as a more nuanced approach to regulating social relations.

The People's War on Drugs displayed a renewed commitment to an all-round approach that highlighted both the 'attack' and 'prevent' arms of crime control, and eschewed the 'shock and awe' tactics of joint police stings and mass rallies. The experience of the public security authorities in simultaneously employing preventative and 'strike' modes contrasts sharply with the 'shock and awe' campaign justice of the past. Nevertheless, despite the increased sophistication of counter-narcotics operations in the 2005–07 campaign, severe punishment, often in the form of the death penalty, remained the weapon of choice for deterring serious drug crime.

China is now one of the world's foremost producers, transit points and consumers of illicit drugs and their precursors, which makes the crackdown on the drug problem a policy priority for criminal justice agencies. But how does this War on Drugs sit with the rise of the 'harmonious society' and 'kill fewer, kill cautiously' rhetoric that started to dominate politico-legal discourse in 2004. Along with the rise in 'harmonious society' discourse, the nation's Supreme People's Court (SPC) began to announce in a number of statements from 2004 that it intended to dramatically reduce the use of the death penalty. Criminal justice authorities in major drug provinces therefore faced a dilemma. Since the party saw the death penalty as its most potent weapon in 'striking hard' against serious drug crime, capital punishment reform risked harming Beijing's capacity to tackle the drug problem. In late 2006 and early 2007, the SPC made a number of bold moves to limit severely the use of the death penalty in the provinces. SPC President Xiao Yang and his lieutenants introduced a new national policy of 'balancing leniency and severity', that demanded that – in the vast majority of capital cases – provincial courts should hand down 'death sentences with a two year reprieve' that would automatically be downgraded to life sentences after this period. But, to complicate the issue even further, Strike Hard policy targeted at drugs and organized crimes remained popular in judicial circles in a number of high-crime provinces such as Yunnan (China's drug capital) and Guangdong (China's itinerant worker capital). This meant that a number of lower courts were happy to go into battle in favour of maintaining Strike Hard when Xiao Yang and the SPC began their 'balancing leniency and severity' onslaught in the media in late 2006 and early 2007, as can be seen from a number of annual reports delivered to provincial people's congresses in late 2006 and early 2007. One such report was from Yunnan Province, which hands down a much higher proportion of severe punishments, including death sentences, than other provinces. The Yunnan provincial court report clearly dismissed Xiao Yang's call to hand down suspended death sentences; it also rejected any significant change in death penalty policy. According to the *Yunnan Daily*, the Court expressed the following view of the new policy of balancing leniency and severity:

> We need to correctly implement and correctly understand the concepts of 'balancing leniency and severity' and 'kill fewer and kill cautiously' . . . Understanding that application of the death penalty for a minority of serious offenders remains a necessity in order to guarantee national security, to protect the interests of the masses, and to guarantee the smooth progress of socialist modernization . . . We need to strengthen our understanding of what is actually happening in society in Yunnan and the importance of acting in the interests of the province . . . Because of the drug situation in Yunnan, the number of death sentences in our province is higher than the national average. Courts at both levels need to be fully cognizant of the fact that reducing the number of death sentences in the province will be a long-term goal, not an immediate process. We need to fully appreciate the lack of acceptance that the public might have of any reduction in the use of the death penalty, and we need to understand the need for the death penalty in protecting social stability . . . We need to follow our established work patterns and not have any sudden increase or reduction in the number of death sentences handed down.[92]

For China to continue rising to even greater economic heights, maintaining social order will necessarily remain a top national priority. Serious crime represents a disruption of the social order and an impediment to market development and economic growth. Thus, it also threatens political stability. Little wonder, then, that China's crime control authorities and national planners at large continue to recognize drug crime as a serious challenge to China's development as a unified, economically strong and powerful nation in the twenty-first century. And little wonder, too, that despite the shift in rhetoric away from traditional campaign catchcries, there is no evidence to suggest that the severe punishment of drug crime was toned down during the People's War, particularly in China's main drug provinces. The above statement by the Yunnan authorities indicates that 'striking hard' – whether or not it is camouflaged as CMPO – remains a priority for high-crime provinces.

6 Fighting the collective

The rise of organized crime

The most common types of serious crime in the PRC in the first decade of the twenty-first century have made the traditional 'shock and awe' style of campaigning increasingly anachronistic. Using campaign justice against simple street crimes and uncomplicated violent crimes may have been considered by some in the party to be effective in the 1980s and 1990s, but in the twenty-first century this line of reasoning has been increasingly difficult to rationalize because those serious crimes that are seen as the biggest threat to social stability are the very crimes that are relatively difficult 'to strike'. While the discussion in Chapter 4 focused on the inadequacies of severe and swift punishment strategies and other social, legal and economic limitations of campaign policy, the discussion in this chapter on the rise of organized crime allows us to see the inadequacy of traditional campaign strategies in fighting certain new categories of crime in particular. We focus here on one major area of crime in contemporary China that is difficult to 'strike hard' using traditional 'united operations' and punishment rituals such as sentencing rallies. Organized and gang crime is difficult to strike hard at because such crimes are hidden, complex and relatively sophisticated. Yet, criminal groups in China form the core of those in the population who commit serious offences. According to scholar Ming Xia, there were around one million criminal groups with a total membership of approximately four million gang members at the turn of the new century. These groups range from small gangs to sophisticated syndicates.[1]

In 2006, a new national specialized struggle was launched against China's latest 'enemies of socialist modernization'; members of organized crime syndicates and gangsters belonging to smaller groups. Policing organized criminal activity involves an attack on two broad categories of groups: loosely organized and largely unsophisticated groups and gangs commonly known as 'dark forces' or 'heinous groups' (*e'shili*) and more mature syndicates known are 'mafia-style syndicates' (*heishehui xingzhi jituan*). The first ten months of this campaign against organized crime recorded speedy results in the media. Police, it was noted, had cracked more than 1,300 heinous gangs and over 100 large mafia-style syndicates, though these figures are widely known to be only the tip of the organized crime iceberg. Many dozens of government officials acting as protective umbrellas for gangs and syndicates were prosecuted. By the end of July 2007, 18 months after the launch of the campaign, 377 syndicate cases involving 4,824 suspects had been sent for trial.

Courts determined 250 of these 377 cases involved mafia-style syndicates while the remaining 127 were prosecuted for lesser crimes under Article 26 of the Criminal Law in 1997 (CL97). In all, 2,749 members of 244 syndicates were convicted for organizing, leading or taking part in mafia-style syndicates and thousands more members were convicted for other serious or violent crimes related to organized gang activities. Just under half of these convicted criminals (49.49 per cent) were either sentenced to imprisonment for a period ranging between five years and a life sentence or were given the death sentence.[2] 'Swiftness' in preparing these cases translated into speedy convictions: within months of arresting suspects, 246 of the syndicate cases were being prosecuted and 177 cases involving multiple defendants were being tried in courts.[3]

Political involvement in the campaign did not go unremarked. At a national teleconference on deepening the fight against gang and syndicate crime in April 2007, the (then) national police chief, Zhou Yongkang, attributed the results of the campaign largely to the efforts of the party's committees in their coordination, supervision and guidance of the work of the courts, prosecutors and police. He also gave credit to a number of key agencies at the forefront of the campaign: the party's Discipline Inspection Commission for uncovering officials who provided protective umbrellas for syndicates; propaganda agencies that helped create public momentum for the campaign; courts and procuratorates that strengthened their resolve to fight organized crime; police agencies that threw full force into the campaigns; and the Ministry of Justice that relocated all recently convicted syndicate members with prison terms longer than ten years to prisons outside their home province and ensured that no-one convicted of criminal syndicate crime would have their sentence reduced while in prison or be eligible for parole at any stage in their sentence.[4] The police chief's statement points not only to the united effort of police, prosecutors and courts as the politico-legal organs of criminal justice but also to how their work is bound firmly to the fiat of party committees. But rather than focusing on the details of the campaign in this chapter, I would like to put the spotlight on the criminal groups themselves, surveying the rise of these organizations, particularly 'mafia-style syndicates' and exploring the implications of such crimes for crime control measures.

Serious crime in China, particularly organized crime has outpaced and has become more sophisticated than traditional campaign-based criminal justice responses. The final part of the chapter questions the wisdom of using traditional campaign tactics to combat a type of crime that has so infiltrated the market in China and is so reliant on corrupt officials that it is extremely difficult to police and prosecute. Strike Hard is now more than ever an inadequate and, indeed inappropriate, means of regulating social relations in an increasingly marketized economy. Almost three decades from the beginning of the reform era, it is far too late to close the door on the structural and economic factors that produce market-induced crime. Such crime is here to stay in China. Campaigns' short-term deterrent value is simply no match for the long-term ambitions of organized criminals and gang members.

We begin by profiling the characteristics and analysing the metamorphosis of organized syndicate and gang crime in China since the 1980s. By understanding these groups and why they have flourished, we can see how unsuitable traditional campaign tactics are for dealing with the new and more complex crimes that have emerged in China's marketized economy.

Overall, two main observations can be made. First of all, organized and gang crime is largely resistant to traditional campaign tactics such as using masses of police and paramilitary personnel in street comb-outs and other 'united operations'. Second, the speed of China's move from state-planned economy to increasingly market economy has outpaced the capacity of the national crime control authorities to curb the exponential growth of serious crime, given the opportunities that marketization has presented for serious crime to flourish. Hence, while the enormous growth in crime rates has been mitigated in recent years, crime cultures in both organized and drug crime have matured and taken on more sophisticated forms. Inevitably, these serious crimes continue to challenge China's socio-political and economic order, and to draw both national policy attention and public concern.

The makeup of gang and syndicate crime

The term used to describe the most worrying type of crime syndicates found in China today – 'mafia-style' organization – is rather cryptic.[5] The following examples of these contemporary 'enemies of socialist modernization' provide some instruction as to their form and scope of activities. In 2001, the local business community of an entire municipality in Yibing City, Sichuan Province, was under the control of two mafia-style criminal gangs. At the funeral of one of the syndicate members, an American godfather-style funeral motorcade stretched for more than 100 metres, with 500 more members walking behind the motorcade to the soundtrack of the Shanghai gangster film 'Shanghai Triad'.[6] The same year in Shenyang City in north-east China, police uncovered a syndicate that provided a powerful illustration of the strength of the political–criminal nexus. It was led by a local People's Congress representative ('big brother'), and its members included a head procurator, a deputy head of the local Bureau of Labour ('godmother'), as well as another local politician and the vice-president of the Shenyang Intermediate People's Court, both female, who were known as the gang's 'concubines'.[7] Further south in Anhui Province, a syndicate led by four brothers used force to obtain contracts to operate copper mines in Anhui between 1996 and 2006.[8] The brothers were sentenced to death (two receiving suspended death sentences) in Hebei Province in November 2006. The syndicate they led stole oil from the Dagong Oilfield Co. in Tianjin, Hebei, Shandong and Anhui Provinces and illegally traded refined oil valued at 4.7 million yuan. It also had its own illegal oil wells, and had used bribes to establish 'protective umbrellas' in government ranks.[9] The brothers' syndicate is just one of the 377 large syndicates involving 4,824 suspects investigated and indicted for trial in the first 18 months of the 2006 national Campaign to 'Strike Hard against Mafia-style Crime'.

In the first 18 months of this national specialized campaign, 244 syndicates were convicted for organizing, leading or taking part in mafia-style actions and thousands more were convicted for other serious or violent crimes related to organized gang activities. This campaign used the policy of 'severely punishing' serious criminal offenders, which strongly encourages judges to impose more severe sentences for crimes targeted by campaigns than for other crimes. Around half of these convicted criminals were given prison sentences that ranged from five years to life or received the death penalty.[10] 'Swiftness' in preparing these cases meant that within months of arrest, 246 of the syndicate cases were in the process of pre-trial investigation and 177 were in the process of being prosecuted in court.[11] By August 2007, 2,749 criminals had been successfully convicted since the start of the campaign in February 2006.[12]

Gang and syndicate crime has been a serious problem in China since the mid-1990s. According to police statistics, in 1979 there were 124,000 small street gangs known to police. By 1993, gang crime comprised 45 per cent of all registered crime in China, and by 1994, there was a total of 151,000 criminal groups, including hundreds of large syndicates, with a total membership of 575,000.[13] As noted in Chapter 3, criminal justice authorities identify three main categories of criminal groups as a major threat to social and economic order in China – 'heinous forces', which are small to medium-sized criminal groups and gangs; mafia-style syndicates; and to a lesser extent, Triads. Smaller and medium-sized 'heinous' gangs are groups that commit mainly street and violent crimes and common extortion activities, which usually have between 10 and 30 members. They are violent but unsophisticated, and usually operate in rural areas and on the industrial outskirts of cities. The second category, mafia-style organizations, constitutes larger groups, also commonly violent but much more sophisticated in structure and operation than the 'heinous forces'. These organizations are involved to a much greater extent in legitimate company enterprises, and use government 'umbrellas' for protection from prosecution, but are less organizationally mature than established Triads outside China. They are classed as mafia-*style* syndicates because their membership is not as tightly controlled as the traditional Triad gangs in Hong Kong and Taiwan.[14] Despite their relative organizational immaturity, in most other ways they closely resemble conventional Triad gangs. Importantly, what sets them apart from smaller organized crime gangs is that they are sufficiently powerful and well connected to enjoy the protection of 'umbrellas' in government and party posts.[15] The main focus of the fight against organized crime in China is the mafia-style syndicate as it is these groups that do the most damage to local economies. According to official sources, Triads have yet to gain a strong foothold in mainland China and are therefore not the focus of counter-organized crime activities, but it is widely acknowledged in the literature that there are a number of Triad groups that operate smuggling rings in Guangdong and Fujian Provinces.[16]

Organized crime groups can be loose, tight or part of a network, according to Kang Shuhua. 'Heinous' groups are loosely organized gangs and groups, and mafia-style syndicates are tightly controlled. Drug-trafficking syndicates, on the other hand, are mostly organized as networks of groups that are often completely independent or semi-independent. Kang Shuhua identifies the following basic characteristics of mafia-style syndicates. First of all, they must have at least three members, who have united to establish a stable and tight organization. Second, they are involved financially in the market economy and have regular contact with legitimate companies and industries. In other words, while their criminal activities are hidden, they have economic ties with legitimate enterprises. For example, they launder money by controlling one or more trades or industries in a geographical region. But unlike established underworld syndicates such as Triads, whose structure and organization relies on ongoing exchanges of goods, economic power and information in order to thrive, mafia-style syndicates are tightly 'closed'. Their third characteristic is that they are mainly motivated by financial gain. Fourth, they have a monopoly over one or more industries in a particular area, and finally, their three basic criminal methods are violence, terror and bribery.[17]

One of China's leading legal scholars, Chen Xingliang, explains that in criminal justice practice the crucial difference between common criminal groups and mafia-style syndicates is that the common criminal group exists to commit individual crimes, while the mafia-style syndicate exists to control a particular part of society or a whole community through criminal activities. By controlling that part of society or community, they are then able to expand their criminal activities. The relationship between the mafia-style syndicate and its community is therefore the most important characteristic of its constitution. Or, to put it another way, 'if we can say that a government is an organization that legitimately controls a society, then a mafia-style syndicate is its opposite: it is an organization that illegitimately controls society'.[18] The difference between a mafia-style organization and a real underworld syndicate such as a Triad, according to Kang Shuhua, is that its scope of activities and its membership are smaller. Most of the mafia-style organizations in China were established by one individual, and most are relatively new, rather than decades old. Most are locally based, unlike the Bamboo gang in Taiwan, which is a nationwide organization. Mafia-style syndicates mainly monopolize smaller industries such as local fruit markets and construction companies, and rely on securing protection from government officials.[19] Syndicate activity is more prevalent in regions bordering Hong Kong, Southeast Asia and countries to China's north and west. Different types of criminal organizations can flourish side by side in the same city. In Huizhou in Guangdong Province, for example, there were three main types of criminal organizations in 2003. These were home-grown syndicates that had taken over particular enterprises or industries, groups with local leadership that employed people from outside the province to do their dirty work, and Hong Kong Triads.[20] Increasingly, Triad organizations have been able either to infiltrate PRC syndicates successfully or establish networks or their own brand of mafia-style syndicate in areas close to Hong Kong. In the district of Longgang in Shenzhen, for example, most mafia-style syndicates have been established by syndicates from across the border. An example of the first type is Zeng Yaoqing's mafia-style organization, which was established in 1999. Zeng was a PRC citizen who went to Hong Kong in the 1990s and joined a Triad syndicate. He returned to the PRC later in the 1990s to establish his own criminal organization. His syndicate expanded to include 70 members and controlled nightclubs and prostitution rings.[21]

Chinese mafia-style syndicates have been involved in six main types of activity since the 1990s: violent acts, including murder and robbery; kidnapping; protection rackets often with 'godfather' figures who control whole streets, roads or villages; criminal acts such as obtaining stolen goods by force; hired hits; and smuggling rackets with links to overseas gangs.[22] They are also actively involved in other areas of serious crime such as money laundering, counterfeiting and drug trafficking. According to a Ministry of Public Security (MPS) circular at the height of the Strike Hard campaign in 2001, organized crime groups routinely engaged in activities such as extortion from local businesses, the operation of underground casinos, murder, robbery, smuggling, forcing women into prostitution, usurping local political power, infiltrating government circles and interfering in judicial matters.[23]

Over the last decade or more, organized crime groups in China have taken new organizational forms, according to scholar Ming Xia, including groups that use legitimate market mechanisms (contracts and payments) rather than illicit transactions; criminal networks comprising discrete groups, which integrate vertically as well as horizontally with traditional hierarchical groups; and groups that operate as legitimate companies and use market mechanisms as their dominant organizational structure.[24] These groups are 'rational entrepreneurs of illicit transactions', whose goal is the pursuit of wealth and power.[25] Like syndicates outside China,

> in assessing which organizational form to choose to achieve their fundamental goals, professional criminals take two factors into consideration: in the short run, tactical efficiency to achieve their goals, and in the long run, strategic security to evade punishment. To maximize both efficiency and security, professional criminals have to first interface with their institutional environment primarily dominated by the state, the economic market, and the family structure.[26]

According to Ming Xia, organized crime groups in China take three different types of organizational format – traditional hierarchies (described above), 'hermit-crab, hybrid organizations', and criminal networks.[27] Most mafia-style syndicates comprise traditional hierarchies that develop from smaller groups in a number of ways. According to Ming Xia, one way is 'spontaneous revival', whereby groups may form based on traditional religious cults or brotherhoods in areas that were once strongholds of traditional secret societies. Groups may also emerge from a process of 'simulated restoration' whereby they develop a reputation and instil fear in their local community by mimicking gangsters in crime movies such as the 'The Godfather' or 'Shanghai Triad', as exemplified by the group described at the beginning of this chapter. Organizations may also form as a result of the return of traditional Triads such as 14K, Waterhouse, Sun Yee On, Wo Shing Wo to Mainland China.[28] 'Hermit-crab hybrid organizations' are those criminal groups that take over the shells of legitimate firms, government offices and enterprises. Criminal networks, on the other hand, are much more flexible, and are able to adapt quickly to changes in market conditions. Ming Xia notes that these networks 'consist of a finite set of actors and a series of linkages, ties, and relationships among criminals and groups'.[29] He classifies them into three types of groupings. The first are multipolar networks, where there are numerous centres or nodes that co-exist. The second are 'cobweb' structures, in which a 'hegemony occupies the centre of a network and other smaller players are allowed to interact among themselves',[30] and the third are 'production and distribution chains' from a producer or supplier to the market. Increasing numbers of organized crime groups that are involved in smuggling and trafficking operate as networks, because such groups are more elusive, loosely structured and thus more capable of evading law enforcement.

The foot-soldier membership of syndicates and gangs has flourished in the past two decades, mainly as a result of the demographics of economic marketization; those who commit syndicate and gang crimes are unsurprisingly and primarily youths (up to 26 years of age). Rural and itinerant workers constitute the gang and syndicate foot soldiers, if not their leadership. The heavy involvement of youths and rural workers in crime in China has been known for decades. At the height of the first peak in youth crime in 1980, between 70 and 80 per cent of all crimes in cities and 60 to 70 per cent of those in rural areas were committed by youths (aged 14 to 25 years old). In the first year of the campaign, the combined average of youth crime (rural and urban) was 60 per cent of total crime, and in 1989 it was 70 per cent. Although the figure fell to 57 per cent in 1990, the types of crime youths were committing were of more concern to the authorities – 60.83 per cent were serious crimes.[31]

The genesis of organized crime in contemporary China

While mafia-style syndicates gained ground in China from the 1990s, their antecedents, the 'hooligan gangs', evolved relatively quickly at the beginning of the post-Mao period. Hooligan gangs were less sophisticated organizationally than today's syndicates and gangs, but were sufficiently disruptive to prompt the new government under Deng Xiaoping to condemn them as a serious threat to both social order and national economic development. Hooligan gang members were the main target of the first Strike Hard campaign – more than 664,000 suspected members of local 'hooligan gangs' were detained for questioning during the campaign, and most were prosecuted for hooliganism and other gang-related crimes such as robbery and theft.[32]

One problem facing the leadership on the eve of the first Strike Hard campaign in 1983 was the fact that the new Criminal law in 1979 (CL79) did not refer to organized crime as such. The National People's Congress (NPC), moved in September 1983 to introduce a legislative basis for punishing hooligan gangs 'swiftly and severely', issuing two legislative 'Decisions' that dealt with gang crime as it related to 'hooligan criminal organizations'. The most lethal was the NPC 'Decision of the Standing Committee of the National People's Congress Regarding the Severe Punishment of Criminals who Seriously Endanger Public Security' (2 September 1983), which branded ringleaders or members of hooligan gangs who committed violent crime with lethal weapons as having committed crimes of hooliganism that would attract the death sentence. Article 160 of the

Criminal Law defined the sentencing options for hooligan crime that were originally set in the CL79 before the decision to 'strike hard' through capital punishment was taken:

> Where an assembled crowd engages in affray, creates disturbances, humiliates women or engages in other hooligan activities that undermine public order, if the circumstances are flagrant, the offenders shall be sentenced to fixed-term imprisonment of not more than seven years, criminal detention or public surveillance.

The Decisions were subsequently criticized by experts for failing to provide adequate detail of the kinds of activities that constituted such crimes.[33] The confusion was not helped by the pivotal CCP Central Committee Document 31 of 1983, which failed to mention hooligan criminal *organizations*, instead referring only to hooligan gangs,[34] as evident in the document's description of gangs:

> These hooligan gang elements are new dregs of society produced under the new historical conditions, elements of the underground society. By killing and impermissible behavior, by raping women, hijacking airplanes and boats, setting fires and explosions and other such cruel means, they cruelly injure and kill the innocent masses. They hate socialism and pose an extremely great threat to public security. We must recognize the nature of hooligan gangs . . . Hooligan gang elements must be taken in one fell swoop; hooligan leaders must be resolutely killed off.[35]

Hooligan gangs were not sophisticated organized crime syndicates, but rather were offenders who had come together to commit public order offences. Notwithstanding their lack of tight organization, the social harm they were believed to have caused was considered serious in both nature and scope. In other words, the object of hooligan attacks was not identified as individuals as such (and such attacks were not seen as an infringement of the rights of the person) but the public order itself.[36] Victims were not targeted specifically, and these crimes were not premeditated, so what was infringed upon was construed as the sense of 'order' itself. The definition of 'order' here, therefore, extended beyond the conventional meaning of 'public order'; it referred to both practical and moral order in the public sphere.[37] Assault committed as a crime of hooliganism was not considered common assault, since common assault referred to assault in which the victim was a specified target, as the result of a specific dispute.[38] In short, the unique characteristic of hooligan crime in the 1980s was that its manifest behaviours were relatively unpredictable, and it is this unpredictability that was considered a threat to the public and moral order.[39]

These characteristics of hooligan crime were not made clear to courts during the first offensive of the 1983 Strike Hard campaign. Despite this legal vagueness, courts fell over each other in their rush to punish any crime remotely analogous with the vague descriptions set out in the CCP's Document 31, as the following example shows:

> Under the leadership of Guan, Peng, and Ma, the gang instigated a string of street fights in residential areas from July 1982. The most serious occasion involved over forty gang members from opposing gangs using wooden batons and iron rods. Three bystanders sustained minor injuries. With knife in hand, Guan led the gang to an electronics technical college and beat up two students for no apparent reason, as the victims were not known to the perpetrators. One of the victims was injured, requiring eleven stitches in his head. On another occasion, the gang took a home-made pop-gun to a cinema and assaulted strangers outside the venue for sadistic pleasure. On another occasion, at the Bureau of Food and Beverages and later at the local train station, they again assaulted a stranger for sadistic pleasure. In the most serious incident, the gang damaged property in over thirty residences in the course of a street fight. Over the three-hour period, local residents were too petrified to leave their homes, and the gangs stopped fighting only when the police arrived. This gang also committed acts of theft valued at 250 yuan in cash and 1,560 yuan in goods. On 3 December 1983, the Shizuishan Intermediate Court sentenced Guan to death and Peng and the other ringleaders to prison terms. All appealed, but the Higher Court upheld the original sentences.[40]

The most severe punishment, the death penalty, was applied to this case, based on the 2 September 1983 NPC Decision that made hooligan gang crime a capital offence. The most severe form of punishment available was meted out in the above case, despite the fact that the violent act was not carried out in a crowded public area; nor was the threat to the public grave. In the case of Guan and the other defendants, the only occasion on which they were involved in fighting was in a public arena, a cinema. Moreover, Guan did not start a gang fight in this venue; he merely assaulted two people, neither of whom was a members of a rival gang.[41] Clearly, the 'gang' in the above description did not even come close to meeting the criteria for a conventional crime organization as outlined in the law, as its crimes were not serious or premeditated assaults. Despite this heavy-handedness, tactics of severe and swift punishment did little to curb the rise in gang crime after 1986, as we see below.

The rise of the 'heinous' criminal organization **(e'shili)**

As we have noted previously, as a result of the first Strike Hard campaign, 664,000 suspected members of 'hooligan gangs' were detained for questioning – this comprised 29 per cent of all suspects detained for questioning during the three years of Strike Hard.[42] According to author Kang Shuhua, those gangs that were not captured during the campaign rapidly expanded in size and complexity of operation, becoming more secretive, hidden and tightly organized.[43] As post-Mao reforms began to remove the Chinese state's financial responsibility to its citizens, the socio-economic landscape was marked by growing poverty, especially outside the cities, alongside opportunities to make money, especially in the cities. Under these conditions, hooligan groups evolved into 'local heinous criminal gangs' that began to control resources and industries in particular geographical areas. They exerted control over entire villages in rural areas and city outskirts and became known as 'village tyrants', 'city tyrants' or 'highway tyrants'. Today's more sophisticated organized crime groups have evolved from these beginnings.

The first mature organized crime syndicates began to appear in the late 1980s and early 1990s. For example, a syndicate that came to the notice of police in 1990, which was led by Song Yongjia, Wang Weifan, and Hao Weitao, had a membership of 47, five of whom were police officers. The group had 26 firearms in its possession. Its crimes included kidnapping, assault, rape, robbery and gambling. Song was a deputy manager of a Harbin–Hong Kong joint venture company, and Wang was manager of a popular dance hall. In the space of seven years, they were involved in 72 armed street fights with rival gangs, 15 kidnappings, and killed 20 people and seriously injured 63 others. They had 62 'protective umbrellas' in government posts, five of whom were section heads of local government. On 9 June 1991, the Heilongjiang Provincial Higher Court sentenced 14 members of the group to death.[44]

Hooligan gangs were no longer the threat to public order that they had been perceived to be in the mid-1980s. Much larger and more threatening groups were emerging. The Pingyuan incident of 1992 demonstrated that a new and powerful era of organized crime was on the horizon. From 31 August to 20 November 1992, an extraordinary Strike Hard-style drive was launched in Pingyuan district in Yunnan Province. This was the first time that a large-scale Strike Hard drive had targeted such a small geographical region, which had only 1,000 residents. Pingyuan is a small ethnic minority area populated by a Moslem community in the Yunnan border region. Pingyuan district, a junction between Yanshan and Wenshan counties, is a small township community. Because of its status as an ethnic minority community, Pingyuan became a haven for criminal syndicates – partly the result of a long-held criminal justice policy of treating crimes committed by members of ethnic minority groups with relative leniency. In the small township, there were a dozen drug trafficking syndicates, which had a complex transnational drug network with traffickers in Burma and Taiwan. It was one of the 20 largest sources of illegal firearms in the country and a centre for pornography production.[45] Ma Huichun, Bao Guo and Lin Hongwen were in control of one 'mafia-style syndicate', and their organization had control over the local government of the township and surrounding villages, as well as the local mosque. The local government, party officials and religious leaders were all members of the syndicate. (The Moslem leader and the local party secretary were later determined to be ringleaders.) The syndicate controlled 10 drug trafficking organizations in the area and had become a major transport link for smuggling drugs out of the country.[46]

From 1985 to August 1992, police in the region had solved 834 drug trafficking cases (involving 113.38 kilograms of heroin and 982.44 kilograms of opium). All of the heroin and 50 per cent of the opium had come from Pingyuan. During this period, police in the area had also confiscated 159 military-style automatic firearms and 1,440 handguns manufactured by the syndicate, 20,000 bullets, and a host of other weapons.[47] Criminals from 24 provinces or cities around China travelled to

Pingyuan to purchase firearms. The syndicate constructed a fortress wall around the township and an underground tunnel system. It had attacked the local police and government offices on 31 different occasions in retaliation for the arrest of some of its members. It also took protection money from local mines, and from local users of the highway leading into and out of town, as well as protection money from prostitutes. In addition, it offered protection to more than over 200 fugitives from all over the country. The syndicate refused to pay local government taxes, refused to have identity cards or residential registration, and refused to register its vehicles.[48]

The Yunnan Province Party Committee Secretary unsuccessfully attempted to send a working party to the area in October 1991 to investigate the extent of the crime problem. Members of the syndicates shot and killed them, along with the police who accompanied them. Realizing that Pingyuan's criminals were too powerful for provincial authorities, in August 1992, the Yunnan provincial government and Party Committee wrote to the Central Party Committee (CPC) and the State Council asking Beijing to intervene. On 31 August, more than 3,000 military police descended on Pingyuan and surrounding villages. The Ministry of Public Security sent armed police and established a liaison group with responsibility for reporting incidents to the CPC and the Ministry of Public Security and for relaying messages back to the armed police. With 3,000 police now surrounding the township, police issued warnings to residents to surrender, blocking off transport routes and the town's water supply. Eventually, they opened fire on the township. The fighting lasted 81 days before they were able to safely enter the township, where 854 people were taken into custody and 994 firearms confiscated, along with 10.47 million yuan in cash and two kilograms of gold.[49] Seven criminals were eventually sentenced to death, and one was given a suspended death sentence. Only two were killed in the battle.[50] Clearly, the Pingyuan incident showed – if nothing else – that organized criminal syndicates had the potential to threaten a region's social stability and economic order and to have an impact on the national economy.

The rise of mafia-style syndicates

The term 'organized crime' remained loosely defined in criminal justice and legal circles until the early 1990s. In 1990, the Guangdong provincial Politico-legal Committee issued a definition of underworld crime, stating that the Triad crime syndicates that were emerging in China had begun either as branches of Triad syndicates across the border in Hong Kong or as indigenous crime syndicates controlled by Triads across the border. The provincial Politico-legal Committee made a distinction between these groups and what it coined 'mafia-style syndicates' which the committee defined as criminal organizations with a known name, a stable leadership, internal rules and a disciplinary code, their own procedures for recruitment, and a scope of operation limited to one geographical area or a particular industry. These groups were not considered to be controlled by overseas Triad syndicates, but many in Guangdong had connections with Triads.[51] Two types of mafia-style syndicate began to emerge in Guangdong: groups that crossed the border from Macao or moved across from Shenzhen into Guangzhou, and home-grown groups that grew out of gangs. Some home-grown groups recruited professionals from outside China to join their organizations.[52]

The first mention of the term 'mafia-style crime' by the Ministry of Public Security (MPS) came in October 1992 at a national MPS conference on group crime. The Ministry attributed six main characteristics to mafia-style organizations:

1 they are groups that developed in structure and sophistication from 'heinous criminal groups';
2 their criminal activities are limited to a particular geographical area;
3 their crimes are professional in nature, and they continue to commit crimes over a relatively long period;
4 they enjoy a stable membership;
5 they have a definite economic base and are able to control a sizeable portion of businesses in a particular area or a sizeable portion of one type of business; and
6 they make use of corrupt police and government officials.[53]

By 1993, gang and syndicate crime comprised 42 per cent of all registered crime in China, according to Kang Shuhau.[54] Gangs and larger syndicates were being apprehended in their thousands. Police in Guangdong Province, for example, reported that from January 1991 to March 1993 they had broken up 800 underworld syndicates and 'mafia-style syndicates', with a total of 3,917 members. While the term 'mafia-style' syndicate was not yet defined in law, its use to describe a mid- to large-sized syndicate became widespread in criminal justice circles from the mid-1990s.[55] Because the term 'mafia-style' syndicate was yet to be defined in the Criminal Law, police statistics at the time did not differentiate between large-scale syndicates and gangs.

By the time the Criminal Law was revised in 1997 (CL97), three clear types of crime group had emerged in China. The lowest level comprised largely unsophisticated and fluid gangs or groups. The mid-level organized groups were called 'syndicates with the characteristics of the underworld' (mafia-style syndicates), and the high-level syndicates were the Triads and other established underworld syndicates that had moved across the Hong Kong border or from Taiwan into China.[56] The CL97 has made participating in, organizing or leading a mafia-style organization a criminal offence, with punishments ranging from three to ten years imprisonment. In addition to this sentencing range, members are also punished for individual crimes such as robbery, extortion and murder. Once a court determines that a defendant is a member of a syndicate, other crimes that they have committed are dealt with more severely than would be the case if they were not affiliated with a syndicate.

Difficulties in defining mafia-style crime

While the CL97 was an important legislative development in the fight against organized crime, in practice the courts found Article 294 difficult to apply because the legal criteria for determining that an organization was a mafia-style organization and not an ordinary criminal group hinged on whether or not the organization had the protection of state functionaries.[57] Many syndicates were therefore only able to be prosecuted under the lesser Article 26(1), combined with discrete criminal activities such as robbery, extortion and so on that were covered elsewhere in the law.[58] For example, on 12 November 1998, Zhang Ziqiang was sentenced to death after being found guilty of illegally trading in explosives and smuggling firearms, robbery, and kidnapping with violence. Ye Jihuan and three other ringleaders in Zhang's organization were also sentenced to death, two others received death sentences with a two-year reprieve, and 28 other members received life imprisonment and other lengthy custodial sentences; in addition, 660,000 million yuan in capital and cash was confiscated. Zhang Ziqiang was 43 years old when arrested. He had migrated to Hong Kong, returning to Guangzhou in the 1990s and joining forces with the criminal syndicate leader Ye Jihuan and his organization to form a large syndicate known as Da Fuhao (The Syndicate of the Rich and Powerful). In October 1997, the syndicate purchased explosives and automotive firearms in Mainland China and smuggled them into Hong Kong. The following month, they bought 181 kilograms of gunpowder and 2,000 detonators, and smuggled them from Guangdong to Hong Kong in seafood containers. In collusion with a Hong Kong syndicate, they robbed nine high-end jewellery stores, stealing gold worth 5.7 million Hong Kong dollars, and opening fire on Hong Kong police in the course of the robberies. They later robbed two more jewellery stores in Kowloon, stealing 1.8 million HK dollars in gold. Earlier, in 1996, the syndicate had kidnapped the son of Hong Kong's most successful businessman, Li Jiaqiang, spending 1.4 million yuan to finance the crime – including the purchase of firearms, cars and a farm to hide the victim. They obtained one billion Hong Kong dollars in ransom money and later released their victim. In 1997, Zhang organized the kidnapping of another Hong Kong businessman, Guo Ziyi, obtaining 600,000 Hong Kong dollars in ransom.[59]

In 2000, the Supreme People's Court attempted to clarify the difference between ordinary criminal organizations that could be charged under the lesser Article 26 and mafia-style organizations by defining the latter in a 'Judicial Explanation'. The Explanation stated that Article 294 Section 1 of the Criminal Law of the People's Republic of China refers to syndicates that simultaneously possess *all* of the following characteristics:

1. they are relatively stable, possess a relatively large membership, and a definite line of leadership;
2. they embark on criminal and illegal activities for economic interests. Such syndicates must have a firm economic base that exists to support the routine work of the syndicate;
3. they employ violent or threatening means or similar methods to commit crimes in a well-organized fashion; and
4. they use bribery or threats to lure or compel government officials to participate in syndicate activities or to obtain protection from them in order to take control

of a particular trade or industry or seriously damage the economic order or way of life in an area.[60]

The Explanation's statement that a criminal organization would need to exhibit all of these characteristics for a charge to be successfully prosecuted meant that prosecutors would have to prove the organization had the protection of a state functionary. This created further problems, which were not solved until the Standing Committee of the NPC issued a legislative interpretation, removing the requirement for a government functionary to be providing the organization with protection from the criteria. Even with this provision removed, police found the investigation of syndicate cases difficult owing to their lack of experience in solving complex organized crime cases. Criminologists Wu Jianqiang and Cao Yi were commissioned by the MPS in 2004 to collate case study literature to be used in training police at public security academies. In the examination of the make-up of present-day mafia-style syndicates that follows, the first three case studies are taken from Wu and Cao's study.

Some cases

Liang Xiaoming the corrupt police officer

The Liang Xiaoming case was the first case in China to be successfully prosecuted using Article 294 (1) in the CL97. The two-year trial, which involved 15 court sessions, beginning in 1998 and ending in 2000, was one of the longest trials in PRC court history. Liang Xiaoming and Zhang Zeyu were convicted of organizing a mafia-style syndicate – Article 294(1) – along with a string of other offences, and were sentenced to death. Four others were convicted of murder and wilful injury resulting in death, and were also sentenced to death; 28 other defendants were given life and other long custodial sentences. The case was broken in the northern city of Changchun in 1998 when 58 syndicate members were arrested. At the time of the arrests, the syndicate was running four legitimate enterprises that included a hotel, two nightclubs and a car repair business, and had 20 million yuan in capital. Liang was born in 1966. In 1995, he used a forged university degree and a fake resume that claimed he was section head of a private security firm to obtain a position as a criminal detective in Changchun City. As a police officer, he was able to boast that he had extensive networks in government and in the law; he also had 35 party and government officials providing protection for the syndicate, including 12 senior officials and people's congress delegates, 5 prosecutors, 4 judges and 15 police officers. The trial involved the prosecution of 70 criminal cases, including four murders, 33 serious assaults, and several million yuan in illegally obtained property. The organization was run as a tightly controlled hierarchical system with Liang at the top of the pyramid. On the level below were his 'senior officials' and on the third level his 'junior officials'. The bottom level comprised the syndicate's standard members. Members were required to swear eternal allegiance to the syndicate, and were not permitted to leave for any reason.[61]

Liu Yong and the case of the SPC intervention

The infamous Liu Yong and his syndicate provide an example of a 'hermit-crab'-type syndicate.[62] Liu Yong began his criminal career in the 1980s as leader of a hooligan gang, which developed into a full-blown criminal organization in the early 1990s and into a mafia-style organization in the mid-1990s. By this time, his syndicate had acquired a local Holiday Inn, a supermarket and a club, and had established a company called the Shenyang Jiayang Group. Liu Yong was born in 1960. He bribed his way to becoming a delegate in the Shenyang Municipal People's Congress. In 1982, he began a number of ventures, including a real estate business. He eventually ran 26 legitimate businesses that employed 2,500 people and had 700 million yuan in capital. His Jiayang Group Enterprise had a Triple A rating.[63] In 1997, Liu Yong was elected as a provincial People's Congress delegate. The Shenyang court president had become his 'concubine' in the group, and he had bought off the mayor of Shenyang, the head procurator, and the deputy mayor. When the prosecution indicted him and began investigations, they made their evidence and documentation available to the corrupt prosecutor.[64] The case was tried in 2002. Liu Yong's syndicate was recognized by the court as a mafia-style syndicate and was prosecuted under Article 294(1) of the Criminal Law; Liu and 22 other members of the syndicate were convicted on a string of further charges including wilful injury resulting in death, robbery, conducting an illegal business, and illegal use of firearms.[65] Initially, he was found guilty and sentenced to immediate execution. The provincial Higher Court refused to ratify the sentence, resentencing him to a suspended death sentence with a two-year reprieve.[66] The members of his syndicate were found guilty of 16 criminal charges in total, but not a premeditated murder charge. The Higher People's Court therefore rationalized that Liu Yong's syndicate was not recognized as sufficiently 'heinous' to support a death sentence. This decision created uproar in the Chinese media, with journalists and members of the public arguing that the provincial court's decision was influenced by Liu's political and financial ties to staff in the provincial court and the prosecution. The Supreme People's Court (SPC) intervened in December 2003, ordering a retrial of the case in the Jinzhou Intermediate Court. In an extraordinary turn of events, for the trial, Jinzhou court judges were replaced by judges from the SPC, who sentenced Liu Yong to immediate execution. The SPC ratified the decision and he was executed immediately.

Tang Lifeng, his thugs and the would-be mayor

This case went to trial in November 1999. Tang Lifeng received the death penalty for a string of offences that included murder and organizing and leading a mafia-style syndicate. Fellow member Jun and other members also received the death penalty for murder. Yan Mengguo and 36 others received sentences of life imprisonment. Tang Lifeng was born in 1970. His syndicate was formed in 1998, and by 1999 more than 100 individuals were involved in the organization, 26 of them as full members. Syndicate members committed acts of rape and murder to obtain protection money. They formed a tightly organized syndicate – all members wore a black uniform, had crew cuts, and they were organized into military-like squadrons whose members received a steady monthly income of 1,000 yuan. They were also involved in making threats to voters in local elections. In 1999, the older brother of one key member, Cheng Jianchao, made it known that he wanted to be a village mayor, but pre-election polling showed that he would not win. Chen took 40-odd uniformed thugs to harass and threaten voters into voting for his brother. The syndicate's 'protective umbrella' was deputy bureau head of the PSB in Ruzhou City, Henan.[67]

Yang Xiaolin, Feng Man and their legitimate companies

On 5 July 2006, the Chongqing Higher Court publicly sentenced syndicate head Yang Xiaolin and 16 of his syndicate members. Yang received the death penalty.[68] The Yang Xiaolin case involved 17 defendants, all locals. Beginning in 2004, they had run drug trafficking activities and organized prostitution rings, extortion activities and high-interest loan rackets. The organization worked under the guise of a legitimate company. Yang was company director, his wife Xiong Jiandi was general manager, and Wang Shiyi, the only member of the gang with a university education, was general staff manager. Syndicate membership involved a clear division of labour and a well-established system of profit distribution: Yang received 30 per cent of all profits, the other members shared 57 per cent, and 13 per cent went into a pension/insurance fund for members who were injured or sent to prison. The syndicate had a monthly board meeting for key members. It paid professional assassins to murder Cai Guohua, a drug trafficker from a rival gang. The assassin, Lu Yongjun, was also sentenced to death.[69]

On 20 January 2004, Chongqing Higher Court sentenced Feng Man to 20 years imprisonment. Feng Man was the director of a registered real estate agency. The company had 21 board members, who were also the 21 'dragon head' leaders, each with men under them. In order to achieve a monopoly of the real estate market in the area, they committed a string of offences including murdering two people and injuring 80 others, and illegally obtained 1.8 million yuan through threats and extortion. They established a building company, a real estate agency, a body corporate services company and a home design and painting company, basically monopolizing the Bannan district in Chongqing. Their authority outranked that of the local council.[70]

The Hu brothers and the takeover of a quarry

The first case against a mafia-style syndicate successfully tried in Beijing was the trial of the syndicate led by Hu Yadong and Hu Yafeng. The trial ran from 11 to 19 July 2006. In all, 34 people were indicted, and the trial involved 53 separate charges, including crimes committed by the brothers, in conjunction with their lawyer, a city official in charge of council regulations in Xunyi district. A separate case involving three police officers connected to the syndicate was tried at a later date.

The Hu brothers were born in Xunyi district, which was also where their syndicate operated. They committed their first crime on 5 August 1996. They stole a car, cutting off the ear of the driver in the course of the crime, which was motivated by revenge. The Hu brothers were the owners of the Dong Dong Car Repair Shop, and the victim was the chief car mechanic for a rival repair shop. The case was tried on 17 December 1996 at the Xunyi Basic Court. The perpetrator of the ear-cutting incident was Wang Hongqing, who received six years imprisonment; his accomplice, Zhang Zhenya, was sentenced to four years imprisonment for robbery. The Hu brothers fled the scene and escaped prosecution. Xunyi Basic People's Court judgment notice stated that the assault had been ordered by Hu Yadong but that he had fled the scene. Hu remained free and unpunished for another 10 years. The procuratorate revealed during the 2006 trial that, in 1996, Hu Yadong had managed to visit the defendants secretly at the Xunyi district watchhouse by paying off a police officer who was guarding the defendants. During the pre-trial investigation in 1996, Hu Yadong offered money to Liu Haiying, the investigating officer, who subsequently demanded that the assault investigation be closed and sent to the procuratorate for indictment without pursuing the Hu brothers. In December 1997, Liu Haiying received the promised 70,000 yuan from Hu.

Zhang Qiuchen, a licensed lawyer, was also prosecuted in 2006. He was legal adviser to the syndicate and the lawyer in the 1996 case. He participated in the syndicate's activities after the trial in 1996, and his crimes included the extortion of a total of 80,000 yuan by deception using his legal letterhead. Zhang was arrested in November 2005. The syndicate's main criminal activities included stealing and the selling of stolen goods. In October 1999, Hu Yadong was indicted for these offences. Xunyi Basic Court sentenced him to three years imprisonment. After his release in 2001, the syndicate presented Hu with a Mercedes-Benz 600.

On 7 October 2002, on orders from Hu Yadong, two members of the syndicate stabbed and seriously wounded Zhang Hongpo, an employee of a rival car repair business. Even though the police forensic officer determined that the injury was extremely serious, the case was not registered as a crime by the local police, who were in the employ of the brothers. In April 2004, the syndicate entered into a new business venture, illegally taking over production at a local quarry that supplied rock and sand for building material. The 30 or so members of the syndicate guarded the quarry, and refused to allow its legitimate employees to enter. The police were called on four occasions to report this takeover, but the first time they arrived at the site to investigate, there was an altercation between the police officers and syndicate members in which the police were injured. An armed police squad was then called in and shots were fired. Over 200 quarry trucks that the gang stole from the quarry owners were confiscated, but mysteriously reappeared at the quarry the following day. The syndicate painted the surname 'Hu' on the sides of the trucks and took control of the 9-kilometre route from the quarry to the main road leading to Xunyi – only trucks bearing the Hu name were allowed to use the road. Between April 2004 and January 2005, when the syndicate abandoned the quarry, it lost 13 million yuan in revenue and the syndicate made a profit of 2.4 million yuan. The syndicate only eventually abandoned the quarry because it had been mined out.

Protective umbrellas in the case included the watchhouse police officer, Xunyi criminal detectives and other police who were in collusion with the syndicate. The Hu syndicate case was transferred to the Beijing Intermediate Court and investigated by the Beijing Municipal police. The indictments were written up by the Beijing procuratorate rather than the local prosecution officials.

The trial of the Hu brothers' syndicate began in Beijing Intermediate Court on 11 July 2006. Nine court vehicles were used to transport the 34 defendants to the court. Although the trial began at 9:30 a.m., members of the public began to line up as early as 7:30 a.m. to obtain tickets to watch the proceedings in the gallery. The procurator was Li Lianjia, Deputy Procurator-General of Beijing. The indictment took 30 minutes to read, and its main gist was that the Hu brothers were charged with organizing and leading a mafia-style syndicate. Other charges against the syndicate included two counts of serious assault, one count of illegally purchasing firearms, one count of using firearms in the course of a crime, 20 counts of extortion, 14 counts of provoking violent fights, two counts of conducting an illegal business, one count of forging government documents, one count of corruption, one count of harbouring a criminal suspect, one count of possessing stolen property, one count of destroying evidence, two counts of illegal gambling, and one count of illegally detaining an individual.[71]

On 12 August 2006, the Beijing No. 2 Intermediate Court publicly pronounced sentencing in Beijing's first mafia-style case. Hu Yadong and Hu Yafeng were convicted of organizing and leading a mafia-style syndicate, along with a string of other crimes, and were sentenced to 20 years and 19 years in prison respectively. They were each fined 2.62 million yuan. The other 32 syndicate members were all convicted of various crimes, including participating in a mafia-style syndicate, and their sentences ranged from 18 months to 18 years. The Judgment Notice ran to 140 pages.

The judge explained in a media statement that the key piece of evidence in determining that the group was a mafia-style syndicate was the fact that it had 'protective umbrellas' in government positions. The inquiry and debate stages of the trial had exposed five police officers as providing 'protective umbrellas', the most senior of whom was a superintendent. The judge reported that cases of these police officers were currently undergoing adjudication, and they had been indicted on charges of corruption and allowing a suspect to flee a crime.[72]

Concluding remarks: serious crime and the marketization of the economy

The case studies we have just considered are testament to the intricate relationships between the market and the new forms of crime that have emerged as a consequence of economic modernization in China. The serious crimes that have been the focus of this and the previous chapter have not simply evolved in parallel with the development of the market in China but have been inextricably linked with the process of marketization. Introducing the market to work in tandem with the state has precipitated, enabled and now sustained these criminal activities. It has done so by fostering the socio-economic and political conditions that have created both the capacity and the will for criminal action. Put simply, the evolution of serious crime in the post-Mao era is largely the product of the two principal forces simultaneously at work in China's economic transition – withdrawal of the state from determining economic production/distribution, and the introduction of the market to replace the state. Both are the product of Chinese planners who seek to engineer this enormously difficult transition under direction of the Chinese leadership and both are crucial aspects of the political philosophy of reform – to deregulate the economic and, to some extent, the political life of the nation.

The withdrawal of the state from supplying goods, services, jobs and income led to social and economic dislocation, as well as need and opportunity, as the security of the iron rice bowl quickly slipped away. Its replacement by the market set in train new forces of supply and demand and the capacity to do both. At least in theory, the people gained the capacity and the will to engage in the market through money and other capital, as well as the freedom to buy, sell, produce, move, take risks and make profits, and the desire to consume beyond the state plan. The poverty and basic need that were created where 'theory' did not work, especially in rural areas where market conditions could not be fostered, meant that crime was seen as a means to wealth or simply survival.

For crime gangs, the evolving market created the capacity to demand and be supplied to; and for drug criminals, it provided the capacity to supply and respond to a demand. Experience in these new market conditions and the 'savvy' and infrastructure developed through that experience have fuelled growth in both types of crime. It is, therefore, inevitable that our discussion of drug and organized crime has led to an examination of the relationship between serious crime and marketization, as Chinese planners have gradually discarded the socialist plan in favour of the market.[73]

The Hu brothers had the capacity *to demand* to take over the rock and sand quarry on the outskirts of Beijing because they had the money to pay for the activities that enabled them to do so – from 'buying' protection from the local public security bureau that provided the syndicate's security umbrella, to painting 'Hu' on the trucks they confiscated. Market conditions gave the evicted quarry owners the capacity to own and operate the quarry that they eventually *supplied to* the extortionate syndicate members. Market conditions also enabled the syndicate to make 2.4 million yuan in profit and the quarry owners to lose 13 million yuan in revenue. In a similar vein, it was the operation of the market that gave drug traffickers the capacity *to supply* (or at least try to supply) the 6,000 small packs of heroin inside the bottles of imported skin cream that Customs officials found in Xinjiang and the 20-plus kilograms of pure heroin that the Hongqilafu police found in the preserved dates from Pakistan. Market conditions give prospective drug buyers the capacity *to create demand* for the product by fostering their financial capacity to purchase. Market operations, in this case through international trade, also enabled the legal international trade in skin cream and dates that facilitated the illegal trade in heroin.

Two issues that facilitate our understanding of the situation relate to the connection between conceptualizing China's market development and the rise in the incidence of serious crime. Both involve the creation of market conditions and the role/responsibility of the state in regulating them.[74] First, serious crime impedes the development of an open market. From the very beginning of post-Mao China's market development, serious crime has been a structural impediment or at least a disincentive to the type of open market conditions that the state is trying to create. Chinese economic planners understand that people will be disinclined to pursue a business if they believe extortionists could threaten it or take it from them with impunity, or that traffickers could use their cargo for passage of illegal substances. The appeal of entering into any commercial transaction wanes if criminal intervention can and possibly will disrupt, diminish or prevent the accumulation and maximization of profit. Confidence and trust are necessary for markets to operate effectively in a mixed economy. Chinese planners seeking to develop the market as part of the Chinese economy surely need to appreciate the potential costs that the prospect of serious crime can present through commercial opportunities forfeited by the erosion of confidence and trust.

The second and related issue is that, while emerging markets in China may have been ripe for regulation to prevent crime entering or taking a foothold, the inexperience of planners regarding what, how and how far to regulate in order to prevent crime inhibited preventive action. This presented a particularly difficult dilemma when the new ethos sought to deregulate rather than re-regulate. The state's preferred strategy was to control crime through campaign justice-style punishment, rather than re-regulate the market with laws that may also have impeded market development. Chinese authorities were, therefore, unprepared for both the surge in serious crime that accompanied the social and economic dislocation caused by introduction of the market, and the capacity of free market conditions to inspire and provide fertile soil for criminal activity. The extraordinary growth in crime throughout the reform period and until very recently suggests that, in the early years after market reform began, inexperience in market regulation and eagerness to maintain market growth left the way open for some forms of serious crime to flourish without effective restraints.

Campaigns may have provided a short-term deterrent to some of the new types of crime that the push to open markets promoted so effectively, but it did not prove a recipe for a stable economic and political environment or a 'harmonious society'. While the rate of growth in serious crime appears to have slowed in recent years, crime had already reached levels that threaten to disrupt social, economic and political stability. The final chapter will conclude the story of campaigns; their failure, their future and how this key theme of stability has continued to surface in debates on the appropriateness and efficacy of 'severe and swift punishment' in an era in which serious crime is deeply embedded in the structure of the economic and political 'marketplace'.

7 The end of campaign justice?

There have been compelling reasons for the Chinese state to cast campaigns as instrumental to what it labels the national Reform program. Reform has entailed the complex and fraught process of introducing market regulation of economic behaviour alongside the role of the state, in a society in which the Maoist authorities had previously outlawed the market. Post-Mao Chinese authorities have used campaigns in an attempt to outlaw the serious crime that market forces have both inspired and enabled. Campaigns are thus cast as means to help achieve reform. The taut regulatory muscle of campaigns has served to help secure the order and social stability on which China's mixed economy, the reform program and the Chinese Communist Party depend. Campaigns are also a way for the party-state to respond to the serious surge in crime without the need to acknowledge the possible contribution of the party itself and its unprecedented reform program to the crime problem.

With roots that reach deep into the criminal justice system of the Mao period, campaigns are also a product of an earlier political ethos. In the 'friend' and 'enemy' binary of post-Mao campaign-style criminal justice practice, serious criminals became the 'enemies' of the state. This post-Mao 'political struggle' against serious crime has focused on national economic development goals rather than on ideological purity. Its fuel has been legalized 'shock and awe' deterrence rather than mass commitment. Campaign justice pursued what we could consider criminal justice 'with Chinese characteristics' while the Chinese state pursued what it called, accommodatingly, 'socialism with Chinese characteristics'. Campaign policy is a distinctively political response to the surge in serious crime that unsettled the post-Mao social, economic and political landscape.

This volume has examined the politics of policing serious crime, tracing the rise and fall of campaign justice in China, with the first part of the book (Chapters 1 to 3) focusing on the rise and the second part focusing on the fall, or more precisely, the inability of campaigns to control serious crime. The Introduction identified three main manifestations of the political in campaigns. Three distinct threads of the political – one ideological, another organizational and third, institutional politics – informed the storyline of why campaigns persisted in contemporary China. Chapter 1 interrogated the *when* (when campaigning proliferated). Chapter 2 examined the *what* of campaign-style justice: what its template comprises –

its foundation stone, scaffolding and bricks and mortar – and what manifestation of political struggle existed in campaign justice in the Reform era. Here we argued that policing serious crime in this era of economic transformation was no longer conceived in terms of class enemies, yet, it continued to operate within the discourse of the political. The political was, therefore, transformed rather than diluted or removed; or to put it another way, the political function of policing serious crime was repoliticized rather than depoliticized. The focus then shifted to explore the *how* (how a campaign is implemented both nationally and in regions) in Chapter 3, a survey of the Strike Hard campaign of the twenty-first century from 2001 to 2003 which found that the basic ethos and strategies of this campaign did not differ fundamentally from those of the first Strike Hard from 1983 to 1986. A consequence of this was the failure of the 2001–03 campaign to produce lasting results and this failure led to an unprecedented attack on campaign justice from within senior police circles. Chapters 4, 5 and 6 addressed a second concern of this study: the factors and events that led to decline in campaign justice's prominence. Chapter 4 examined the beginnings of cracks in the campaign façade. The problems of campaign justice had been known to senior police for a considerable time, but it was only during the period from 2002 to late 2003 that a chorus of criticism from both junior and senior police urged party authorities to break free from the dominance of the campaigning mentality. This chapter took stock of the effects of campaigns on crime, crime control and the legitimacy of the law through the eyes of those at the coalface. We found that the post-2001 political landscape was increasingly tolerant of domestic criticism of human rights and procedural justice abuses that campaigns encourage. These criticisms from police were unequivocal: striking hard does not work to curb serious crime. Striking hard frustrates efforts by local police to create sound preventative policing practices. The Strike Hard-initiated fast tracking of case investigations inevitably conflicts with the careful and meticulous police investigation work that might normally follow conventional policing practice. Cracking criminal cases at great speed cannot be compared favourably to solid basic police work. These are just a few of Strike Hard's failings.

The following two chapters put the spotlight on crime rather than on crime control. An examination of drug crime and organized crime in Chapters 5 and 6 illustrates a crucial point about the downfall of campaign justice, which was the party authorities' choice to prioritize Strike Hard over crime prevention in the era of economic transformation. The newly emerging markets in China were arguably an opportunity to impose certain market regulations that would prevent crime from gaining a foothold. But, eagerness to fast-track economic reform occluded the prioritizing of preventive action. The new 'fast-track' ethos resulted in the deregulation rather than re-regulation of the economy. The choice made to control serious crime through Strike Hard-style punishment rather than to re-regulate the market with laws (which could have potentially impeded market development) meant that the wave of serious crime linked to the social and economic dislocation caught China's leaders unawares. Inexperience in market regulation and enthusiasm to maintain market growth permitted some forms of serious crime to flourish, and it is these types of crime – organized and drug crime – that fail to respond to the deterrent message of campaigns.

Some scholars who study the politics of crime control in the USA argue that a distinct late-modernist mentality of governance has emerged in the decades since the 1960s where crime and the risk of crime have become the prism through which a whole range of social policies are now approached. David Garland, in his book *The Culture of Control*, argues that the move away from instrumental or utilitarian punishment philosophies in the USA such as rehabilitation, toward retributive and punitive goals, has occurred in tandem with a shift in decision-making away from judges to legislators. He attributes this shift to a constellation of features which characterize late modernity, such as the insecure economy, a 'hedonistic consumer culture that combines extensive personal freedoms with relaxed social controls', a 'pluralistic moral order that struggles to create trust relations between strangers who have little in common', and a '"sovereign" state that is increasingly incapable of regulating a society of individuated citizens and differentiated social groups'. He asserts that the 'risky, insecure character of today's social and economic relations is the social surface that gives rise to our newly emphatic, overreaching concern with control and to the urgency with which we segregate, fortify and exclude'.[1] Garland also argues that a sense of general insecurity within communities that is a by-product of the economic and social conditions of late-modernity has led to the development of a mentality of risk management in American society whereby people have grown to expect an instant governmental response to their feelings of insecurity. This has allowed legislators to place themselves on a 'war footing' in relation to crime, and to exercise direct control over sentencing levels.[2]

A rather different thematic thread of unequivocally political hue has run through the chapters of this study as a way of navigating through the complex array of issues that comprise criminal justice practice in contemporary China. The thread is in essence an argument about the political function of policing and punishing serious crime, which is this: in the post-Mao period, the political function of criminal justice practice as it applies to serious crime remained integral to the *raison d'être* of the state rather than having been diluted or removed from the reform agenda. The political goal in sight, however, was not run on the fuel of any Maoist call to class warfare as it was in the past, but reflected a particular vision of economic modernization, one that placed social stability and social order at the top of state priorities. This was the case despite the continued use of Maoist nomenclature and practice in anti-crime campaigns. Despite the political pre-eminence given to stability-order, it nevertheless became an increasing elusive goal given the fracturing social consequences that economic upheaval bore on communities across the nation. One of the implications for this continued prominence of the political is that anti-crime campaigns remained stubbornly mired in the Mao-style ethos and format of political struggle. We found, however, that in the first years of the twenty-first century, campaign justice became overwhelmingly recognized in professional circles as an anachronistic social control mechanism that was hopelessly unable to restrain the types of emerging offences such as drug and organized crime that were the products of the new market economy.

This chapter concludes the volume by exploring the failures and the future of Strike Hard in China. Strike Hard's failures are examined through a review of what Chinese academics and practitioners see as the key problems with severe and swift punishment. These failures point directly to the problems that develop when law is cast as a political vehicle for political ends. Here we focus on the legal, social and institutional implications of 'severely and swiftly' punishing serious crime by examining what some critical observers have identified as a 'vicious cycle' of harshness and leniency – or at least less severe harshness – that has constructed the culture of campaign justice throughout the post-Mao reform period. We examine how Chinese scholars and criminal justice practitioners interpret the way in which the high levels of conflict, dislocation and instability created by unprecedented economic growth have precipitated the state's 'swift and severe' response to serious crime. Many argue that in some ways this extreme response may have intensified rather than mitigated conflict, dislocation and instability.

In the Introduction, we introduced the argument that the policing and punishing of serious crime in China can be understood by tracing three threads of 'the political': one ideological, another organizational and third, institutional politics. Almost three decades since the beginning of the campaign juggernaut, we find that campaigns have dropped dramatically in frequency, the theatrics and their shock and awe rhetoric. The most dynamic aspects of 'the political' that are alive and well today in these practices is the institutional politicking within criminal justice organs, particularly the SPC. This study concludes by exploring Strike Hard's future through a brief examination of some of the recent and momentous changes to the death penalty policy and practice in China that has been made possible through attempts by the SPC to thwart the party's reliance on Strike Hard.

Justice-related problems with striking hard

We begin this final evaluation of the doing and undoing of campaign justice with two incidences which remind us that the guiding ethos of campaign justice has remained alive, if not well, in twenty-first-century China. On 19 October 2006, the Guangzhou Comprehensive Management of Public Order (CMPO) Committee held the third-quarterly meeting of the year to discuss and reflect on the crime situation for the year to October and make plans for anti-crime activities for the final three months of the year. Guangzhou Municipal Politico-legal Affairs Committee secretary, Zhang Guifang, stated at the meeting that while for the previous months in 2006, the number of recorded crimes had declined by 9.8 per cent, the New Year holiday time (i.e. high-crime period) was nevertheless fast approaching and itinerant workers would be preparing, one way or another, to 'take home the fattened pig' to celebrate the New Year in their home provinces. 'We are now confronted with two distinct battlefronts: one on the street [i.e. bag snatching and common theft] and another in the home [i.e. break and enter crime]', he asserted.[3] He then announced that the Guangdong Higher Court had agreed to the police request to lower the existing monetary standard at which a theft offence in Guangzhou could be charged and criminally prosecuted. While stealing property valued at 2,000 yuan was once sufficient grounds to indict a suspect, now the value would be reduced to 1,000 yuan. That is to say, whereas stealing property valued at 1,000 yuan would until that time have been dealt with as a summary offence and dealt with through the system of administrative punishment, now offenders would face criminal prosecution. This new measure, Zhang added, was to 'help the police to fight crime with a stronger fist'.[4] In effect, readjusting these figures meant a change in the standard by which police distinguish between crime and misdemeanours. This move was classic campaign mentality. What were called 'Strike Hard' operations against crime in Guangzhou City began in August 2006 and concluded in November. Each week from August onwards, Strike Hard joint operations were planned in which police and other security forces launched 'dragnets' across the city to apprehend active criminals and fugitives. The first joint operation on 22 August involved 23,000 police officers and 49,000 other public and private security officers throughout the city including military police and private security guards. Security forces performed 3,800 stop-and-searches on vehicles and made checks on over 20,000 venues and residences. By 8:00 p.m. that evening, over 700 suspects had been brought in for questioning. The 'Strike Hard Joint Operation' targeted muggings, armed robberies and break-and-enter theft.[5]

A year after this Strike Hard Operation, in August 2007 in Xinjiang Province in China's west, Xinjiang Higher Court President, Rosa Ismail, announced that courts at all levels in Xinjiang would continue to give cases involving national security top priority. Courts, he said, were required to place strong pressure on the three evils (terrorists, separatists and fundamentalists) because these three groups were the greatest threat to social stability in Xinjiang. He added that the criminal activities of these groups included murder, bombings, drug trafficking and arson, are all crimes that endangered social stability, which indicated that the provincial court would allow local courts to prosecute suspected members of these groups using common criminal charges not necessarily related to national security. In adjudicating cases related to those classed as belonging to the 'three evils', he explained that the policy 'is to hand down the most serious punishment possible within the scope of the law' that is, to give them the highest possible punishment and to execute a proportion of these criminals in accordance with the provisions in the Criminal Law.[6]

> Even though a criminal may be involved in crimes related in one way or another to the three evils, we will nevertheless implement the policy of balancing leniency with severity on a case by case basis, that is, to separate heads of groups who are principal offenders from non-principals; and for those who have been forced or those deceived into committing criminal acts or those criminals who have given police important information, the courts will consider leniency. When adjudicating cases involving the three evils, judges must be unswerving in attitude and must pursue . . . a relentless attack against those who the lead forces of the three evils.[7]

Both the Guangzhou and Xinjiang scenarios above exemplify campaign justice as a product of the machinery of a socialist politico-legal system. They also serve as examples of the continued call to 'strike hard' in the first years of the first decade of the twenty-first century. As we have argued throughout this volume, campaigns are quintessentially a form of political struggle against the enemies of economic modernization. In the Guangzhou example, we find that legal elasticity is applied to the definition of what constitutes 'theft' in order to widen the Strike Hard dragnet. In the Xinjiang example, legal elasticity is applied by ordering judges to hand down the 'most serious punishment' possible within the existing laws to those targeted by criminal justice authorities. This persistent use of elasticity in particular in relation to severe and swift punishment had not gone uncontested in criminal justice and academic circles in late twentieth-century China. One of the promising developments in criminal justice research over the last decade has been the proliferation of criminology journals both within police academies and in academic and judicial settings. This recent growth in the number of journals parallels the increase in the variety and contentiousness of debates on key issues identified by Chinese criminologists and legal experts.

Criminologists and legal experts who point to the failure of campaigns tend not to do so in the general media, but reserve their criticisms for specialist law and criminology journals that do not have a wide public distribution. Two distinct sets of problems with the policy of severity and swiftness, in particular, are identified in the literature that points to the failures of Strike Hard in 2001–03. The first is that 'severity' policy is difficult to control, and that criminal justice agencies routinely overstep the mark. The dramatic oscillations between severity and leniency during different periods and in different parts of the country inhibit the capacity to implement campaigns effectively. Second, scholars and practitioners warn against the 'chop suey' form of justice that campaigns encourage, including tactics that often serve to de-legitimize the authority of the law and law enforcers. These criticisms form a compelling argument against the most extreme elements of campaign policy, if not the basic culture of 'heavy-penaltyism' at their very core.

Overstepping the Strike Hard mark: severity

We begin this survey of the critics' attacks on Strike Hard's 'attack' arm with a statement by scholar Wang Wenyuan in 2005 that cynically mocks typical Strike Hard propaganda and gives some sense of the degree of loathing that campaigns inspire in some areas of criminology.

> By now, everyone is familiar with the call to 'strike hard' and the people applaud loudly every time they hear it. Criminals run like rats running across the streets when they hear the word Strike Hard, limping like homeless dogs with nowhere to go. The members of the masses who have become victims of crime no longer continue to nurse their grievances . . . Strike Hard makes the masses deliriously happy to a point where all they fear is that Strike Hard might not even be tough enough . . . There are very few people who are suspicious of the benefits of Strike Hard because many important and major crimes are

> solved during campaigns . . . Strike Hard fulfils the wishes of both God and the people. All those who support Strike Hard do so with cheers and raised arms. This might be considered Strike Hard's greatest significance . . . But Strike Hard's significance actually goes beyond this. Its second area of significance is that the term 'Strike Hard' is itself the symbolic measuring stick that is used to gauge the efficacy of the law, and is a reflection of the attitudes of both the law's makers and its enforcers. It also reflects the idiosyncratic pleasures of public security politicians and authorities: they take great pleasure in the 'kill one to scare a hundred' idea.[8]

Wang does seek to make a serious point about Strike Hard policy: Strike Hard has been commonly rationalized as a way to animate or rejuvenate the punishment tasks of criminal justice agencies that, from time to time, like their counterparts worldwide, are accused of being too soft on crime. Wang notes that, prior to a campaign, it is not uncommon to hear politicians and criminal justice authorities warning that 'the power to enforce the law is insufficient'. Then suddenly you will find them saying that they will 'add fuel to the enforcement power of the law' by starting a new Strike Hard initiative. Surely, Wang argues, this can hardly be a matter of 'striking hard' if the situation prior to its introduction was one in which 'the power to enforce the law [was] insufficient'. Wang continues: 'It is commonly said that we need to strike hard when "law enforcement has gone soft". That's the equivalent of saying that you haven't been doing the job expected of you as set out in the law'. What is required, he suggests, is a return to the respect of law rather than the current reliance on Strike Hard, which amounts to 'overshooting the mark to strengthen the crooked to excess'.[9]

The practice of 'overshooting the mark to strengthen the crooked to excess' is manifest in Strike Hard's main weapon – harsh punishment – which is directed at criminals who fall within campaign targets. Judge Li Yuanhe from the Chongqing Higher People's Court and Judge Yu Tianmin from the Chongqing Intermediate People's Court attested in 2003 that Strike Hard policy results in far too much emphasis being placed on the task of getting a case to the stage of prosecution, and far too little on the sentencing rationale for individual cases. This occurs both because the range of penalty options in the criminal law is too wide, and because little emphasis is placed on the mitigating or aggravating circumstances of individual crimes. The common Strike Hard philosophy is that, as long as the judge has correctly determined the category of crime under prosecution, it makes little difference to the court whether a convicted criminal receives a few more or less years' imprisonment, as all penalties fall within the legitimate scope of the criminal law. This engenders further problems, according to Li and Yu. The initial sentencing decision processes involve the examination of the social (or in the case of property offences, the material) consequences of the crime in order to determine the length or type of punishment. At appeal, or in petition applications from prisoners, the appellate court only considers applications in which the original sentence was incorrect in the extreme. An appeal is never upheld if the application only entails increasing or reducing a sentence by a few years.

A second problem with Strike Hard, the judges argue, is that, in practice, courts routinely dispense the heaviest possible penalty under the law. This partly occurs for historical and cultural reasons, but also partly because this is how the public like it and, just as importantly, because Strike Hard policy itself engenders a fear of criticism from political superiors: courts would rather be criticized both within and outside the system for handing down heavy sentences than for handing down sentences that may be deemed too light, for fear of being accused of not correctly implementing Strike Hard policy.[10] In all these arguments, the underlying assumption is that 'acting in accordance with the law' should entail fair treatment of individual cases, a right endorsed in law.

In a similar vein, Judge Huang Xiangqing from the Shanghai Intermediate Court argues that when severity policy is invoked during Strike Hard campaigns and specialized drives, mitigating circumstances are seldom considered in sentencing. Courts usually go directly to the heaviest penalty under the law. For instance, if a judge gives less than eight years' imprisonment in a robbery case, the penalty is not considered to be severe enough, because robbery is considered to be a crime that 'seriously endangers public order'. Very few robbery cases receive sentences of between three and five years, because judges seldom consider three to five years as a sentencing option. In theory, the extent to which a crime has 'seriously endangered public order' is the measuring stick for the severity with which that crime is viewed, the judge explains. The important point here is that the determination of whether a crime is 'serious' or not should be made on a case-by-case basis, not by considering all robbery cases to 'seriously endanger public order'. The Criminal Law provides judges with the discretion to punish robbery cases with relative leniency or severity depending on the particular circumstances of the crime. 'Robbery' is a category of crime that inevitably falls within the scope of the Strike Hard 'severity and swiftness' policy during campaigns, as Strike Hard is aimed at crimes that seriously endanger public order. While authorities stipulate that the policy of severity should only be applied during Strike Hard and specialized campaigns, Judge Huang asserts that 'severity' has been continuously applied to the punishment of robbery cases for the last ten years. Thus, he claims, 'we can either admit that we have been experiencing a continual Strike Hard for the last ten years [against robbery] or that we have lost the integrity of the law in respect to sentencing. Take your pick'.[11] Part of the problem lies in the slippery nature of the term 'serious' as it is applied here. As You Wei and Xie Xiaomei argue, the very concept of 'serious' – whether encapsulated in the term 'serious violent crime' or the catchcry 'seriously affecting the public's sense of security' – has no standard meaning in Criminal Law in China. While Strike Hard is charged with targeting serious crime, there is no clear demarcation in Strike Hard policy between serious and non-serious crimes because the concept of 'serious' is itself unclear.[12]

Chop suey justice

We established in an earlier chapter that the routine application of the policy of the 'two basics' during Strike Hard campaigns meant that judges only need to establish that the 'basic' facts of a case are clear and the 'basic' evidence is conclusive to convict a suspect of a particular crime.[13] One legal expert points out that the 'two basics' do not satisfy the requirements of the Criminal Procedural Law (CPL), which states that only when the facts of a case are 'categorically clear' and the evidence is 'compelling' (*zhengju queshi chongfen*) can a criminal be pronounced guilty of a crime. He argues that because Strike Hard policy relies only on satisfying the 'two basics', procedural propriety can in no way be guaranteed during Strike Hard operations.[14]

One Sichuan Province police academy researcher, Zhong Yuhua, aptly characterized flexible practices such as the 'two basics' as indicative of the 'chop suey' approach to criminal justice.[15] Chop suey justice refers to the way in which criminal justice practices are all thrown together and stirred in one pot, treating different situations in the same way. This campaign-style flexibility contrasts with its procedural opposite, 'the assembly line' model of justice, in which a case is handed progressively down the line from the police, to the prosecution, and finally to the courts. Zhong believes that campaign justice as experienced in the Strike Hard campaign in 2001, can be described as 'chop suey' justice to the extent that it is administered under the leadership of the party and the government; cases are often handled jointly by the three organs of criminal justice through joint case-handling offices; and the prosecution and courts routinely practice 'joining in the investigation and prosecution before the assigned time'. These are all common campaign practices. Zhong argues that 'chop suey' justice does not comply with the principles set out in the Criminal Procedural Law, and judges who employ these practices are not independent administrators of justice: 'They are stage actors who perform in cohorts with the police and the prosecution to prosecute criminals. This is completely against the procedural law that stipulates a separation of tasks between the three agencies'.[16] Zhong maintains that such practices amount to a system of bogus justice, and notes dryly that in this system of 'chop suey' justice, the difference between the three arms of justice is no more than the difference between the three arms of the military – the army, the navy and the air force.[17]

Not only is there a problem of 'overdoing severity' during campaigns and drives, according to public security officer Rao Yuanming; the tendency to 'overdo severity' is matched by a tendency to 'overdo leniency' by offering lenient treatment to some criminals in exchange for surrendering to police. As he explains:

> We have a local government policy now that offers leniency to fugitives; they are guaranteed a lenient sentence if they surrender by a certain date. The result of this is that although the rate of capturing fugitives improves in the short term, it also brings with it a mountain of negative side effects. For example, many criminal suspects flee to the countryside immediately after they commit a crime and then return to the city to surrender once they hear the policy of leniency is in force . . . This results in a situation whereby 'the more fugitives you chase the more there are'.[18]

Another obvious problem with 'chop suey' justice is that cases are routinely rushed through the courts. The policy of 'swiftness' that characterizes Strike Hard and other specialized drives forces many police to file cases for prosecution with minimal evidence, only to be returned for further investigation before indictments are given or overturned at appeal. In Fujian Province, for example, between January and November 2001, 26 per cent of cases were rejected by the prosecution and ordered to undergo further investigation. In some areas the figure was 54 per cent.[19] This attests to the fact that during the Strike Hard campaign of 2001–03 there was a strong emphasis on cracking cases, while the tasks of case management took a backseat. For police concerned with fulfilling clear-up rate quotas, the objective is catching criminals – not successfully mounting the case against them. This also means that a thorough investigation of the criminal record of an accused is seldom undertaken during drives. At the local level, there are minimum quotas for the number of arrests to be made within a specific time. All efforts are thus focused on making arrests in order to meet these quotas, and the scope of criminal justice is expanded to include cases that would normally be dealt with through the system of administrative punishment.[20]

Contestation from the judge's bench: the Supreme People's Court and Strike Hard's future

Given Strike Hard's longevity and the myriad of problems it presents judges, policing practitioners and law reformers alike, what attempts have been made to undermine this policy from within judicial circles that implement it? We know from Chapter 4 that in 2002 and 2003, police in China attempted to thwart the over-reliance on Strike Hard policy by publishing a series of critiques in public security journals. Since the mid-1990s, legal reformers in China, particularly senior judges in the Supreme People's Court (SPC), have also been attempting to limit the scope and force of the 'severe and swift punishment' meted out in lower courts. A breakthrough came in late 2006 with the party's Resolution on Harmonious Society and with the return to the SPC of the authority to review and approve all death sentences in China. In this final section, I discuss how reformers have attempted to turn around the culture of heavy-penaltyism in light of the new rhetorical atmosphere of tolerance and harmony that emerged from President Hu Jintao's 'socialist harmonious society' Resolution of October 2006. Important changes to the application of the death penalty since late 2006, particularly in relation to the implementation of a new criminal justice policy of 'balancing leniency and severity' have empowered some in the SPC to limit both the use of Strike Hard policy and the number of death sentences handed down by local courts in the first instance; the focus has been on how to interpret what actually constitutes the most 'serious crime'.

One reason for the extensive use of the most severe of severe punishment, the death penalty, relates to the allocation of authority – and specifically the authority to review death sentences – between the different bodies in the judicial system. In the 1979 Criminal Law, the SPC, the nation's highest court, was given ultimate responsibility for death penalty decisions. In 1983, however, the SPC was required by legislative directive to delegate its authority to review the vast majority of death sentences handed down by municipal intermediate people's courts to provincial higher people's courts.[21] This delegation of authority was intended to facilitate the large-scale 'severe and swift punishment' of serious criminal offenders that had been generated by the nation's first Strike Hard campaign which began that year. By being forced to delegate authority to the provincial courts, the SPC relinquished its power to control the criteria for applying the death penalty, which in the hands of the provincial higher people's courts produced the greater number of 'severe' death sentences whose deterrent value was expected to be instrumental in Strike Hard's success at controlling crime.[22]

The authority to review and approve all death sentences in China was returned to the SPC on 1 January 2007, after a period of over two decades in the hands of provincial courts. For over 20 years, provincial judges performed decision-making at two judicial levels in the same procedure, reviewing the appellate case of a condemned criminal as well as ratifying its own appeal decision. The NPC amendment of Article 13 of the Organic Law of the People's Court of 31 October 2006 reversed the NPC Decision of 2 September 1983. The 1983 Decision delegated the power to review and approve death sentence decisions from the SPC to provincial courts for cases of homicide, rape, robbery, bombing and other crimes that seriously endangered public security and damage social order.[23] This Decision was originally taken in order to accommodate the Strike Hard policy of 'severe and swift punishment' against serious criminal offenders who were targeted during China's first 'Strike Hard' campaign.[24]

In the intervening years, the main issue regarding application of the death penalty was uncertainty of the law, which derived from two sources. One was inconsistency in imposing the death penalty during anti-crime campaigns and non-campaign periods; the second was geographical differences across jurisdictions. These inconsistencies, together with the increasing number of miscarriages of justice exposed in the media, triggered escalating calls in the 1990s to reign in the authority of provincial courts as the final decision-makers in death penalty cases. In 2002, the level of authority to approve death penalties was formally raised as an issue at the 16th Party National Congress. By October 2005, the SPC had explicitly signalled its takeover of this power in the Second Five-Year Program for the Reform of the People's Court.

Chief Justice Xiao Yang, China's then head of the SPC and a tireless legal reformer had initiated meetings with law academics to discuss the leniency and severity balance as early as mid-2006,[25] and issued a number of media statements in November that year. But his big move to dilute the potency of heavy-penaltyism came on 28 December 2006 with two major media statements on the eve of the SPC takeover of the system for approving death sentences. In the first media statement, the SPC wheeled out 'balancing leniency with severity' as its Trojan horse in the death penalty debate, declaring it a new foundational policy for criminal justice in China. The 1997 Criminal Law (CL97) allows for a wide range of discretionary criminal sentences, with the possibility for sentences to be reduced on the grounds of mitigating circumstances. In this context, Xiao Yang announced that criminals in capital cases who surrendered to authorities and criminals who provided important evidence in a criminal case, along with non-principal offenders, would escape immediate execution. Instead, for these convicted criminals, an execution should not be enforced immediately after sentencing, and a two-year suspended death sentence should be handed down as an alternative punishment, automatically reverting to a life sentence after the two years.[26] This would lead to a dramatic and immediate reduction in the number of people executed in China.

For other types of cases – homicides that escalated from domestic or civil disputes, where the perpetrator immediately confessed to a crime and would be able to offer financial compensation to the victim's family – the lower courts were told by the SPC not to consider the death sentence as the first and only alternative. While Xiao Yang insisted that the policy of 'swiftness and severity' would be maintained, he crucially added that it would be reserved for the *most* heinous criminals. To affirm that the SPC would continue to apply the death penalty but only to the small minority of criminals who required the most severe punishment, he added that 'In cases where the evidence is clear and where the death penalty is applicable, we will continue to apply the death penalty and we will not be limp wristed about it'.[27]

Xiao Yang delivered a second speech that day to clarify just how limited lower courts would be in their use of the death sentence after 1 January 2007. He announced that in the near future the SPC would draw up unified national standards for evidence applied to capital cases. These standards would clearly stipulate that to apply the death sentence to a case, 'all the facts must be clear and the evidence compelling'.[28] He claimed that in applying these two principles, courts would return to the 'original' intent and stipulations of the Criminal Procedure Law. But in putting forward these new standards, Xiao Yang was in fact nullifying the use of the 'two basics' in capital cases that had been a mainstay of Strike Hard policy for years.[29] As we recall from Chapter 2, the 'two basics' lower the standards of evidence by which Strike Hard-targeted cases are judged. Judges need only be satisfied that, first, the *basic* facts are clear, and second, the *basic* evidence is conclusive. The term 'basic' in this context means that the key facts are those that can be considered the main components of the crime and the 'essential evidence' is the only evidence required to ascertain criminality and guilt. Note that in reviewing death penalty cases, the SPC would hear, where possible, each defendant's defence in person. Alternatively, in some cases, the defendant would be permitted to write a response to the panel of three SPC judges reviewing the case. Further expanding on post-January 2007 SPC death penalty approval policy, Xiao Yang explained that from that day on, if the three-person panel agreed that the facts were unclear, the evidence was inconclusive, the sentence was too harsh or there were procedural irregularities, then the panel would use its authority under the law to reject the provincial application for approval. However, if there were dissent within the panel, the case would need to go to a specially arranged SPC judicial committee. Where the judicial committee convened to discuss a disputed case, the Head of the Supreme People's Procuratorate or his/her deputy, would be required to attend the meeting to listen to the cases but would not be allowed to participate in discussions. This required attendance serves as both a disincentive mechanism for prosecutors at lower levels to insist on the death penalty at trial of first instance for anything but the most heinous crimes, and an encouragement to lower courts to hand down custodial sentences or suspended death sentences.[30]

Xiao Yang followed his major policy speeches in late December 2006 with a series of SPC 'Judicial Opinions' to lower courts a few weeks later. These expanded on the importance of applying the policy of balancing leniency and severity to individual cases. He explained that cases in which the facts were not clear and the evidence not abundant would not be accepted by the SPC and would be returned to the lower courts for retrial or re-sentencing. Cases in which the facts were clear and evidence was sufficient but which were seen by the SPC to have been sentenced too harshly would also be rejected and sent back to the provinces for re-sentencing. Cases rejected due to unclear facts or insufficient evidence would all need to be retried at the Intermediate Court level.[31]

The most important document to be issued since the 1 January 2007 hand-back of authority was a joint 'Opinion' of the SPC, the Supreme People's Procuratorate (SPP), the MPS and Ministry of Justice, promulgated on 9 March 2007. The document's 52 articles outline the specific procedures for each of the four institutions in the SPC's approval process for the death sentence. One of the most clever and interesting aspects of the document may be the lip service it pays to Strike Hard policy, which is followed immediately by a string of measures that would effectively thwart many traditional Strike Hard strategies. Although Article 3 of the Opinion announced that the four organs would need to 'continue to maintain Strike Hard policy as a method of punishment', and would continue to pursue 'political struggle' against serious criminal offenders, the rhetoric had much less teeth than previous Strike Hard exhortations.[32]

The undermining of Strike Hard appeared in the document where judicial organs were urged to continue, when required, to implement Strike Hard policy 'correctly, fully and precisely', but crucially, only towards an *extremely* small minority (*ji shao*) of offenders whose crimes were *extremely* serious (*ji yanzhong*). The judicial organs were to sentence these criminals to death in accordance with the policies of harmonious society and 'killing fewer, killing cautiously'. Many of the strict procedural regulations outlined in the Opinion either neutralized or frustrated the use of traditional Strike Hard tactics such as 'severe and swift justice' and the 'two basics'. Judicial organs were told not to overlook procedural justice in favour of substantive justice, and not to rely on 'attacking crime' at the expense of guaranteeing a defendant's rights. To be sure, 2007 was a momentous year in the contemporary history of criminal justice in China.

Strike Hard's legacy: the culture of 'kill more'

A key argument put forward in this book is that the politicization of law through campaign justice has had serious consequences for China's attempts to professionalize the ranks of criminal justice and promote a socialist rule of law. Whatever the view of the campaign advocates who have dominated national policy on serious crime until very recently, it can be argued that striking hard at crime through severe and swift punishment may have even encouraged greater volume and gravity of 'serious crime', for two main reasons. First, campaign policy led to a dramatic increase in the number of capital crimes under the Criminal Law, and with non-capital crimes, encouraged judges to hand down longer custodial sentences than would otherwise have been the case. Second, mass imprisonment of public order offenders produced a conga line of hardened and unreformed ex-criminals who, upon release from prison, formed most of the leadership of the army of gang and syndicate members we find in China today. As Chen Xingliang has put it, '"strike hard" and "crime" have been locked into a seesaw struggle in a protracted war against each other'.[33] Many criminals who first entered the prison system in the 1980s grouped together and re-entered society as hooligan gangs, and in the following decade, developed into heinous gangs and then into mafia-style syndicates.[34] Hence, while the party-state has made serious offenders the enemy of modernization and social stability, these offenders have made society their enemy.

The SPC's attempts to limit the application of the death penalty described above have not been about eliminating Strike Hard policy completely. The real point of the debate is related to whom to strike hard and how to limit Strike Hard's scope. Opinion on whom to strike hard varies from opinions by some senior party officials who believe that criminal justice authorities should severely punish a broad range of offenders, to a much more narrow range as put forward by the SPC. How to strike hard is now being renegotiated, including measures aimed at curtailing the immediate execution of those given the death penalty and handing down alternative punishments. In a less perceptible way, the debate which occurred in the wake of changes to the death penalty has been about SPC attempts to diminish the power of Strike Hard by banning a number of practices that the SPC finds dubious and by limiting the types of criminal circumstances that attract the death penalty. At issue here is how each of the various key players (in the SPC and the Politburo especially), interprets the relationship between the goal of harmonious society and the threat of social instability. It is also about the different interpretations of these legal and political bodies about how to achieve social stability. The SPC's Xiao Yang argued that harmonious society can only be achieved by anodizing the brutalizing effect that overzealous use of the death penalty has wrought on society. In this view, a less brutal, more humane, punishment regime is the legal horse that pulls the harmonious society cart. The Politburo's Luo Gan, on the other hand, claimed that 'struggle' through harsh punishment produces social stability which in turn produces a harmonious society.[35]

Strike Hard's presumed efficacy in dealing with serious crime over the last two decades is powerfully tied to an assumption about the potential of harsh punishment to curb social instability. The politburo's line on harsh punishment at the end of 2006 and the beginning of 2007 had been well rehearsed in the decades leading up to the death penalty changes on 1 January 2007. It is that only striking hard can bring about social stability, and only social stability can bring about harmonious society. SPC Chief Xiao Yang introduced a different perspective when he opened up Strike Hard as a crime-fighting strategy to competition from other sources that he argued may also procure social stability. As he illustrated in an interview in

Liaowang, China's largest new weekly internet magazine in February 2007, Strike Hard is just one of numerous possibilities for protecting social stability.

> Maintaining a policy of balancing leniency and severity is a way of promoting social stability. Attacking crime is a way of protecting social stability . . . Resolving social contradictions is also a means of protecting social stability . . . Likewise, maintaining Strike Hard policy also protects social stability. Upholding and respecting individual rights is another way of protecting social stability.[36]

Xiao Yang argued his case firmly in 2007: while serious crime must be punished severely in accordance with the law, and while courts still need to be resolute when firmness is needed, the application of severe punishment must have its basis within the law. Judges, he maintains, must correctly differentiate the severity of crimes, and once this has been done, the criminals whose crimes are not severe must be treated more leniently.[37] Importantly in judging capital cases, he claims, 'When there is a choice either to kill or not to kill, always choose not to kill'.[38]

As noted above, provincial courts were delegated the responsibility for reviewing and approving death sentences handed down by inferior courts to accommodate the policy of severe and swift punishment at the start of the nation's first and bloodiest Strike Hard campaign in 1983. Here was a template for the overzealous use of Strike Hard's severe and swift punishment against serious criminal offenders and a reason for the continually high number of executions in China. The 'kill more' criminal justice culture was a product of the Strike Hard campaign of the 1980s. The number of executions has increased exponentially during Strike Hard campaigns and specialized drives. The culture of heavy penaltyism nourished by these conditions was virtually guaranteed.

Today the death penalty can still be applied to 68 types of offences. But the majority of criminals who are executed have been found guilty of committing a much smaller repertoire of very serious crimes such as murder, manslaughter, serious assault, robbery, rape, and drug trafficking. These crimes are the most frequent campaign targets.[39] Nevertheless, Chen Guangzhong, Professor of Law at the University of Politics and Law in Beijing, argues that it is not simply the large number of offences in the Criminal Law of 1979 that encourages the overuse of capital punishment or the material conditions of China that have made the death sentence so widespread in China since the early 1980s. He claims that the overuse of the death penalty is directly attributable to the Strike Hard principle of meting out mandatory severe punishment encapsulated in the well-rehearsed 1983 dictum that, in cases where the death penalty may be applicable, 'When there is a choice to kill or not to kill, choose to kill; the majority should be killed' (*kesha kebusha sha, duoshu dou dei sha*).[40]

In the new millennium, an increasingly large and vocal chorus of scholars and experts in China have argued against abuses and miscarriages of justice, particularly through capital punishment, along with an unprecedented degree of anti-campaign coverage in the press. Yet, to argue against Strike Hard policy solely on the grounds that it fails both in crime deterrence and in 'rule of law' may be missing an important point about Strike Hard policy, according to at least one researcher. While most academics and criminal justice researchers in China claim that Strike Hard is primarily a criminal justice policy, and proceed to pick at its bones through legal argument, Li Chuan's view is one of the few that are conspicuously different. Li, a researcher at the Shandong Police Academy, argues that Strike Hard was fundamentally political and should be treated that way:

> Strike Hard is an ideological tool of propaganda . . . the victory of Strike Hard lies not in the results of campaigns but in the actual launching of a campaign as a political statement that demonstrates the legitimacy and the political power of the party and government.

This, says Li, is much more important for Strike Hard's political deployment than fighting crime.[41]

Arguments that warn us not to expect to find legal DNA in a creature that is essentially political have some explanatory power, but they should not detract from the now increasingly recognized perspective that the goals of campaigns are unrealistic at best, which has consequences for the carriage of justice at the grassroots. In 1983, Deng Xiaoping announced that the first (and at the time, it was assumed the only) Strike Hard campaign would eliminate serious crime in China. In the 2001–03 campaign, the goals were only marginally less lofty: 'to effect a fundamental turnaround in public order within two years'. As one commentator has queried:

> Why, in the three main Strike Hard campaigns, have we been unable to break out of the cycle that crime 'cannot be completely defeated nor can it be completely prevented'? It's simple. Attacking crime doesn't eliminate crime. The ebb and flow in crime rates are closely connected to social contradictions, so significant reductions in crime cannot come about simply through the efforts of the criminal justice agencies.[42]

These social contradictions include the widening disparity between rich and poor, a significant point when we recognize that China has one of the largest gaps between rich and poor in the world today.

Nowadays, researchers and practitioners alike acknowledge that campaigns alone will not solve the serious crime problem. While the campaign shell will most probably disappear in the decade ahead, it is unlikely that Strike Hard policy, no matter how it is diluted, will disappear entirely in the near future. Certainly, the developments described in this chapter do not suggest a complete end to the practice of severe and swift punishment. After all, it is not the courts or police that own Strike Hard policy – it is the party. The party still leads police and courts in policy matters relating to crime control. Campaigns are initiated by the Central Party Committee's Politico-legal Affairs Committee in Beijing and run under the leadership of the party at national, provincial, municipal and county levels. This includes party organizations run within each court from the basic level up to the SPC. The SPC cannot refuse outright to participate in anti-crime drives.

Moreover, as we found in the conclusion to Chapter 5 on the People's War on Drugs, the debate about the future of campaign justice is complex and not simply a clear-cut 'two-line struggle' between criminal justice agencies and the party. Strike Hard policy targeted at drugs and organized crime remains popular in judicial circles in a number of high crime provinces such as Yunnan, China's drug capital, and Guangdong, China's itinerant worker capital. A number of lower courts were happy to go into battle against their superior court, the SPC, in favour of retaining Strike Hard policy when Xiao Yang and the SPC began the 'balancing leniency and severity' onslaught in the media in late 2006 and early 2007, as can be seen in annual provincial police and court reports delivered to provincial people's congresses in late 2006 and early 2007. As noted in the conclusion to Chapter 5, one such report in December 2006 from Yunnan, China's chief drug province, which has the nation's highest rate of executions and generally hands down a much higher proportion of harsh punishments including death sentences than other provinces, dismissed Xiao Yang's urging to issue suspended death sentences. Despite continued support for *Yanda* policy in some provinces, one of the most positive developments in the 2006–07 debate on heavy penaltyism has been the ability of the SPC, and to a lesser extent the Ministry of Public Security, to weave 'harmonious society' rhetoric into their own set of arguments.

Concluding remarks: wither campaign justice?

So, we may ask, wither campaign justice? Let us consider some further developments in late 2007 and in 2008. In October 2007, Luo Gan retired as head of the Politico-legal Affairs Committee in China. His replacement was Zhou Yongkang, the former national Minister of Public Security. As noted previously, Zhou had been a restrained critic of campaign justice in the past. In December 2007, Chief Justice Xiao Yang announced to *Xinhua* news that for the first time in the history of the PRC, the annual number of suspended death sentences (which would revert to life sentences after two years) exceeded the number of death sentences with immediate execution. In the same month, the SPC Deputy President announced that the number of death sentences in China in 2007 had declined by a huge 33 per cent.[43]

In December 2007, Xiao Yang was nominated and short-listed for China's 'Person of the Year' in a national on-line poll. On 10 March 2008, he retired. The same day, it was announced at the annual National People's Congress that Xiao Yang's replacement as President of the SPC would be none other than one of Luo Gan's right-hand men in the Politico-legal Affairs Committee, Wang Shengjun, a political bureaucrat with no legal training. At his final address to the sitting National People's Congress in March 2008, Xiao Yang observed that 15 per cent of cases sent to Beijing for death sentence approval in 2007 had been rejected by the SPC and sent back to the provinces for retrial or re-sentencing. In the same week, a *Xinhua* news journalist reported on the claim by an international human rights organization that as many as 8,000 people are executed in China each year. The news report neither denied nor acknowledged the accuracy of the figure, but invited comment from Liu Renwen, an SPC legal advisory committee member in charge of researching execution processes. As one of China's senior experts on the death penalty process, Liu responded that China's leading legal experts are now in agreement about the significance and prospect of abolishing the death penalty in China. It is the general public who are most opposed to the move, according to Liu.[44] On 21 March 2008, SPC Deputy President Jiang Xingchang announced that changes to the death penalty application had already had a positive effect on the incidence of violent crime, which declined in 2007, a year that was decidedly short on campaign offensives. Intentional homicides were down by 6.8 per cent, kidnapping by 4.3 per cent, serious assault resulting in death (manslaughter) by 6.1 per cent and robbery by 3.1 per cent.[45] These data sharply contradict the claim about the deterrent effect of harsh punishment.

The politiburo's response to this blatantly anti-death penalty announcement came less than one month into the tenure of its new handpicked President of the Supreme People's Court. The new Chief Justice Wang Shengjun made a comment during a routine inspection visit to courts in Guangdong Province that courted national headlines. In a defiant return to the political nomenclature of Strike Hard in its glory days, Wang announced that,

> We need to maintain the adjudication policy of 'balancing leniency and severity', continuing to make good use of the 'severity' aspect of the policy. At present, incidences of crime are at an extremely high rate, therefore, those cases that should be treated with harsh punishment must be treated with harsh punishment in order to satisfy the expectations of the masses.[46]

More importantly, he went on to emphasize that in relation to capital cases, the policy of 'balancing leniency and severity' should involve three main judicial decision-making criteria: 'The first is the relevant legal stipulations [in relation to routine sentencing criteria within the Criminal Law], the second is the current situation in relation to crime rates and third is the sentiments of the masses'. Not content with this rhetorical bombshell, the likes of which had not be uttered for years, Wang went on to stress that, 'Some may not understand why it is important to make the "feelings of the masses" a criterion. This emphasis is the only way to reconcile positive legal outcomes of a case with positive outcomes for society in general'.[47]

Anti-crime campaigns are the Chinese state's far-reaching response to serious crime, and therefore deserve careful and critical analysis – just as serious crime deserves a careful critical response by Chinese authorities. Campaigns and serious crime are both serious concerns in China. Both have made a palpable impact on Chinese society, governance and policing. The campaign process has made a spectacle of punishment – not just to punish but also to deter. Its performative spectacle reaches across society at all levels, and its judicial decentralization means that considerable power is exercised at the local level, even in areas where access to legally trained and experienced personnel is poor. Through their characteristic approach of 'swiftness and severity', campaigns have seen millions of Chinese incarcerated and thousands put to death. Campaign justice has diminished the prospects for achieving justice in a nation whose report card on human rights has for some time been recognized by national governments, community organizations, and concerned individuals outside China as very poor. The mapping of the campaign landscape provided in this book therefore casts critical light on the important issue of how the state regulates serious crime.

Campaigns have offered a bridge, albeit an unsteady one, between the aspirations of a rule-governed society (expressed as 'the socialist rule of law') on the one hand, and the impact of unprecedented economic reforms that have produced new forms of social instability. The financial and professional limitations placed on criminal justice institutions curbed the development of a system of 'rule-governed order' as a viable legal culture. But, the promises of socialist democracy and the socialist 'rule of law' had already been made to the public when the first Strike Hard campaign was introduced in 1983 and these promises could not be completely withdrawn. This led to the difficult marriage between the aspiration to a socialist rule of law and hard-line justice, the product of which was a series of strategies built around the rhetoric of punishing 'severely and swiftly' but doing so 'in accordance with the law'.

The discussion about campaign justice in this chapter, in particular the survey of the SPC's ambitious reforms, is arguably the beginning of a civilizing process in relation to the death penalty and the culture of heavy penaltyism. As in eighteenth- and nineteenth-century Europe, the elites are leading this drive. Language played an enormous role in the civilizing process in Europe through the popularization of vocabulary such as 'benevolence' and 'charity'. In contemporary China, too, language cast in terms such as 'harmonious society' rhetoric is playing a real role in reform on the death penalty. However, the upsurge in 'benevolence' and 'harmony' in China today, as was the case in Europe two centuries ago, needs not only to be expressed in language, but in a determination on the part of social reformers to 'ameliorate the human lot and to reduce the amount of sheer physical cruelty in the world'.[48] Weakening the culture of heavy penaltyism has a long way to go before we see a stable, uniform and regularized practice of punishing serious crime throughout China. Attempts by Xiao Yang and the SPC to sharpen the definition of 'extremely serious crime' in order to narrow the definition of which categories of criminal find their way to China's gallows is indeed a momentous step. And as this volume has suggested, senior police have also played their part in Strike Hard's fall from grace. The next phase in moving towards a more stable and just regime will be in the hands of legislators, who will need to make substantial changes to the Criminal Law to limit further the fast and loose application of severe punishment, particularly the death penalty. The landscape of serious crime and severe punishment in China is surely set to stay richly textured with politics for at least the foreseeable future.

Notes

Introduction

1 See, for example, David Garland, *The Culture of Control: crime and social order in contemporary society*.

2 Two different types of 'order' are articulated in Chinese criminal legal theory as the main objects of criminal activity (*fanzui de keti*) that attract Strike Hard treatment. They are the social order (*shehui zhixu*) and the public order (*shehui zhi'an*). The 'social order' is a general term that refers to a state of stability in society characterized by a highly ordered and stable social environment. A sound social order is manifest in orderly and stable economic production and social relations in the community. Violent and contact crimes such as homicide, rape, arson, assault, kidnapping and armed robbery threaten the public's sense of security. The 'public order' on the other hand is a phenomenon that encompasses both the material (economic) and the ideological/behavioural realm and includes crimes such as property offences (mainly theft), organizing prostitution rings and manufacturing pornographic materials. In all campaigns, the interpretation of the social danger of certain crimes has informed the response of criminal justice agencies to particular categories of crime. See Liu Hua, 'Hooliganism', p. 57.

3 Lin Zhongliang, *Geji danwei zhengfa wei de zhineng ji hongguan zhengfa gongzuo* (The Functions and Macroscopic Tasks of the Politico-legal Affairs Work of Politico-legal Affairs Committees at all Levels of Government), p. 338.

4 Ibid.

5 Jiang Pusheng, 'Yanda zhengzhi douzheng de huigu yu sikao' (A reflective look back at the Strike Hard campaign), p. 39.

6 Lu Zhuo, 'Dui xian jieduan yanda zhengzhi douzheng de lixing sikao' (A rational reflection on this current stage of the Strike Hard campaign), p. 33.

7 Ibid.

8 As Borge Bakken explains, financial incentives encourage police to engage in 'creative accounting' because they are paid by the rate of solved cases. Police therefore 'improve' statistics for solved crime by reducing the number of reported crime cases, and inflating the number of solved cases in police records. Borge Bakken, 'Moral panics, crime rates and harsh punishment in China', p. 75.

9 In the 22 years from the start of the first Strike Hard campaign in 1983 to the end of 2005, over 120 million people were formally arrested, detained and charged with a criminal offence in China (almost one tenth of the nation's current population). And in 2005, over 1.4 million people were serving prison sentences in China. These figures exclude the millions who have been charged with committing unlawful acts and have been dealt with under the system of administrative punishment. Many of these people who have committed misdemeanours have served or are still serving up to three years in 'reeducation through labour' facilities that are not part of the criminal justice system

but the administrative punishment system run by police. See Li Jingui, 'Kuanyan xiangji shi woguo jiben xingshi zhengce' (Balancing leniency and severity is a fundamental criminal justice policy in China), http://review.jcrb.com/zyw/n124/ca514495.htm (accessed 30 September 2007).

10 For the most insightful study of the death penalty to date outside China, see David T. Johnson and Franklin E. Zimring, *The Next Frontier: national development, political change and the death penalty in Asia*, pp. 225–86. For a discussion of the estimated annual number of executions, see pp. 231–42.

11 Chen Xingliang, 'Kuanyan xiangji xingshi zhengce yanjiu' (A study of the criminal justice policy of balancing leniency and severity), p. 19.

12 For a discussion of the implementation of severe and swift punishment prior to the first Strike Hard campaign in 1983, see Susan Trevaskes, *Courts and Criminal Justice in Contemporary China*.

13 The 'Statute on the Punishment for Counterrevolutionary Activity' identified three main types of crime that fell into the categories of the counterrevolutionary offences aimed at overthrowing the popular democratic regimes and undermining the people's democracy: first, political crimes such as treason, espionage, incitement, assassination and sabotage; second, crimes relating to corruption (for example, bribery) and, third, social crimes against the person, including assault and murder. Albert P. Blaustein, 'Introduction', *Fundamental Legal Documents of Communist China*, p. xix. Note that many of the definitions for crimes listed in the 1951 Act have their precedent in the Punishment of Counterrevolutionary Crimes Act of the Chinese Soviet Republic in 1934. The 1934 Act makes reference to similar crimes including assassination, espionage and political sabotage. See translation of 'Statute of the Chinese Soviet Republic on Punishment for Counter-Revolutionary Crimes (1934)', in W.E. Butler, *The Legal System of the Chinese Soviet Republic 1931–1934*, pp. 204–08. Note also that there were other minor regulations in the 1950s which include the Order of the State Administrative Council Concerning the Strict Prohibition of Opium and Other Narcotics, 1950; the Provisional Regulations for the Surveillance of Counterrevolutionary Elements, 1952; and the Provisional Regulations on Penalties for Undermining the State Monetary System, 1951; the Provisional Regulations on Safeguarding State Secrets, 1951; and the Regulations on Reform Through Labour, 1954.

14 The punishments listed in the Statute on Penalties for Corruption are broader in scope than those outlined in the Statute of Punishment for Counterrevolutionary Activity and include almost the entire gamut of punishments available. This included 'supplementary' punishments such as reprimand, fine, confiscation of property, deprivation of political rights, suspension of sentence and 'principal' punishments such as fixed term imprisonment, life imprisonment and the death penalty. For a summary of punishments see translated excerpts from a series of lectures on criminal law by the Teaching and Research Office for Criminal Law of the Central Politico-legal Cadres' School, *Chung-hua jen-min kung-ho-kuo hsing-fa tsung-tse chiang-i*, translated in Jerome Cohen, *The Criminal Process in the People's Republic of China, 1949–63: an introduction*, pp. 514–30, 535, 211–12. Hereafter referred to as 'The Lectures'. Also see Blaustein's translation, 'Statute on Penalties for Corruption (1952)', in Blaustein, *Fundamental Legal Documents of Communist China*, pp. 227–29.

15 Blaustein, *Fundamental Legal Document of Communist China*, p. xxi.

16 Borge Bakken, 'The culture of revenge and the power of politics: a comparative attempt to explain the punitive', p. 174.

17 Ibid., p. 178.

18 Ibid., p. 180.

19 Ibid., p. 170. For further arguments against the 'culture' thesis, see Ibid., pp. 178–80.

20 David Garland, 'Concepts of culture in the sociology of punishment', p. 437.

21 Ibid., p. 438.

22 Ibid. (my emphasis).
23 Daqing and Dazhai are the two cities in northern China that Mao Zedong's Supreme Directives put forward as model cities in the 1960s. Rich in oil and gas from the Daqing oilfield, Daqing was to host industries that would take advantage of these energy resources, to serve as a model of good practice in industry and healthcare. Dazhai, a village in Shanxi Province, was its agricultural counterpart. With the slogan 'Learn from Dazhai,' it was made a national agricultural model for China's farmers.
24 Shenzhen is the biggest of the four Special Economic Zones (SEZs), set up in 1979 as the national model for Deng Xiaoping's new economic reforms.
25 Michael Dutton makes this observation. For an examination of police work in the Suppression of Counterrevolutionaries Campaign see Michael Dutton, *Policing Chinese Politics: a history*, pp. 160–79.
26 Ibid., p. 298.
27 Ibid., p. 16.
28 As he notes, Maoist China lived life politically and, in the process, transformed everything into a binary political question framed in the language of class. No longer would class operate as a purely economic category. Instead, it became the crucial point of decision dividing the world of Mao into friend and enemy. Ibid., p. 304.
29 Ibid., p. 4.
30 Ibid., p. 12.
31 Ibid., p. 19.
32 Ibid., p. 18.
33 Ibid.
34 Ibid.
35 Ibid., p. 19.
36 Ibid., pp. 299–300.
37 David Garland, *The Culture of Control: crime and social order in contemporary society*, p. 133.
38 Jonathan Simon, *Governing Through Crime: how the war on crime transformed American democracy and created a culture of fear*, pp. 112–13.
39 This claim is explored at length in Chapter 2.
40 Mao Zedong, 'Jiguanqiang he paijipao de laili ji qita', (The origin of machine guns and mortar among other things) in Zhongyang wenxian yanjiushi, *Jianguo yilai Mao Zedong wengao* (Mao Zedong's Works Since the Establishment of the PRC), p. 452.
41 'Mao Zedong huijian meiguo qianzongtong lichade nikesong de nu'er zhuli nikesong-aizenhaowei'er he nikesong de nuxu daiwei aizenhaowei'er de tanhua jilu' (Mao Zedong's talk with Julie Nixon-Eisenhower (daughter of former president Richard Nixon) and David Eisenhower (Nixon's son-in-law), Zhonggong zhongyang danganguan, *Bada yilai zhonggong zhongyang wenjian ji* (Selected Documents of the Central Party-Government since the Eighth Party Congress, Volume 12 (1976), unpublished Central Party-Government materials, 1997, p. 17.
42 Trevaskes, *Courts and Criminal Justice in Contemporary China*, p. 215.
43 'PRC's Xinjiang executes 15 criminals after public sentencing', *Xinjiang ribao* (Xinjiang Daily), 16 November 2001, FBIS Document no.: FBIS-CHI-1204.
44 Tanner, 'State coercion and the balance of awe', p. 646.
45 Robert Grafstein, 'Legitimacy of political institutions', p. 58, cited in John Brigham, *The Cult of the Court*, p. 30.
46 Garland, *Punishment and Modern Society*, p. 282.
47 Ibid. A more detailed analysis of Garland's observation is made in Susan Trevaskes, *Courts and Criminal Justice in Contemporary China*, p. 21.
48 Garland, *Punishment and Modern Society*, p. 285.
49 Han Yanlong, *Zhonghua renmin gongheguo fazhi tongshi* (A Comprehensive History of the Legal System in the People's Republic of China), pp. 870–71; Murray Tanner

notes that other sources put the figure at over two million. See Murray Scot Tanner, 'Campaign-style policing in China and its critics', p. 175.

50 See Tanner, 'Campaign-style policing in China and its critics', p. 175.

51 Harold Tanner, *Strike Hard!: anti-crime campaigns and Chinese criminal justice 1979–1989*,; Murray Scot Tanner, 'State coercion and the balance of awe: the 1983–1986 "Stern Blows" anti-crime campaign', pp. 93–125; and Trevaskes, *Courts and Criminal Justice in Contemporary China.*

52 Borge Bakken, *The Exemplary Society: human improvement, social control and the dangers of modernity in China*, p. 394.

53 Zeng Guangwen, *Beijingzhi: gong'anzhi* (The Beijing Annals: chronicles of the Beijing Public Security), p. 148.

54 The complete listing of nationally initiated specialized drives and larger Strike Hard campaigns from 1986 to 2007 on p. 43 of this book brings home this key point about Strike Hard's relentlessness.

55 Guo Xingguo, *Jianguo yilai gongan gongzuo dashi yaolan* (National Overview of Public Security Work Since the Establishment of the People's Republic), pp. 645–1299 and Bi Xiqian and Chen Juan, 'Yanda zhengzhi douzheng de huigu yu zhanwang' (A look back and a look ahead at the Strike Hard rectification campaign), pp. 45–50.

1 The rise of campaign justice

1 Sarah Biddulph's *Legal Reform and Administrative Detention Powers in China* is the only English-language study to discuss a specialized struggle, the 'Six-evils' campaign, which was primarily against minor not serious crime.

2 Borge Bakken, 'Moral panics, crime rates and harsh punishment in China', pp. 67–68.

3 This account of party leadership in Strike Hard 1983–86 is primarily from the restricted access publication, Guo Xingguo, *Jianguo yilai gongan gongzuo dashi yaolan* (An Outline of the Chronicles of Public Security Work Since Liberation); (hereby referred to in-text as *The Chronicles*) and from restricted public security annals at grassroots level. *The Chronicles* is an internally circulated reference resource for public security bureaucrats and all former heads of public security since the 1980s including Liu Fuzhi, the Minister of Public Security at the time of the first Strike Hard, provided materials, verified and signed off on the events described.

4 Guo, *Jianguo yilai gongan gongzuo dashi yaolan,* p. 534.

5 For more details on the targets of the 1983–86 campaign, see Harold M. Tanner, *Strike Hard!: anti-crime campaigns and Chinese criminal justice 1979–1989*; Murray Scot Tanner, 'State coercion and the balance of awe: the 1983–1986 "Stern Blows" anti-crime campaign', pp. 93–125 and Susan Trevaskes, *Courts and Criminal Justice in Contemporary China.*

6 These figures are recorded in Zhao Ying, *Guizhou shenpanzhi* (Annals of Trial Work in Guizhou), p. 339 and Zhao Rixin, *Liaoning shenpanzhi* (Annals of Trial Work in Liaoning), Neibu chugao (Draft document for internal circulation), p. 365, (no publication year recorded).

7 Mu Yumin, *Beijing jingcha bainian* (One Hundred Years of Policing in Beijing), p. 608.

8 Tanner, *Strike Hard!*, p. 98.

9 Qian Qiang, Li Yaojie and Li Suoping, 'Qianlun zhuanxiang douzheng de jiben tezheng' (An outline of the basic characteristics of specialized struggles), p. 38.

10 Chen Jiping, *Zhongguo shehui zhi'an zonghe zhili nianjian 2001–2002* (2001–2002 Yearbook of Comprehensive Management of Public Order in China), p. 646.

11 Qian *et al.*, 'Qianlun zhuanxiang douzheng de jiben tezheng', p. 36.

12 'Sichuan kuangbiao xingdong diyiyi' (The first battle of 'Operation Hurricane' begins in Sichuan), *Renminwang* (People's Daily online), www.people.com.cn/GB/shehui/43/index.html, (accessed 28 April 2001).

13 Ibid.
14 Qian *et al.*, 'Qianlun zhuanxiang douzheng de jiben tezheng', p. 37.
15 Ibid.
16 Ibid.
17 Susan Trevaskes, 'Propaganda work in Chinese courts: public trials and sentencing rallies as sites of expressive punishment and public education in the People's Republic of China', pp. 5–23.
18 For example, even in the twenty-first century, the number of crimes committed in the Beijing district sub-bureaus of Chaoyang, Haidian and Fengtai districts accounted for 50 per cent of the total number of crimes committed in the entire city, even though these districts had only 30 per cent of the city's criminal detectives. See Qian *et al.*, 'Qianlun zhuanxiang douzheng de jiben tezheng' p. 37. On police funding, see Fu Hualing, 'Zhou Yongkang and the recent police reform in China', pp. 241–53 and Fu Hualing and D.W. Choy, 'Policing for profit: fiscal crisis and institutionalized corruption of China's police', pp. 537–52.
19 Qian *et al.*, 'Qianlun zhuanxiang douzheng de jiben tezheng', p. 37.
20 Ibid.
21 Huang Jianmin (ed.), *Guangxi shenpanzhi* (The Annals of Court work in Guangxi), p. 207.
22 Ibid.
23 Zeng Guangwen, *Beijingzhi: gonganzhi* (The Beijing Annals: chronicles of the Beijing public security), p. 148.
24 Ibid., p. 149.
25 Guo, *Jianguo yilai gongan gongzuo dashi yaolan*, p. 797.
26 Mu Yumin, *Beijing Jingcha bainian*, p. 711.
27 Ibid., p. 712.
28 Ibid.
29 Guo, *Jianguo yilai gongan gongzuo dashi yaolan*, p. 798.
30 Ibid., p. 889.
31 Ibid., p. 912.
32 Ibid., p. 964.
33 Ibid., p. 986.
34 Ibid., p. 1009.
35 Ibid., p. 1046.
36 Ibid., p. 1068.
37 Ibid., p. 1070.
38 Ibid., p. 1072.
39 Mu, *Beijing Jingcha bainian*, p. 722.
40 Ibid., p. 722.
41 Ibid.
42 At the same time, because some police stations at the local level were still without intranet access, the Ministry of Public Security made 36,000 CDs of the wanted list of criminals who police were to find within three months. In Beijing, around 4,000 fugitives were caught during the campaign, the majority as a result of the intranet database.
43 Lin Zhongliang, *Geji danwei zhengfa wei de zhineng ji hongguan zhengfa gongzuo* (The Functions and Macroscopic Tasks of the Politico-legal Affairs Work of Politico-legal Affairs Committees at all Levels of Government), p. 359.
44 See for instance, Jing Yingming, 'Yanhai diqu gonggong anquan fazhan zhanlue de Beijing guandian he moshi' (Background, issues and patterns in the development of public security in coastal regions), p. 99.
45 See Murray Scot Tanner, 'Campaign-style policing in China and its critics', p. 183.
46 See Tanner, 'Campaign-style policing', p. 177.
47 Ibid.
48 Ibid., p. 178.

49 Ibid.
50 Ibid.
51 A detailed examination of 'comprehensive management of public order' appears in Chapter 5.
52 Tanner, 'Campaign-style policing', p. 182.
53 Ibid.
54 Ibid., p. 184.
55 Guo, *Jianguo yilai gongan gongzuo dashi yaolan*, pp. 1300–01.
56 Ibid., p. 1302.

2 The campaign template

1 The author would like to thank the British Journal of Criminology for permission to use an earlier version of some of the contents of this chapter from the originally published SusanTrevaskes, 'Severe and Swift Justice in China', *British Journal of Criminology* 47 (1), 2007, pp. 23–41.
2 Lin Zhongliang, *Geji danwei zhengfa wei de zhineng ji hongguan zhengfa gongzuo* (The Functions and Macroscopic Tasks of the Politico-legal Affairs Work of Politico-legal Affairs Committees at all levels of Government), p. 177.
3 Ibid., p. 361.
4 Ibid.
5 A. James Gregor, *The Ideology of Fascism: the rationale of totalitarianism*, p. 353. Cited in Larry Cata Backer, 'The party as polity, the communist party, and the Chinese constitutional state: a theory of state-party constititutionalism', *Journal of Chinese and Comparative Law* 16 (1), 2009, p. 150.
6 'Wenge zuofeng zaixian: cunming beibixuan liejiren' (A throwback to the cultural revolution: villagers pronounced as 'bad seeds'), www.Chinanews.com/2001-10-19/26/131804.html (accessed on 19 October 2005).
7 Ibid. Anyone who refused to participate in the vote was fined 200 yuan. Despite Tang's declaration that the campaign had been launched by the Central Party Committee's Politburo and that every person must select five bad seeds, attempts to force villagers to vote were unsuccessful because villagers were unwilling to nominate their neighbours. As one villager explained: 'We don't know who is a bad seed. We don't have drug-users. We're so poor we don't have enough to eat. We don't own anything worth stealing. Do we look like we have money to drink alcohol? So we simply could not vote. We don't know anyone in these categories.' The voting resumed the following night, but the villagers still couldn't decide on even one bad seed. Only Deputy Mayor Tang voted for someone: a 14-year-old boy who had been sent to the meeting to represent his family. When the Deputy Mayor called his father's name at the attendance roll, the boy had responded in place of his father, inducing the deputy mayor's ire. After five nights, 70 people were finally selected, mostly by the local government and party representatives in the village. One was Lu Duke, who was fined 500 yuan (including a 200 yuan fine for allowing his wife to plant crops on government land). With no money for the fine, he arranged for a loan, which came through 24 hours later and thus inspired a further 500 yuan fine. As a result, Lu Duke fled the village. Two brothers were each fined 250 yuan and required to do four days community service, but on the fifth day they were required to select two more bad seeds in their place before they were allowed to return home. Unwilling to provide any names, they were tied to a tree for hours and fined another 1,200 yuan. These brothers also fled the village. A retired local bank manager and his two sons were selected by local cadres. One of the sons was beaten and ran away, while the other son was not even aware of his new classification and continued working in a neighbouring town.
8 Deputy Mayor Tang announced that his act was an attempt to defraud the party, fined the man 350 yuan, and made him stand in a corner for eight hours. Another resident also

nominated himself, his wife and two children, which Tang declared to be 'an act of defrauding the Communist Party' because he had 'only' nominated four people, and forced the man to stand in a corner for 16 hours. Similar actions were repeated in surrounding villages, with some villagers forced to sell their few possessions, even down to the family cow.

9 Wang Keqin, 'Gongxuan lieji yinbao baozi heimu' (Scam of pronouncing 'bad seeds' exposed).

10 Ibid.

11 Zhao Jianming, 'Yanda bairi gongjian huizhan dakai xumu' (The curtain opens on the public security's 'hundred day decisive battle' to assault fortified positions).

12 Punishment would be both financial and through means such as forced public apologies. Success would be measured in numbers. As Xu explained: 'In this decisive battle, we have four rock-solid regulations . . . [First], with regard to municipal sub-bureaus that haven't met the required quotas, the sub-bureau heads and other senior officers will not be eligible to receive their annual bonus. Any good work done before the campaign that might have been counted towards their bonus, will be disregarded . . . [Second], not only will these unsuccessful municipal sub-bureau heads receive this treatment, their entire staff – police and administrators – will also not be eligible for their annual bonus . . . [Third], the three worst performing municipal heads [of the total of 15 sub-bureaus] will be ineligible to receive bonuses or promotions, regardless of whether or not they fulfil their quotas . . . [Fourth], the bureau head and his/her chief of criminal investigations in charge of the three worst performing municipal sub-bureaus will be called to Shenyang to give a public self-criticism.' See Liu Chenjun, 'Liaoning kaizhan bairi yanda' (Liaoning launches a hundred-day Strike Hard).

13 Ibid.

14 'Zhejiang taixun zai dianyingyuan li shenpan tanguan, sanbai ming gangbu peiou pangting' (Three hundred officials' wives attend the criminal trial of a corrupt official in a cinema in taixun County, Zhejiang Province), *Chongqing chenbao* (Chongqing Morning Post), 23 September 2005, p. 1.

15 Ibid.

16 Ibid.

17 Roger Cotterrell, *Law's Community: legal theory in sociological perspective*, p. 4.

18 Ibid.

19 Perry Keller, 'Sources of order in Chinese law', p. 721.

20 Ibid., p. 754.

21 Lin Hua (ed.), *Zhongguo falu jichu* (The Foundations of Chinese law), p. 18.

22 Chou En-lai, 'Report on the work of the government', given at the 4th meeting of the 1st session of the NPC, 26 June 1957, *Chung-hua jen-min kung-ho-kuo fa-ling hui-pien* (Collection of laws and decrees of the People's Republic of China), pp. 93–94, (Excerpt in Jerome Cohen, *The Criminal Process in the People's Republic of China, 1949–63: an introduction*, p. 297).

23 Ibid., p. 297.

24 A. Vyshinsky, *The Law of the Soviet State*, p. 50, cited in Phillip M. Chen, *Law and Justice: the legal system in China 2400 BC to 1960 AD*, p. 77.

25 As Philip Chen notes: 'It is a theory which has to produce "legal principles". But these legal principles are not the positive law that is to be established on the basis of these principles. If they are to be "legal" principles, they are legal not in the sense of positive law, but in the sense of norms of an ideal law, the law that ought to be established in a socialist society. It stands to reason that these principles are the ideal norms of a socialist law.' Chen, *Law and Justice*, p. 73. Perry Keller takes up this point. Keller argues that the instrumentalist conception of law in China developed closely along the lines of Vyshinsky's idea of law as the positive expression, in normative form, of current Party policy. See Keller, 'Sources of order in Chinese law', p. 721.

26 The punishments listed in the Statute on Penalties for Corruption are broader in scope than those outlined in the Statute of Punishment for Counterrevolutionary Activity and include almost the entire gamut of punishments available. This included 'supplementary' punishments such as reprimand, fine, confiscation of property, deprivation of political rights, suspension of sentence and 'principal' punishments such as fixed term imprisonment, life imprisonment and the death penalty. For a summary of punishments see translated excerpts from a series of lectures on criminal law by the Teaching and Research Office for Criminal Law of the Central Political-Legal Cadres' School (ed.), *Chung-hua jen-min kung-ho-kuo hsing-fa tsung-tse chiang-i*, translated in Jerome Cohen, *The Criminal Process in the People's Republic of China, 1949–63: An Introduction*, pp. 514–30, 535, 211–12. Hereafter referred to as 'The Lectures'. Also see Blaustein's translation, 'Statute on penalties for corruption, (1952), in Blaustein, *Fundamental Legal Documents of Communist China*, pp. 227–29.

27 Blaustein, *Fundamental Legal Document of Communist China*, p. xxi.

28 Peng Zhen's 'Explanation of the Draft Act of the PRC for Punishment of Corruption' notes that the Act was based on the 'experience that has been accumulated during the "three-anti" and "five-anti" movements'. Peng Chen (Deputy Chairman of the Political-Legal Committee of the Government Administrative Council of the Central People's Government), 'Explanation of the Draft Act of the PRC for Punishment of Corruption', *Hsin-hua yueh-bao* (New China Monthly), pp. 23–24, translation in Cohen, *The Criminal Process in the People's Republic of China*, p. 312.

29 Dong Biwu, quoted in Wu Jianfan, 'Building China's New Legal System', John R. Oldman (ed.) *China's Legal Development*, pp. 19–20.

30 Peng Zhen, (11 May 1951) cited in James Brady, *Justice and Politics in People's China: legal order or continuing revolution?*, p. 91.

31 Shen Chun-ju, Speech made to the third session of the first National Committee of the CPPCC on 28 October 1951, cited in Philip Chen, *Law and Justice*, p. 88.

32 S.B. Thomas, *Government and Administration in Communist China*, p. 106.

33 With regard to the 'nature' of a crime, an act of larceny, for example, would be considered a crime but an act of 'taking advantage in a small way' would not be. An act of uttering 'backward words and deeds' would be less socially dangerous than a crime of 'counterrevolutionary provocation and incitement'. 'The Lectures' explain that: 'A judgement as to what kind of act is a serious act can generally be made on the basis of peoples' social practice. In judicial practice, we regard as criminal acts counterrevolutionary acts which infringe the people's democratic system of our country, homicide which infringes the lives of others, robbery, rape, etc.' See 'The Lectures', in Cohen, *The Criminal Process in the People's Republic of China*, p. 330.

34 'The Lectures', in Cohen, *The Criminal Process in the People's Republic of China*, p. 333.

35 Susan Trevaskes, *Courts and Criminal Justice in Contemporary China*, p. 95.

36 Article 2, Chapter 1, General Provision, *Criminal Law of the People's Republic of China*, p. 11.

37 Zhao Zhenjiang (ed.), *Zhongguo fazhi sishinian* (Forty Years of the Chinese Legal System), p. 54.

38 For example, according to one text, law in the post-1978 period embodies the nature of the 'broad masses' (*guangfan de renminxing*); it possesses a genuinely democratic nature (*zhenzheng de minzhuxing*), a highly scientific nature (*gaoji de kexuexing*) and a genuinely just nature (*zhenzheng de zhengyixing*). See Lin, *Zhongguo falu jichu*, pp. 15–17.

39 Ronald Keith and Zhiqiu Lin, *New Crime in China: public order and human rights*, p. 10.

40 Deng Xiaoping, 'The present situation and the tasks before us', *Selected Works of Deng Xiaoping* (1975–82), p. 227, cited in Keith and Lin, *New Crime in China*, p. 10.

41 Keith and Lin, *New Crime in China*, pp. 10–11.

42 Article 13, *Criminal Law of the People's Republic of China*, Beijing: China Legal System Publishing House, 2000, p. 17.
43 Du Xichuan and Zhang Lingyuan, *Chinese Legal System: a general survey*, p. 104.
44 Ronald C. Keith, *China's Struggle for the Rule of Law*, pp. 154–55.
45 Keith and Lin, *New Crime in China*, p. 20.
46 Chen Xingliang, 'Kuanyan xiangji xingshi zhengce yanjiu', p. 17.
47 Ibid.
48 Ibid., p. 18.
49 Ibid.
50 Chen Xingliang, 'An examination of the death penalty in China', p. 37.
51 Jiang Zhu, 'Stress improving public order at national meeting', *Xinhua* News 3 April 2001, FBIS-CHI-2001–0403.
52 Ibid.
53 Ibid.
54 As head of the Politico-legal Affairs Committee within the Party's Central Committee, Luo Gan was the nation's most central player in the formulation of criminal justice policy at the time and was therefore instrumental in Strike Hard policy-making.
55 Guo, *Jianguo yilai gongan gongzuo dashi yaolan*, p. 1375.
56 Lin, *Zhengfa wei de zhineng ji hongguan zhengfa gongzuo*, p. 368.
57 Ibid., p. 177.
58 Ibid., p. 1.
59 Ibid., pp. 32–33.
60 Ibid., p. 34.
61 From an organizational perspective, the secretary of the Politico-legal Affairs Committee is the director of CMPO Committee (the directorship is a part-time position). All standing members of the Politico-legal Affairs Committee take 'front bench' senior membership positions in the CMPO Committee. The full-time administrator, the secretary-general of the CMPO Committee, is also the secretary-general in the Politico-legal Affairs Committee. The Politico-legal Affairs Committee and the CMPO Committee operate physically out of the same office. The day-to-day work of the CMPO Committee is, in practice, carried out under the directorship of the Politico-legal Affairs Committee. 'Back bench' members of the CMPO Committee are bureau heads of government, culture, education, finance and tax offices. Lin, *Geji danwei zhengfa wei de zhineng ji hongguan zhengfa gongzuo*, p. 400.
62 The Report of the 16th Party Congress in 2002, Lin points out, makes it clear that to perfect the tasks of reform and development, the Party must maintain a long-term, harmonious social environment. Lin, *Zhengfa wei de zhineng ji hongguan zhengfa gongzuo*, p. 181.
63 Lin, *Geji danwei zhengfa wei de zhineng ji hongguan zhengfa gongzuo*, p. 177.
64 Ibid., p. 178.
65 Ibid.
66 Ibid., p. 180.
67 Lin, *Geji danwei zhengfa wei de zhineng ji hongguan zhengfa gongzuo*, p. 361.
68 Ibid., p. 369.
69 Wang Zhiqing, *Xiaoyi gonganzhi* (Annals of Xiaoyi Public Security Work), p. 181.
70 Ibid.
71 Ibid.
72 'Henan gongkai xuanpan 1,168 yanzhong xingshi fanzui fenzi' (1,168 serious criminal offenders publicly sentenced in Henan), www.people.com.cn/GB/shehui43/index/.html, 23 April 2001 (accessed 25 August 2001).
73 'Shanghai dui yipi yanzhong baoli fanzui jinxing jizhongxuanpan' (A batch of serious violent offenders sentenced en masse in Shanghai), *Renmin wang Fajie dongtai* (People's Daily online: legal trends), www.people.com.cn/GB/shehui/43/index. html, 12 April 2001 (accessed 9 September 2001).

74 Xu Xiaogang, 'Shenhua renshi qianghua cuoshe, tuidong yanda zhengzhi douzheng shenru fazhan' (Deepen understanding and strengthen measure, expatiate a deepened development of the Strike Hard campaign'), p. 38.
75 Xu, 'Shenhua renshi', p. 38.
76 Lin, *Zhengfa wei de zhineng ji hongguan zhengfa gongzuo*, p. 368.
77 'Henan Zhengzhou juxing gongpu dahui shimin hecai, zhuanjia zhiyi' (Public arrest rallies held in Zhengzhou Henan, residents applaud but the experts call the practice into question), *Xinhua* News, www.xinhuanet.com/legal/2007–09/10/content_669564_1.htm, 10 September 2007 (accessed 10 September 2007).
78 Ibid.
79 Ibid.
80 Trevaskes, *Courts and Criminal Justice in Contemporary China*, pp. 173–76.
81 Ibid., pp. 104–08.
82 Ibid., p. 98.
83 Tanner, *Strike Hard*, p. 91.
84 For a detailed and insightful account of administrative punishment in China see Sarah Biddulph, *Legal Reform and Administrative Detention Powers in China.*
85 Sun Guoyang, 'Xingshi yituhua shiyexia "strike hard" de lixingsikao' (A rational reflection on the implementation of an integrated vision of criminal justice work into the Strike Hard campaign), p. 99; and Zhuang Huining, 'Renmin fayuan zai strike hard zhengzhizhong tuilian duiwu (The people's courts' training of contingents during Strike Hard), p. 31.
86 For a more detailed account of 'swiftness', see Susan Trevaskes, 'Severe and swift justice in China', pp. 28–30.
87 Zou Wei, Zhang Dechang and Chen Wenquan, 'Lun xinshiqi de yanda fangzhen', (On Strike Hard policy' in the New Age) *Guizhou jinggua zhiye xueyuan xuebao*, pp. 14–17.
88 Trevaskes, *Courts and Criminal Justice in Contemporary China*, p. 175.
89 'Shanghai dui yipi yanzhong baoli fanzui jinxing jizhongxuanpan' (A batch of serious violent offenders sentenced en masse in Shanghai), *Renmin wang fajie dongtai* (People's Daily online: legal trends), www.people.com.cn/GB/shehui/43/index.html, 12 April 2001 (accessed 9 September 2001). This is press statement by the Court President, Shanghai Higher People's Court, 21 April 2001.
90 'Decision of the Standing Committee of the National People's Congress regarding the severe punishment of criminals who seriously endanger public security', *The Laws of the People's Republic of China (1983–1986)*, p. 32.
91 For a more detailed examination of the hooligan as a campaign target, see Harold M. Tanner, *Strike Hard!: anti-crime campaigns and Chinese criminal justice 1979–1989*; Murray Scot Tanner, 'State coercion and the balance of awe: the 1983–1986 "Stern Blows" anti-crime campaign', pp. 93–125 and Trevaskes, *Courts and Criminal Justice in Contemporary China.*
92 Sun, 'Xingshi yitihua shiyexia "yanda" de lixing sikao', p. 99.
93 Susan Trevaskes, 'Propaganda work in Chinese Courts', pp. 6–8.
94 Trevaskes, *Courts and Criminal Justice in Contemporary China*, p. 60.
95 Ibid., pp. 60–61.
96 Ibid., pp. 71–73; and Susan Trevaskes, 'Severe and swift justice in China', pp. 23–41.
97 *Yanchang wanbao* (Yancheng Evening News), 25 April 2001.
98 Trevaskes, *Courts and Criminal Justice in Contemporary China*, pp. 71–73; and Trevaskes, ' Severe justice in China', pp. 23–41.
99 'Henan Zhengzhou juxing gongpu dahui shimin hecai, zhuanjia zhiyi' (Public arrest rallies held in Zhengzhou Henan. Residents applaud but experts call the practice into question) *Xinhua* News, www.xinhuanet.com/legal/2007-09/10/content_669564_1.htm, 10 September 2007 (accessed 10 September 2007).

100 For a detailed examination of sentencing rallies see Susan Trevaskes, *Courts and Criminal Justice in Contemporary China*, pp. 59–80.
101 'Sichuansheng fayuan yanli daji yanzhong xingshi fanzui gongzuo huiyi', (Sichuan Province Court work conference on striking hard at serious crime) *Renmin fayuan nianjian 1990* (The Yearbook of the People's Courts 1990), p. 630.
102 Harold Garfinkel, 'Conditions of successful degradation ceremonies', p. 420.
103 For a more detailed examination of this argument, see Trevaskes, *Courts and Criminal Justice in Contemporary China*, pp. 21–24.
104 Perry Keller, 'Sources of order in Chinese law', p. 754.
105 Murray Scot Tanner, 'State coercion and the balance of awe: the 1983–1986 "Stern Blows" anti-crime campaign', p. 94.
106 Ibid., p. 95.
107 Cai Songyun (ed.), *Yiyangshi gonganju wei Hunan de difangzhi zhunbei cailiao* (Preparatory Material for the Hunan Province Chronicles by the Yiyang Public Security Bureau), unpublished materials.
108 Tanner, 'State coercion and the balance of awe', p. 97.
109 Ibid., pp. 97–98.
110 Ibid., p. 96.
111 Michael Dutton, *Policing Chinese Politics: a history*, p. 279.
112 As Michael Dutton explains, 'Theoretically, this type of dual leadership was challenged by the demand for police to professionalize, specialize, and obey the rule of law. These demands pointed to the need to strengthen professional, technical, and legal leadership over local police branches. Yet this was being argued at the very time that financial pressures militated against any strengthening of this type of leadership. Basically, whoever paid the bills played the tune, and on the ground, an ever-increasing portion of the financial burden for local policing was being pushed onto the shoulders of local governments rather than onto professional, technical, or legal leadership bodies.' See Dutton, *Policing Chinese Politics: a history*, p. 279.
113 Fu Hualing, 'Zhou Yongkang and the recent police reform in China', pp. 246–47. As Fu explains, 'the police complained that by doing non-police work illicitly imposed by the local political authority, scarce police resources were diverted from crime control to other "real" police work, straining police–public relations and discrediting the police', pp. 246–47.
114 Murray Scot Tanner and Eric Green, 'Principals and secret agents: central versus local control over policing and obstacles to "rule of law" in China', p. 646.
115 Ibid.

3 Striking hard in the new millennium

1 An earlier version of this chapter was originally published in the Australian and New Zealand Journal of Criminology. See Susan Trevaskes, '"Strike Hard 2001": form and strategy in a Chinese anti-crime campaign', pp. 272–92.
2 Chen Xingliang, 'Kuanyan xiangji xingshi zhengce yanjiu' (A study of the criminal justice policy of balancing leniency and severity), p. 20.
3 I use these stages to describe the details of the 1983–86 campaign in Susan Trevaskes, *Courts and Criminal Justice in Contemporary China*, pp. 115–44.
4 While the figure of 3.69 million crimes in 2000 seems relatively insignificant given China's population of 1.3 billion, crime rate figures need to be placed in the context of a system that first, suffers from a chronic level of under-reporting and second, regards most cases of theft as misdemeanours not crimes. The figure of 3.69 million may also mask the real problem of crime in China because most minor theft is not registered officially as a crime and is punished administratively either through the system of 'reeducation through labour' (*laodong jiaoyang*) in which offenders are sent to institutions for

a period up to three years or, for extremely minor offences, through the issuing of fines or formal police warnings (*jiaoyu shifang*). The determination of what is to be considered an indictable offence is measured against an internal system of 'standards for measuring indictable offences' (*li'an biaozhun*). For example, according to these standards, minor theft, which is theft involving money or property valued under 1,000 yuan (US$125.00) in urban areas and 300 yuan (US$40.00) in rural areas, is not regarded as an indictable offence.

5 Benshu bianxiezu (ed.), *Yanda douzheng yu shehui zhian ganbu duben* (Readings for Cadres on the Strike Hard Campaign and Public Order), pp. 45–46.

6 For the official Xinhua news release outlining the aims of the campaign see 'Zhongguo zai quanguo fanweinei kaizhan yanda zhengzhi douzheng zhongdian daji san zhong fanzui' (China begins a nationwide Strike Hard campaign focusing the attack on three crime categories), *Xinhua* News, 3 April 2001.

7 Chen Jiping, *Zhongguo shehui zhi'an zonghe zhili nianjian 2001–2002* (2001–2002 Yearbook of comprehensive management of public order in China), p. 104. (Hereafter referred to as *Nianjian 2001–2002*.)

8 Zhou Lu, *Dangshi shizheng fanzuixue* (Contemporary Substantive Issues in Criminology), pp. 136–37.

9 Kang Shuhua, *Dangdai Zhongguo fanzui zhuti* (Crime Issues in Contemporary China), pp. 190–94.

10 Kang Shuhua, *Dangdai Zhongguo fanzui zhuti*, pp. 190–94.

11 Ibid., pp. 190–94.

12 *Nianjian 2001–2002*, p. 106. (These amounted to 65.5 per cent of the total number of cases and they were considered dangerous crimes because they occurred in domestic residences.)

13 *Nianjian 2001–2002*, p. 106.

14 Lu Zhuo, 'Dui xian jieduan yanda zhengzhi douzheng de lixing sikao' (A rational reflection on this current stage of the Strike Hard campaign), p. 33.

15 These figures are quoted in 'China preparing to wage new Strike Hard anti-crime campaign', *Xinhua* News, 5 April 2001, available in English from FBIS: Document no. FBIS-CHI-2001-0405.

16 Jiang Zhu, 'Stress improving public order at national meeting', *Xinhua* News, 3 April 2001, available in English from FBIS: FBIS-CHI-2001-0403.

17 'China preparing to wage new Strike Hard anti-crime campaign', *Xinhua* News, 5 April 2001, available in English from FBIS: Document no. FBIS-CHI-2001-0405. In addition to the three main categories, individual provinces were encouraged to add to this list, their own local crime targets. See 'Zhongguo zai quanguo fanweinei kaizhan yanda zhengshi douzheng zhongdian daji san zhong fanzui' (China begins a nationwide Strike Hard campaign focusing the attack on three crime categories), *Xinhua* News, 3 April 2001.

18 For a summary of the conference, see 'National public order work conference held in Beijing' *Xinhua* News, 3 April 2001, available in English from FBIS: Document no. FBIS-CHI-2001-0403.

19 Ming Xia gives this estimate. See Ming Xia, 'Assessing and explaining the resurgence of China's criminal underworld', p. 166.

20 Lu Gengsong, 'Zhongguo heishehui xianzhuang fenxi' (An analysis of the make-up of mafia-style syndicates) *Yancheng wanbao* (Yancheng Evening News), 24 May 2001, http:www.people.com.cn?GB/shehui/46/index.html (accessed 25 August 2001); and Zhou Liangtao, 'Lun heishehui xingzhi de zuzhi' (On the organization of mafia-style syndicates), in Li Zhongxin (ed.), *Lun heishehui xingzhi fanzui wenti yanjiu* (Research issues on mafia-style organized crime).

21 Lu Gengsong, 'Zhongguo heishehui xianzhuang fenxi'.

22 Benshu bianxiezu, *Yanda douzheng yu shehui zhian ganbu duben.*

23 Kang Shuhua, *Dangdai Zhongguo fanzui zhuti*, pp. 318–24.

24 Lu Gengsong, 'Zhongguo heishehui xianzhuang fenxi'.

25 'Roundup of PRC crime crackdown drive', *Xinhua* (News), 10 April 2001, available in English from FBIS: Document no. FBIS-CHI-2001-0410.

26 Lu Gengsong, 'Zhongguo heishehui xianzhuang fenxi'.

27 Ibid.

28 'Shanxi yanda qudele jieduanxing chengguo' (Some progressive successes gained in the Strike Hard campaign in Shanxi), *Zhongguo qingnianbao* (China Youth Daily), 8 June 2001.

29 'Nanjing bannian liushisan ge tanguan luoma' (63 corrupt officials in Nanjing brought down in the past six months), *Jiangnan shibao* (South China Times), 24 July 2001, p. 1.

30 Lu Gengsong, 'Zhongguo heishehui xianzhuang fenxi'.

31 Ibid.

32 'PRC Public Security Ministry issues circular on fighting crimes', *Xinhua* News, 26 April 2001, available in English from FBIS: Document no. FBIS-CHI-2001-0426.

33 'PRC's Xinjiang executes 15 criminals after public sentencing', *Xinjiang ribao* (Xinjiang Daily), 16 November 2001.

34 'Xinjiang reports achievements in Strike Hard drive', *Xinjiang ribao* (Xinjiang Daily), 31 May 2001, available in English from FBIS: Document no. FBIS-CHI-2001-0619.

35 'Terrorism crackdown starts in Xinjiang region of China', 10 October 2001, FBIS-CHI-2001.

36 'AFP cites Xinjiang Legal Daily on anti-crime campaign', AFP, *Daily Report*, 14 November 2001, available in English from FBIS: Document no. FBIS-CHI-2001-1114.

37 Ibid.

38 For a description of the Yining incident see James Millward, 'Violent separatism in Xinjiang: a critical assessment', pp. 16–17.

39 Incomplete or incorrect reporting on the details of politically motivated crimes in Xinjiang was not limited to the Strike Hard campaign. James Millward notes that in March 1999, Xinjiang Governor Abdulahat Abdurishit had claimed that 'thousands' of bombings, assassinations and other incidents had occurred in 1999, and party documents at the same time had claimed 380 such incidents in 1998 alone. Given the government's reluctance to report details of the majority of alleged politically motivated crimes in Xinjiang, it is perhaps not surprising that in 2002 when Xinhua news agency released China's most comprehensive report on separatism in Xinjiang to date that details on the number of citizens killed and injured in separatist uprisings or terrorist attacks did not tally up correctly. Millward notes that in the preface of the Chinese government report titled 'East Turkistan terrorist forces cannot get away with impunity' issued by the Information Office of the State Council, alleges that 162 people had been killed by terrorist acts in the 1990s and 440 others injured yet the body of the document only enumerates 57 deaths. Ibid., p. 12.

40 'Anfan Aposile yu Aihamade yi weihai guojia anquanzui bei pan sixing' (Abdulmejid and Abdulahmad convicted of crimes of threatening national security, are executed' *Yili Wanbao* (Yili Evening News), http://72.14.253.104/search?q=cache:nNyt11YaJGgJ:news.xinhuanet.com/newscenter.htm, 16 October 2001 (accessed 31 August 2007). For a detailed account of the 1997 incident see Liu Hantai and Du Xingfu, *Zhongguo daji dongtu baogao* (A Report on China's Fight against East Turkestan Groups), p. 10.

41 Ibid., p. 18.

42 'Cengjing zhizao duoqi baoli kongbu shijian de dongtu zuzhi toumu bei chujie' (Head of East Turkestan organization who had committed numerous violent terrorist acts is executed) *Wurumuqi wanbao* (Urumqi Evening News), http://72.14.253.104/search?q=cache:nNyt11YaJGgJ:news.xinhuanet.com/newscenter.htm, 22 October 2003 (accessed 31 August 2007).

43 Mu Yumin, *Beijing jingcha 100 nian*, p. 740. In the two years of the campaign, the Beijing police cracked 99,668 criminal cases, detained 76,185 suspects and caught

6,551 fugitives. The biggest improvements were witnessed in large public places like railway stations. The success of the campaign in Beijing, according to Mu Yumin, lay in the emphasis paid to maintaining standards of crime prevention. Another ingredient in the Beijing success story was the close attention paid to misdemeanour crimes, with 50,179 people either fined or sent to reform through education, a 21.6 per cent increase from the previous two years. The rate of crime incidents dropped by 15.5 per cent in the first year of Strike Hard in Chaoyang, Haidian and Fengtai districts and 27.5 per cent after the second year of Strike Hard. According to Mu, the secret of their success was that there was a clear-cut distribution of tasks between plain clothed police who were solely responsible for criminal investigations and uniformed police at stations and on street patrol who were responsible for crime prevention. This tripartite division of labour along with the help of community groups and para-policing units (including private security firms) were the main stated reasons for the success of Strike Hard in Beijing. Mu, *Beijing jingcha 100 nian*, p. 743.

44 *Nianjian 2001–2002*, p. 444.

45 In 2003, there were 70,989 crimes registered by the Beijing police, 12,485 of which were Strike Hard-targeted crimes. The crime rate was down a modest 0.5 per cent from the previous year. *Zhongguo shehui zhian zonghe zhili nianjian 2003* (The Comprehensive Management of Public Order Yearbook for China 2003), p. 233.

46 Jilinsheng gonganting, *Shiji zhijiao de jilin gongan gongzuo* (Public Security Work in Jilin at the Turn of the Century), p. 11.

47 Ibid.

48 Ibid., p. 32. Note that Jilin Province also focused on the following targets in Strike Hard 2001: (1) mafia-style syndicates and gang crime; (2) large-scale hold-ups; (3) murder, robbery and kidnapping; (4) bag-snatching and theft; and (5) border control law and order issues in areas bordering on North Korea. There were four province-wide simultaneous public arrest and sentencing rallies organized including 'public send-offs to reeducation through labour prison rallies' (*gongkai song laodong jiaoyang*). In 2001, more than 70,000 cases were cracked, an increase in the clear-up rate of more than 60 per cent. More than 10,000 fugitives had been apprehended and 2,014 gangs and mafia-style syndicates (including 17 large syndicates and 363 medium sized criminal groups) were smashed. The following year, from January to September 2002, 2,662 members of gangs and mafia-style syndicates had been apprehended. See *Nianjian 2001–2002*, pp. 704, 727.

49 'Jilin uses Strike Hard to force out starving Koreans', *South China Morning Post*, 25 May 2001, p. 7; and 'China steps up repatriation of North Korean refugees: medical charity says people who return face reprisals', *Washington Post*, 23 June 2001, A16.

50 Ibid., p. 749.

51 Ibid., pp. 749–50.

52 'Sichuan "kuangbiao" xingdong diyiyi' (The first battle of 'Operation Hurricane' begins in Sichuan), *Renminwang* (People's Daily online), www.people.com.cn/GB/shehui/43/index.html 21 April 2001 (accessed 28 April 2001).

53 'Zhibiao zhongxia de huangtang' (The arrest quota system turns into a farce), *Fazhibao* (Legal Daily News), 22 April 2001.

54 'Wuhan 'yanda' diyizhanyi, 135 ming dupu taofan luowang' (135 wanted criminals caught in the net in the first phase of Strike Hard in Wuhan), *Changjiang Ribao* (Changjiang Daily), 29 May 2001, www.people.com.cn/GB/shehui43/index/.html (accessed 25 August 2001).

55 'Qingdao yingzao yanda gaoya taishi' (Qingdao authorities exert maximum Strike Hard pressure), *Renminwang* (People's Daily online), 4 July 2001, www.people.com.cn/GB/shehui43/index/.html (accessed 25 August 2001).

56 'Xinjiang reports achievements in Strike Hard drive', *Xinjiang ribao* (Xinjiang Daily), 31 May 2001, available in English from FBIS: Document no. FBIS-CHI-2001-0619.

57 Zou Wei, Zhang Dechang and Chen Wenquan, 'Lun xinshiqi de "yanda" fangzhen' (On Strike Hard policy in the new age), pp. 14–17.
58 'Xinjiang party secretary addresses meeting on public order', *Xinjiang ribao* (Xinjiang Daily), 16 April 2001, available in English from FBIS: Document no. FBIS-CHI-2001-0521.
59 'Yinian dasi shier ren, jingcheng "damengun" ermo bei pan sixing' (The 'head bashing' monsters, killers of 12 people within a year in the capital are sentenced to death), *Jiangnan shibao* (Southern China Times), 26 July 2001, p. 3.
60 'Anhui fayuan gao xiaolu pan'an chu'e' (Anhui courts highly effective in trying heinous criminals), *Renmin ribao* (People's Daily) (hereafter cited as *RMRB*), 24 July 2001, p. 6.
61 Zhang, Fusan, 'Jiji kaizhan yanda zhengzhi douzheng, weihu he cuijin gaige kaifang fazhan wending' (Urgently launch the Strike Hard campaign: protect and promote the stability of the economic reforms), p. 243.
62 Zhang, Fusan, 'Sifabu guanyu jinyibu jiaqiang Yanda zhengzhi douzheng gongzuo de tongzhi' (Ministry of justice notice on further strengthening Strike Hard campaign work), *Nianjian 2001–2002,* p. 256.
63 'Beijing jieri tixun yanda yifan' (Strike hard suspects interrogated during the holiday period), *Beijing qingnian bao* (Beijing Youth Daily), 8 August 2001.
64 'Yanda zhengzhi douzheng quanmian zhankai' (The Strike Hard campaign begins in earnest), *RMRB*, 18 April 2001, p. 9.
65 'Teshi tezuo, zhongan zhongchu, zhangzhoushi jiancha jiguan quanli touru yanda' (Special matters require special handling, serious cases require serious punishment: Zhangzhou municipal procuratorate engage in striking hard in force), www. people.com.cn/GB/shehui43/index/.html, 6 May 2001 (accessed 25 August 2001).
66 'Yanda zhengzhi douzheng quanmian zhankai' (The Strike Hard campaign begins in earnest), *RMRB,* 18 April 2001, p. 9.
67 'Carrying out struggle to "strike hard" and put things in order, strengthening public order work', *Xinhua* News, 3 April 2001, available in English from FBIS: Document no. FBIS-CHI-2001-0404.
68 'Xinhua round-up on PRC's strike hard anti-crime campaign', *Xinhua* News, 11 April 2001, available in English from FBIS: Document no. FBIS-CHI-2001-0411.
69 'Beijingshi yanda zhengzhi zhuangxian douzheng quanmian zhankai' (The Strike Hard campaign in Beijing is launched extensively throughout the city), *Renminwang* (People's Daily online), www.people.com.cn/GB/shehui43/index/.html, 11 April 2001 (accessed 25 August 2001).
70 'Guangzhou juxing gongpu gongpan dahui' (Joint public arrest and sentencing rally held in Guangzhou), *RMRB,* 12 April 2001, p. 1.
71 'Xinhua round-up on PRC's Strike Hard anti-crime campaign'.
72 'Shanghai dui yipi yanzhong baoli fanzui fenzui jinxing jizhong xuanpan' (A batch of serious criminal offenders sentenced en masse in Shanghai), *Renminwang* (People's Daily online), www.people.com.cn/GB/shehui43/index/.html, 12 April 2001 (accessed 25 August 2001).
73 'At least 89 executed in one day in PRC's strike hard campaign', Hong Kong AFP, *Daily Report*, 12 April 2001, available in English from FBIS: Document no. FBIS-CHI-2001-0412.
74 'Guangdong gedi gongkai chuli 5,000 yifan' (5,000 suspects publicly arrested across Guangdong Province), *RMRB*, 19 April 2001, p. 1.
75 'Henan gongkai xuanpan 1168 yanzhong xingshi fanzui fenzi' (1,168 serious criminal offenders publicly sentenced in Henan), www.people.com.cn/GB/shehui43/index/. html, 23 April 2001 (accessed 25 August 2001); and 'Sichuan "kuangbiao" xingdong diyiyi'.
76 Ibid.

77 'Xinjiang reports achievements in strike hard drive', *Xinjiang ribao* (Xinjiang Daily), 31 May 2001, available in English from FBIS: Document no. FBIS-CHI-2001-0619.
78 Ibid.
79 The crime reporting system in China has long suffered from a chronic level of under-reporting. Many police stations have two different crime records on file: one for internal-use-only that records the real incident report rate; the other, a falsified record. Police reports hide the large number of cases that they are aware of but have not yet solved, and many only report incidents officially as 'cases on file for investigation' (*li'an lu*), once they have actually cracked the case so that favourable evaluations can be made by comparing the number of cases on file for investigation and the number of case that have been solved.
80 *Nianjian 2001–02*, p. 107.
81 Ibid.

4 Cracks in the campaign armour

1 Chen Jiping, *Zhongguo shehui zhi'an zonghe zhili nianjian 2001–2002* (2001–2002 Yearbook of Comprehensive Management of Public Order in China), p. 109 (hereafter referred to as *Nianjian 2001–2002*).
2 'Teshi tezuo, zhongan zhongchu' (Special matters require special handling, serious cases require serious punishment), *Fuzhou renminwang* (Fuzhou People's Daily online), www.people.com.cn/GB/shehui43/index/.html, 6 May 2001 (accessed 10 August 2001).
3 'Execution toll passes 1,000 in Chinese crackdowns,' *Sydney Morning Herald*, 11 June 2001, p. 14; and '1,781 executed in three-month frenzy: amnesty,' *The Age* (Melbourne), 7 July 2001, p. 24.
4 *Nianjian 2001–2002*, p. 109.
5 Ibid.
6 Ibid., p. 110.
7 Ibid., p. 109.
8 Ibid., p. 111.
9 'Zhongyang shehui zhian zonghe zhili weiyuanhui guanyu yinfa "2002 quanguo shehui zhian xingshi fenxi baogao" de tongzhi' (Notice concerning the 2002 national comprehensive management of public order crime report published by the CPC Comprehensive management of public order committee, 14 March 2003), in Chen Jiping, *Zhongguo shehui zhian zonghe zhili nianjian 2003* (2003 Yearbook of comprehensive management of public order in China), p. 12 (hereafter referred to as *Nianjian 2003*).
10 The number of cases tried was greater than the number of arrests because many cases that went to trial that year were carried over from the previous year.
11 *Nianjian 2003,* p. 12.
12 Ibid., p. 13.
13 Ibid.
14 Xu Xiaogang, 'Shenhua renshi qianghua cuoshe, tuidong yanda zhengzhi douzheng shenru fazhan' (Deepen understanding and strengthen measure, expatiate a deepened development of the Strike Hard campaign), p. 38.
15 'Yanda zhengzhihou de ruogan sikao' (Some 'post-Strike Hard' campaign reflections), *Zhejiang gongan gaodeng zhuanke xuexiao xuebao* (Journal of Zhejiang Police College: Public Security Studies) 2, 2004, p. 82.
16 Ibid.
17 Ibid., p. 83.
18 Ibid.
19 Ibid.

20 Zheng Jianguo, 'Lun youhua yanda celue' (On optimizing Strike Hard tactics), *Gongan xuankan: Zhejiang gongan gaodeng zhuanke xuexiao xuebao* (Public Security Journal: Zhejiang Police Academy) 2, 2005, p. 82.
21 Ibid.
22 Ibid., p. 83.
23 Liu Xuegang, 'Yanda liuxia de yihan' (Some lamentable things that Strike Hard has left in its wake), *Liaowang xinwen zhoukan* (Outlook News Weekly) 32, 2003, p. 46.
24 Ibid., p. 48.
25 Guo Xingguo, *Jianguo yilai gongan gongzuo dashi yaolan* (An Outline of the Chronicles of Public Security Work Since Liberation), pp. 594–95.
26 Ibid., pp. 594–95.
27 'Xingshi yitihua shiyexia yanda de lixing sikao' (A rational reflection on implementing an integrated vision of criminal justice work into the Strike Hard campaign), *Jiangsu jinggong xueyuan xuebao* (Journal of the Jiangsu Police Academy) 4, 2004, p. 99.
28 Xiao Xiong, 'Guanyu yanda rougan wenti de sikao' (Reflections on some problems with Strike Hard), *Shanghai gongan gaodeng zhuanke xuexiao xuebao* (Journal of the Shanghai Police Academy) 15 (1), 2005, p. 17.
29 Sun Guoyang, 'Xingshi yitihua shiyexia yanda de lixing sikao', p. 99.
30 Ibid.
31 Zhai Jinping, 'Yanda yu gongan gaige' (Strike hard and reforms in public security), p. 26.
32 Chen Zili, 'Yanda zhengzhi douzheng jiujing ruhe shenru' (How the Strike Hard campaign can have a deep impact), p. 23.
33 Li Shuangqi, 'Fujiansheng yanda gongzuo diaocha baogao' (Survey results on Strike Hard work in Fujian Province), p. 89.
34 Ibid., p. 90.
35 Ibid.
36 Ibid.
37 For an analysis in English of underreporting crime, see Borge Bakken, 'Comparative perspectives on crime in China', pp. 70–79; Olivia Yu and Lening Zhang, 'The under-recording of crime police in China: a case study', pp. 252–63; and Ni He and Ineke H. Marshall, 'Social production of crime data: a critical examination of Chinese crime statistics', pp. 46–64.
38 Note that Mu Yumin also makes this claim. See Mu Yumin, *Beijing Jingcha bainian* (One Hundred Years of Policing in Beijing), p. 636.
39 Rao Yunming, 'Yanda zhengzhihou de rougan sikao', p. 83.
40 Li Chuan, 'Dangqian yanjiuzhong de si ge wuqu' (Four inaccuracies regarding the current research on Strike Hard), p. 7.
41 Mu Yumin, *Beijing Jingcha bainian*, p. 636.
42 Ibid., p. 637.
43 Rao Yunming, 'Yanda zhengzhihou de rougan sikao', p. 83.
44 Li Yaoming and Chen Jiwei, 'Guanyu gonggu he fazhan yanda zhengzhi douzheng chengguo de sikao (Some reflections on consolidating and developing the success of the Strike Hard campaign), p. 22.
45 Xu Yingui, Zhou Ying and Cao Cheng, 'Shilun yanda zhengce de falu yiji qi duice' (Preliminary assessment of Strike Hard policy on basic legal principles and some other measures), p. 75.
46 Liu Xuegang, 'Yanda liuxia de yihan', p. 46.
47 Ibid.
48 Li Shuangqi, 'Fujiansheng Yanda gongzuo diaocha baogao', p. 92.
49 Ibid.
50 Ibid.
51 Chen Zili, 'Yanda zhengzhi douzheng jiujing ruhe shenru', p. 23.
52 Liu, 'Yanda liuxia de yihan', p. 46.

53 Ibid.
54 Lu Zhuo, 'Dui xian jieduan yanda zhengzhi douzheng de lixing sikao' (A rational reflection on this current stage of the Strike Hard campaign), p. 34.
55 Ibid.
56 Ibid., p. 35.
57 Michael Dutton, *Policing Chinese Politics: a history*, p. 279.
58 Lu Zhuo, 'Dui xian jieduan yanda zhengzhi douzheng de lixing sikao', p. 35.
59 Wei Zhenzhong, 'Queshi gaohao zhuitao gongzuo tuidong yanda zhengzhi douzheng shenru kaizhan' (Successfully perform the task of apprehending fugitives to advance the deeper impact of Strike Hard campaign on crime), p. 23.
60 Ibid.
61 Ibid.
62 Ibid.
63 Ibid.
64 Jiang Yanhu, 'Dangqian yanda zhengzhi douzhengzhong cunzai de wenti duice' (Existing problems and countermeasures related to the latest Strike Hard campaign), p. 6.
65 Ibid., p. 9
66 Jiang Pusheng, 'Yanda zhengzhi douzheng de huigu yu sikao' (A reflective look back at the Strike Hard campaign), p. 40.
67 Ibid., p. 39.
68 Ibid., p. 41.
69 See Zhong Yuexiong, 'Zhian fangkong jizhi de shijian' (Practices of the system of crime prevention), in Ma Xiangjin (ed.), *Jingwu xinlun* (New Theories of Policing), p. 20.
70 This comment was made to the author by a senior police officer present at the meeting.
71 Zhang Guoxing and Li Jingping, 'Xin xingshixia jiaqiang he gaijin dang dui gongan gongzuo de lingdao' (Strengthening and improving Party leadership over public security work in the new period of policing), in *Lun zhanlue jiyuqi gongangonagzuo de gaige yu chuangxin* (Reforms and Ideas for Strategies of Public Security Work in an Age of Transformation), p. 9.
72 Interview with a senior police officer (July 2005).
73 Ibid.
74 *Lun zhanlue jiyuqi gongangonagzuo de gaige yu chuangxin*, p. 9.
75 Zhang Guoxing and Li Jingping, 'Xin xingshixia jiaqiang he gaijin dang dui gongan gongzuo de lingdao', p. 23.
76 Ibid.
77 Ibid.
78 John Delury, '"Harmonious" in China', p. 25.
79 Lin Zhongliang, *Zhengfa wei de zhineng ji hongguan zhengfa gongzuo*, p. 386.
80 'Luo Gan qiangdiao: yao jianchi Yanda fangzhen, jiaqiang zhian guanli' (Luo Gan stresses that authorities must continue with Strike Hard policy and strengthen the management of public order), www.Chinaacc.com/new/2003_11%5C31113081914.htm, (accessed 10 December 2003).
81 'Luo Gan calls for continuation of China's Strike Hard campaign', *Xinhua* News, 18 July 2003, available in English from FBIS: Document no. FBIS-CHI-2003-0718.
82 Lin Zhongliang, *Zhengfa wei de zhineng ji hongguan zhengfa gongzuo*, p. 387.
83 Ibid., p. 388.
84 For a description of the principle of combining punishment with leniency, see Ronald C. Keith, *China's Struggle for the Rule of Law*, pp. 154–55.
85 Lin Zhongliang, *Zhengfa wei de zhineng ji hongguan zhengfa gongzuo*, p. 392.
86 Ibid., p. 386.
87 Ibid., p. 392.
88 Moves to push the prevention to the forefront of crime control were afoot even before

the end of Strike Hard in 2003. See Zhong Yuexiong, 'Zhian fangkong jizhi de shijian' (Practices of the system of crime prevention), in Ma Xiangjin (ed.), *Jingwu xinlun*, p. 20.

89 'Luo Gan qiangdiao: yao jianchi Yanda fangzhen'.

90 Susan Trevaskes, *Courts and Criminal Justice in Contemporary China*, p. 37.

91 Alan Hunt, 'Dichotomy and contradiction in the sociology of law', p. 80.

92 Trevaskes, *Courts and Criminal Justice in Contemporary China*, pp. 34–37.

93 Alan Hunt, 'Dichotomy and contradiction in the sociology of law', p. 77.

94 Ibid., p. 78.

95 Ibid.

96 Mao Lei, 'Duiyu fanzui ruguo queshao zhunque yuce he chongfen de yufang, name, fanji de daijia jiangshi, shifen ang'guide' (If accurate crime rate predictions and ample crime prevention measures are not taken seriously, the cost of all anti-crime activities will soar), *Renmin ribao* (People's Daily), 8 August 2001, p. 9.

97 'Yanda: zouchu sige wuqu' (Strike hard: the four main mistakes), *Renmin ribao* (People's Daily), 8 August, 2001, p. 10.

98 'Beijing Yanda wenming xiemu liangnian gaipan 35 lisixing' (Beijing bows out gracefully and closes the curtain on Strike Hard in a civilized manner, overturning the death penalty on 35 criminals), *Renminwang* (People's Daily online), 9 August 2003 (accessed 1 September 2003).

5 The people's war on drugs

1 At the 16th Party Congress in 2002, it was referred to not as a fixed term but more loosely as 'making society more harmonious' as one aspect of the goal of building a well-off (*xiaokang*) socialist society.

2 'The CCP Central Committee Plenum's resolution on the construction of a harmonious society', *Xinhua* News, 11 October 2006.

3 Willy Wo-Lap Lam, 'Chinks in the armour of the Hu Jintao administration: can a harmonious society emerge in the absence of political reform?', p. 5.

4 Lin Zhongliang, *Geji danwei zhengfa wei de zhineng ji hongguan zhengfa gongzuo* (The Functions and Macroscopic Tasks of the Politico-legal Affairs work of Politico-legal Affairs Committees at all Levels of Government), p. 392.

5 This is with the exception of the long-held annual drug burn-offs and rallies on World Anti-drugs Day on 26 June.

6 Mo Desheng and Jin Changling, *Shehui zhian zonghe zhili zhuanti yanjiu* (A Study of Comprehensive Management of Public Order), p. 262.

7 Li Changming, 'Zousi fanmai hailuoyin 433.95 gongjin Yunnan teda dupin anfan fufa' (Criminals convicted of smuggling and selling 433.95 kilograms of heroin in a major drug case in yunnan have been executed), www.Chinacourt.org/htm/article/200708/17/260403.shtml, 17 August 2007 (accessed 18 August 2007).

8 'Tan Xiaolin deng dufan bei zhixing sixing' (Tan Xiaolin and other drug traffickers are executed), *Xinhua* News, http://news.xinhuanet.com/legal/2004-06/25/content_1547028.htm, 25 May 2004 (accessed 30 May 2004).

9 Ibid.

10 Ibid.

11 Chen Beidi, *Zhongguo xidu diaocha* (An Investigation into Drug Use in China), p. 127.

12 'Tan Xiaolin deng dufan bei zhixing sixing'.

13 Liang Jinyun, Yunnan jindu douzheng xingshi pinggu (Assessment of the situation regarding the people's war on drugs in Yunnan Province), p. 3.

14 Report on 2005 National Counter-Narcotics Activities by the Counter Narcotics Control Commission (released in 2006) www.gov.cn/gzdt/2006-06/26/content_319658.htm.

15 Report on 2006 National Counter-Narcotics Activities by the Counter Narcotics

Control Commission (released in 2007) www.China.com.cn/law/zhuanti/yldp/2007-06/02/content_8333483.htm.

16 Liang Jinyun, 'Yunnan jindu douzheng xingshi pinggu', p. 3.

17 Annual Report on Drug Control in China, 2008, Office of the National Counter-Narcotics Activities.

18 US Department of State 2007 International Narcotics Control Strategy Report (INCSR), p. 279.

19 United Nations Office on Drugs and Crime, Patterns and Trends of Amphetamine-type Stimulants and Other Drugs of Abuse in East Asia and the Pacific, 2006.

20 For a comprehensive study of anti-drug campaigns in the 1980s and 1990s see Zhou Yongming, *Anti-Drug Crusades in Twentieth-Century China: nationalism, history, and state building* and Zhou Yongming, *China's Anti-Drug Campaign in the Reform Era*.

21 Liang Jinyun, 'Yunnan jindu douzheng xingshi pinggu', p. 4.

22 Ibid., p. 1.

23 Zhonglin Chen and Kacheng Huang, 'Drug problems in China: recent trends, countermeasures and challenges', pp. 98–101.

24 Liang Jinyun, 'Yunnan jindu douzheng xingshi pinggu', pp. 3–6.

25 Ibid., p. 5.

26 Ibid.

27 Chen Beidi, *Zhongguo xidu diaocha*, p. 126.

28 Niklas Swanstrom, 'Narcotics and China: An old security threat from new sources', p. 124.

29 'Reports on Crimes, Sentences, Punishments, and Other Judicial-related Activities in the PRC, Monitored from 13 December 2006 to 8 January 2007', *Xinhua* News, OSC Report, 19 January 2007. Document no. 200701191477.1_941323fbf14a7065.

30 Chen Beidi, *Zhongguo xidu diaocha*, p. 121.

31 Ibid. A more recent route begins at any number of ports along the Yangtze River to Chongqing City where the drug shipments are divided and sent overland to Mongolia and Russia.

32 Ibid.

33 Ibid., p. 125.

34 US Department of State 2007 International Narcotics Control Strategy Report (INCSR), p. 279.

35 Sarah Biddulph, *Legal Reform and Administrative Detention Powers in China*, p. 107.

36 Ibid., p. 108.

37 Mo and Jin, *Shehui zhian zonghe zhili zhuanti yanjiu*, p. 261.

38 'Zhonggong zhongyang guowuyuan jiaqiang shehui zhi'an zonghe zhili de jueding' (Central party committee and state council decision on strengthening comprehensive management of public order), 19 February 1991.

39 Ibid. The second main document rationalizing CMPO, the 'Central Party Committee and State Council decision on further enhancing comprehensive management of public order' (5 September 2001), reconfirmed many of the points in the 1991 document but added an official line on the priority that must be given to crime prevention. The document stated that criminal justice organs must 'combine preventing with attacking but to give first priority to preventing crime' (*dafang jiehe, yufang weizhu*). Mo and Jin, *Shehui zhian zonghe zhili zhuanti yanjiu*, p. 271.

40 Mo and Jin, *Shehui zhian zonghe zhili zhuanti yanjiu*, p. 262.

41 Ibid.

42 Ibid., p. 264.

43 'Anti-drugs campaign launched in 10,000 recreation venues in China', *Xinhua* News, 16 October 2006, Available in English from FBIS: FBIS-CHI-20051016.

44 Ibid.

45 'Beijing ups fight against drug abuse at entertainment venues', *Xinhua* News, 23 June 2006, OSC Transcribed Text.
46 'Over 90 per cent of entertainment venues install cameras in Beijing', *Xinhua* News, 13 December 2006, OSC Transcribed Text.
47 For an analysis of the private security regime, see Susan Trevaskes, 'The public/private security nexus in China', pp. 28–55.
48 Ibid.
49 News report from *Renminwang* (People's Daily Online) www.people.com.cn/GB/shehui/46/20011016/582674.html, 16 October, 2001 (accessed on 20 December 2001.) In 2006, security personnel helped to capture 162,000 individuals suspected of committing crimes or misdemeanours, and provided police 220,000 sources of information related to crime incidents. It is reported that in 2006, security guards prevented potential theft of property worth 2.05 billion yuan (US$260,000) and private security companies made 7.5 billion yuan (US$940 million) in profit. See Wang Lili 'Quanguo baoan zongshu da 230 wan ren' (The number of private security personnel in China reaches 2.3 million) *Zhongguo Jianchawang* (China Procuratorate Net) 2007, www.cpd.com.cn/gb/newscenter/2007-02-05/content_728515.htm (accessed on 2 February 2008.
50 Mo and Jin, *Shehui zhian zonghe zhili zhuanti yanjiu*, p. 264.
51 Zhou Yongming, *Anti-Drug Crusades in Twentieth-Century China*, p. 136.
52 Mo and Jin, *Shehui zhian zonghe zhili zhuanti yanjiu*, p. 264.
53 'China's drug commission tells celebrities to stay away from drugs' *Xinhua* News, 31 May 2007, OSC Transcribed Text, Document no. 200705311477.1_bcff0068a15e7a8.
54 Mo and Jin, *Shehui zhian zonghe zhili zhuanti*, p. 264.
55 'China targets primary, middle students to combat drug addiction', *Xinhua* News, 8 January 2007, OSC Transcribed Text, Document no. 200701191477.1_941323fbf14a7065.
56 Ibid.
57 'Two men sentenced to death for drug manufacturing in northwest China', *Xinhua* News, 26 June 2006, OSC Transcribed Text. On the same day, the Supreme People's Court in Beijing released details of five drug traffickers who had been executed. The criminal gang led by Lian Yongming Wu Bing, Liu Hongwei, and Su Chuwen were convicted of multiple counts of drug trafficking and other offences. Lian Yongming and his accomplices set up a network purchasing, transporting and selling 20 kilograms of heroin in ten separate instances in Chongqing, Shanghai and Wuxi. Lian Yongming was also convicted of trafficking 1.4 kilograms in another ten separate instances. In a separate case, Wu Bing transported and arranged others to sell a total of 1.6 kilograms of heroin in eight separate cases while Liu Hongwei was involved in transporting 108 kilograms of heroin in five cases and Su Chuwen 8.8 kilograms in four cases. Four other drug traffickers in Wuxi in Jiangsu Province were also executed on 26 June and another, Qin Tengjun, in Guangzhou three days earlier on 23 June. See 'China announces execution of seven drug traffickers', *Xinhua* News, 25 June 2006, OSC Transcribed Text. Document no. 200706251477.1_6bf500ab15e5a206.
58 Mo and Jin, *Shehui zhian zonghe zhili zhuanti yanjiu*, p. 264.
59 'Zhongguo gong'anbu jindu guanyuan tan zhongguo de jindu gongzuo' (Counter-narcotics officials talk about counter- narcotics work in China), http://ipc.fmprc.gov.cn/chn/cfh/t143074.htm (accessed 14 August 2007).
60 The country's largest compulsory rehabilitation centre outside Kunming City in Yunnan houses up to 10,000 inmates at a time. Inmates are detoxed 'cold turkey' with the help of a herbal medicinal product that is manufactured on site. Inmates work up to eight hours a day in workshops within the facility, the males making machinery parts and the females making national minority dolls for a Taiwanese company. For those who come voluntarily and whose families are sufficiently well-off enough to pay are housed in more luxurious accommodation. There is also a methadone clinic in a

'voluntary rehabilitation' wing of the facility which is separated from the involuntary part of the centre and a clinic attached to the centre for former heroin users in Kunming who travel to the centre to receive treatment. In the voluntary rehabilitation wing, patients, many coming from as far away as Taiwan and Hong Kong for treatment, are offered an array of educational and counselling resources. Involuntary inmates on the other hand, are rehabilitated through work and pay a minimum of 40 yuan per month for food and accommodation, most paying for this service in kind through labour. The recidivism rate is 85–90 per cent. This information is collated from the author's interview with Centre Director (June 2005).

61 Liang Jinyun, 'Yunnan jindu douzheng xingshi pinggu', p. 3.

62 Report on 2006 National Counter-Narcotics Activities by the Counter Narcotics Control Commission (released in 2006) www.china.com.cn/law/zhuanti/yldp/2007-06/02/content_8333483.htm. Note that in June 2006, an MPS Notice announced mandatory detention at compulsory rehabilitation centres for all drug takers and those users caught a second time would be sent to a mandatory reduction through labour facility.

63 Liang Jinyun, 'Yunnan jindu douzheng xingshi pinggu', p. 1.

64 Interview with counter narcotics official, Kunming, 2005.

65 Report on 2006 National Counter-Narcotics Activities by the Counter Narcotics Control Commission www.gov.cn/gzdt/2006-06/26/content_319658.htm.

66 Ibid. Because of the success of police 'defence lines' in the first months of the War on Drugs 2005, the decreased supply of heroin on the street in Yunnan pushed up the price by 31.5 per cent and in areas outside Yunnan, the price rose from 30 to 50 per cent. In Shanghai and Jiangsu Provinces, the price rose to 1,000 yuan per gram, a dramatic rise compared with the start of the year when it was 325 yuan per gram. Given the relative scarcity of supply, there was also an increase in the impurity of street heroin, which was mainly mixed with corn flour. At the beginning of 2005 in Beijing, each gram of heroin was 64.1 per cent pure but by October, it was only 37.7 per cent. In Kunming City, Yunnan Province, in April it was 37 per cent and by June purity had dropped to 23.1 per cent.

67 Ibid.

68 As noted above, 46,300 serious drug crime cases uncovered involved 56,200 suspects, 47,290 of whom had already been formally arrested and indicted for trial. Drugs seized included 5.79 tonnes of heroin, 1.69 tonnes of opium and 5.95 tonnes of ice. Report on 2006 National Counter-Narcotics Activities by the Counter Narcotics Control Commission, www.china.com.cn/law/zhuanti/yldp/2007-06/02/content_8333483.htm.

69 Ibid.

70 Ibid.

71 Report on 2006 National Counter-Narcotics Activities by the Counter Narcotics Control Commission.

72 Report on 2005 National Counter-Narcotics Activities by the Counter Narcotics Control Commission

73 Ibid.

74 'Reports on crimes, sentences, punishments, and other judicial related activities in the PRC monitored from 13 December 2006 to 8 January 2007', *Xinhua* News, 19 January 2007, OSC Transcribed Text, Document no. 200701191477.1_941323fbf14a7065.

75 Ibid.

76 'Compilation of reports on crimes, sentences, punishments, and other judicial related activities in the PRC monitored from 4 to 22 January 2007', *Xinhua* News, 23 January 2007, OSC Transcribed Text, Document No. 200701231477.1_3a1518e20ef22b90.

77 2007 Annual Report on Drug Control in China for 2006 National Counter-Narcotics Activities, CNCC.

78 Ibid.

79 Author interview with a senior MPS counter narcotics official (July 2005).

80 Ibid.
81 Annual Report on Drug Control in China, 2008, Office of the National Counter-Narcotics Control Commission, February 2008.
82 'Drug Lord Sentenced to Death in South China', *Xinhua* News, 26 June 2007, OSC Transcribed Text,. Document No. 200706261477.1_d9a0001e647add29.
83 Li Changming, 'Zousi fanmai hailuoyin 433.95 gongjin Yunnan teda dupin anfan fufa' (Criminals convicted of smuggling and selling 433.95 kilograms of heroin in a major drug case in Yunnan have been executed), www.chinacourt.org/htm/article/200708/17/ 260403.shtml, 17 August 2007 (accessed 18 August 2007).
84 Annual Report on 2007 National Counter-Narcotics Activities by the Counter Narcotics Crime Commission, p. 32.
85 US Department of State 2007 International Narcotics Control Strategy Report (INCSR), p. 279.
86 Annual Report on 2007 National Counter-Narcotics Activities, p. 32.
87 'China police bring in 37 suspected drug trafficking leaders in 2006', *Xinhua* News, 26 June 2007, OSC Transcribed Text, Document no. 200706261477.1_e83700317eba873f.
88 'Reports on crimes, sentences, punishments, and other judicial related activities in the PRC monitored from 13 December 2006 to 8 January 2007', *Xinhua* News, 19 January 2007, OSC Transcribed Text, Document no. 200701191477.1_941323fbf14a7065.
89 'Southwest China court hears cross-border heroin trafficking case', *Xinhua* News, 18 January 2007, OSC Transcribed Text, Document no. 200701181477.1_3374002ea54491d0.
90 Liang Jinyun, 'Yunnan jindu douzheng xingshi pinggu', p. 5.
91 Ibid.
92 'Zhao Shijie: wei jianshe fuyu wenming kaifang hexie yunnan tigao sifa baozheng' (Zhao Renjie: providing legal guarantees for a prosperous, civilized, open and harmonious Yunnan) Yunnan Ribao (Yunnan Daily), 8 December 2006, p. 1, www.yn.xinhuanet.com.gov/2006-12/08/content_873333.htm, 8 December 2006, p. 1 (accessed 12 December 2006).

6 Fighting the collective: the rise of organized crime

1 Ming Xia, 'Assessing and explaining the resurgence of China's criminal underworld', p. 166.
2 'Quanguo yanli daji she hei fanzui, qunian yilai 2,749 ming zuifan huoxing' (2,749 criminals have been successfully convicted since the start of the national strike hard against mafia-style crime last year), *Fazhi ribao* (Legal System Daily), http:www.jcrb.com/200708/ca632350.htm 29 August 2007 (accessed 30 August 2007).
3 'Zhou Yongkang: xiang hei e'shili xuanzhan duoqu dahei chu'e douzheng de shengli' (Zhou Yongkang: war has been declared on criminal syndicates and gangs; police are striving for victories in the struggle against gangs and criminal syndicates), *Fazhi ribao* (Legal System Daily), 27 April 2007, p. 1.
4 Ibid.
5 The term *heishehui xingzhi jituan* can be translated literally as 'syndicates with the characteristics of the underworld'. I use the term 'mafia-style syndicates' as it is the English translation used in English language newspapers and journals in China including *Xinhua* News.
6 'Yiqianwan renmin de qidai' (Carrying the expectations of one billion people), *Renmin Ribao* (The People's Daily), 11 May 2001, p. 4. (Hereafter citied as RMRB). For a detailed examination of the relationship between organized crime and government, see Ko-lin Chin and Roy Godson, 'Organized crime and the political-criminal nexus in China', pp. 5–42.
7 Ibid.

8 Ibid.
9 'Four brothers sentenced to death for running north China crime gang', *Xinhua* News, 17 November 2006, OSC Transcribed Text, Document no. 200611171477.1_526500211524cb01.
10 'Quanguo yanli daji she hei fanzui, qunian yilai 2,749 ming zuifan huoxing'.
11 'Zhou Yongkang: xiang hei e'shile xuanzhan duoqu dahei chu'e douzheng de shengli'.
12 Ibid.
13 Kang Shuhua, *Dangdai Zhongguo fanzui zhuti* (Crime Issues in Contemporary China), Beijing: Qunzhong chubanshe, 2004, p. 313.
14 Lu Gengsong, 'Zhongguo heishehui xianzhuang fenxi' (An analysis of the make-up of mafia-style syndicates) *Yancheng wanbao* (Yancheng Evening News), 24 May 2001; Zhou Liangtao, 'Lun heishehui xingzhi de zuzhi' (On the organization of mafia-style syndicates), in Li Zhongxin, *Lun heishehui xingzhi fanzui wenti yanjiu* (Research Issues on Mafia-style Organized Crime), pp. 43–51.
15 Lu, 'Zhongguo heishehui xianzhuang fenxi'.
16 Ming Xia, 'Organizational formations of organized crime in China: perspectives from the state, markets, and networks', pp. 1–23.
17 Kang Shuhua, *Dangdai Zhongguo fanzui zhuti*, pp. 281–84.
18 Chen Xingliang, 'Guanyu heishehui xingzhi fanzui de lixing sikao' (A rational assessment of mafia-style syndicate crime), Beida wenxian (Unpublished Beijing University document).
19 Kang, *Dangdai Zhongguo fanzui zhuti*, p. 325.
20 Yan Jianping, 'Huizhoushi hei'eshili tuanhuo' in Guangdongsheng jingcha xiehui (ed.), *Guangdong heishehui fanzui wenti yanjiu* (Research on Mafia-style Crime Issues in Guangdong), Beijing: Gong'an daxue chubanshe (restricted circulation), 2003, p. 296.
21 Wang Mingman and Ning Hongtao, 'Shenzhen Longgangqu heishehui xingzhi fanzui xianzhuang' (The current situation concerning mafia-style crime in Longgang district in Shenzhen) in *Guangdong heishehui fanzui wenti yanjiu*, p. 190.
22 Lu Gengsong, 'Zhongguo heishehui xianzhuang fenxi'; Zhou, 'Lun heishehui xingzhi de zuzhi', pp. 43–51.
23 'PRC Public Security Ministry issues circular on fighting crime', *Xinhua* News, 26 April 2001. FBIS-CHI-2001-0426, Document no. CCP20010426000191.
24 Ming Xia, 'Organizational formations of organized crime in China', p. 3.
25 Ibid., 5.
26 Ibid., 5.
27 Ibid., p. 12.
28 Ibid., pp. 13–14.
29 Ibid., p. 17.
30 Ibid., p. 19.
31 Tang Shuhua, *Fanzuixue tonglun* (Debates in Criminology), pp. 206–07.
32 For an analysis of juvenile delinquency in China in the 1980s see Borge Bakken, 'Crime, juvenile delinquency and deterrence policy in China', pp. 29–53.
33 Ronald Keith and Zhiqiu Lin, *New Crime in China: Public Order and Human Rights*, p. 95.
34 Ibid.
35 'Zhongguo zhongyang guanyu yanli daji xingshi fanzui huodong de jueding – jielu (B)' p. 133, cited in Harold M. Tanner, H., *Strike Hard!: anti-crime campaigns and Chinese criminal justice 1979–1989*, p. 91.
36 Han Yanlong (ed.), *Zhonghua renmin gongheguo fazhi tongshi* (A Comprehensive History of the Legal System in the People's Republic of China), p. 712.
37 Trevaskes, *Courts and Criminal Justice in Contemporary China*, p. 120.
38 Ibid., p. 121.

39 Dangdai zhongguo lishi weiyuanwei (ed.), *Dangdai Zhongguo de shenpan gongzuo* (Trial work in Contemporary China) (vol. 1), pp. 342–44.
40 Trevaskes, *Courts and Criminal justice in Contemporary China*, p. 153, citing a case from Zou Xianchao, *Ningxia shenpanzhi* (Annals of Trial Work in Ningxia), p. 206.
41 Ibid.
42 Kang, *Dangdai Zhongguo fanzui zhuti*, p. 308.
43 Ibid.
44 He Bingsong, *Heishehui fanzui jiedu* (Readings on Underworld Crime), p. 6.
45 Guo Xingguo (ed.), *Jianguo yilai gongan gongzuo dashi yaolan* (An Outline of the Chronicles of Public Security Work Since Liberation), p. 912.
46 Wu Jianqiang and Cao Yi, *Zhongguo heishehui xingzhi fanzui wenti yanjiu* (Research issues on Chinese mafia-style syndicates), p. 194.
47 Ibid.
48 Ibid., p. 196.
49 Guo, *Jianguo yilai gongan gongzuo dashi yaolan*, p. 912.
50 Ibid.
51 Zhou Xinjie, 'Guangdong heishehui fanzui ruogan wenti chutan' (A preliminary study of some issues relating to underworld crime in Guangdong Province), in *Guangdong heishehui fanzui wenti yanjiu*, p. 4.
52 Ibid., pp. 7–8.
53 Kang, *Dangdai Zhongguo fanzui zhuti*, p. 278.
54 Ibid., p. 313.
55 Li Wenyan and Tian Hongjie, *Da hei chu'e xingshi falu shiyong jieshu* (Interpreting the Application of Criminal Law in the Campaign against Organized Crime), p. 2.
56 Kang, *Dangdai Zhongguo fanzui zhuti*, p. 275.
57 For a discussion of these difficulties, see Keith and Li, *New Crime in China: public order and human rights*, p. 101.
58 Article 26 of the CL97 states that 'A criminal group refers to a relatively stable criminal organization formed by three or more persons for the purpose of committing crimes jointly'.
59 Wu and Cao, *Zhongguo heishehui xingzhi fanzui wenti yanjiu*, pp. 199–202.
60 'Zuigao fayuan guanyu shenli heishehui xingzhi zuzhi fanzui de anjian juti yingyong falu ruogan wenti de jieshi' (SPC judicial interpretation of certain issues related to the specific application of laws to prosecute mafia-style syndicates), passed at the No. 1148 Judicial Committee meeting. Judicial Interpretation (2000) No 42, available online at www.law-lib.com.
61 Wu and Cao, *Zhongguo heishehui xingzhi fanzui wenti yanjiu*, pp. 197–98.
62 Ming Xia, 'Organizational formations of organized crime in China, p. 14.
63 Ibid., p. 204.
64 Kang, *Dangdai Zhongguo fanzui zhuti*, p. 318.
65 Wu and Cao, *Zhongguo heishehui xingzhi fanzui wenti*, p. 203.
66 Ibid.
67 Ibid., pp. 230–32.
68 Cheng Weifa, 'Chongqing Yanda heishehui xingzhi zuzhi, she hei tuanhuo zhujian gongsihua' (Chongqing strikes hard at mafia-style syndicates, syndicates becoming more and more commercially sophisticated) *Diyi cajing ribao* (First Economic Daily), 7 July 2006.
69 Ibid.
70 Ibid.
71 'Beijing teda shehei tuanhuo 34 ren shoushen, cengyu chengguan hemou fanzui' (34 syndicate members involved in a major mafia-style syndicate case in conspiracy with government officers), http://news.China.com/zh_cn/domestic/945/20060712/13462162.html, 12 July 2006 (accessed 15 July 2006).
72 Hou Shasha, 'Beijing shouli heishehui zuzhi an shi'erri xuanpan' (Sentencing of

Beijing's first mafia-style syndicate case was publicly pronounced on 12 August), *Renmin ribao* (People's Daily), 13 August 2006.

73 Growing interest in the relationship between marketization and crime growth in China has inspired several studies. See, for example, Jianhong Liu, 'Modernization and crime patterns in China', pp. 119–30 and Jianhong Liu, 'Crime patterns during the market transition in China', pp. 613–33.

74 These matters reach deep into the scholarly terrain of political economy which is beyond my immediate concern with crime and crime control in this chapter. I raise them here to draw attention to these issues for others to explore in detail.

7 The end of campaign justice?

1 David Garland, *The Culture of Control: crime and social order in contemporary society*, p. 194.

2 Garland also argues that a sense of general insecurity within communities that was a by-product of the economic and social conditions of late-modernity has led to the development of a mentality of risk management in American society whereby people have grown to expect an instant governmental response to their feelings of insecurity. This has allowed legislators to place themselves on a 'war footing' in relation to crime, and to exercise direct control over sentencing levels. Garland explains the legislative consequences of this fixation with control: '[Political actors'] most pressing concern is to do something decisive, to respond with immediate effect to public outrage, to demonstrate that the state is in control and is willing to use its powers to uphold "law and order" and to protect the law-abiding public. Some . . . laws – such as the reintroduction of the chain gang, boot camps, shaming punishments, and attempts to revive corporal punishment – have a 'made for television' quality that betrays their main purpose. Some – such as mandatory sentences, "truth in sentencing" laws and the expediated death penalty – have an absolutist quality designed to reassure a distrustful public that the system will not betray them once the case goes out of view. Others – such as community notification, sexual predator laws, supermax prisons, electronic monitoring and the recriminalization of juvenile justice – involve public safety considerations of doubtful efficacy and a barely sublimated punitiveness that suggests a complete disregard for the rights of humanity of those being sanctioned. Such policies become particularly salient where a more general insecurity – deriving from the precariousness of social and economic relations in late modern society – is widely experienced and where the state is deemed to have failed in its efforts to deliver physical and economic security to key social groups' (see Garland, *The Culture of Control*, p. 133). Jonathon Simon's book, *Governing Through Crime*, goes one step further than Garland by arguing that 'crime' itself has emerged as the central organizing principle around which political authority in the US is now conceived and exercised. Crime, he argues, has transformed from being one of many social problems to be managed, to being the issue around which political authority is organized. See Jonathan Simon, *Governing Through Crime: how the war on crime transformed American democracy and created a culture of fear*.

3 'Guangzhou lowers the standard at which a theft offence becomes an indictable offence from the theft of 2000 yuan to 1000 yuan worth of property', http://legal.people.com.ca/GB/42735/4937706.html (accessed 28 August 2006).

4 Ibid.

5 'Yanda Fengbao zuotian lingcheng xijuan Guangzhou quanshi' (Strike hard operation storm engulfs the entire city of Guangzhou) *Guangzhou ribao* (Guangzhou Daily), 23 August 2006, p. 1.

6 'Xinjiang fayuan jiang jixu dui sangu shili fanzui caiqu gaoya' (Xinjiang to keep up the pressure on the 'three evil forces'), Zhongguo xinjiang xinwen zhongxin (Xinjiang China news centre), www.chinaxinjiang,cn/news (accessed 31 August 2007).

7 Ibid.
8 Wang Wenyuan, 'Yanda shiyi' (Clearing up some doubts about Strike Hard), p. 46.
9 Ibid.
10 Li Yuanhe and Yu Tianming, 'Yanda xingshi zhengce yu xingfa cailiang (Strike hard criminal justice policy and the range of punishment within the law), p. 40.
11 Huang Xiangqing, 'Yanda xingshi zhengce de zhangwo' (Understanding Strike Hard criminal justice policy), p. 24.
12 You Wei and Xie Xiaomei, 'Fanzuihua yuance yu woguo de yanda zhengce' (Principles of criminality and China's Strike Hard policy), p. 38.
13 See discussion on flexible criminal justice practices in Chapter 3.
14 Sun Guoyang, 'Xingshi yitihua shiyexia yanda de lixing sikao (A rational reflection on implementing an integrated vision of criminal justice work into Strike Hard), p. 99.
15 Zhong Yuhua, 'Dui yanda zhengce de lixing zai renshi' (Rethinking the rationality of Strike Hard policy), p. 68.
16 Ibid.
17 Ibid.
18 Rao Yuanming, 'Yanda zhengzhihou de rougan sikao' (Some post-Strike Hard campaign reflections), p. 82.
19 Bi Xiqian and Chen Juan, 'Yanda zhengzhi douzheng de huigu yu zhanwang (A look back and a look ahead at the Strike Hard campaign), p. 46.
20 Ibid.
21 The SPC retained the authority to review and approve large corruption cases and other major economic crimes.
22 For a more detailed examination of this argument, see Susan Trevaskes, 'The death penalty in China today: kill fewer, kill cautiously', pp. 393–413.
23 The provincial courts were temporarily delegated this power in 1980 and again in 1981.
24 Trevaskes, 'The death penalty in China today', p. 394.
25 See Zhao Lei, 'Zhongguo sifa kaiqi shaosha shidai: congzhong congkuai chengwei lishi henji' (Chinese justice enters a new era of fewer executions: 'severe and swift' punishment becomes a vestige of history), *Nanfang Ribao* (Southern China Daily), 4 January 2007.
26 In China, suspended death sentences are invariably reduced to life sentences within two years of handing down the initial sentence. Those sentenced to death with a two-year reprieve in theory serve a maximum of 24 years. Those given a life sentence are supposed to serve 22 years. In practice, however, the vast majority of prisoners' sentences are routinely reduced. At present, if someone is handed a death sentence with a reprieve, his/her sentence will be reduced to a life sentence within two years. Prisoners serving life sentences can be released after 15 years. See Chen Xingliang, 'Kuanyan xiangji xingshi zhengce yanjiu' (A study of the criminal justice policy of balancing leniency and severity), p. 24.
27 'Zhongguo jiangzai xiaoyou falu kuangjianei yange kongzhi sixing' (China is putting in place strict legal controls on the application of the death penalty), *Xinhua* News, http://news.xinhuanet.com.legal/2006-12/28/content_5542754.htm, 28 December 2006 (accessed 29 December 2006).
28 'Quebao meiyiqi sixing anjian, jingdeqi lishi jianyan' (Ensure that each and every death penalty decision can stand the test of time), *Xinhua* News, http://news.xinhuanet.comm.legal/2006-12/28/content_5542621.htm, 28 December 2006 (accessed 29 December 2006).
29 Ibid. Also see Trevaskes, 'The death penalty in China today', p. 405.
30 Ibid.
31 'Zuigao renmin fayuan guanyu fuhe sixing anjian ruogan wenti de guiding' (Decision of the SPC on several issues relating to the approval of death sentences), Document 2007-4 www.chinacourt.org/flwk/show.php?file_id=116488, 27 February 2007 (accessed 28 February 2007). Although first promulgated as a 'decision' (*jueding*), it

was confirmed later as a judicial interpretation (*sifa jieshi*) which is more authoritative than a decision. Also see Trevaskes, 'The death penalty in China today', pp. 404–06.

32 'Zuigao renmin fayuan zuigao renmin jianchayuan gonganbu sifabu guanyu jinyibu yange yifa ban'an, quebao sixing anjian zhiliang de yijian' (Joint opinion of the supreme people's court, the supreme people's procuratorate, the Ministry of Public Security, and the Ministry of Justice on 'strengthening measures in handling cases strictly in accordance with the law and on 'guaranteeing the quality in the handling of death penalty cases'), 9 March 2007. Hereafter referred to as the 'Joint Opinion'. http: www.chinacourt.org/flwk/show1.php?file_id=116768 (accessed on 14 March 2007). Also see Trevaskes, 'The death penalty in China today', p. 408.

33 Chen Xingliang, 'Kuanyan xiangji xingshi zhengce yanjiu' (A study of the criminal justice policy of balancing leniency and severity), p. 20.

34 Ibid.

35 Trevaskes, 'The death penalty in China today', p. 402.

36 'Zhuanfang zuigao fayuan yuanzhang xiao yang: wei hexie shehui tigong sifa baozheng' (Exclusive interview with SPC president Xiao Yang on providing legal guarantees for the building of a harmonious society), www.chinacourt.org, 6 February 2007 (accessed on 6 February 2007).

37 Ibid.

38 Ibid.

39 The 68 offences include 7 crimes under the category of 'Crimes of endangering national security', 14 under 'Crimes of endangering public security, 16 under 'Crimes of disrupting the order of the socialist market economy, 5 under 'Crimes of infringing upon citizen's rights of the person and democratic rights', 2 under 'Crimes of property violation', 8 under 'Crimes of obstructing the administration of public order', 2 under 'Crimes of impairing the interests of national defence', 2 under 'Crimes of embezzlement and bribery', and 12 under 'Crimes of servicemen's transgression of duties'.

40 Zhao Lei 'Zhongguo sifa kaiqi shaosha shidai: congzhong congkuai chengwei lishi henji' (Chinese justice enters a new era of fewer executions: 'severe and swift' punishment becomes a vestige of history), *Nanfang Ribao* (Southern China Daily), 4 January 2007.

41 Li Chuan, 'Dangqian yanda yanjiuzhong de si ge wuqu' (Four inaccuracies regarding the current research on Strike Hard), p. 3.

42 Sun Guoyang, 'Xingshi yitihua shiyexia yanda de lixing sikao (A rational reflection on implementing an integrated vision of criminal justice work into the Strike Hard campaign), p. 99.

43 'Sifa kongzhi yichujixian, sixing lifa youchi' (Judicial means of controlling the death penalty have now reached their limits. We are waiting on legislative changes to do their part in reform), *Nanfang ribao* (Southern Capital News), http://news.1488.com/news/review/2007/12-24/13-5-39-1.shtml 24 December 2007 (accessed on 19 March 2008).

44 'Faxue zhuanjia cheng: xuejie dacheng feichu sixing gongshi, dan zao minyi fandui' (Legal expert says: members of China's legal fraternity are united in their belief that the death penalty can be abolished, but abolition is not supported by the public', *Xinhua* News http://news.news.xinhuanet,com/legal/2008-03/18/content_7810280.htm,18 March 2008 (accessed on 19 March 2008).

45 Hong Yunteng, Chen Weidong and Liu Renwen, '15% sixing wei hezhunlu shuoming shenme?: sixing fuhe gaige de qishi' (What is the significance of the 15% of death sentence applications to the SPC that have been rejected? Some revelations about reforms to the system of death penalty approvals), *Fazhi ribao*, 21 March 2008, p. 3.

46 Wu Bo, 'Zuigao fayuan yuanzhang: "qunzhong ganjue ying zuowei pan sixing yiju zhiyi"' (President of the SPC says: 'the feelings of the masses should be one criteria for judicial decision-making in capital cases'), *Xinhua* News, 11 April 2008.

47 Ibid.

48 Keith Thomas, *Man and the Natural World: changing attitudes in England 1500–1800*, London: Allen Lane, 1983, p. 175.

Bibliography

Selected bibliography of English language sources

Backer, Larry Cata, 'The party as polity, the communist party, and the Chinese constitutional state: a theory of state-party constititutionalism', *Journal of Chinese and Comparative Law* 16 (1), 2009, pp. 101–64. Available online at http://papers.ssrn.com/sol3/papers.cfm?abstract_id=1325792.

Bakken, Borge, 'Crime, juvenile delinquency and deterrence policy in China', *The Australian Journal of Chinese Affairs* 30, 1993, pp. 29–53.

—— 'Editor's introduction', *Chinese Sociology and Anthropology* 27 (3), Spring 1995, pp. 3–18.

—— *The Exemplary Society: human improvement, social control and the dangers of modernity in China*, New York: Oxford University Press, 2000.

—— 'Moral panics, crime rates and harsh punishment in China', *The Australian and New Zealand Journal of Criminology* 37, 2004, pp. 67–90.

—— 'Comparative perspectives on crime in China', in Borge Bakken (ed.), *Crime, Punishment and Policing in China*, Lanham MD: Rowman & Littlefield Publishers, 2005.

—— 'The culture of revenge and the power of politics: a comparative attempt to explain the punitive', *Journal of Power* 1 (2), 2008, pp. 169–87.

Biddulph, Sarah, *Legal Reform and Administrative Detention Powers in China*, New York: Cambridge University Press, 2007.

Blaustein, Albert P., *Fundamental Legal Documents of Communist China*, South Hackensack, NJ: F.B. Rothman Publishers, 1962.

Brady, James, *Justice and Politics in People's China: legal order or continuing revolution?* London: Academic Press, 1982, p. 91.

Brigham, John, *The Cult of the Court*, Philadelphia: Temple University Press, 1987.

Butler W. E. (ed.), *The Legal System of the Chinese Soviet Republic 1931–1934*, New York: Transnational Publishers Inc., 1983.

Chen, Albert H. Y., *An Introduction to the Legal System of the People's Republic of China*, Hong Kong: LexisNexus, 2004.

Chen Jianfu, *Chinese Law: Towards an Understanding of Chinese Law, its Nature and Development,* The Hague/London/Boston: Kluwer Law International, 1999.

—— *Chinese Law: context and transformation*, Leiden/Boston: Martinus Nijhoff, 2008.

Chen Jianfu, Li Yuwen, Jan Michiel Otto (eds), *Implementation of Law in the People's Republic of China*, The Hague/Boston: Kluwer Law International, 2002.

Chen, Phillip M., *Law and Justice: the legal system in China 2000 B.C. to 1960 A.D.* New York/ London: Dunnellen Publishing Company, 1973.

Chen Xianglong and Qiu Xinlong, 'The relationship between crime and punishment', *Social Sciences in China*, Third Issue, September 1988, pp. 180–99.

Chen Xingliang 'An examination of the death penalty in China', *Contemporary Chinese Thought* 36 (3), 2005, pp. 35–52.

Chen Zhonglin and Kacheng Huang, 'Drug problems in China: recent trends, countermeasures and challenges', *International Journal of Offender Therapy and Comparative Criminology* 51 (1), 2007, pp. 98–109.

Chin Ko-lin and Roy Godson, 'Organized crime and the political-criminal nexus in China', *Trends in Organized Crime* 9 (3), 2006, pp. 5–42.

Cohen, Jerome, *The Criminal Process in the People's Republic of China, 1949–63: an introduction*, Cambridge, MA: Harvard University Press, 1968.

Cohen, Stanley, *Folk Devils and Moral Panics: the creation of the Mods and Rockers*, New York: St Martin's Press, 1980.

Cotterrell, Roger, *Law's Community: legal theory in sociological perspective*, Oxford: Clarendon Press, 1995.

Counter Narcotics Control Commission, Report on 2006 National Counter-Narcotics Activities (released in 2007). Available online at www.china.com.cn/law/zhuanti/yldp/2007-06/02/content_8333483.htm.

Criminal Law of the People's Republic of China, Beijing: China Legal System Publishing House, 2000.

Criminal Procedural Law of the People's Republic of China, Beijing: China Legal System Publishing House, 1999.

Damaska, Mirjin, *The Faces of Justice and State Authority: a comparative approach to the legal process*, New Haven/London: Yale University Press, 1986.

Delury, John, '"Harmonious" in China', *Policy Review* 148, 2008, pp. 35–44.

Deng Xiaoping, *Selected Works of Deng Xiaoping* (1975–1982), Beijing: Foreign Languages Press, 1984.

Deng Xiaoping, *Selected Works of Deng Xiaoping Volume III (1982–1992)*, Beijing: Foreign Languages Press, 1994.

Dowdle, Michael W., 'Heretical laments: China and the fallacies of "rule of law"', *Cultural Dynamics* 11 (3), 1999, pp. 287–314.

Du Xichuan and Zhang Lingyuan, *Chinese Legal System: a general survey*, Beijing: New World Press, 1990.

Dutton, Michael R., *Policing and Punishment in China: from patriarchy to the people*, Cambridge: Cambridge University Press, 1992.

—— *Policing Chinese Politics: a history*, Durham, NC, and London: Duke University Press, 2006.

Ericson, Richard V., Patricia M. Barnanek and Janet B. L. Chan (eds), *Representing Order: crime, law, and justice in the News Media*, Buckingham: Open University Press, 1991.

Finder, Susan, 'The supreme people's court of the people's republic of China', *Journal of Chinese Law* 7, 1993, pp. 145–224.

Findlay, Mark, '"Independence" and the judiciary in the PRC', in Kanishka Jayasuriya (ed.), *Law, Capitalism and Power in East Asia: the rule of law and legal institutions*, London: Routledge, 1999, pp. 281–99.

Fu Hualing and D. W. Choy, 'Policing for profit: fiscal crisis and institutionalized corruption of China's police', in Stanley Einstein and Manachem Amir (eds), *Police Corruption:*

paradigms, models and concepts – challenges for developing countries, Huntsville, TX: OICJ Press, 2003, pp. 537–52.

Fu Hualing, 'Zhou Yongkang and the recent police reform in China', *The Australian and New Zealand Journal of Criminology* 38 (2), 2003, pp. 241–53.

Garfinkel, Harold, 'Conditions of successful degradation ceremonies', *The American Journal of Sociology* 61 (5), 1956, pp. 420–24.

Garland, David, *Punishment and Modern Society: a study in social theory*, Chicago: University of Chicago Press and Oxford University Press, 1990.

—— 'Punishment and culture: the symbolic dimensions of criminal justice', *Studies in Law, Politics and Society* 11, 1991, pp. 191–222.

—— *The Culture of Control: crime and social order in contemporary society*, Chicago: University of Chicago Press, 2001.

—— 'Concepts of culture in the sociology of punishment', *Theoretical Criminology* 10 (4), 2006, pp. 419–47.

Garland, David and Peter Young (eds), *The Power to Punish: contemporary penalty and social analysis*, Atlantic Highlands, NJ: Humanities Press, 1983.

Grafstein, Robert, 'Legitimacy of political institutions', *Polity* 14, 1981, pp. 51–70.

Gregor, James, *The Ideology of Fascism: the rationale of totalitarianism*, New York: The Free Press, 1969.

He Baogang, *The Democratization of China*, London: Routledge, 1996.

He Ni and Ineke H. Marshall, 'Social production of crime data: a critical examination of Chinese crime statistics', *International Criminal Justice Review* 7, 1997, pp. 46–64.

Hunt, Alan, 'Dichotomy and contradiction in the sociology of law', in Piers Beirne and Richard Quinney (eds), *Marxism and Law*, New York: John Wiley & Sons, 1982, pp. 74–101.

Jayasuriya, Kanishka, 'Corporatism and judicial independence within statist legal institutions in East Asia', in Kanishka Jayasuriya (ed.), *Law, Capitalism and Power in East Asia: the rule of law and legal institutions*, London: Routledge, 1999, pp. 173–204.

Jiang Zhu, 'Stress improving public order at national meeting', *Xinhua* News, 3 April 2001, FBIS-CHI-2001-0403.

Johnson, David T. and Franklin E. Zimring, *The Next Frontier: national development, political change and the death penalty in Asia*, New York: Oxford University Press, 2009.

Keith, Ronald C., *China's Struggle for the Rule of Law*, London: St Martin's Press, 1994.

Keith, Ronald C. and Zhiqiu Li, *Law and Justice in China's New Marketplace*, New York: Palgrave, 2001.

—— *New Crime in China: public order and human rights*, London and New York: Routledge, 2006.

Keller, Perry, 'Sources of order in Chinese law', *The American Journal of Comparative Law* XLII, 1994, pp. 711–59.

Lacey, Nicola, Celia Wells and Dick Meure (eds), *Reconstructing Criminal Law: critical perspectives on crime and the criminal process*, London: Weidenfeld and Nicolson, 1998.

Lam, Willy Wo-Lap, 'Chinks in the armour of the Hu Jintao administration: can a harmonious society emerge in the absence of political reform?', *China Perspectives* 72, 2007 (3), pp. 4–11.

Lin, Chris X., 'A quiet revolution: an overview of China's judicial reform', *Asian-Pacific Law & Policy Journal* 4 (2), 2003, pp. 293–314.

Liu Hua, 'Hooliganism', *Chinese Sociology and Anthropology* 27 (3), Spring 1995, pp. 57–63.

Liu Jianhong, 'Crime patterns during the market transition in China', *British Journal of Criminology* 45, 2005, pp. 613–33.

—— 'Modernization and crime patterns in China', *Journal of Criminal Justice* 34, 2006, pp. 119–30

Lubman, Stanley B., *Bird in a Cage: legal reform in China after Mao*, Stanford, CA: Stanford University Press, 1999.

Manning, Peter, *Police Work: the social organization of policing*, Cambridge, MA: MIT Press, 1977.

Mao Tse-tung, 'On the correct handling of contradictions among the people', in *Selected Works of Mao Tse-tung Volume 5*, Peking: Foreign Languages Press, 1973, pp. 384–421.

—— 'On the people's democratic dictatorship', in *Selected Works of Mao Tse-tung Volume 4*, Peking: Foreign Languages Press, 1973, pp. 411–24.

Mathieson, Thomas, 'General prevention as communication', in R. A. Duff and David Garland (eds), *A Reader on Punishment*, Oxford: Oxford University Press, 1994, pp. 218–37.

Meithe, Terance D. and Hong Lu, *Punishment: a comparative historical perspective*, Cambridge: Cambridge University Press, 2005.

Millward, James, 'Violent separatism in Xinjiang: a critical assessment', *Policy Studies* 6, East-West Centre Washington. Available online at www.eastwestcenter.org/fileadmin/stored/pdfs/PS006.pdf.

Munro, Donald J, 'Belief control: the psychological and ethical foundations', in Amy Auberacher Wilson *et al.* (eds), *Deviance and Social Control in Chinese Society*, New York: Praeger, 1977, pp. 14–36.

—— *The Concept of Man in Contemporary China*, Ann Arbour: University of Michigan Press, 1977.

Nathan, Andrew J., *China's Transition*, New York: Columbia University Press, 1997.

Office of the National Counter-Narcotics Activities, Annual Report on Drug Control in China, 2008, Beijing: National Counter-Narcotics Control Commission, 2008.

Oldman, John. R. (ed.), *China's Legal Development*, New York: M. E. Sharpe, 1986, pp. 19–20.

Peerenboom, Randall, *China's Long March Toward Rule of Law*, Cambridge: Cambridge University Press, 2002.

—— 'Out of the pan and into the fire: well-intentioned but misguided recommendations to eliminate all forms of administrative detention in China', *Northwestern University Law Review* 98 (3), 2004, pp. 991–1104.

Potter, Pitman, *The Chinese Legal System: globalization and local legal culture*, London and New York: Routledge, 2001.

Sarat, Austin and Thomas R. Kearns (eds), *Law in Everyday Life*, Ann Arbour: University of Michigan Press, 1993.

—— *Law in the Domains of Culture*, Ann Arbour: The University of Michigan Press, 1998.

Shao Daosheng, *Preliminary Study of China's Juvenile Delinquency*, Beijing: Foreign Language Press, 1992.

Sibley, Susan, 'Making a place for cultural analysis of law', *Law and Social Inquiry* 17, 1992, pp. 39–62.

Simon, Jonathan, *Governing Through Crime: how the war on crime transformed American democracy and created a culture of fear*, Oxford/New York: Oxford University Press, 2007.

Swanstrom, Niklas, 'Narcotics and China: an old security threat from new sources', *China and Eurasia Forum Quarterly* 4 (1), 2006, pp. 113–31.

Tanner, Harold, *Strike Hard!: anti-crime campaigns and Chinese criminal justice 1979–1989*, New York: East Asian Program, Cornell University, 1999.

Tanner, Murray Scot, 'State coercion and the balance of awe: the 1983–1986 "stern blows" anti-crime campaign', *The China Journal* 44, 2000, pp. 93–125.

—— 'Campaign-style policing in China and its critics', in Borge Bakken (ed.), *Crime, Punishment, and Policing in China*, Lanham, MD: Rowman & Littlefield, 2005, pp. 171–88.

Tanner, Murray Scot and Eric Green, 'Principals and secret agents: central versus local control over policing and obstacles to "rule of law" in China', *The China Quarterly* 191, 2007, p. 646.

The Laws of the People's Republic of China 1983–1986, Beijing: Foreign Language Press, 1987.

Thomas, Keith, *Man and the Natural World: changing attitudes in England 1500–1800*, London: Allen Lane, 1983.

Thomas, S. B., *Government and Administration in Communist China*, Westport, CT: Greenwood Press, 1974, p. 106.

Trevaskes, Susan, 'Courts on the campaign path: criminal court work in China's "yanda 2001" anti-crime campaign', *Asian Survey* 42 (5), 2002, pp. 673–93.

—— 'Public sentencing rallies in China: the symbolizing of punishment and justice in a socialist state', *Crime, Law and Social Change* 39, 2003, pp. 359–82.

—— '"Strike hard 2001": form and strategy in a Chinese anti-crime campaign', *Australian and New Zealand Journal of Criminology* 36 (3), 2003, pp. 272–92.

—— 'Propaganda work in Chinese courts: public trials and sentencing rallies as sites of expressive punishment and public education in the People's Republic of China', *Punishment and Society* 6 (1), 2004, pp. 5–21.

—— *Courts and Criminal Justice in Contemporary China*, Lanham, MD: Lexington Press, 2007.

—— 'Severe and Swift Justice in China', *British Journal of Criminology* 47 (1), 2007, pp. 23–41.

—— 'The public/private security nexus in China', *Social Justice* 34 (3–4), 2007, pp. 28–55.

—— 'The death penalty in China today: kill fewer, kill cautiously', *Asian Survey* 43 (3), 2008, pp. 393–413.

United Nations Office on Drugs and Crime, Patterns and trends of amphetamine-type stimulants and other drugs of abuse in East Asia and the Pacific 2006.

US Department of State, International Narcotics Control Strategy Report (INCSR), 2007.

Winn, Peter A., 'Legal ritual', *Law and Critique* 2, 1991, pp. 207–32.

Xia Ming, 'Assessing and explaining the resurgence of China's criminal underworld', *Global Crime* 7 (2), 2006, pp. 151–75.

—— 'Organizational formations of organized crime in China: perspectives from the state, markets, and networks', *Journal of Contemporary China* 17 (54), 2008, pp. 1–23.

Yu, Olivia, 'The under-recording of crime police in China: a case study', *Policing: An International Journal of Police Strategies and Management* 22 (3), 1999, pp. 252–63.

Zhang Qianfan, 'The people's court in transition: the prospects of the Chinese judicial reform', *Journal of Contemporary China* 12, 2003, pp. 69–101.

Zhang Yong, 'Recent developments in Chinese criminal justice', *Asia Pacific Law Review* 8 (1), 2000, pp. 77–104.

Zhou Yongming, *Anti-Drug Crusades in Twentieth-Century China: nationalism, history, and state building*, Lanham, MD: Rowman & Littlefield, 1999.

—— *China's Anti-Drug Campaign in the Reform Era*, Singapore: World Scientific Press, 2000.

Selected bibliography of Chinese language sources

Bai Hucheng (ed.), *Yulin diqu shenpanzhi* (Annals of Court Work in Yulin District), Xi'an: Shaanxi renmin chubanshe, 1995.

Benshu Bianxiezu (ed.), *Yanda douzheng yu shehui zhian ganbu duben* (Readings for Cadres on the Strike Hard Campaign and Public Order), Beijing: Zhonggong zhongyang dangxiao chubanshe, 2000.

Bi Xiqian and Chen Juan, 'Yanda zhengzhi douzheng de huigu yu zhanwang' (A look back and a look ahead at the strike hard rectification campaign), *Zhongguo renmin gongan daxue bao* (*Journal of the Chinese People's Public Security University*) 2, 2003, pp. 45–50.

Cai Songyun (ed.), *Yiyangshi gonganju wei hunan de difangzhi zhunbei cailiao* (Preparatory Material for the Hunan Province Chronicles by the Yiyang Public Security Bureau), unpublished materials (undated).

Chen Beidi, *Zhongguo xidu diaocha* (An Investigation into Drug Use in China), Beijing: Xinhua chubanshe, 2006.

Chen Jiping (ed.), *Zhongguo shehui zhi'an zonghe zhili nianjian 2001–2002* (2001–2002 Yearbook of Comprehensive Management of Public Order in China), Beijing: Zhongguo chang'an chubanshe, 2003.

Chen Xingliang, 'Guanyu heishehui xingzhi fanzui de lixing sikao' (A rational assessment of mafia-style syndicate crime), Beida wenxian (Unpublished Beijing University document), 2005.

—— 'Kuanyan xiangji xingshi zhengce yanjiu' (A study of the criminal justice policy of balancing leniency and severity), *Faxue zazhi* (*Jurisprudence Magazine*) 1, 2006, pp. 17–25.

Chen Zexian (ed.), *Sixing zhongwei guanzhu de jiaodian* (The Death Penalty and its Control: A Global Focus), Beijing: Gongan daxue chubanshe, 2005.

Chen Zili, 'Yanda zhengzhi douzheng jiujing ruhe shenru' (How the Strike Hard campaign can have a deep impact), *Gongan yanjiu* (*Public Security Research*) 5, 2002, pp. 23–26.

—— 'Yanda zhengzhi douzhengjiujing ruhe shenru?' (How can the yanda campaign sustain a deep impact?) *Gongan yanjiu* (*Public Security Research*) 5, 2003, pp. 45–50.

Chongqing chenbao (*Chongqing Morning Post*), 'Zhejiang taixun zai dianyingyuan li shenpan tanguan, sanbai ming gangbu peiou pangting' (Three hundred officials' wives attend the criminal trial of a corrupt official in a cinema in Taixun County, Zhejiang Province), 23 September 2005, p. 1.

Counter Narcotics Control Commission, Report on 2005 National Counter-Narcotics Activities by the Counter Narcotics Control Commission (released in 2006). Available online at www.gov.cn/gzdt/2006-06/26/content_319658.htm.

—— Report on 2006 National Counter-Narcotics Activities by the Counter Narcotics Control Commission (released in 2007). Available online at www.china.com.cn/law/zhuanti/yldp/2007-06/02/content_8333483.htm.

—— Annual Report on 2007 National Counter-Narcotics Activities by the Counter Narcotics Crime Commission, p. 32.

Dai Peng, 'Xinshiqi de juece zuzhi yu shishi' (The policy, organization and implementation of yanda in the new era), *Zhongguo renmin gongan daxuebao* (*Journal of the Chinese People's Public Security University*) 3, 2003, pp. 27–31.

Dai Ruilin (ed.), *Hebeisheng shenpanzhi* (Annals of Trial Work in Hebei Province). Shijiazhuang: Hebei renmin chubanshe, 1994.

Dangdai zhongguo lishi weiyuanwei (ed.), *Dangdai zhongguo de shenpan gongzuo* (Trial work in Contemporary China (vol. 1)), Beijing: Dangdai zhongguo chubanshe, 1993.

Gao Mingxuan (ed.), *Xin zhongguo xingfa lifa wenxian ziliao* (Documents on Criminal Legislation in the New China) Volume 1, Beijing: Renmin gongan daxue chubanshe, 1998.

Gao Qingxiang, 'Yanda zhengzhi jiesuhou ruhe baochi shehui changzhi jiuan' (How can long-term law and order be maintained in the wake of the yanda campaign?) *Gongan yanjiu* (*Public Security Research*) 4, 2003, pp. 61–65.

Gonganbu zhengce falu yanjiushi (eds), *Zhifa shouce: daji xingshi fanzui zhuanji* (Vol. 4) (Law Enforcement Manual: combating crime), Beijing: Qunzhong chubanshe, 1984.

Gonganbu zhengzhi bu (eds), *Yanzhong baoli fanzui anli pingxi* (Critique and Analysis of Violent Criminal Cases), Beijing: Qunzhong chubanshe, 1998.

Guo Daohui (ed.), *Dangdai faxue zhengming shilu* (Records of Contentious Issues in Contemporary Jurisprudence), Hunan: Hunan chubanshe, 1998.

Guo Jisheng (ed.), *Fayuan guanli gailun* (Outline of Court Management), Beijing: Renmin fayuan chubanshe, 1992.

Guo Xingguo (ed.), *Jianguo yilai gongan gongzuo dashi yaolan* (An Outline of the Chronicles of Public Security Work Since Liberation), Beijing: Qunzhong chubanshe, neibu faxing, 2003.

Han Yanlong (ed.), *Zhonghua renmin gongheguo fazhi tongshi* (A Comprehensive History of the Legal System in the People's Republic of China), Beijing: Zhonghua zhongyang dangxiao chubanshe, 1998.

He Bingsong (ed.), *Heishehui fanzui jiedu* (Explanations of Organized Crime), Beijing: Zhongguo jiancha chubanshe, 2003.

Hou Honglin, *Xingshi zhengce de jiazhi fenxi* (An Analysis of Criminal Justice Policy Values) PhD Dissertation. Beijing: Zhongguo zhengfa daxue yanjiushengyuan, Zhongguo zhengfa daxue, 2004.

Huang Jianmin (ed.), *Guangxi shenpanzhi* (The Annals of Trial Work in Guangxi), Nanning: Guangxi renmin chubanshe, 2000.

Huang Xiangqing, 'Yanda xingshi zhengce de zhangwo' (Understanding yanda criminal justice policy) *Zhengzhi yu falu* (*Politics and the Law*) 7, 2001, pp. 23–26.

Jai Dongjun and Guo Zhangcheng, *Yanda xingshi zhengce: fanfanzui de zhongguo jingyan* (Strike Hard Criminal Justice Policy: China's experience in countering crime), Beijing: Zhongguo renmin gongan daxue chubanshe, 2008.

Jiang Pusheng, 'Yanda zhengzhi douzheng de huigu yu sikao' (A reflective look back at the Strike Hard campaign), *Gongan Yanjiu* (*Public Security Studies*) 7, 2003, pp. 40–43.

Jiang Yanhu, 'Dangqian yanda zhengzhi douzhengzhong cunzai de wenti duice' (Existing problems and countermeasures related to the latest Strike Hard campaign), *Gongan yanjiu* (*Public Security Studies*) 3, 2002, pp. 6–11.

Jilinsheng gonganting (ed.) *Shiji zhijiao de jilin gongan gongzuo* (Public Security Work in Jilin at the Turn of the Century), Beijing: Zhongguo renmin gongan chubanshe, 2005.

Kang Shuhua, *Dangdai Zhongguo fanzui zhuti* (Crime issues in Contemporary China), Beijing: Qunzhong Chubanshe, 2004.

Lan Quanpo, *Qishi nian falu yaolan* (Outline of Seventy Years of Law), Beijing: Falu chubanshe, 1997.

Li Changming, 'Zousi fanmai hailuoyin 433.95 gongjin Yunnan teda dupin anfan fufa' (Criminals convicted of smuggling and selling 433.95 kilograms of heroin in a major drug case in Yunnan have been executed). Available online at www.chinacourt.org/htm/article/2007-08/17/ 260403.shtml, 17 August 2007 (accessed 18 August 2007).

Li Chuan, 'Dangqian yanda yanjiuzhong de si ge wuqu' (Four inaccuracies regarding the current research on Strike Hard), *Zhongguo xingshi zazhi* (*Criminal Justice in China*) 2, 2003, pp. 3–7.

Li Jingui, 'Kuanyan xiangji shi woguo jiben xingshi zhengce' (Balancing leniency and severity is a fundamental criminal justice policy in China), *Zhengyiwang* (Justice online). Available online at http://review.jcrb.com/zyw/n124/ca514495.htm, 12 July 2006 (accessed 30 September 2007).

Li Shuangqi, 'Fujiansheng yanda gongzuo diaocha baogao' (Survey results on Strike Hard work in Fujian Province), *Zhongguo xingshi zazhi* (*Chinese Criminal Justice*) 13 (2), 2002, pp. 88–97.

Li Wenyan and Tian Hongjie, *Da hei chu'e xingshi falu shiyong jieshu* (Interpreting the Application of Criminal Law in the Campaign against Organized Crime), Beijing: Qunzhong chubanshe, 2001.

Li Xuntao, 'Zhuanbian zuofeng zhenzhua shigan quebao yanda zhengzhi douzheng liangnian weiqi mubiao ruqi shixian' (Tranform the style of work and get right on the job to ensure that the objectives of the yanda campaign are met by the scheduled time), *Gongan yanjiu* (*Public Security Research*) 5, 2002, pp. 12–14.

Li Yaoming and Chen Jiwei, 'Guanyu gonggu he fazhan yanda zhengzhi douzheng chengguo de sikao' (Some reflections on consolidating and developing the success of the strike hard campaign), *Zhejiang gongan gaodeng zhuanke xuexiao xuebao* (*Journal of Zhejiang Police College: Public Security Studies*) 4, 2003, pp. 18–22.

Li Yuanhe and Yu Tianmin, 'Yanda xingshi zhengce yu xingfa cailiang' (Yanda criminal justice policy and the range of punishment within the law), *Renmin sifa* (*People's Justice*) 5, 2003, pp. 38–40.

Li Zhongxin (ed.), *Lun heishehui xingzhi fanzui wenti yanjiu* (Research issues on mafia-style organized crime), Beijing: Zhongguo renmin gongan daxue chubanshe, 2000.

Lian Shanggang (ed.), *Ban'an guifan* (Standards for Case Management), Beijing: Renmin fayuan chubanshe, 1995.

Liang Guozhen (ed.), *Luoding gonganzhi* (Annals of Public Security Work in Luoding), Luoding: neibu ziliao, 1997.

Liang Jinyun, 'Yunnan jindu douzheng xingshi pinggu' (Assessment of the Situation Regarding the People's War on Drugs in Yunnan Province), *Yunnan jingguan xueyuanbao* (*Yunnan Police Academy Journal*) 2, 2006, pp. 1–7.

Lin Hua (ed.), *Zhongguo falu jichu* (The Foundations of Chinese Law), Guangzhou: Zhongshan daxue chubanshe, 1992.

Lin Zhongliang, *Geji danwei zhengfa wei de zhineng ji hongguan zhengfa gongzuo* (The Functions and Macroscopic Tasks of the Politico-legal Affairs Work of Politico-legal Affairs Committees at All Levels of Government), Beijing: Changan chubanshe, 2004.

Liu Chenjun, 'Liaoning kaizhan bairi yanda' (Liaoning launches a hundred-day Strike Hard), *Liaoshen wanbao* (*Liaoning Shenyang Evening News*), 20 September 2005, p. 1.

Liu Hantai and Du Xingfu (eds.) *Zhongguo daji dongtu baogao* (A Report on China's Fight against East Turkestan Groups), Urumqi: Xinjiang renmin chubanshe, 2003.

Liu Shangyu (ed.), *Heishehui fanzui yu duice* (Organized Crime and Police Countermeasures), Beijing: Qunzhong chubanshe, 1997.

Liu Xinsheng (ed.), *Xuzhou gonganzhi* (Annals of Public Security Work in Xuzhou), Xuzhou: neibu faxing, 1994.

Liu Xuegang, 'Yanda liuxia de yihan' (Some lamentable things that Strike Hard has left in its wake), *Liaowang xinwen zhoukan* (*Outlook News Weekly*) 32, 2003, pp. 45–47.

Lu Gengsong, 'Zhongguo heishehui xianzhuang fenxi' (An analysis of the make-up of mafia-style syndicates) *Yancheng wanbao* (*Yancheng Evening News*), 24 May 2001. Available online at www.people.com.cn?GB/shehui/46/index.html (accessed 25 August 2001).

Lu Zhuo 'Dui xian jieduan yanda zhengzhi douzheng de lixing sikao' (A rational reflection on this current stage of the Strike Hard campaign) *Gongan yanjiu* (*Public Security Studies*) 8, 2001, pp. 32–37.

Mo Desheng and Jin Changling, *Shehui zhian zonghe zhili zhuanti yanjiu* (A Study of Comprehensive Management of Public Order), Beijing: Qunzhong chubanshe, 2003.

Mu Yumin, *Beijing jingcha bainian* (One Hundred Years of Policing in Beijing), Beijing: Gongan daxue chubanshe, 2004.

Ning Yuce (ed.), *Qingxu fayuan baogao* (Report on Qingxu Court), Shanxi: neibu faxing, 1998.

Ou Sanren, 'Yanda chuangxin quyi' (A Discussion on some yanda innovations), *Xiangtan shifan xueyuan xuebao* (*Journal of Xiangtan Normal University*) 26 (4), 2004, pp. 37–40.

Peng Ke (ed.), *Xingfaxue zixue kaoshi dagang* (An Outline of Criminology for Self-Study), Beijing: Beijing daxue chubanshe, 1992.

Qian Hui and Bi Jianlin (eds), *Zhongguo renmin gongheguo fazhi dashiji* (Chronicle of Events of the Legal System of the People's Republic of China), Jilin: Jilin renmin chubanshe, 1992.

Qian Qiang, Li Yaojie and Li Suoping, 'Qianlun zhuanxiang douzheng de jiben tezheng' (An outline of the basic characteristics of specialized struggles), *Gongan yanjiu* (*Public Security Studies*) 3, 2004, pp. 36–40.

Qiu Chuangjiao (ed.), *Yunnan shenpanzhi* (Annals of Trial Work in Yunnan), Kunming: Yunnan renmin chubanshe, 1996.

Rao Yuanming, 'Yanda zhengzhihou de ruogan sikao' (Some post-Strike Hard campaign reflections), *Zhejiang gongan gaodeng zhuanke xuexiao xuebao* (*Journal of Zhejiang Police College*: *Public Security Studies*) 2, 2004, pp. 82–84.

Renmin fayuan nianjian bianji weiyuanhui (ed.), *Renmin fayuan nianjian 1990* (Yearbook of the People's Courts: 1990). Beijing: Xinhua chubanshe, 1993.

Renmin fayuan nianjian bianji weiyuanhui (eds), *Renmin fayuan nianjian 1991* (Yearbook of the People's Courts: 1991), Beijing: Xinhua chubanshe, 1994.

Song Zhansheng (ed.), *Zhongguo gongan baike quanshu* (Encyclopedia of Public Security in China). Jilin: Jilin renmin chubanshe, 1990.

Su Huiyu and Sun Wanhuai, 'Yanda fangzhen de zingshi faxue sikao' (A reflection on the jurisprudential aspects of yanda policy) *Faxue* (*Jurisprudence*) 1, 2001, pp. 26–32.

Sun Guoyang 'Xingshi yitihua shiyexia "yanda" de lixing sikao' (A rational reflection on implementing an integrated vision of criminal justice work in yanda campaigns), *Jiangsu jinggong xueyuan xuebao* (*Journal of the Jiangsu Police Academy*) 4, 2004, pp. 97–102.

Tang Shuhua, *Fanzuixue tonglun* (Debates in Criminology), Beijing: Beijing daxue chubanshe, 1992.

Wang Huizhang and Sun Feixiang, 'Shilun yanda de mingyun guisu' (Preliminary assessment of the fate of yanda policy), *Hebei faxue* (*Hebei Jurisprudence*) 11, pp. 129–33.

Wang Jianguo, 'Guanyu jianli yanda jingchangxing gongzuo jizhi de sikao' (Reflections on the normalization of the system of yanda), *Hunan gongan zhuanke xuexiao xuebao* (*Journal of Hunan Public Security College*) 18 (6), pp. 21–24.

Wang Keqin, 'Gongxuan lieji yinbao baozi heimu' (Scam of pronouncing 'bad seeds' exposed), *Zhongguo Jingji Shibao* (*China Economic Times*), 18 July 2003.

Wang Li, 'Yanda yu yange gongan xingshi zhifa de sibian' (Analysis of yanda and public security's strict enforcement of the criminal law) *Zhongguo renmin gongan daxuebao* (*Journal of the Chinese Public Security University*) 104 (4), 2003, pp. 20–24.

Wang Lili, 'Quanguo baoan zongshu da 230 wan ren' (The number of private security personnel in China reaches 2.3 million) *Zhongguo Jianchawang* (China Procuratorate Net), 2007. Available online at www.cpd.com.cn/gb/newscenter/2007-02-05/content_728515.htm (accessed on 2 February 2008).

Wang Luwei, 'Chuangxin fazhan yanda sixiang quebao shehui changzhi jiuan' (Innovate and develop yanda thought to ensure a prolonged period of law and order*), Gongan yanjiu* 11, 2003, pp. 25–28.

Wang Mingliang, *Yanda de lixing pingjia* (A Rationale Appraisal of Yanda), Beijing: Beijing daxue chubanshe, 2004.

Wang Wenyuan, 'Yanda shiyi' (Clearing up some doubts about Strike Hard), *Shehui* (*Society*) 5, 2005, p. 46,

Wang Zhimin and Zhao Ruigang (eds), *Yanhai diqu gonggong anquan fazhan zhanyue* (The Development Strategies for Public Security in Coastal Regions), Beijing: Qunzhong chubanshe, 1989.

Wang Zhiqing (ed.) *Xiaoyi gonganzhi* (Annals of Xiaoyi Public Security Work), Taiyuan: Shanxi Guji chubanshe, 2000.

Wang Zhongfang (ed.), *Zhongguo shehui zhan zonghe zhili lilun yu shijian* (The Theory and Practice of China's Comprehensive Management of Public Order), Beijing: Qunzhong chubanshe, 1989.

Wei Zhenzhong, 'Queshi gaohao zhuitao gongzuo tuidong yanda zhengzhi douzheng shenru kaizhan' (Successfully doing the job of capturing fugitives to expediate the deeper impact of yanda on crime), *Gongan yanjiu* (*Public Security Research*) 2, 2002, pp. 21–24.

Wu Jianqiang and Cao Yi (eds). *Zhongguo heishehui xingzhi fanzui wenti yanjiu* (Research Issues on Chinese Mafia-style Syndicates), Beijing: Gongan daxue chubanshe, 2005.

Wu Lei (ed.), *Zhongguo sifa zhidu* (China's Judicial System), Beijing: Renmin daxue chubanshe, 1992.

Xiao Xiong, 'Guanyu yanda rougan wenti de sikao' (Reflections on some problems with Strike Hard), *Shanghai gongan gaodeng zhuanke xuexiao xuebao* (*Journal of the Shanghai Police Academy*) 15 (1), 2005, pp. 16–17.

Xining gonganju (ed.), *Xining gonganzhi* (Annals of Public Security Work in Xining), Qinghai: neibu faxing, 1994.

Xinjiang ribao (*Xinjiang Daily*), 'PRC's Xinjiang executes 15 criminals after public sentencing', 16 November 2001, FBIS Document no.: FBIS-CHI-1204.

Xu Xiaogang, 'Shenhua renshi qianghua cuoshe, tuidong yanda zhengzhi douzheng shenru fazhan' (Deepen understanding and strengthen measure, expatiate a deepened development of the Strike Hard campaign) *Gongan yanjiu* (*Public Security Studies*) 8, 2001, pp. 38–40.

Xu Yingui, Zhou Ying and Cao Cheng, 'Shilun yanda zhengce de falu yiji qi duice' (Preliminary assessment of Strike Hard policy on basic legal principles and some other measures), *Nanjing shehui kexue* (*Social Sciences in Nanjing*) 1, 2003, pp. 74–77.

Xu Zhubao, 'Goujian yanda changxiao gongzuo jizhi' (Constructing a system to sustain enduring results in yanda work), *Qunzhong* (*The Masses*) 1, 2005, pp. 37–47.

Yan Jianping, 'Huizhoushi hei'eshili tuanhuo' in Guangdongsheng jingcha xiehui (ed.), *Guangdong heishehui fanzui wenti yanjiu* (Research on Mafia-style Crime Issues in Guangdong), Beijing: Gongan daxue chubanshe (restricted circulation), 2003.

Yanda douzheng yu shehui zhian ganbu duben (Readings on the Strike Hard Campaign and Comprehensive Management of Public Order), Beijing: Zhonggong zhongyang dangxiao chubanshe, 2001.

Yang Shi and Li Ran, 'Yifa congzhong congkuai de laili' (The origins of severity and swiftness in accordance with the law), in Guo Daohui *et al.* (eds), *Zhongguo dangdai faxue zhengmin shilu* (Records of Contentious Issues in Contemporary Jurisprudence), Hunan: Hunan renmin chubanshe, 1998, pp. 277–84.

You Wei and Xie Xiaomei, 'Fanzuihua yuance yu woguo de Yanda zhengce' (Principles of criminality and China's Strike Hard policy) *Falu kexue: xibei zhengfa daxue xuebao* (*Law And Science: Journal of the Northwestern Politics and Law University*) 1, 2003, pp. 38–43.

You Wei and Xie Xiaomei, 'Yanda zhengce de huigu yu kexue dingwei' (A look back at yanda and its scientific merits) *Huadong zhengfa xueyuan xuebao* (*Journal of the Huadong College of Law and Politics*) 1, 2004, pp. 48–52.

Yu Gaizhi, 'Lun yanda de yaosu dixianji xingfa xiaoyi' (On some key issues regarding the punitive effects of yanda) *Faxue* (*Jurisprudence*) 12, pp. 40–42.

Yu Guoxing, 'Zhengque baowo yanda zhengzhi douzheng fanxiang ying zhuyi si ge wenti' (Four issues that need to be taken into consideration in order to correctly understand the direction to take in the yanda campaign), *Gongan yanjiu* (*Public Security Research*) 9, 2001, pp. 8–13.

Zeng Guangwen, *Beijingzhi: gonganzhi* (The Beijing Annals: chronicles of Beijing Public Security), Beijing: Beijing chubanshe, 2003.

Zhai Jinping, 'Yanda yu gongan gaige' (Strike Hard and reforms in public security), *Zhongguo renmin gongan daxuebao* (*Journal of the Chinese People's Public Security University*) 104 (4), 2003, pp. 25–28.

Zhang, Fusan, 'Jiji kaizhan yanda zhengzhi douzheng, weihu he cuijin gaige kaifang fazhan wending' (Urgently launch the Strike Hard campaign: protect and promote the stability of the economic reforms), 6 April 2001, in Chen Jiping (ed.), *Zhongguo shehui zhi'an zonghe zhili nianjian 2001–2002* (2001–2002 Yearbook of Comprehensive Management of Public Order in China), Beijing: Zhongguo chang'an chubanshe, 2003, pp. 240–45.

—— 'Sifabu guanyu jinyibu jiaqiang Yanda zhengzhi douzheng gongzuo de tongzhi' (Ministry of Justice notice on further strengthening Strike Hard campaign work), in Chen Jiping (ed.), *Zhongguo shehui zhi'an zonghe zhili nianjian 2001–2002* (2001–2002 Yearbook of Comprehensive Management of Public Order in China), Beijing: Zhongguo chang'an chubanshe, 2003, pp. 287–88.

Zhang Guoxing and Li Jingping, 'Xin xingshixia jiaqiang he gaijin dang dui gongan gongzuo de lingdao' (Strengthening and improving Party leadership over public security work in the new period of policing), in *Lun zhanlue jiyuqi gongangonagzuo de gaige yu chuangxin* (Reforms and Ideas for Strategies of Public Security Work in an Age of Transformation), Beijing: Gongan chubanshe, 2005.

Zhang Huasong, 'Yanda xingshi zhengce yu fanzui yufeng' (Yanda's criminal justice policy and crime prevention), *Jiangsu jinggong xueyuan xuebao* (*Journal of Jiangsu Police Academy*) 18 (1), 2003, pp. 20–24.

Zhang Peitian and Zhang Hua, *Jinxiandai zhongguo shenpan jiancha zhidu de yanbian* (Changes in the Modern and Contemporary System of Trial and Prosecution in China), Beijing: Zhengfa daxue chubanshe, 2004.

Zhao Bingzhi, 'Yandazhong xingfa shiyong rougan wenti yanjiu' in *Xingshi fazhi fazhan yanjiu baogao*, Beijing: Zhongguo renmin gongan daxue chubanshe, 2002.

Zhao Bingzhi (ed.), *Xingshi fazhi fazhan yanjiu* (Research Reports on Developments in Criminal Law), Beijing: Gongan daxue chubanshe, 2004.

Zhao Jianming, 'Yanda bairi gongjian huizhan dakai xumu' (The curtain opens on the public security's 'hundred day decisive battle' to assault fortified positions), *Liaoning ribao* (*Liaoning Daily News*), 20 September 2005, p. 1.

Zhao Rixin (ed.), *Liaoning shenpanzhi* (Annals of Trial Work in Liaoning), Liaoning: Neibu chugao (Draft document for internal circulation: no publication year recorded).

Zhao Xichen, 'Yanda zhengzhi douzheng lilun yu shijian yantaohui zongshu' (Summary report of views on the theory and practice of yanda), *Faxue Luntan* (*Legal Forum*) 17 (4), 2002, pp. 92–93.

Zhao Ying (ed.), *Guizhou shenpanzhi* (Annals of Trial Work in Guizhou), Guiyang: Guizhou renmin chubanshe, 1999.

Zhao Yuezeng, 'Jianchi Yanda fangzhen, shenhua yanda zhengzhi douzheng' (Maintain yanda policy and deepen the impact of the campaign), *Gongan yanjiu* (*Public Security Research*) 8, 2001, pp. 41–43.

Zhao Zhenjiang (ed.), *Zhongguo fazhi sishinian* (Forty Years of the Chinese Legal System), Beijing: Beijing daxue chubanshe, 1990.

Zheng Jianguo, 'Lun youhua yanda celue' (On optimizing Strike Hard tactics), *Gongan xuankan: Zhejiang gongan gaodeng zhuanke xuexiao xuebao* (*Public Security Journal: Zhejiang Police Academy*) 2, 2005, pp. 82–85.

Zhong Yuexiong, 'Zhian fangkong jizhi de shijian' (Practices of the system of crime prevention), in Ma Xiangjin (ed.), *Jingwu xinlun* (New Theories of Policing), Beijing: Renmin gongan daxue chubanshe, 2004, pp. 20–28.

Zhong Yuhua, 'Dui yanda zhengce de lixing zai renshi' (Rethinking the rationality of Strike Hard policy), *Gansu zhengfa xueyuan xuebao* (*Journal of the Gansu Institute of Political Science and Law*) 8, 2003, pp. 63–70.

Zhonggong zhongyang danganguan (eds), *Bada yilai zhonggong zhongyang wenjian ji* (Selected Documents of the Central Party-Government since the Eighth Party Congress), Volume 12 (1976), unpublished Central Party-Government materials, 1997.

Zhongguo gongan nianjian bianjibu (eds), *Zhongguo gongan nianjian 2001* (Yearbook of Public Security in China), Beijing: Qunzhong chubanshe, 2001.

Zhongguo shehui zhian zonghe zhili nianjian 1991–1992 (Yearbook of Comprehensive Management of Public Order in China: 1991–1992), Beijing: Falu chubanshe, 1996.

Zhongguo shehui zhian zonghe zhili nianjian 1993–1994 (Yearbook of Comprehensive Management of Public Order in China: 1993–1994), Beijing: Falu chubanshe, 1997.

Zhongguo shehui zhian zonghe zhili nianjian 1995–1996 (Yearbook of Comprehensive Management of Public Order in China: 1995–1996), Beijing: Falu chubanshe, 1998.

Zhongguo shehui zhian zonghe zhili nianjian 1997–1998 (Yearbook of Comprehensive Management of Public Order in China: 1997–1998), Beijing: Chang'an chubanshe, 2000.

Zhongguo shehui zhian zonghe zhili nianjian 1999–2000 (Yearbook of Comprehensive Management of Public Order in China: 1999–2000), Beijing: Chang'an chubanshe, 2002.

Zhongguo shehui zhian zonghe zhili nianjian 2001–2002 (Yearbook of Comprehensive Management of Public Order in China: 2001–2002), Beijing: Chang'an chubanshe, 2003.

Zhongguo shehui zhian zonghe zhili nianjian 2003 (The Comprehensive Management of Public Order Yearbook for China 2003), Beijing: Zhongguo changan chubanshe, 2004.

Zhongguo sifa zhidu ziliao xuanbian bianjizu (ed.), *Zhongguo sifa zhidu ziliao xuanbian* (Selected Materials on the judicial System in China), Beijing: Renmin fayuan chubanshe, 1991.

Zhongyang wenxian yanjiushi (eds), *Jianguo yilai Mao Zedong wengao* (Mao Zedong's Works Since the Establishment of the PRC), Beijing: Zhongyang wenxian chubanshe, 1993.

Zhongyang zhengfawei yanjiushi (ed.), *Jianlai jianquan yanda jingchangxing gongzuo tizhi diaoyan wenji* (Reports on the Work System for Establishing the Regularization of Yanda into Everyday Police Work), Beijing: Changan chubanshe, 2004.

Zhou Liangtao, 'Lun heishehui xingzhi de zuzhi' (On the organization of mafia-style syndicates), in Li Zhongxin (ed.), *Lun heishehui xingzhi fanzui wenti yanjiu* (Research Issues on Mafia-style Organized Crime), Beijing: Zhongguo renmin gongan daxue chubanshe, 2000.

Zhou Lu, *Dangshi shizheng fanzuixue* (Contemporary Substantive Issues in Criminology), Beijing: Renmin fayuan chubanshe, 2004.

Zhou Xinjie, 'Guangdong heishehui fanzui ruogan wenti chutan' (A preliminary study of some issues relating to underworld crime in Guangdong Province), in *Guangdong heishehui fanzui wenti yanjiu*, 2003.

Zhou Zhenxiang and Shao Jingchun (eds), *Xin Zhongguo fazhi jianshe 40 nian yaolan* (Outline of Forty Years of the Construction of the Legal System in the New China), Beijing: Qunzhong chubanshe, 1990.

Zhuang Huining, 'Renmin fayuan zai yanda zhengzhizhong tuilian duiwu' (The people's courts' training of contingents for yanda), *Liaowang xinwen zhoukan* (*Outlook News Weekly*) 33, 2001, pp. 30–31.

Zou Wei, Zhang Dechang and Chen Wenquan, 'Lun xinshiqi de "yanda" fangzhen' (On Strike Hard policy in the new age), *Guizhou jinggua zhiye xueyuan xuebao* (*Journal of the Guizhou Police Academy*) 3, 2002, pp. 14–17.

Zou Xianchao, *Ningxia shenpanzhi* (Annals of Trial Work in Ningxia), Yinchuan: Ningxia renmin chubanshe, 1998.

Zuigao fayuan yanjiushi (ed.), *Renmin fayuan wunian gaige gangyao* (Outline of the Five Years Reform Plan for the People's Courts), Beijing: Renmin fayuan chubanshe, 2000.

'Zuigao renmin fayuan guanyu fuhe sixing anjian ruogan wenti de guiding' (Decision of the Supreme People's Court on issues relating to approval of death sentences), Document 2007-4 Available online at www.chinacourt.org/flwk/show.php?file_id= 116488 (accessed 28 February 2007).

'Zuigao renmin fayuan guanyu shenli heishehui xingzhi zuzhi fanzui de anjian juti yingyong falu ruogan wenti de jieshi' (SPC judicial interpretation of certain issues related to the specific application of laws to prosecute mafia-style syndicates) Passed at the No. 1148 Judicial Committee Meeting. Judicial Interpretation (2000) No 42. Available online at www.law-lib.com.

'Zuigao renmin fayuan zuigao renmin jianchayuan gonganbu sifabu guanyu jinyibu yange yifa ban'an, quebao sixing anjian zhiliang de yijian' (Joint opinion from the Supreme People's Court, the Supreme People's Procuratorate, the Ministry of Pubic Security, and the Ministry of Justice on further measures to apply the law strictly in case work and to ensure the quality of decision making in capital cases), 11 March 2007. Available online at http: www.chinacourt.org/flwk/show1.php?file_id=116768 (accessed on 14 March 2007).

Zuigao renmin jianchayuan gongsuting and gonganbu xingshi jianchaju (eds), *Yanli daji weihai shehui zhixu fanzui: falu shiyong zhidao* (A Guide to the Application of Laws to Sternly Combat Crimes Endangering Social Order), Beijing: Zhongguo jiancha chubanshe, 2002.

Zuo Weimin and Zhou Changyun, *Bianqian yu gaige fayuan zhidu xiandaihua yanjiu* (Research on the Changes and Reforms in the Modernization of the Court System). Beijing: Falu chubanshe, 2000.

Index

UNIV DUNELM

DURHAM UNIVERSITY LIBRARY
3 0104 01599823 4

Durham
University
Durham University Library

Please return or renew this item by the last date shown below or the date shown on your Self-Issue receipt.

If this item is requested by another user it may be recalled and a revised due date will be given. The item MUST be returned by the revised due date. Fines are incurred on overdue books.

www.durham.ac.uk/library/